"This book is an impressive feat of C. S. L (the presence of the greatest Christian p est Christian prose storytellers) and fo treatment of that theme, which admirat accuracy in detail with 'big picture' wis moral practice."

Peter Kreeft, Professor of Philosophy, Boston College
Author of *C. S. Lewis for the Third Millennium*,
Between Heaven and Hell*, and *Back to Virtue

"This is an immensely impressive work. It is what scholarship ought to be— perspicacious, *readable*, measured, and exhaustive (in the good scholarly sense of that word). I found myself continually delighted on page after page. Lovers of Dante and Lewis will find themselves 'surprised by joy.'"

Thomas Howard, former Professor of English, best-selling author of
Narnia and Beyond: A Guide to the Fiction of C. S. Lewis

"This carefully researched, lucidly written study fills a much-needed gap in Lewis scholarship. It not only traces the profound impact that Dante had on Lewis's fiction; it identifies the Beatrice character in each novel that imparts grace and revelation to the protagonist."

Louis Markos, Professor of English and Scholar in Residence
Houston Baptist University

"I am impressed with the care Dr. Daigle-Williamson has taken in reading primary and secondary sources and bringing them into conversation with each other. It is an extraordinary accomplishment requiring mastery of Dante and of Lewis and of the most important scholarly work on both authors. I have argued for years that in order to understand Lewis, you must understand Dante. Now—at last!—this thoughtful study demonstrates why this is true. *Reflecting the Eternal* is a very important book. I highly recommend it."

Diana Pavlac Glyer, Professor of English, Azusa Pacific University
Author of *The Company They Keep: C. S. Lewis and*
J. R. R. Tolkien as Writers in Community

"Marsha Daigle-Williamson's book has helped me better know and appreciate my countryman Dante Alighieri. (Contemporary hermeneutics are correct in claiming that a work cannot be fully understood except retrospectively by the the fruit it produces and the influence it exercises.) In this comparison of Dante and Lewis, flashes of truth burst forth that illuminate the journey on earth for people today as it did for people in the Middle Ages and in all times. Both authors point to the same goal—the eternal—and offer the same map, Christian revelation."

Raniero Cantalamessa, O.F.M. Cap., Preacher to the Papal Household

"Virgil guided Dante through Hell and accompanied him through Purgatory; George MacDonald guided Lewis through *The Great Divorce.* In an intellectually exciting way, Marsha Daigle-Williamson has guided her readers through a double journey: Lewis's novels as they were influenced by Dante. The great spiritual journey is illuminated!"

Joe R. Christopher, Professor Emeritus of English
Tarleton State University, author of *C. S. Lewis: A Checklist of Writings*
about Him and his Works* (in collaboration) and *C. S. Lewis

"In this brilliant and comprehensive study, Marsha Daigle-Williamson shows how C. S. Lewis not only quotes Dante but also—and more importantly— transfuses the soul, as it were, of the *Divine Comedy* into his own major writings. One aspect of the importance of Lewis is his honesty. This is amply demonstrated in the careful analysis of nine works of Lewis, from *The Pilgrim's Regress* to *Till We Have Faces*; our understanding of them will never be the same. Monumental."

John Bremer, Director, Institute of Philosophy
Author of *C. S. Lewis, Poetry, and the Great War*

"Marsha Daigle-Williamson's *Reflecting the Eternal: Dante's* Divine Comedy *in the Novels of C. S. Lewis* is a thoughtful, thorough, and astute study of Dante's influence upon Lewis's fiction. While some readers may have noted general Dantean echoes in books such as *The Screwtape Letters*, *The Great Divorce*, and *Perelandra*, fewer will have seen Dante's influence on the Chronicles of Narnia and *Till We Have Faces*. Daigle-Williamson expertly draws out these connections in a compelling and fascinating manner. This is a must book for both general readers and Lewis experts."

Don W. King, author of *C. S. Lewis, Poet: The Legacy of His Poetic Impulse*,
***Plain to the Inward Eye: Selected Essays on C. S. Lewis*,**
and *The Collected Poems of C. S. Lewis: A Critical Edition*

"In this well-researched and thoroughly documented study, Daigle-Williamson provides overwhelming evidence that Dante's *Divine Comedy* served as both source and influence for Lewis's fiction. Her work fills a significant gap in C. S. Lewis scholarship, supporting the bold claim that Dante's masterpiece is, in fact, the model for Lewis's fiction. To her credit, the author has created a book that will satisfy, not only literary critics, but general readers and fans of Lewis's fiction looking for a deeper appreciation of Lewis's artistry, theology, and imaginative vision."

Gary L. Tandy, Professor of English, George Fox University
Author of *The Rhetoric of Certitude: C. S. Lewis's Nonfiction Prose*

REFLECTING *the* ETERNAL

REFLECTING *the* ETERNAL

Dante's *Divine Comedy* in the
Novels of C. S. Lewis

MARSHA DAIGLE-WILLIAMSON

HENDRICKSON
PUBLISHERS

**Reflecting the Eternal: Dante's *Divine Comedy*
in the Novels of C. S. Lewis**

© 2015 by Marsha Daigle-Williamson

Hendrickson Publishers Marketing, LLC
P. O. Box 3473
Peabody, Massachusetts 01961-3473

ISBN 978-1-61970-665-1

Printed in the United States of America

First Printing—October 2015

Library of Congress Cataloging in Publication Data

A catalog record for this book is available from the Library of Congress

Hendrickson Publishers Marketing, LLC ISBN 978-1-61970-665-1

To J. C., who first gave me the idea

Contents

Acknowledgments

I have been writing this book on and off for almost thirty years now. Producing a book can be likened to raising a child: it takes a village. I would like to thank the "village" that supported me during this project.

First, this book would not be in print if it were not for Carl Z. Nellis who, after a chance encounter at a conference, single-handedly acted as a liaison between me and his fellow editors at Hendrickson to promote my book. Subsequently, as my editor, his suggestions were always thoughtful and judicious, and his manner in handling my expressed preferences for this or that detail during the book's production was always gracious and kind.

Thanks also go to Joe R. Christopher and Don King (both of whom have written excellent books on Lewis) for their encouragement over the years to move forward with this project. I need to thank my four main readers who gave me valuable feedback about the readability of the book: my husband Peter S. Williamson, my university colleagues Dr. Charles Morrisey and Dr. Robert H. Woods Jr., and my friend Christine Helrigel. Behind this project and holding it up in prayer are several people who are relieved to be able finally to cross this off their lists (in alphabetical order): Jeannette Barbacane, Jan Belanger, Linda Duffy, Mariel La Fleur, Sharon Foster, Julia Glas, Yolanda Gonzalez, Paula Holtz, Dr. Pamela Jackson, Christine Jones, Jeane Larson, Dorothy Morsfield, Jim and Juliet Pressel, Lidija Balciunas Thomas, and countless others.

Had I waited until I found *all* the links between Lewis and Dante, this book would never have gone to print. I am certain, therefore, that readers will find omissions as well as errors (hopefully not too many), and for the omissions and errors I have no one to thank but myself.

Abbreviations

Works by C. S. Lewis

GD	*The Great Divorce: A Dream.* London: Geoffrey Ellen, 1945. Reprint, New York: Macmillan, 1946.
OSP	*Out of the Silent Planet.* London: John Lane, 1938. Reprint, New York: Macmillan, 1965.
Per.	*Perelandra.* London: John Lane, 1943. Reprint, New York: Macmillan, 1965.
PR	*The Pilgrim's Regress: An Allegorical Apology for Christianity, Reason and Romanticism.* London: Geoffrey Bles, 1933; 2nd ed. rev. with a new preface. London: Geoffrey Bles, 1944.
SC	*The Silver Chair.* New York: Macmillan, 1953.
SL	*The Screwtape Letters.* London: Geoffrey Bles, 1942. Reprint, with a new preface. New York: Macmillan, 1961.
THS	*That Hideous Strength.* London: John Lane, 1945. Reprint, New York: Macmillan, 1965.
TWHF	*Till We Have Faces: A Myth Retold.* London: Geoffrey Bles, 1956.
VDT	*The Voyage of the "Dawn Treader."* New York: Macmillan, 1952.

Dante Alighieri's *Divine Comedy*

Inf.	*Inferno*
Purg.	*Purgatorio*
Par.	*Paradiso*

La Divina Commedia, Scartazziniano edition. Ed. Giuseppe Vandelli. Milan: Ulrico Hoepli, 1965.

Introduction

Clive Staples Lewis (1898–1963) was a professor and scholar of medieval and Renaissance literature at Oxford University and later at Cambridge. He was also a literary critic, lay theologian, poet, essayist, novelist, cultural critic, philosopher, Christian polemicist, and literary historian. He is known and admired for his intelligence, his wit, his storytelling, and his skill at communicating complex concepts in simple and accessible ways. He has become one of the most widely read and translated Christian authors of the twentieth century with books on topics ranging from Christian apologetics to literary criticism. His fiction and popular theological works continue to be best-sellers, and the recent filming of books from The Chronicles of Narnia series has helped bring his stories to a new generation.

Books about Lewis abound, treating various aspects of his career, his personal life, and his writings. So why another book on Lewis? In studying Lewis's novels, readers and scholars who have analyzed his characters, themes, imagery, and sources have discovered that Lewis's novels are replete with echoes of the great classics of Western literature. However, no book so far has examined in depth the significant role that Dante's *Divine Comedy* plays in the composition of Lewis's novels and the parallels to that poem that abound in his novels. This is a significant gap since, as I argue throughout the book, there is perhaps no classic that is as important to understanding Lewis's art as Dante's *Divine Comedy*. In fact, Lewis employs Dante's masterpiece as the major literary model for his fiction, and the themes he treats in his novels are fundamentally the same as Dante's. In one of his essays, Lewis writes, "A Source gives us things to write about; an Influence prompts us to write in a certain way." An examination of Lewis's novels demonstrates that Dante, according to Lewis's own definition, was both a source and an influence for him.

This book is for Lewis fans, teachers of Lewis and their students, Lewis critics and scholars, Dante lovers, and general readers. Readers will learn more about the ideas, structural patterns, and narrative details in Lewis's novels that have links to Dante's poem. They will see how a modern author can make use of a predecessor's material—and in this case, how he can successfully incorporate medieval elements into modern stories. Writers of religious fiction can learn how Lewis and Dante express theological and spiritual principles in literary depictions of spiritual life. The book will be of use in any high school or college class that includes Lewis's work as it describes a vital feature that runs throughout his novels.

For the sake of readers who may not be very familiar with Dante and *The Divine Comedy*, a brief introduction is in order. Dante Alighieri (c. 1265–1321) was a poet, a linguist, and a philosopher from Florence, who is known in Italy as *il Sommo Poeta* ("the Supreme Poet"). Dante's works include a linguistic treatise, a political treatise and a philosophical treatise. His *New Life* (*La Vita Nuova*), a collection of love poems set within a prose narrative, recounts the history of his love for a young woman in Florence named Beatrice Portinari, whom he saw only twice before her untimely death at the age of 24 (and who subsequently figures prominently in his poetic masterpiece).

Dante is best known, however, for his lengthy poem *The Divine Comedy* (*La Divina Commedia* or just the *Commedia*). Narrated in the first person, this poem tells the story of a man who has lost his way and is spiritually transformed by a journey through hell, purgatory, and heaven. As he travels through the afterlife and sees historical and mythological characters in each realm, he learns about the essence of sin (hell), the importance of overcoming vice and growing in virtue (purgatory), and the joyful bliss of souls united to God (heaven). During this journey Dante's pilgrim is guided first by the Roman poet Virgil and then by Beatrice. Dante's storytelling abilities, his descriptions, his well-drawn and unforgettable characters, his imagery, and his literary presentation of Christian truths have earned him a permanent place in the canon not only of Western literature but of world literature as well. It is this masterpiece that Lewis draws on to tell his stories.

Understanding the relationship between Lewis's fiction and Dante's poem is important because, although it is no secret that Lewis's imagination was shaped by the medieval and Renaissance literature he loved so much, his appreciation and understanding of Dante provide a major key to the shape of that literary imagination. The links between his fiction and Dante's poem demonstrate Lewis's lifelong belief that the modern age has much to learn from the past—in this case, from an author in the distant past whose story, characters, literary techniques, and Christian worldview are still relevant today. They demonstrate Lewis's consummate artistry in the variety of ways he adapts features from that poem. They shed light on Lewis's meaning in all his novels, since the spiritual truths he teaches are the same as Dante's, illustrating that certain basic Christian themes transcend time, culture, and denominations. The specific adaptations Lewis makes of *The Divine Comedy* also provide his indirect commentary on that medieval masterpiece. Dante, by his own admission in the poem, acknowledged that he learned his literary craft from Virgil's *Aeneid* and that he was following in that poet's footsteps. So too Lewis, in the composition of his novels, followed in the footsteps of the author who was perhaps his main guide, Dante.

The Organization of This Book

Each of the chapters discusses one of Lewis's novels in the chronological order of its publication. This chronological order enables readers to track and evaluate the development of Lewis's varied uses of Dante's poem in his novels. Each chapter begins with a brief introduction and plot summary of one of Lewis's novels, followed by a discussion of that novel's fictional world and its inhabitants and the way they reflect Dante's imaginary universe. It next describes the similarities between the main character and Dante's pilgrim and traces the patterns in his or her journey that parallel journey patterns in *The Divine Comedy*. Finally, each chapter concludes with a discussion of the character who fulfills a function analogous to that of Beatrice in *The Divine Comedy*, i.e., a character who serves as a channel of grace and revelation and as an instrument of transformation for the main character. (Lewis always depicts the protagonist's meeting with this character using narrative details imported from the meeting between Dante's pilgrim and Beatrice at the top of Mount Purgatory in the Garden of Eden.)

Chapter 1 provides a framework or context for the book's discussions by addressing Lewis's general approach to literary predecessors and helps explain why Lewis thought it was not only permissible but appropriate for an author to draw on past authors. It also details his admiration for Dante, which remained constant throughout his life, and concludes with a brief plot summary of Dante's *Divine Comedy.*

Chapter 2 deals with *The Pilgrim's Regress* (1933). Lewis constructs the geography of this imaginary world with literary techniques from Dante. In addition, the journey of Lewis's pilgrim John echoes events from the journey of Dante's pilgrim in the *Inferno* and *Purgatorio.* In this novel Lewis presents his interpretation of Dante's Beatrice most fully, which can help readers to recognize the Beatrice figures in his subsequent novels. This is the only novel in which an inanimate object (rather than a personal being) fulfills a Beatrician role.

Chapter 3 describes *Out of the Silent Planet* (1938). In this book Lewis constructs a modern Christian cosmos that incorporates features from Dante's medieval cosmos. His hero Elwin Ransom, who resembles Dante's pilgrim in a variety of ways, undergoes a journey whose significance parallels that of the journey in the *Inferno* and echoes events from the *Paradiso.* The ruling spirit of the planet Malacandra (Mars) is Beatrice's parallel here.

Chapter 4 considers *The Screwtape Letters* (1942). Lewis's depiction of hell incorporates several parallels to concepts that shape Dante's hell. In addition, the "patient" (the young Christian man being tempted) goes through three stages of spiritual development that correspond to the three-phase journey of Dante's pilgrim, and the young woman he loves is patterned after Beatrice.

Chapter 5 looks at *Perelandra* (1943), the second novel of the Ransom trilogy. Lewis's story is again set in the imaginative Christian cosmos he presented in *Out of the Silent Planet*, but this time on the planet Venus. The mini-journey of the narrator at the beginning of the book reflects the journey in the *Inferno* while

Ransom's adventures parallel the journey in the *Purgatorio*. His vision of the Great Dance at the end of the novel condenses visions and images of light from the *Paradiso*. Here it is a couple, the Perelandrian Adam and Eve, who act and speak like Beatrice.

Chapter 6 completes the discussion of Lewis's trilogy. Ransom reappears in *That Hideous Strength* (1945) and resembles Dante's pilgrim in a unique way. The journeys are ended for Ransom and the pilgrim, so now they assist others on their spiritual journeys. The spiritual journeys in this novel occur for a young couple, Mark and Jane Studdock: Mark's progressive involvement with a scientific institute, the National Institute of Coordinated Experiments (N.I.C.E.), parallels the descent of Dante's pilgrim into hell, while Jane's involvement with a small group of Christians echoes the ascent of Dante's Mount Purgatory. In this novel that features two characters on spiritual journeys, Lewis presents the reader with two Beatrice figures.

Chapter 7 deals with *The Great Divorce* (1946), which is often called Lewis's *Divine Comedy* because it deals with the state of souls in the afterlife. However, the links are much deeper than this shared theme. Lewis's techniques for constructing the afterlife mirror Dante's mode of designing a physical realm that represents spiritual realities. For many of his narrative details, Lewis reassembles and condenses material from Dante's poem. He blends two or more settings, characters, events, and dialogues into new wholes producing a highly compressed version of significant sections of Dante's narrative. The narrator in *The Great Divorce* resembles Dante's pilgrim in ways not seen in any other Lewis novels. In this novel multiple characters that come down from Mountains in the east, and in particular the guide George MacDonald and Sarah Smith, fulfill Beatrician functions.

Chapter 8 treats The Chronicles of Narnia (1950–1956) together. In this series, Lewis employs typology to shape and narrate events that are similar to biblical events, a narrative approach used by Dante. Two Narnian novels explicitly echo *The Divine Comedy*. The first part of the journey in *The Voyage of the "Dawn Treader"* (1952) reflects Dante's design of Mount Purgatory, while the second part condenses events and images from the *Paradiso*. *The Silver Chair* (1953) presents a journey under the earth that echoes some features of Dante's *Inferno*.

Chapter 9 analyzes Lewis's last novel, *Till We Have Faces* (1956). Written as a first-person narrative, this book recounts the spiritual journey of a woman in pre-Christian times who comes to recognize herself as a sinner and repents. Lewis adapts a classical myth for his story in a way that parallels Dante's procedure for adapting myths. Lewis also uses Dante's moral criteria for assessing the spirituality of a pagan. Before her conversion, the protagonist Orual is reminiscent of some of the souls in Dante's *Inferno* and *Purgatorio*, while the narration of her spiritual awakening at the end of the story echoes details from the *Inferno* and from Dante's garden scene at the end of the *Purgatorio*. Orual's half-sister Psyche functions as Beatrice on two separate occasions. The first involves a failed attempt to lead her sister to faith in the deity while the second occasion is successful.

In concluding, chapter 10 summarizes the different kinds of links between Lewis and Dante. It also includes an overview of Lewis's ongoing patterns in three areas: his construction of fictional worlds, his journey narratives, and his Beatrice figures.

How conscious and deliberate are these parallels to Dante on Lewis's part? On several occasions in response to specific queries from readers, Lewis confirms that particular parallels with Dante in his novels are intentional. Otherwise, Lewis is silent. We can only wish that readers had asked him more questions. However, the sheer number of specific allusions and parallels are evidence, at the very least, that Dante's poem was an integral part of Lewis's thinking.

Whether or not *all* my examples of Lewis's parallels to Dante were directly intended by Lewis, there can be no doubt that he approached *The Divine Comedy* as an archetypal account of the Christian journey that bears repeating to a new generation. Dante's powerful poem presents in literary form what the Bible has to say about redemption and damnation, about human freedom, and about how human beings should live. In fashioning his stories to teach those same truths, Lewis follows in the footsteps of a master who had accomplished that task for his own generation. It is a tribute to Lewis's art and his understanding of Dante's poem that he could succeed at recasting so much of Dante's story into language and imagery accessible to the modern reader without requiring the reader's prior acquaintance with Dante's medieval masterpiece.

Lewis and Dante are ultimately connected because Lewis's novels not only retell the important truths of *The Divine Comedy* but also make direct use of material from that work to accomplish his task. Although *The Great Divorce* has sometimes been referred to as Lewis's *Divine Comedy*, I would argue that the entire corpus of Lewis's novels comprises his *Divine Comedy*.

Lewis scholar Alister E. McGrath comments, "Lewis was deeply conscious of standing within a tradition of literary, philosophical, and theological reflection, which he extended and deepened in his own distinctive manner. There is more that remains to be discovered about Lewis's rich intellectual vision. . . . Half a century after his death, the process of receiving and interpreting Lewis has still only begun." This book is an attempt to discover more of "Lewis's rich intellectual vision."

Two brief notes are in order as to what readers can and cannot expect from this book. First, this book is not about Lewis's life, all his fictional themes, all the other authors he draws on, all the layers of echoes that pertain to some events or characters, or the connections between his novels and his personal life. It focuses only on *The Divine Comedy* as a major strand that is woven throughout Lewis's fiction, so some things that readers might expect or consider as "essential to be said" may be left unsaid here.

Second, the notes at the end of this book are for readers who are interested in more details about Dante's poem, in my agreements, disagreements, and debts to other Lewis and Dante scholars, or in the original quotations in Italian. These notes may be disregarded by readers whose primary interest is simply to learn how C. S. Lewis creatively adapts and employs Dante's *Divine Comedy* in his novels.

CHAPTER ONE

Lewis, Dante, and Literary Predecessors

In his 1919 essay "Tradition and the Individual Talent," T. S. Eliot, a contemporary of C. S. Lewis and a major figure in English letters, claimed that every new writer will find a place in literature only if he is solidly in line with tradition, if his work fits with the "*whole* existing order" of literature that is created by the "monuments" of previous writers. The writer must have a historical sense that "involves a perception, not only of the pastness of the past, but of its presence." In fact, for Eliot, the significance of any author lies in "his relation to the dead poets and artists" that came before him, and "not only the best, but the most individual parts of his work may be those in which the dead poets, his ancestors, assert their universality most vigorously." Eliot's remarks here refer to poetry. What they say applies to literature in a much broader sense. C. S. Lewis himself used the term "poetry" in a similar way. "By poetry," Lewis wrote, "I mean, as the renaissance critics meant, imaginative literature whether in prose or verse."

While writing The Chronicles of Narnia, the Ransom trilogy, or *The Screwtape Letters*—the "imaginative literature" for which so many of us know him—C. S. Lewis was certainly conscious of the achievements of previous writers. He expressed his approach to literary predecessors throughout his writing career in works of literary criticism as well as in his essays on a variety of topics, public lectures, letters, and religious writings. Over the course of his writing career, Lewis remained remarkably consistent in his views on literature. His overall approach to literature derives from classical and medieval traditions and is steeped in Christian thinking about creativity. Lewis's ideas about the purpose of literature, the role of the author, the proper subject matter of storytelling, and the role of literary predecessors in an author's creative process can best be understood in the light of these traditions.

For Lewis, the purpose of art, including literature, and therefore the role of the artist, including the writer, is "to teach and to delight." In *The Personal Heresy* (1939), Lewis writes that "the old critics were perfectly right when they demanded of literature the *utile* and the *dulce, solas* and *doctrine*, pleasure and profit." A year later, Lewis restates this position in a letter by saying that the arts "are only healthy when they are either a) Definitely the handmaids of religious, or at least moral, truth—or b) Admittedly aiming at nothing but innocent recreation or entertainment." With these statements, Lewis reaffirms an approach to literature that was accepted by ancient, medieval, Renaissance, and neo-classical authors and that has only recently been challenged in modern times. Despite whatever formula was used in any given age to express the concept, it has generally been held that the purpose of literature is either instruction or entertainment or both.

In upholding that tradition, however, Lewis is aware that he is consciously opposing a modern trend that redefines the role of the artist:

> Until quite recently—until the latter part of the last century—it was taken for granted that the business of the artist was to delight and instruct his public. . . . All this has changed. In the highest aesthetic circles one now hears nothing about the artist's duty to us. It is all about our duty to him. . . . We [now] owe him "recognition." . . . The bard does not exist in order to delight the tribe; the tribe exists in order to appreciate the bard.

In rejecting this trend, Lewis condemns the notion that poets are "a separate race of great souls or mahatmas" and that "the end which we are supposed to pursue in reading . . . is a certain contact with the poet's soul." In other words, Lewis believes an author is not to be the focus of attention but is to be the channel for communicating truths to others; he or she is not meant to be "a spectacle but a pair of spectacles." Lewis likewise opposes the notion that T. S. Eliot championed in his defense of James Joyce's *Ulysses,* i.e., that "a man of genius is responsible to his peers, not to a studio full of uneducated and undisciplined coxcombs." Lewis insists, instead, that the bard does indeed exist for the sake of the tribe and that he is indeed responsible to more than just his peers. According to Lewis, an artist's indifference to the audience "is not genius nor integrity; it is laziness and incompetence"—particularly if the role of the artist, and the purpose of literature, is to teach and delight the public that is now being held in disdain.

As for what constitutes the proper subject matter for the art of literature, Lewis's view is based partly on the tradition of "pleasure and profit" for the reader, and partly on an application of New Testament Scriptures to the literary texts. In *The Discarded Image*, Lewis describes the concept of literature held by medievalists and sums up his own position equally well: "Literature exists to teach what is useful, to honour what deserves honour, to appreciate what is delightful," and if that be the case, then the content of literature should be "useful, honourable, and delightful things." Lewis reaffirms this concept in his essay on "Christianity and Literature." According to Lewis,

> Our whole destiny seems to lie in . . . acquiring a fragrance that is not our own but borrowed, in becoming clean mirrors filled with the image of a face that is not ours. . . . Applying this principle to literature, . . . we should get as the basis of all critical theory the maxim that an author should never conceive himself as bringing into existence beauty or wisdom which did not exist before, but simply and solely as trying to embody in terms of his own art some reflection of eternal Beauty and Wisdom.

For Lewis, then, the proper subject matter of literature consists in values or truths that are superior to literature and for whose sake literature exists.

In terms of literary predecessors, this meant that Lewis's approach to writing was intentional "imitation," receiving inspiration and ideas from writers of the past and at times purposely echoing them as part of adding layers of meaning to his own work. As Lewis noted in *The Personal Heresy*, this way of seeing creative work is a centuries-old tradition. When Virgil, for instance, has Aeneas unsuccessfully attempt to embrace the shade of his dead wife Cruesa three times, he is echoing the passage from Homer in which Odysseus tries to greet his dead mother in Hades. Dante's pilgrim replicates that action with the very same result when he sees his dead friend Casella on the shores of purgatory (see *Purg.* 2.76–81).

This echoing of his predecessors enriches the scene by drawing the stories of Homer and Virgil into *The Divine Comedy*. In the same way, Lewis's novels are enriched by the many stories he draws on.

Lewis's approach to "imitation," in addition to being a centuries-old tradition in Western literature, is also explicitly based on his reading of the New Testament. In "Christianity and Literature," Lewis points out that "in the New Testament the art of life itself is an art of imitation: can we, believing this, believe that literature is to aim at being 'creative,' 'original,' and 'spontaneous'[?]" Although Lewis derives his rationale here for "imitation" from Church teaching, this kind of approach to one's predecessors is the procedure that was generally recommended and adopted by Western writers until the modern period. Despite the variations that occurred in the interpretation and application of the concept of "imitation" during successive literary ages, there was at least a consensus that predecessors were to be respected, studied, and followed. Literary achievements were models for new authors, deep wells for inspiration, sign-posts to assist and guide them along the well-trod path that lay before them.

As Lewis points out, the emphasis that was placed on "originality" and "creativity" as literary ideals since the Romantic period led to a negative appraisal of "imitation" during Lewis's lifetime: "We certainly [now] have a general picture of bad work flowing from conformity and discipleship, and of good work bursting out from certain centres of explosive force . . . which we call men of genius." For Lewis, however, "imitation" and "originality" are not mutually exclusive terms. There is room for originality in Lewis's literary theory, but it is not to be achieved by consciously setting oneself off from one's predecessors as some recent theories purport. In fact, according to Lewis, when originality is raised to the status of an ideal in and of itself, it becomes self-defeating. In *Mere Christianity*, he contends that "in literature and art, no man who bothers about originality will ever be original: whereas if you simply *try* to tell the truth (without caring twopence how often it has been told before) you will, nine times out of ten, become original without ever having noticed it." Originality, then, is a by-product that can occur when an author has his or her sights set on higher goals.

Given his views on originality, Lewis maintains that the imitation of predecessors is a valid and necessary factor in the writing of good literature, as any writer tries "to tell the truth." This approach results, in Lewis's case, in a profound affinity between his fiction and the vast body of writings that comprise European literature. His novels abound with echoes of Edmund Spenser, Homer, St. Augustine, John Milton, William Shakespeare, Virgil, Jonathan Swift—the list is as long as Lewis's reading list. Lewis's creative use of the work of past writers provides a rich experience for any reader familiar with the Western literary tradition.

However, the works echoed in Lewis's fiction are seldom directly alluded to or quoted. Their presence tends to be woven into the fabric of Lewis's novels in such a way that a reader's lack of familiarity with those works constitutes no hindrance to the enjoyment of Lewis's writing. Although erudition on the part of readers is not required to understand his stories and their messages, recognizing the ways in which he draws on his literary heritage enhances one's appreciation for Lewis's masterful artistry.

It is in this context that we can consider Lewis's admiration for and "imitation" of Dante, beginning with a short history of his relationship to *The Divine Comedy*. Lewis began reading Dante's *Inferno* in Italian in February 1917 with his tutor William Kirkpatrick, and by October 1918 he was reading through the *Purgatorio*. During Christmas of 1920 he acquired the Oxford edition of the entire *Divine Comedy*. In January 1930 he writes in a letter to his childhood friend Arthur Greeves that the *Paradiso* "has really opened a new world to me. . . . I should describe it as feeling more *important* than any poetry I have ever read," and Lewis later tells him, "I think it [*Paradiso*] reaches heights of poetry which you get nowhere else."

Lewis continued reading Dante's poem thereafter. In a letter to Arthur Greeves written in January 1930, Lewis reports that he and Owen Barfield were reading *The Divine Comedy*, and the *Paradiso* in particular, during a four-day visit. Six months later, in a letter to Greeves on July 8, Lewis says he and Barfield finished the *Paradiso*. The next year, Lewis again writes to Greeves that he and Barfield had "splendid talks and reading of Dante."

In 1937, Lewis joined the Dante Society at Oxford. According to Humphrey Carpenter, Lewis and Colin Hardie, the classical tutor at Magdalen College, read Dante aloud together in weekly evening sessions before World War II. At Dorothy L. Sayers's request, Lewis offered ongoing feedback to her about her translation of *The Divine Comedy* beginning in the the late 1940s.

Lewis's high regard for Dante and his poem remained undiminished throughout his life. In 1936, in his award-winning work of literary criticism *The Allegory of Love*, he states, "Dante remains a strong candidate for the supreme poetical honours of the world." In 1940 he writes, "I think Dante's poetry, on the whole, the greatest of all the poetry I have read." George Sayer, a former student and a biographer of Lewis, confirms that Dante was Lewis's favorite poet and that his "love for *The Divine Comedy* was lifelong."

Lewis's esteem for Dante can be demonstrated by the abundance of references to *The Divine Comedy* throughout his writings. Lewis is reputed to have remembered everything he read and had an "astonishing verbatim memory," so it is not surprising that continual references to what he considered as "the greatest of all the poetry I have read" would emerge in his works and letters. Lewis's three essays on Dante appear posthumously in *Studies on Medieval and Renaissance Literature* (1966) with seven mentions of him in that book's other essays. He mentions Dante thirty-nine times in *The Discarded Image* (1964), his book on the medieval worldview; twenty-three times in *The Allegory of Love* (1936), his book on courtly love and the development of allegory; and nineteen times in his commentary on *Arthurian Torso* (1948), Charles Williams's unfinished lyric cycle on the Arthurian legend. These references make it clear that Lewis looked to Dante as a model and a leading representative of what was best in the Middle Ages.

What is perhaps more telling is that books on topics that do not deal with medieval and Renaissance literature and worldviews also include multiple references to Dante. In the three volumes of *The Collected Letters of C. S. Lewis*, Lewis refers to Dante or his poem over seventy-five times and recommends the poem to some correspondents as necessary reading. The multiple references that appear for decades throughout all his various kinds of writings indicate that Dante was always close to the surface of Lewis's mind.

Given Lewis's admiration for Dante's art and his profound knowledge and understanding of *The Divine Comedy*, we can turn to the ways in which Lewis's literary imitation of Dante is evident in his novels. Crucially, Lewis followed Dante in presenting perennial Christian truths to his readers and used the form of the journey narrative as a framework for conveying these teachings. In terms of form, Lewis's fiction is tied intimately to Dante's *Divine Comedy* in a variety of ways:

1. Lewis occasionally paraphrases or quotes Dante directly.

2. Lewis's choice of vocabulary, phrasing, and inclusion of odd details can at times only be explained as tipping his hat to Dante.

3. Throughout Lewis's fiction, settings, characters, events, and dialogues from *The Divine Comedy* reappear in new adaptations or in new combinations.

4. Some metaphors from Dante become literal events in Lewis's stories.

5. Lewis's protagonists resemble Dante's pilgrim through specific parallel details, and their journeys are shaped to mirror several journey patterns in Dante's poem.

6. Finally, Lewis's construction of imaginary worlds follows techniques that Dante uses to translate spiritual and theological concepts into concrete images.

Because of the subtle ways in which Lewis adapts Dante's material to modern situations, the ever-present *Divine Comedy* most often lies below the surface of Lewis's fiction and may not be visible at first glance. The following brief plot summary of Dante's poem may be helpful to some readers. The theological significance invested in these narrative details by Dante, and then in turn by Lewis, will be discussed as they reappear in Lewis's novels in their transformed shapes.

The Divine Comedy

Dante Alighieri's *Divine Comedy* (also called *La Divina Commedia* or just the *Commedia*) was written at the beginning of the fourteenth century and deals with the state of souls after death. He expresses the theme of his poem as showing how a human being "by his merits or demerits in the exercise of his free will . . . is deserving of reward or punishment by justice." Hoping to direct his readers to God, he says his purpose in writing is "to remove those living in this life from a state of misery and to bring them to a state of happiness." Dante's clear aim was to bring enlightenment to his readers that would lead to change. Although written from a medieval Catholic viewpoint, the poem for the most part presents basic doctrines that Christians from all denominations accept: hell is reserved for unrepentant sinners, heaven is the dwelling place of God and the redeemed, and people still living on earth must turn from their sin and live righteous lives.

Dante's poem is divided into three major parts that represent the three realms of his afterlife—the *Inferno* (*Hell*), the *Purgatorio* (*Purgatory*), and the *Paradiso* (*Heaven*). It is further divided into sections called cantos that consist of 115 to 160 verses. After an introductory canto, thirty-three cantos are dedicated to each realm, adding up to 100 cantos (a number representing fullness and completeness for Dante). The poem tells the story of a man in midlife who has departed from the path of truth and finds himself lost in a dark wood. Virgil, the classical Roman poet and author of the *Aeneid*, is divinely appointed to offer him a journey through the afterlife as his only way back to the right path. Virgil leads him through hell and purgatory, and Beatrice, a woman in Florence whom Dante loved and who had died prematurely, leads him through the realms of heavens and then into the spiritual heaven beyond space and time, the true dwelling of God and the redeemed, which he calls the Empyrean.

Some features of Dante's narrative described here appear only once in Lewis's fiction; other features appear again and again, although always in new creative ways. Given Lewis's position on the imitation of literary predecessors, his prodigious memory, and his proven admiration for Dante, it should come as no surprise that this is the case.

Inferno

Dante's hell, located under the earth, is funnel-shaped and is divided into nine concentric circles where sinners are punished. Each circle has a guardian, a creature from classical mythology that embodies that circle's sin, and a distinct punishment that Dante calls a *contrapasso*—a punishment that reflects the particular sin. (For example, murderers who shed the blood of others are immersed in a river of boiling blood, receiving for all eternity the essence of what they chose in life.)

Once past the entrance to hell, Virgil and the pilgrim see souls in hell's vestibule who refused to take a stand for good or evil when they were alive, so in line with their choices in life, they are rejected by both heaven and hell. After crossing the classical river Acheron into hell, Virgil and the pilgrim visit Limbo where, according to medieval theology, unbaptized righteous pagans live in unfulfilled desire for God. The next four circles of hell are for punishments of sins of the flesh, i.e., sins of incontinence that are linked to emotions and passions: lust, gluttony, avarice/prodigality, and wrath.

Virgil and Dante next arrive at the iron walls of the City of Dis (another name for Hades) that separate the five upper circles of hell from the four lower circles. Unlike sins that indulge the flesh and are linked to passions, the transgressions punished in these lower circles are premeditated sins of the heart and mind: heresy, violence, fraud, and treason. When Virgil and the pilgrim are refused entrance to this lower hell, an unnamed angel arrives to open the gate of Dis and enforce God's will for the pilgrim's journey to continue. After seeing the sixth circle of heretics, the pilgrim and his guide visit the last three circles, each of which has several subdivisions. The seventh circle is divided into separate rings that punish three kinds of violence: (1) against others (murder, destruction of others' property), (2) against self (suicide), and (3) against God (blasphemy, sodomy, usury). The eighth circle is subdivided into ten circular ditches called *Malebolge* (literally, "evil pouches"), each lower than the one above it. Ten kinds of fraud are punished here in different ways: seduction, flattery, simony, sorcery, civil graft, hypocrisy, theft, deception, sowing of discord, and the falsifying of various things. The last circle is divided into four zones corresponding to different kinds of treason: against family, against country, against guests, and against benefactors. At the bottom of this ninth circle, which is the center point inside the earth, a three-faced Satan (a parody of the Trinity) with six wings is encased in ice up to the middle of his chest. To leave hell, Virgil and the pilgrim climb down one of Satan's legs and follow a subterranean tunnel that leads to the earth's unexplored southern hemisphere.

Purgatorio

Emerging from hell, Virgil and Dante arrive at the shore of the island where Mount Purgatory is located. Souls destined for heaven are transported here in a boat piloted by an angel to begin the process of purification. Ante-purgatory, the grassy area around the base of the mount, is populated by souls who delayed repentance and are now delayed from ascending the mount. Mount Purgatory has seven successive circular ledges where souls are being purged of each of the seven capital sins: pride, envy, anger, sloth, avarice, gluttony, and lust—in that sequence from bottom to top. As each of these sinful dispositions is purged, souls simultaneously grow in virtue through their meditation on sacred and secular examples of that virtue and its corresponding vice. (For example, the proud, carrying heavy stones on their backs, are bent over and thus have their eyes cast down as they meditate on biblical and classical examples of humility carved on the side of the cliff and examples of pride carved on the path they walk. The weight of the load that each one carries is proportionate to the amount of pride needing to be cleansed.)

Since Mount Purgatory is inaccessible because of the high wall around it, Dante's pilgrim is supernaturally transported to its gate by a heavenly lady (Lucia) who is intervening to assist the pilgrim. The angel guardian at the mountain's gate inscribes seven P's ("P" for *peccatum*, sin) on the pilgrim's forehead that indicate the seven vices that need to be purged on the mountain's ledges. As Dante's pilgrim climbs the stairs that connect one ledge to another, the angel guarding those particular stairs removes one "P," signifying the pilgrim's cleansing from that sinful attitude.

After going through the wall of fire on the last ledge (lust), the pilgrim finds himself in the original Garden of Eden. He and Virgil are welcomed by a woman named Matilda and then watch a procession of several allegorical figures: men representing the books of the Old and New Testaments, seven nymphs representing the theological and cardinal virtues, and a gryphon representing the human and divine natures of Christ. Beatrice arrives in the chariot being pulled by the gryphon, and the pilgrim is reunited with her at this point.

Beatrice first greets the pilgrim by rebuking him for having departed from the path of righteousness after her death and chronicles his misdeeds. The pilgrim, who had expected a joyous reunion with the woman who had been a channel of God's grace for him on earth, experiences a series of conflicting emotional reactions during this time, acknowledges his sin, and is cleansed in Eden's two streams, Lethe and Eunoë. The pilgrim next sees symbolic reenactments, interpreted by Beatrice, of the history of the Christian church and its future victory over evil.

Paradiso

As Beatrice gazes on God and the pilgrim gazes at her, they rise up through each of the nine spheres of heaven (the classical and medieval divisions of heaven in the Ptolemaic model of the universe at that time). Redeemed souls display the different degrees of blessedness they enjoy in the Empyrean, their true dwelling, by appearing to the pilgrim in each of the seven planetary spheres (Moon, Mercury, Venus, Mars, the Sun, Jupiter, and Saturn). In the eighth sphere of the Fixed Stars (the constellations), the pilgrim sees symbolic visions of the whole host of heaven. In the ninth sphere, which is referred to as the Prime Mover (or the *Primum Mobile*) and is responsible for the rotation of the other eight spheres below it, he sees the nine orders of angels who administer God's reign throughout the universe.

The pilgrim then moves beyond the physical universe and enters into the spiritual heaven of the Empyrean. Beatrice returns to her heavenly seat, and St. Bernard of Clairvaux, a twelfth-century mystic, helps orient the pilgrim as he sees successive symbolic visions of the court of heaven. In his last vision of the redeemed, he sees them in white robes seated in circular rows, which he compares to a white rose, gazing at a point of light (God). As he gazes at God and experiences a mystical vision and understanding of the incarnation, his will and desire "revolve" around God because having seen God, he too, like the rest of the universe, is now moved by God's love.

CHAPTER TWO

The Pilgrim's Regress

Introduction

Lewis's first novel, *The Pilgrim's Regress: An Allegorical Apology for Christianity, Reason and Romanticism* (1933), is an allegorical novel recording his intellectual conversion to Christianity. Prior to his conversion, Lewis had published a collection of lyric poems, *Spirits in Bondage: A Cycle of Lyrics* (1919), and a long narrative poem, *Dymer* (1926), so this prose novel marks a new direction in his writing and is his first book as a Christian. Lewis had been studying medieval allegory since 1928 (which resulted in his next published work, *The Allegory of Love* in 1936), so he was well versed in the allegorical mode of writing.

This novel was written in two weeks during a holiday visit in August 1932 to his childhood friend, Arthur Greeves. For the 1943 edition, Lewis added a preface to explain the major allegories in the book as well as headlines at the top of each page to clarify the meaning of characters and events, since some readers had difficulty understanding the book.

In this novel, the protagonist John, who lives in the eastern shire of Puritania (legalistic religion), glimpses an island far off in the west that attracts him with longing and desire for its beauty. Eager to escape the oppressive rules of the Landlord (God), who owns the land and dwells in the nearby Eastern Mountains, John travels west to reach his island, accompanied for some of the way by a fellow-traveler, Vertue. During his journey on the Main Road that stretches from east to west, he encounters characters north and south of the road who represent philosophical, theological, and literary schools of thought. They either question the island's existence or offer substitutes and different opinions about its meaning. He crosses the canyon that divides the inhabited section of the world from its far-western part with help from Mother Kirk (the Christian church) by entering into a pool that comes up through a tunnel on the other side of a cliff (baptism). When he reaches the island in the far west, he is shocked to discover it is actually the back side of the Eastern Mountains (God's dwelling) that he tried to leave behind. He can only reach these mountains, his true desire, by retracing his steps—hence his "regress" from west to east.

The Pilgrim's Regress has most often been compared to John Bunyan's *The Pilgrim's Progress*, and at first glance, they seem very much alike. Lewis's title is clearly a play on Bunyan's title and signals to the reader that there is a connection between them. Both are dream-vision narratives that record a spiritual journey within a Christian framework. Both stories use personifications of immaterial realities. Occasional events in Lewis's novel are reminiscent of Bunyan's story, such as John's imprisonment by the giant of Zeitgeistheim (home of the Spirit of the Age), which recalls the imprisonment of Bunyan's hero, Christian, by Giant Despair. Close scrutiny of *The Pilgrim's Regress*, however, reveals that its relationship to Bunyan's allegory tends to be limited to its title and its similar allegorical form. Layers underneath have significant correlations with Dante's *Divine Comedy*. But first, a quick look at the allegorical form of Lewis's novel.

Lewis classified medieval allegory as "secular allegory" (because it derives from pagan sources) or as "religious allegory" (because it derives from the Bible). In secular allegory, which Bunyan uses, the author creates *visibilia*, fictionalized personifications, to express emotions, states of mind, theological concepts, and so forth. The personification is in a one-to-one relationship with the character, place, or event signified and has no identity apart from it. Bunyan's Mr. Worldly Wiseman represents worldly wisdom and nothing else; the Slough of Despond represents the state of depression and nothing more; when Bunyan's pilgrim is freed from the dungeon of Giant Despair, that event signifies a person's freedom from the oppression of despair—and only that. In this kind of allegory, the literal story is merely a vehicle for the deeper meaning, the "veil" through which the real story is meant to be grasped.

On the other hand, religious allegory (also called "the allegory of theologians" and "scriptural allegory") is the mode of allegory that Dante writes, and it has very little, if any, personification. The story's characters and settings are presented as historical and are not merely vehicles for hidden truth since they have their own meaning and significance on the literal level. The interpretation of a character, a setting, or an event is not restricted to a single meaning, as it is in secular allegory. Dante's Virgil, for example, represents, according to Charles Williams, "Virgil, and poetry, and philosophy and the Institution or the City" or, in Dorothy L. Sayers's view, Virgil is "the Natural Man in his perfection . . . the idea of Empire . . . humanistic ethics . . . Natural Religion." Whichever of these two interpretations (among many) more accurately describes Dante's Virgil is irrelevant here; the point is that he is intended to be interpreted on multiple levels. In terms of events, the ascent of Mount Purgatory by Dante's pilgrim not only depicts his journey up a steep mountain, but it also simultaneously signifies the purification of his soul from sinful inclinations, the transformation of his mind, and his growth in virtue. Religious or scriptural allegory, then, differs from secular allegory by its use of historical figures and places, as opposed to personifications, and by its potential for multiple interpretations, as opposed to a single, restricted one.

Although Bunyan primarily uses personification of immaterial reality and Dante primarily uses historical characters and locations, there are examples in both works of occasional points of crossover, as when Bunyan's pilgrim encounters Moses, who can hardly be called an invented personification, or when Dante personifies the books of the Bible and the theological and cardinal virtues in the procession in the Garden of Eden (see *Purg.* 29.83–150).

Lewis uses secular allegory for *The Pilgrim's Regress* rather than scriptural allegory. There are at least two reasons why he may have made this choice. First, Lewis's story has a single interpretation rather than multiple ones: Lewis is chiefly recounting *one* stage of his spiritual development, namely, his intellectual conversion to Christianity. His progress, as described in the book's preface, "from 'popular realism' to Philosophical Idealism . . . to Pantheism . . . to Theism . . . to Christianity" does not entail several levels of significance. Second, the characters in Lewis's allegory represent philosophies and various schools of religious and literary thought

in Britain prior to his conversion in 1931, so the embodiment of
these abstract entities is more simply and accurately rendered
through personification. A personification like Mr. Enlightenment
in Book II, 1, for example, would more clearly signify that particular philosophy than a character like Voltaire, who would, as a historical figure, carry other meanings like "philosophical novelist"
or "precursor of the French Revolution"—meanings that would be
irrelevant to the story and would thus detract from a clear and
focused expression of a character's intended significance.

Nevertheless, although Lewis's mode of allegory ties him to *The
Pilgrim's Progress*, the geographical design of Lewis's fictive world
and the journey of his pilgrim through that world are quite different from Bunyan's story. One critic has even remarked that "Lewis's
emulation of Bunyan in *The Pilgrim's Regress* is . . . almost entirely
unlike Bunyan." I would agree. But I would heartily disagree with
his conclusion that "Lewis did not understand Bunyan well" because I think Lewis most surely did. In writing *The Pilgrim's Regress*,
Lewis emulated Bunyan, but not *only* Bunyan. Many of the major
differences between *The Pilgrim's Progress* and Lewis's work can be
explained by observing the ways that Lewis merged Bunyan's style
with features of Dante's *Divine Comedy*. Even in writing secular
allegory, Lewis relied heavily on the structure of Dante's universe
and on the journey of Dante's pilgrim.

Lewis's Fictional World and Its Inhabitants

Although Lewis's imaginary world in *The Pilgrim's Regress* does
not resemble the earth and heavens depicted in Dante's poem, the
design of his fictional world draws on Dante's pattern for constructing a geography that has spiritual significance. Bunyan's fictive world is a "blank world," so to speak, dotted with allegorical
places that lack internal design. Except for the departure of his
hero Christian from the City of Destruction and his arrival at the
Celestial City, there is a randomness to the shape of that world:
Doubting Castle could have been placed closer to, or further from,
the Slough of Despond without doing harm to the story. In contrast, Dante's universe and Lewis's fictional world—in addition to
the significance of the specific locations—are shaped by an overall

meaning that results, in both cases, in imaginative worlds that have a depth and complexity not found in Bunyan's.

In *The Divine Comedy*, Dante makes geographical features equivalent to spiritual realities through the use of an overarching metaphor. The Sun represents God (as well as grace, truth, light, and love) and serves as the reference point for the layout of his universe. Every area is spiritually defined by its geographical relationship to the Sun. Hell, in its traditional setting under the earth, is the region farthest from the Sun and is cut off from its light, thus representing separation from God. Mount Purgatory reaches up toward the Sun, so its ascent represents movement toward God. The heavens are the location of the Sun where increasing light represents increasing union with God.

With the Sun as his key metaphor, Dante constructs the subdivisions in his three realms as elaborations of this fundamental pattern. The circles of hell are located at a greater and greater distance from the Sun, indicating increasing levels of the gravity of a given sin. The ascending ledges of Mount Purgatory are progressively closer to the Sun, indicating increasing levels of acquired virtue and decreasing gravity of the capital sins being purged. In the heavens, the spheres are filled with successive increases in light, indicating increasing levels of blessedness. The spiritual condition of any soul in Dante's universe can be deduced merely by its location in this scheme because the very geography of this universe is itself a tacit message.

The overall geography of Lewis's fictional world likewise reflects spiritual reality and does so through a metaphor that regulates its whole design. In *The Pilgrim's Regress*, the Eastern Mountains (God's dwelling place) metaphorically represent Truth and functions analogously to Dante's Sun; that is, these mountains determine the spiritual significance of each location in this world. Since east represents Truth, the central section of this world lying west of the Eastern Mountains necessarily represents error. The nineteen shires and their cities that comprise this inhabited section represent thought systems that are all departures from Truth, but the degree of error in any given system is indicated by that shire's proximity to or distance from the east. The shire of Pagus, for instance, lies farther west than the shire of Puritania, which indicates that, in Lewis's eyes, pagan philosophy entails more serious error than Puritanism. The

uninhabited far-west region on the other side of the canyon lies
beyond the shires of error and represents a *vision* of truth because
the Eastern Mountains can only be viewed, but not reached, from
this vantage point. The far west is the starting point in the quest for
truth, and it is from this point that the actual journey to the east
begins. The very design of Lewis's world, like Dante's, carries an
unspoken message.

In addition to an overall design that reflects the story's message, the nineteen shires of Lewis's inhabited middle region are
divided into two major categories whose significance is tied to the
significance of the two main divisions of Dante's hell. Insofar as
the five upper circles of Dante's hell and its four lower circles are
cut off from the Sun, both areas signify departures from grace, but
they are of different kinds. The upper circles of hell represent the
passionate, spontaneous sins of the flesh or of incontinence (lust,
gluttony, avarice/prodigality, and wrath). The lower circles represent more serious cold-hearted, premeditated sins of the mind or
will (heresy, violence, fraud, and treason).

Lewis includes a similar kind of contrast in his distinction between the southern and northern areas of his fictional world. Since
north and south both lie west of the Eastern Mountains, they represent departures from Truth, but they are of different kinds. In
his preface, Lewis distinguishes between south and north through
their inhabitants: "The Southerners are . . . boneless souls whose
doors stand open day and night . . . with readiest welcome for
those . . . who offer some sort of intoxication," while "Northerners
are the men of rigid systems, whether skeptical or dogmatic." In
other words, the errors of the Southerners are due to their emphasis on passion, emotion, self-indulgence, and are reflected in such
names as the shire of Orgiastica and the city of Aphroditopolis.
The errors of the Northerners are due to their emphasis on cold,
abstract, cerebral systems and are reflected by such shire names
as Dialectica and Cruelsland. Lewis's south, then, roughly corresponds to Dante's upper circles of hell, the sins of the flesh, while
his north corresponds to Dante's lower circles of premeditated sins.

Although all three parts of Dante's universe (hell, purgatory,
heavens) have subdivisions, Lewis's three-part world (Eastern
Mountains, the middle region, the far west) has no subdivisions
except in the inhabited middle region. However, his internal

structure of that region echoes a pattern found in Dante's hell. For example, souls in the seventh circle who shed the blood of others are immersed in a river of boiling blood, but the extent of any given sinner's submersion—from one's ankles to whole-body submersion—is determined by and correlated to the amount of blood that person shed (see *Inf.* 12.103). All murderers are guilty of the same sin—and are, therefore, at the same distance from the Sun—but their relative degrees of guilt are indicated through a corresponding intensity of that punishment.

The central section of Lewis's world is also designed to distinguish between degrees, in this case degrees within a given error. Lewis indicates this by the location of a shire farther south and farther north of the Main Road. For example, directly south of Pagus (pagan philosophy) lie Golnesshire (lechery) and farther south, Occultica (practice of the occult). All three of these shires are characterized by the same error of materialism and are thus equidistant from the east; but by being farther away from the Main Road, the southernmost shires represent that error, according to Lewis, in its progressively extreme forms.

Unlike the personified locations in Bunyan's allegory that function just like the characters, as helps or hindrances along the pilgrim's path, specific locations in Dante's universe and Lewis's world have a different function from that of the characters. Hell, for instance, is the setting for the pilgrim's encounters with Francesca in the circle of lust or with Farinata in the circle of heretics, but the pilgrim does not interact with any region in the afterlife per se. Likewise, the specific locations in Lewis's world serve merely as the settings for John's interactions with the characters there. Locations in Dante's threefold universe represent the possible spiritual states of a soul that are perennial (sin, spiritual growth, and blessedness), while his characters are past or contemporary representatives of those sins or virtues. The characters one would meet there would thus vary according to the timeframe of the journey, but the geographical structure of that spiritual universe remains the same.

Similarly, Lewis's world represents perennial categories of philosophical and theological systems, while his characters represent modern representatives of those categories. A shire like Zeitgeistheim is found in every century, but not until the twentieth century would one encounter Sigismund (Freudianism) there. The characters would vary from age to age, but the map of that world and its significance remains the same.

By creating a world whose structure has perennial significance but whose characters are contemporary to his pilgrim, Lewis succeeds—as Dante did before him—in the simultaneous depiction of the local/specific and the perennial. This intersection of the local/specific and the perennial results for both authors in a story that is at once rooted in time and timeless.

Any discussion of the similarity in geography between the world in *The Pilgrim's Regress* and Dante's must necessarily include a description of the Valley of Wisdom in Books VII, IX, X, because Lewis closely patterns it after the first circle of Dante's hell, Limbo, the dwelling of righteous pagans. One of Lewis's epigraphs for Book VII is his translation of *Inferno* 4.40–42 in which Virgil explains his presence in Limbo: "Through this [lack of faith in Christ] and through no other fault we fell, / Nor being fallen, bear other pain than this /—Always without hope in desire to dwell."

Lewis parallels his Valley of Wisdom to Dante's Limbo through a series of details that mimic his description of that place and the visit of Dante's pilgrim there.

(1) The journey of Dante's pilgrim in hell always involves a downward direction. When John approaches Wisdom's house, he "went on, always downhill" (Book VII, 4).

(2) The souls in Dante's Limbo dwell in a castle in a grassy area encircled by a river (see *Inf.* 4.106–108, 118). John sees a house in the middle of a wide lawn that is encircled by a river (see Book VII, 6).

(3) Although the rest of Dante's hell is dark, his pilgrim sees "a light that overcame the dark hemisphere there" (*Inf.* 4.68–69); John sees (since it is night) that "lamps were already lit within" the house (Book VII, 6).

(4) Dante's pilgrim recognizes, among other souls, "the master of knowledgeable men [Aristotle], seated in the midst of the family of philosophers" (*Inf.* 4.131–132). John recognizes "Wisdom, sitting among his children, like an old man" (Book VII, 6).

(5) The souls in Dante's Limbo have "serious, slow-moving eyes . . . and seldom spoke but did so with soft voices" (*Inf.* 4.112–114). Wisdom and his children have "resigned voices . . . [and] faces, so quiet" (Book VII, 10).

(6) Dante lists several virtuous pagans in Limbo only by their first names: Camilla, Aeneas, Zeno, and so on (see *Inf.* 4.121–144); Lewis lists the names of Wisdom's children only by their first names: Karl (Marx), Rudolph (Steiner), Benedict (Spinoza), and so on (Book VII, 10).

Lewis's use of these details clearly suggests the setting and atmosphere of Dante's Limbo. Wisdom's house is the last place that John visits before he crosses the canyon to enter the far-western section of that world. If one were to leave Dante's hell through Limbo, it would be the last place visited before reentering the earth. Perhaps Lewis's parallel is a signal that just as someone emerging from Limbo would be leaving hell and sin behind, so too John is about to leave behind the inhabited world with its error and deception concerning his island.

Lewis's suggested link between Wisdom's house and Dante's Limbo becomes explicit during John's return journey east. His newly appointed guide for that segment of the journey, Slikisteinsauga (whetstone eyes), explains that during John's initial journey west, this place was called the Valley of Wisdom, "But now that you are going East you may call it Limbo, or the *twilit porches of the black hole*" (Book X, 3; italics added)—a poetic description and commentary on Lewis's part of Dante's first circle that has light but could be called a "porch" with respect to the rest of his dark hell. In Dante's Limbo, one hears "only the sounds of sighs" (*Inf.* 4.26), and John now hears only "the sound of their sighing" (Book X, 3). John's guide then paraphrases and repeats the last verse from the *Inferno* used at the beginning of Book VII: "It is their doom to live for ever in desire without hope" (Book X, 3).

In *The Divine Comedy* souls are in Limbo because "the merit they had was not enough; they did not have baptism, the doorway to faith" (*Inf.* 4.34–36) and because "they did not worship God the way they should have" (*Inf.* 4.38). Virgil explains, "Not what I did but what I did not do caused me to forfeit being able to see the lofty sun [God] you seek" (*Purg.* 7.25–26). Lewis offers a moral as well as a theological explanation for the presence of Wisdom's family in his version of Limbo, saying they have kept alive "the deep desire of the soul but through some fatal flaw, of pride or sloth . . . or timidity, have refused . . . the only means to its fulfillment" (Book X, 3). Despite these different rationales, the point both authors are making is that nobility of life or philosophical wisdom do not suffice for salvation. As one Dante scholar points out, "If there are some truths which it is indispensable for a man to know, and he doesn't know them, then no matter how much else he does know he might just as well know nothing."

In brief, every part of Dante's fictional universe has significance in its representation of the spiritual states of sin, purgation, or blessedness. Similarly, Lewis's fictional world, which is depicted on the map accompanying the novel and includes locations John never even visits, is designed to represent a world of truth and error, and every area is labeled to make that meaning clear to the reader. Lewis's world, by its internal design, its significance, its function, and its similar Limbo, is a sister world to the world in Dante's *Divine Comedy*, because the dialectic of truth and error—like the dialectic of sin and grace—remains universal for human beings in every age.

John's Journey

Like the fictional world in *The Pilgrim's Regress*, the shape of this journey finds its counterpart in Dante's *Divine Comedy* rather than in Bunyan's story. *The Pilgrim's Progress* recounts a simple, straightforward journey for the most part: Christian is converted at the very beginning and leaves the City of Destruction to reach the Celestial City. He overcomes moral hindrances and receives assistance along the way to reaching his goal.

The journey in *The Pilgrim's Regress*, on the other hand, occurs in three distinct phases that parallel the general contours of the Dantean journey. In *The Divine Comedy* during the journey through hell, Dante's pilgrim undergoes the first stage of his conversion, which involves coming to understand the nature of sin; his passage through the nine circles and out of hell signifies his repudiation of sin. The first segment of John's journey, from east to west, deals with his intellectual struggle to learn the truth about the island. In this phase, he learns to repudiate the various errors about his island and discovers that the Eastern Mountains represent his true desire. Dante's pilgrim, during a journey that always proceeds downward and farther away from the Sun, passes through circles that represent increasingly more serious sin. Likewise, Lewis's protagonist, traveling farther away from the east, journeys through areas that represent increasingly more serious error. In other words, the journey *west* in Lewis's novel philosophically and morally parallels the journey *down* in the *Inferno*.

The second segment of the journey for Dante's pilgrim in the *Purgatorio* deals with the pilgrim's moral development. In this phase the seven P's (for *Peccatum*, representing the seven sinful dispositions common to humanity) that are inscribed on his forehead at the gate of Mount Purgatory are removed during his arduous ascent of the mount, signifying the cleansing of his soul from evil inclinations and his growth in virtue. The second segment of John's journey, the pilgrim's "regress" eastward through the same territory, deals with his moral development as well. In this phase, he develops moral fortitude by resisting the lure of *Luxuria* (lust) in the south (see Book X, 7) and by slaying the dragon of the north "so that [his heart] could never again flutter with panic or with greed" (Book X, 8). During his journey east, John sees the true ruling inhabitants of the world he had just passed through: *Superbia* (pride), *Ignorantia* (agnosticism), and *Luxuria* (lust)—in that order—from west to east. Insofar as *Superbia* and *Luxuria* correspond to pride and lust, the first and last sinful dispositions on Dante's mount, John's journey east reflects a purgatorial pattern as well. Dante's pilgrim climbs upward through ledges on Mount Purgatory where decreasingly serious evil dispositions are purged. In a similar fashion John, traveling east, goes through areas of decreasing degrees of error. In other words, the journey *east* in Lewis's novel philosophically and morally parallels the journey *up* in the *Purgatorio*.

Although Dante geographically distinguishes hell and purgatory, Lewis creates the theological distinction between them by using the same terrain but having John receive spiritual vision as he journeys back through it. John is told that the very different world he now sees "is just as it was when you passed it before, . . . but your eyes are altered. You see nothing now but realities" (Book X, 2). Both authors, however, imply a theological kinship between those two realms. Dante's hell involves *punishment for sin* while purgatory involves *cleansing from sin*. Similarly, John *encounters error* during his journey west and *overcomes error* on his journey east.

The major event that divides the first two legs of John's journey occurs when he reaches his island and discovers it is inaccessible from the west, and that turning point bears similarity to the arrival of Dante's pilgrim in Mount Purgatory's Garden of Eden. For both pilgrims, arrival at the previously desired goal becomes a new beginning. The journey for both protagonists up to this point has not been the final journey to the true good but rather preparation for the journey that leads to the true good, God.

Both Dante and Lewis indicate this transition point by major shifts in pattern for the remainder of the journey. In Dante's poem, there is a change in the direction of the journey—away from the earth and up into the heavens—as well as a shift in the mode of travel. The pilgrim is no longer walking but is propelled upward by the force of his spiritual desires (see *Par.* 2.18–20). In Lewis's novel, this change takes the form of a reversal in the direction of the journey: John must now "regress" eastward to find what he truly desires, for "the way to go on . . . is to go back" (Book IX, 6).

The chapter in Lewis's novel in which John learns he must retrace his steps is titled "Nella Sua Voluntade"—a phrase from the famous passage in the *Paradiso* in which a redeemed soul says, "*In His will* is our peace" (*Par.* 3.85; italics added). In paraphrasing part of Dante's verse for his chapter title, Lewis intends to convey John's disposition of overcoming his initial disappointment and peacefully acquiescing to retrace his steps.

Both pilgrims are given guides noted for their powers of vision for this new phase of the journey: Beatrice, replacing Virgil, is endowed with "perfect vision" (see *Par.* 5.5) and helps the pilgrim understand what he sees. John is led by the angel Slikisteinsauga whose "sight was so sharp that the sight of any other who travelled with him would be sharpened by his company" (Book IX, 6).

The pilgrims also receive special vision themselves to equip them for this next phase of the journey. Although Dante's pilgrim has seen the spiritual realities of the afterlife from the very beginning, after his reunion with Beatrice his vision is transformed and expanded. Gazing at her, he is changed within (see *Par.* 1.67–69) and is able to withstand successive increases of light from sphere to sphere, until he has the capacity for visions of God. John's knowledge of the truth about the island has transformed his sight; now he sees the terrain differently because he himself is different. John had journeyed west a natural man and had seen the current inhabitants of the country as men and women; now he journeys east as a spiritual man and sees the spiritual beings that perennially inhabit the land. He had originally seen cities and normal countryside; now he sees that the region south of the Main Road consists of "swamps and jungle sinking almost at once into black cloud," while the region north of the Main Road is a land of "crags rising within a few paces of the road into ice and mist and, beyond that, black cloud" (Book X, 1).

Although there are distinctions between the errors of the south and north, as reflected in the different types of terrains, both areas lead to "black cloud." The distinctions that initially seem significant are swallowed up by the similarity that levels them. The black cloud signifies mental darkness and confusion, and those who depart for the Main Road, whether to the south or the north, end up, like all of Dante's souls in hell, as those "who have lost the good of the intellect" (*Inf.* 3.18).

The third segment of the journey for Dante's pilgrim concludes with his arrival in the Empyrean (God's dwelling beyond the physical universe) where he experiences union with God. Similarly, the third segment of John's journey—and the novel ends as he *begins* this phase—is the journey across the brook (representing death) into the Eastern Mountains, representing union with God.

Although all three segments of the journey in *The Divine Comedy* are allotted equal attention and equal space (thirty-three cantos each), Lewis's narration of the journey westward takes up the bulk of the novel (Books I–IX). The journey eastward is given little space (Book X), and the journey into the Eastern Mountains is alluded to but not described in the very last chapter, where the narrator remarks that "they were already at the brook, but . . . I did not see them go over" (Book X, 10). However, Dante is dealing with all the possible states of a soul's relationship to God, while Lewis is focusing on the story of his recent intellectual conversion. In a 1941 letter, Lewis explains that the "reason why John's return journey is so simple in the book is that I hadn't then begun traveling it and knew v. [*sic*] little about it." Despite these narrative differences, the general pattern of the three segments of John's journey parallels the three stages of the Dantean journey in a way that makes Lewis's hero similar to Dante's pilgrim.

Beatrice

The meeting between Dante's pilgrim and Beatrice in the Garden of Eden takes up the last five cantos of Dante's *Purgatorio*, and according to Lewis the last quarter of the *Purgatorio* "is the heart of the whole book." It is therefore not surprising that—in a similar fictional world with a similar fictional pilgrim—this major event of the Dantean journey finds an echo in *The Pilgrim's Regress*. This is the novel in which Lewis most clearly sets forth his understanding of Beatrice's role in Dante's poem. In *The Pilgrim's Regress*, it is John's island that functions as Beatrice—that is, as a channel of grace—and it is in John's apprehensions of the island that he has what Lewis calls "Beatrician experience."

When John first sees the island in the far west, it gives him intense joy, arousing in him a desire and a longing that propel him to begin his journey. According to Lewis, "joy (as distinct from mere pleasure, still more from amusement) emphasises our pilgrim status: always reminds, beckons, awakens desire." In his autobiography, Lewis says that this joy "is distinct . . . even from aesthetic pleasure . . . [and] must have the stab, the pang, the inconsolable longing." Lewis refers to this dialectic of joy and desire as *Sehnsucht* here (and elsewhere). This German word, which means "longing," recalls both the vocabulary and the ideology of the Romantic school.

Romanticism, a nineteenth-century movement throughout Europe in literature, music, and painting, was characterized, among other things, by an emphasis on imagination and emotions rather than reason. It involved a revolt against traditional social and artistic conventions and brought a new appreciation for nature. What Lewis says he meant by "romantic" when he wrote *The Pilgrim's Regress* "was a particular recurrent experience which dominated my childhood and adolescence . . . of intense longing . . . [and] the mere wanting felt to be somehow a delight."

Although Lewis's notion of longing and joy can be associated with Romanticism, that joy and desire also parallel the experience of Dante's pilgrim. When Dante's pilgrim first saw Beatrice prior to the events in the poem, the sight of her impelled him to begin to pursue the right path, and she was his inspiration to advance spiritually. After her death and his subsequent departure from righteousness, the pilgrim's desire for the joy that would come from a reunion with Beatrice becomes the initial motivating force for undertaking his journey.

Both Dante's Beatrice and John's island have been the occasion of dramatic personal experiences—"known" channels of good, "known" sources of joy—and as such, each continues to be an impetus for the journey particularly when obstacles dampen the desire or quench the will to continue forward. For Dante's pilgrim, Beatrice is his constant thought. When he refuses to go through the wall of fire on the ledge of lust on Mount Purgatory because it will burn him, only one motive is able to prod him forward: "This wall is what stands between you and Beatrice" (*Purg.* 27.36). John is likewise spurred on by continual reminiscences of the island; at times he catches fleeting glimpses of it, at times he sees it in night visions, but those glimpses keep him moving forward.

Lewis, like Dante, addresses the issue of substitutes for the true good along the journey. Beatrice explains that at an earlier time for Dante's pilgrim, she "sustained him with my countenance: showing him my youthful eyes, I led him with me towards the right path" (*Purg.* 30.121–123). After her death, however, the pilgrim "abandoned me [Beatrice] and gave himself to others" (*Purg.* 30.126). Dante's pilgrim confesses in the Garden of Eden that "worldly things with their false joys turned my steps *as soon as I no longer saw your face*" (*Purg.* 31.34–36; italics mine). In losing sight of Beatrice, his standard, his spiritual journey was derailed.

Lewis uses verses from *The Divine Comedy* to discuss this very point in his novel. One of the four epigraphs for Book II—the book in which John begins to accept substitutes for his island—is Lewis's translation of *Purgatorio* 30.131–132: "Following false copies of the good, that no / Sincere fulfillment of their promise make." John is distracted early in his journey, for instance, by brown girls and then by Media Halfways in the city of Thrill (all representing lust) who promise that they are really what he is looking for. Other instances of distraction and confusion occur throughout his journey.

The deception of "false copies of the good" is explained near the end of John's journey west by the hermit Mr. History. John's vision of the island, like other visions people have had, "tends inevitably to be confused with common or even with vile satisfactions lying close at hand, yet which is able, if any man faithfully live through the dialectic of its successive births and deaths, to lead him at last where true joys are to be found" (Book VIII, 9). Despite detours and sidetracks by both John and Dante's pilgrim, John's island, like Beatrice, functions as the kind of standard that, according to Lewis, if "faithfully followed, would retrieve all mistakes, head you off from all false paths." By clinging to his vision of the island, John is ultimately not deceived by the Southerners who offer various substitutes for it or by the Northerners who deny its very existence for various reasons.

Lewis makes the analogy between John's island and Dante's Beatrice explicit when John learns from Mr. History that throughout the ages, the Landlord (God) has sent different kinds of pictures (metaphors) to men in an effort to bring them to himself:

> What is universal is not the particular picture, but the arrival of some message . . . which wakes this desire and sets men longing for something East or West of the world. . . . The strangest shape it ever took was in Medium Aevum, . . . a picture of a Lady! . . . [One man] carried this new form of the desire right up to its natural conclusion and found what he had really been wanting. He wrote it all down in what he called a *Comedy*. (Book VIII, 9)

Lewis makes plain that John's island is, like Beatrice, one of the many shapes that the "image" of good can take, and that they are both "pictures" sent from "the Landlord." The island, like Beatrice, functions as a kind of lighthouse that has led the pilgrim thus far but now points beyond itself, to the final joy, to the ultimate good that is desired.

Lewis solidifies his analogy between Beatrice and the island by using narrative details about the pilgrim's arrival in the Garden of Eden to describe John's arrival at the island: the status of the pilgrims is similar, the landscape is similar, and the pilgrims' initial experiences are similar.

As he is about to reach his island, John is in a spiritual position corresponding to that of Dante's pilgrim awaiting Beatrice's arrival. Dante's pilgrim has just accomplished the ordeal of his journey. He has seen the horrors of hell, ascended the mount, passed through the ledge of fire, and will be cleansed in the rivers Lethe and Eunoë. John has similarly accomplished the ordeal of his journey. He has traveled through the world of error, has been imprisoned and released, has overcome deceptions, and has been cleansed (baptized) in the pool at the bottom of the canyon.

The setting for John's arrival at the island echoes the setting for the meeting with Beatrice in the garden in a number of respects. For John, "It was early in the morning" (Book IX, 5). The far-western area of John's world is "a place very ancient . . . deep in the silence of forests." The virgin warrior Reason, who had assisted John earlier in his journey, reappears to accompany him at this point. John walks "*westward* along the banks of a *clear river* [italics added]." He is in a place that is described as being, "in some sort, lying rather at the world's beginning, as though men were born travelling away from it"—a description that recalls the Garden of Eden.

For Dante's pilgrim it is a "new morning," and he wanders "deep within the ancient woods" (*Purg.* 28.23) Virgil (who represents reason, among other things) walks with Dante's pilgrim in the garden until Beatrice arrives. Dante's pilgrim strolls *westward* along the banks of Lethe, which is *clearer* than any river on earth. While John walks in a garden that hearkens back to Garden of Eden, Dante's pilgrim is in the original garden itself.

John's experience, when he does reach the island, is also similar to that of Dante's pilgrim. In both cases, attainment of the original goal comes with unexpected and unwelcome surprises. In the *Purgatorio*, the initial reunion is not a happy occasion but a day of reckoning. This Beatrice is not the tender, understanding Beatrice the pilgrim had been longing to see. This is Beatrice seen from a different angle—Beatrice as judge, chiding the pilgrim and insisting on his confession of culpability for having left the right path (see *Purg.* 31.22–30). John too sees his island from a different angle—as the back of the Eastern Mountains. It is "different from his desires, and so different that, if he had known it, he would not have sought it" (Book IX, 5). Nevertheless, in both cases the unwelcome surprises give way to joy as each pilgrim moves forward to attain his ultimate desire.

John's island, like Dante's Beatrice, is not the true goal of the journey. It is only an image (although a true image) of the desired good; each is a channel (but not the source) of the joy the pilgrim desires. This clearly intentional parallel between Dante's Beatrice and John's island does not eliminate the differences between the two—the island is an inert object while Beatrice is a living person.

Even so, Beatrice and the island are theologically equivalent inso-far as both illustrate Lewis's belief that God can use all of creation, from inanimate nature to living beings, to attract individuals to himself, and Lewis's choice of a static object rather than a person to be the "Beatrice" of this story serves to highlight this concept. In fact, the novel's narrator underscores this very point about the variety of channels that God can use: when John finally sees his island, "what the others [with John] saw I do not know: but John saw the Island" (Book IX, 5).

Conclusion

As noted above, Lewis considers the meeting between Dante's pilgrim and Beatrice as a literary archetype of a spiritually transfor-mative encounter and names it the "Beatrician experience." Readers will see new Beatrices again and again in Lewis's fiction. No future Beatrice in Lewis's fiction will be inanimate, however. Lewis leaves behind the idea of nature as this kind of image for the good and, in his future writing, always gives this Beatrician function to a living being. Likewise, Lewis continually redraws the scene in Dante's Garden of Eden throughout his work, casting it and recasting it in a number of different variations.

In his *Allegory of Love*, Lewis comments that "the art of read-ing allegory is as dead as the art of writing it, and more urgently in need of revival if we wish to do justice to the Middle Ages." At the beginning of this chapter, I noted that Lewis's choice of the title *The Pilgrim's Regress* would immediately recall Bunyan's allegory for readers, preparing the reader for Bunyan's mode of storytelling (secular allegory) and suggesting that the story involves a spiri-tual journey. The difficulty of such allegories for modern readers involves both the unfamiliar form and the medieval assumptions about human beings and types of characters and landscapes that are generally foreign to them. Nevertheless, *The Pilgrim's Regress* can serve as a good introduction to secular allegory for a mod-ern reader. The story deals with philosophies or movements that are recognizable (Romanticism, Freudianism, Humanism, and so forth), and Lewis uses carefully drawn images to reflect the essence of those abstract concepts.

Although it is perhaps the least read of Lewis's novels, it is significant that, as Joe R. Christopher aptly remarks, "the number of motifs and ideas in *The Pilgrim's Regress* that reappear in Lewis's later works indicates both how quickly his ideas matured and how little they changed."

The multitude of resonances between *The Pilgrim's Regress* and *The Divine Comedy* indicates that Dante's poem is a dominant paradigm for this novel. At the beginning of Lewis's writing career, Dante's fictional universe becomes a model for the construction of a fictional world. Lewis uses the journey through hell, purgatory, and heaven as a model for John's journey to the west, east, and beyond. Dante's Beatrice is taken up by Lewis as a precursor of John's island. Lewis never wrote another allegorical novel, but themes and features of *The Divine Comedy* are woven into the rest of his fiction in ways that are tailored to whatever genre he takes up.

CHAPTER THREE

Out of the Silent Planet

Introduction

Following the publication of *The Pilgrim's Regress* and *The Allegory of Love*, Lewis wrote a science fiction novel, *Out of the Silent Planet* (1938), the first of three novels that together comprise his Ransom trilogy.

In this novel, which Lewis called "a thriller about a journey to Mars," Elwin Ransom, a middle-aged Cambridge philologist, is abducted by the scientist Edward Rolles Weston and his business partner Dick Devine and taken to Malacandra (Mars) as a possible sacrifice for its inhabitants. Ransom escapes from his captors upon arrival, and the bulk of the novel records his adventures as he learns about the language, history, culture, and spiritual condition of the planet's three *hnau* (rational species): the Hrossa, Séroni, and Pfifltriggi. He becomes aware that the Malacandrians, in sharp contrast to people on Earth, live together peacefully according to the will of their deity Maleldil. When the planet's chief ruling spirit, the Oyarsa of Malacandra, summons Ransom, Weston, and Devine for interviews and hears Weston's plan to colonize other planets, even at the price of exterminating their inhabitants, the Oyarsa commands Weston and Devine to leave and never to return. Ransom, when given the choice to stay or go, decides to return home but is commanded to be on guard against any evil the other two men might still do.

Lewis took up the science fiction genre for at least four reasons. First, it can encompass a broad range of stories—space journeys, exotic adventures, time travel, utopias, and dystopias. Second, it can lend itself to a wide variety of purposes that range from futuristic speculation to satire. Third, Lewis was particularly interested in the fact that science fiction could "be filled by spiritual experiences." Outer space could become an analog for inner space, and other planets could become the stage for a discussion of spiritual, ethical, and philosophical issues.

Fourth, Lewis had a polemical motive for writing science fiction:

> What immediately spurred me to write [*Out of the Silent Planet*] was Olaf Stapledon's *Last and First Men* [1930] . . . and an essay in J. B. S. Haldane's *Possible Worlds* [1927] both of wh. [*sic*] seemed to have the desperately immoral outlook which I try to pillory in Weston. I like the whole inter-planetary idea as a *mythology* and simply wished to conquer for my own (Christian) pt. [*sic*] of view what has always hitherto been used by the opposite side.

Science fiction becomes a fictional forum for Lewis to challenge certain philosophical trends in the scientific community—and to challenge even science fiction itself, because at the time of his writing that genre was a primary vehicle for the dissemination of the trends he opposed.

Some scholars have called this novel "Lewis's imitation" or "creative alteration" of H. G. Wells's *First Men in the Moon*. Lewis, in fact, structures the basic plot in *Out of the Silent Planet* as a polemic against *First Men in the Moon* by paralleling many details of Wells's plot and then adding the character Ransom as a contrast to counter the viewpoint of Wells's two main characters, Cavor and Bedford. Lewis's Weston and Devine mirror Wells's team of an amoral scientist and a capitalist: Weston (like Cavor) is motivated by the desire to colonize a planet for man's posterity, while Devine (like Bedford) is interested in a potentially lucrative enterprise. Wells's duo has experiences that confirm their negative preconceptions about life beyond our planet that outer space is a black void and that the universe is filled with death and hostile aliens. Lewis's Weston and Devine have the same set of assumptions as their Wellsian counterparts, but their assumptions block a true perception of reality and pervert what they see. Lewis thus leaves Wells's storyline and two main characters fairly intact but demonstrates the error of their negative preconceptions (and Wells's worldview) through Ransom's perspective as he learns that the universe is full of life, goodness, and beauty and is inhabited by joyful and peaceful non-terrestrials.

Lewis's story thus stands as a contrast to Wells's novel, but it also stands in contrast to the novel that Lewis called "his real model," David Lindsay's *Voyage to Arcturus* (1920). Lindsay raises philosophical and spiritual dilemmas during the moral odyssey of his space voyager, but his attempt to distinguish good and evil fails and the novel ends in confusion and despair. Lewis describes Lindsay as "the first writer to discover what 'other planets' are really good for in fiction" and as the one "who first gave me the idea that the 'scientifiction' appeal could be combined with the 'supernatural' appeal." That is the only debt Lewis owes Lindsay, however, since he found that Lindsay's "spiritual outlook is detestable, almost diabolist I think, and his style crude."

One of the main factors that distinguishes Lewis's book from those of Wells and Lindsay is that he is restoring a Christian character to the cosmos that the science fiction writers of his time had universally discarded. In so doing, Lewis draws on *The Divine Comedy* as a model. He follows Dante's methodology for constructing an imaginative vision of a Christian cosmos by combining elements from science, philosophy, and mythology into a cohesive new unity. In addition, *The Divine Comedy* provides Lewis with a prototype of a journey into the heavens whose significance is primarily spiritual, so Lewis draws from patterns of that prototype for Ransom's journey and for his meeting with this novel's "Beatrice."

Lewis's Cosmos and Its Inhabitants

In Lewis's fictional cosmos, the universe is ruled by Maleldil, its Creator, and supervised by eldils (angelic beings) who dwell in Deep Heaven (outer space). Every planet in the solar system is overseen by a chief eldil or ruling spirit—called "Oyarsa" in Malacandra's Old Solar language—who rules the inhabitants by means of the eldils subordinate to him. The only planet excluded from this system is Thulcandra (Earth). When Earth's Oyarsa became "bent" (evil), he was exiled from Deep Heaven and confined to the air of his planet. Since that time, there has been no communication between Earth and Deep Heaven.

Lewis's cosmos differs from Dante's in two respects that necessarily accommodate a twentieth-century framework. First, the theological foundation of *The Divine Comedy*, which assumes a Christian readership, is no longer universally accepted or understood, so Lewis invents new names, symbols, and metaphors for his cosmos to parallel a Christian construct. Second, the Ptolemaic system, the classical and medieval model of the universe underlying Dante's poem, has been displaced, so Lewis bases his cosmos on the modern solar system.

Nevertheless, some features of Lewis's cosmos reflect the Ptolemaic universe of Dante's poem, which he describes this way in *The Discarded Image*:

> The central (and spherical) Earth is surrounded by a series of hollow and transparent globes, one above the other, and each of course larger than the one below. These are the "spheres," "heavens." . . . Fixed in each of the first seven spheres is one luminous body. Starting from Earth, the order is the Moon, Mercury, Venus, the Sun, Mars, Jupiter, and Saturn. . . . Beyond the sphere of Saturn is the *Stellatum* [the constellations], to which belong all those stars that we still call "fixed" because their positions relative to one another are, unlike those of the planets, invariable. Beyond the *Stellatum*, there is a sphere called the First Movable or *Primum Mobile*. This, since it carries no luminous body, gives no evidence of itself to our sense; its existence was inferred to account for the motions of all the others.

Some scholars have noted medieval features in Lewis's imaginary cosmos, given his love and respect for the Middle Ages, but the characteristics he incorporates have specific connections to Dante's interpretation of that medieval universe. The heavens are once again filled with the glory of the biblical Creator and are peopled with creatures who delight to do his will. Like Dante, Lewis achieves the imaginative representation of his cosmos by a synthesis of concepts from science, classical philosophy, and classical literature as he adapts that material to be in harmony with Christian truth. Drawing from the same storehouse of classical material as Dante—as well as from *The Divine Comedy* itself—Lewis follows Dante by ascribing the same spiritual significance that Dante did to certain physical features of the cosmos.

Lewis's cosmos reflects Dante's cosmos primarily in three ways: the retention of Dante's spiritual interpretation for Aristotle's distinction between Nature and Sky, the presence of angelic agents in the heavens who function like Dante's, and an allusion to Dante's interpretation of the music of the spheres.

First, Dante's Ptolemaic cosmos is shaped in line with Aristotle's division of the universe into Nature (*physis*) and Heaven or Sky (*ouranos*). "Nature" comprises the region of earth and air below the moon; it is composed of the four elements (fire, water, earth, and air) and is subject to change and corruption. "Heaven" comprises the area from the Moon and beyond; it is composed of the fifth element (ether) and is eternal and incorruptible.

In *The Divine Comedy*, in which the physical always mirrors the spiritual, this classical division of the universe becomes a reflection of the spiritual division in the universe. The sublunary region—Earth, including hell and purgatory—is the place of sin, evil, and imperfection while the heavenly region, under God's rule, is the place of grace and perfection. Dante specifically refers to Aristotle's two categories in his poem when Beatrice describes the point of light representing God: "The *heavens* and *all nature* are dependent on that point" (*Par.* 28.41–42; italics added). Dante weaves some implications of Aristotle's distinction into his pilgrim's journey as well. On Earth, Dante's pilgrim is subject to the sublunary rules of time, space, and the downward pull of gravity, so he becomes weary and needs sleep in the *Purgatorio*. During his journey into the unchangeable and incorruptible heavens, however, Dante's pilgrim can travel enormous distances instantly and never tires. Having been cleansed on Mount Purgatory and thus spiritually "freed from hindrance" (*Par.* 1.139–140), he is now also physically freed in the heavens as well. According to the *spiritual* law of gravity, he is automatically drawn upward toward God by the force of his spiritual desires (see *Par.* 2.19–20). Although his example of this law in the heavens is purely his invention, Dante's spiritual extrapolations are based on Aristotle's postulation of the diverse nature of these two regions.

Lewis cannot retain Aristotle's distinction between Nature and Sky because of modern physics, but he retains that division metaphorically to indicate the spiritual division of his cosmos. The sublunary and the heavens are still diametrically contrasting regions because the sublunary is under the rule of the Bent One, while the heavens are under the rule of Maleldil. These two separate regions, then, continue to differ spiritually for their respective inhabitants, just as they do in Dante's poem.

Second, according to Christian tradition, there are nine orders of angels, and Dante correlates those angels with the nine Ptolemaic spheres by making them responsible for rotating them. In shaping his angels, Dante draws on classical suppositions concerning the rotators of the spheres, and he extracts what can harmonize with the Christian doctrine of angels. He adapts Plato's notion of celestial beings and Aristotle's notion of spiritual intelligences to shape his Christian angels, making them "the intelligences that move these stars" (*Par.* 8.109–110), with each sphere having its own intelligence (see *Par.* 28.78).

With remarkable ingenuity, Lewis finds a way to incorporate angelic beings in his modern cosmos who act like their classical and medieval counterparts. Although the rotators of the Ptolemaic spheres disappeared when modern science chased them from the sky, Lewis peoples his heavens with chief eldils, supernatural beings who are in charge of rotating what is left—the planets. Adopting Dante's syncretistic methodology, Lewis shapes his chief eldils as a blend of classical mythological gods, Plato's demigods, and Dante's angels. Like the gods of mythology, each of the ruling eldils has individual characteristics traditionally associated with a given planet: Malacandra's chief eldil, for example, is masculine and warlike, and one of the chief colors of his planet is red. Like Plato's demigods, each Oyarsa is a transcendent being who rules over a specific planet. And finally, like Dante's angels, each Oyarsa is considered an angelic intelligence and is also a "rotator"—although of a planet now instead of a sphere.

Angels are typically thought of as worshipping God, waging spiritual battles, and guarding human beings, but Dante adds a specific function for his angels that Lewis adopts: angels partake in forming a planet's life-forms and thereby leave their characteristic imprint on them. Dante distinguishes between primary (or direct) creation by God—angels, human beings, the heavens, the elements—and secondary creation in which God acts in collaboration with other agents. For Dante, the angels and the planetary spheres they rule are responsible for shaping the characteristics of the earth's flora and fauna (see *Par.* 2.139–140; 7.133–135). Lewis indirectly introduces this concept in *Out of the Silent Planet* insofar as the planet reflects the characteristics of its Oyarsa. However, he makes it explicit in *Perelandra* when that planet's Oyarsa explains that "my face" can be seen in the water, the islands, the trees, the sky, and the animals. King Tor confirms this when he tells the Oyarsa of Venus, "We have often wondered whose hand it was that we saw in the long waves and the bright islands. . . . We saw dimly that to say 'It is Maleldil' was true, but not all the truth. . . . We take it [this planet] by *your gift* [italics added] as well as by His."

Lewis's lesser eldils are also fashioned in Dante's manner of fusing classical and Christian concepts, this time from Plato, Apuleius, and Augustine. Plato believes the creatures dwelling in the heavens, *daimones*, are all good spirits who are intermediaries between the planet-gods and men. Apuleius makes these creatures both good and evil but restricts them to the sublunary regions. Saint Augustine, like Apuleius, believes that *daimones* are restricted to the sublunary region, but he considers all of them evil. Lewis reconciles these various theories by adopting the notion of eldils being both good and evil (Apuleius), with good eldils dwelling in the heavens (Plato) and evil eldils inhabiting the sublunary region (Augustine).

Although Lewis's chief and lesser eldils represent a fusion of ancient and medieval prototypes, their fundamental identity is that of Dante's angels, because as intermediaries between Maleldil and all of creation, they are Lewis's version of biblical angels. In shaping his eldils, Lewis says that he "was v. [*sic*] definitely trying to smash the 19th century *female* angel. I believe *no* angel ever appears in Scripture without exciting terror: they always have to begin by saying 'Fear not.'" Lewis once remarked about angels in literature that "those of Dante are the best. Before his angels we sink in awe." In his essay "Dante's Similes," Lewis describes the angel of Dis in the *Inferno* as "surely the best angel ever made by a poet." It is, therefore, not surprising that Lewis would have looked to Dante's synthesizing approach for the shaping of his own splendid twentieth-century angels.

The third way that Dante's universe is echoed in Lewis's cosmos is through his indirect allusion to the music of the spheres. The music of the spheres, despite differences in its exact description by the ancients, was a universally accepted feature of the Ptolemaic universe. When the spheres rotated, they each produced a musical note that together comprised either a seven-note chord or an eight-note chord. Dante does not attempt to settle the dispute as to the number of notes in the heavenly chord, but his pilgrim does indeed hear music as soon as he rises from the earth (see *Par.* 1.76–78, 82). However, as always, Dante ascribes spiritual significance to that particular phenomenon: The music is not due primarily to the physical movement of the spheres but to the harmony of hymns of praise sung by the redeemed as the pilgrim rises from sphere to sphere.

Lewis handles the notion of the music of the spheres in the same way he handles other elements of Dante's Ptolemaic universe: Since he cannot incorporate its literal significance into his story, he incorporates Dante's spiritual interpretation of it. In all classical accounts, Earth does not participate in the music of the heavens because it is stationary, and Cicero explicitly notes that the heavens are "not silent" in contrast to the Earth, which is silent. The "silent planet," then, could be said to be one of Earth's names in the Ptolemaic scheme. In Lewis's novel, the term "silent planet" is meant to describe Earth's lack of communication with the rest of Deep Heaven after the Bent One was confined to its atmosphere. As the Oyarsa of Malacandra explains, Thulcandra "alone is outside the heaven, and no message comes from it." However, since Earth is under the rule of the Bent One, it is also the only planet that does not participate in joyful praise of Maleldil. In this regard, the name "silent planet" is consistent with Dante's spiritual interpretation of the music of the spheres.

Both Dante and Lewis, in line with the Platonic principle that the visible is patterned after the invisible, ascribe spiritual significance to the accepted scientific facts of their time. For Dante, the nine Ptolemaic spheres represent an exact reflection of the nine states of blessedness in the Empyrean (the true heaven beyond the physical universe). Dante also accepts the Ptolemaic concept that the Earth casts a conical shadow into the first three spheres of Moon, Venus, and Mercury. He interprets that scientific notion spiritually by placing in those three spheres the blessed whose lives, though now redeemed, were significantly shadowed by earthly imperfection.

Lewis, in a primary example of that same procedure, incorporates modern science in shaping his eldils. In Einstein's physics, light is the swiftest matter in motion that can be seen by the human eye without technical apparatus, making a body whose motion exceeds the speed of light invisible. Lewis extrapolates from this scientific tenet a plausible explanation for the traditional belief in the invisibility of angels. Although Lewis's eldils are corporeal beings, their normal motion exceeds the speed of light and thus renders them invisible, but when they decelerate their movement, they become visible to human beings. Lewis uses science here to "explain" the spiritual phenomena of angels appearing to people throughout the centuries.

In addition to the angelic beings who dwell in Deep Heaven, the inhabitants of Malacandra also reflect Dante's cosmos in recalling Dante's redeemed in the *Paradiso*. Dante's heavenly souls are in constant communion with God, and the creatures on this planet likewise dwell in constant spiritual awareness of their deity and his angelic messengers. Just as Dante's blessed are located in higher and higher spheres, so too each group of Malacandrians dwell in higher and higher places on the planet. The Pfifltriggi live on the plains and work underground in the mines, the Hrossa live higher up in the valleys, and the Séroni live higher up still in the hills. Dante's redeemed all share the Beatific Vision and form one harmonious community, but each of the nine groups of souls enjoys that vision in varying degrees. The utopian society on Malacandra is likewise comprised of separate groups that together form one harmonious community. Malacandra's three groups of *hnau* function in diverse capacities and are endowed with distinctly different abilities: the Pfifltriggi are miner-artisans; the Hrossa are farmer-poets; the Séroni are astronomer-scientists. In both "heavenly societies," however, inequality exists within a larger framework of equality; diversity exists within the larger framework of unity. In the *Paradiso* the basis for unity lies in the souls' adherence to the divine will. As one soul in heaven famously says, "In His will is our peace" (*Par.* 3.85). On Malacandra, the unity between these separate groups is likewise founded upon submission to Maleldil's will, and peace is also the direct result of their joyful obedience to Maleldil. The Malacandrian Oyarsa, in a rephrase of the substance of Dante's famous verse, tells the visiting Earthmen, "If you were subjects of Maleldil you would have peace" (*OSP* 140).

Incorporating what he could from Dante's cosmos, Lewis's cosmos results in being simultaneously modern and medieval, but also specifically Dantean. In his cosmos, the physical is an indicator of the spiritual, as it is in Dante's. His primary goal in the construction of such a cosmos, however, is to demonstrate the Christian tenet that Jesus Christ is Lord of the universe. Once again in our own time, as Dante had earlier written, "The glory of the One who moves all things permeates the universe" (*Par.* 1.1–2).

Ransom and His Journey

Lewis's partial restoration of Dante's cosmos, of course, paves the way for the possible appearance of someone like Dante's pilgrim. Although Ransom has been compared to J. R. R. Tolkien, Owen Barfield, Charles Williams, and even Lewis himself, scholars seem to have overlooked that he also bears several clear marks of his medieval kinsman from the very beginning of the trilogy.

(1) Dante's pilgrim is meant to represent Everyman; he is named only once, and that comes late in the poem. Ransom is first introduced only as the "Pedestrian" (*OSP* 7)—a kind of modern Everyman—and is referred to three times this way before we are told his name. One scholar believes that Lewis, by calling Ransom a "Pedestrian" at first, not only gives him the status of an "Everyman, but he also places him in the Dantean Dark Wood."

(2) Dante's pilgrim at the beginning of the poem is "in the middle of the journey of our life" (*Inf.* 1.1). According to Psalm 90:10, a human being's life-span is seventy years, or eighty if he or she is strong, so if Dante is taking Scripture as his measure in this case, the midpoint of life means that Dante's pilgrim is thirty-five to forty years old. Ransom is specifically described as "about thirty-five to forty" (*OSP* 7).

(3) Dante's pilgrim, as a poet and as the author of a linguistic treatise, *On Eloquence in the Vernacular* (*De vulgari eloquentia*), has a special interest in language and words. Ransom, as a philologist, has a professional interest in language and words.

(4) Just as Dante's pilgrim is turned back at the beginning of the story (from climbing the mountain) and is left confused in a dark wood in early evening, so Ransom is turned back (from the inn where he was to stay) and is left confused on an unfamiliar country road in early evening—a variation of Dante's dark wood experience.

At this narrative point, their adventures begin—Dante's pilgrim to the three realms of the afterlife and Ransom to Malacandra.

Similar pilgrims can imply similar journeys. One scholar suggests that Ransom resembles "a character out of Bunyan, one whose outer journey will reflect his soul's progress." Although it is true that Ransom's journey is a spiritual one, Ransom is not an allegory the way Bunyan's characters are since he is a multifaceted character like Dante's pilgrim. In fact, the Malacandrian journey recalls the pilgrim's journey in the *Inferno* and does so in four ways: parallel details at beginning of the journey, the significance of the journey, the ongoing demeanor of the pilgrim, and parallel details at the end of the journey.

First, several points of convergence occur at the beginning of both journeys. Dante's pilgrim does not initiate his journey; it has been ordained by heaven. Similarly, Ransom does not initiate his journey and later discovers that a heavenly Oyarsa had summoned him (see *OSP* 120). As Dante's pilgrim is about to begin his journey into the afterlife, he swoons, loses consciousness, and wakes to find himself having crossed the Acheron River into another realm (see *Inf.* 3.133–136). Before Ransom's journey begins, he is drugged, loses consciousness, and wakes to find himself en route to another world. While unconscious, Dante's pilgrim is mysteriously transported into a new realm typically reached in a small boat; Ransom is transported in a small spaceship. In a stylistic parallel, loss of consciousness for Dante's pilgrim is recorded in the last two verses of a canto (see *Inf.* 3.135–136), and Ransom's loss of consciousness is recorded in the last sentence of a chapter (*OSP* ch 2).

Given these suggestive parallels to the beginning of the journey in the *Inferno*, it is not surprising that the significance of Ransom's first journey parallels the significance of the first part of the journey for Dante's pilgrim. For both pilgrims, it is the beginning of their spiritual education. In the *Inferno*, the pilgrim is gradually instructed as to the nature of sin and evil; he witnesses sinners undergoing their various punishments and sees the essence of each sin reflected through the nature of its punishment. Ransom is likewise gradually brought to understand the depth and nature of sin and evil, in his case through the contrast he increasingly discovers between life on Malacandra and life on Earth. During his stay with the Hrossa, Ransom puzzles over why the natural instincts of these creatures "so closely resembled the unattained ideals of that far-divided species Man whose instincts were so deplorably different" (*OSP* 74). He moves to a state of acute embarrassment in his interaction with the Séroni who "were astonished at what he had to tell them of human history—of war, slavery and prostitution" (*OSP* 102). The effortless moral superiority of the Malacandrians becomes a tacit indictment of humanity's history and its fallen state. When his Hrossa friend Hyoi is shot and killed by Weston, Ransom acknowledges, "We [Earthmen] are all a bent race. . . . We are only half *hnau*" (*OSP* 81). His admission points to the fact that Earthmen have rational faculties like all *hnau*, but they are morally defective.

A third major similarity between the journeys concerns the emotional demeanor of the pilgrims. Dante's pilgrim is well known for his fear and timidity at almost every step of the way during his journey through hell. Ransom is likewise fearful at many points of his Malacandrian adventure, and at the end of his time there, the Oyarsa highlights this ongoing characteristic: "You are guilty of no evil . . . except a little fearfulness" (*OSP* 142).

Finally, Ransom's departure from Malacandra, like the beginning of his journey, includes a number of parallel details to the departure of Dante's pilgrim from hell. In order to leave the last circle of hell, Virgil and Dante's pilgrim must move past Satan. His six enormous flapping wings pose a danger, so Virgil "waited and watched for the right time and place . . . when the wings were stretched out enough" (*Inf.* 34.71–72). Leaving hell, and having seen the three faces of Satan described as yellow, red, and black, Virgil and Dante's pilgrim climb down one of Satan's legs and then turn upside down to reverse course (see *Inf.* 34.109–111)—an event that Lewis says involves "a science fiction element in *The Divine Comedy*." When Dante's pilgrim reaches the end of the tunnel out of hell, he exits "through a small round opening" (*Inf.* 34.138).

When the Earthmen are commanded to leave Malacandra, Weston carefully needs to plot the exact timing for takeoff since a danger is posed by the position of the two planets and the angle of solar rays (see *OSP* 140). Ransom, after liftoff, sees the sand deserts "appearing as illimitable stretches of *yellow* and *ochre* [red] . . . [and a] "*black* sky" (*OSP* 144–45; italics added). Ransom then goes "to the lower side of the sphere into the chamber which was now *most completely upside down"* (*OSP* 143; italics added). When Ransom's spaceship lands on Earth, he also exits through a small round hole, the spaceship's "manhole" (*OSP* 150). Ransom's trip takes exactly ninety days (see *OSP* 141), a multiple of nine, a number that was structurally significant for Dante in both his *Divine Comedy* and in *La Vita Nuova* (*New Life*), his collection of poems and prose.

The details at the beginning and end of this journey that parallel those in the *Inferno* function as bookends to enclose a journey whose primary significance is similar to that of Dante's pilgrim in hell. Just as Dante learns about the true nature of sin and evil during his journey through hell, so too Ransom becomes acutely aware of the specific ongoing evils of his planet.

Although Ransom's education about evil theologically and philosophically parallels that of Dante's pilgrim in the *Inferno*, Lewis's narrative also includes echoes of scenes, characters, and events from the *Paradiso*, for the journey in this novel is also a journey into the heavens. One such parallel concerns being blocked from perceiving the truth because of preconceived notions. When Dante's pilgrim first rises into the heavens, he believes he is still on Earth, so he does not understand what he sees. Beatrice tells him, "Your false perception is clouding your mind so that you are not seeing what you would see if you had shaken it off" (*Par.* 1.88–90). When he tells Beatrice what he thinks causes moon spots, he is told, "Your belief is steeped in error" (*Par.* 2.61–62). Ransom also has false notions and erroneous beliefs—in this case derived from the worldview in certain scientific circles and in most science fiction literature—that must be dealt with before he can perceive the truth. And Ransom's false notions are often adjusted by correctives that are in line with features from Dante's narrative.

The two main areas in Ransom's thinking that need correction involve, first, outer space and, second, extraterrestrial beings. He had "the dismal fancy" of outer space as "the black, cold vacuity, the utter deadness, which was supposed to separate the worlds" (*OSP* 32). Once he is in outer space, however, Ransom undergoes an experience similar to that of Dante's pilgrim, who rises up into the heavens precisely at noon and sees ever-increasing light from then on (see *Par.* 1.43–45). Once Ransom is in space, he sees "there were no mornings here, no evenings . . .—nothing but the *changeless noon*" (*OSP* 29; italics added); and on his return journey, space is again described as "the ocean of *eternal noon*" (*OSP* 146; italics added). On the other side of the ship that shows the night, Ransom sees throughout the heavens "*celestial* sapphires, rubies, emeralds and pin-pricks of burning gold" (*OSP* 31; italics added)—jewels that Dante uses as metaphors for the blessed in different locations throughout his heavens. Ransom now sees outer space—using Dante's word for the true heaven—as an "*empyrean* ocean of radiance" (*OSP* 32; italics added).

This initial adjustment in Ransom's thinking begins to establish a link with Dante's heavens, which are filled with life, abundance, and light. It also begins to establish the fundamental contrast between Lewis's cosmos and the cosmos as depicted in most science fiction literature of Lewis's day, which is characterized by darkness, hostility, and death—characteristics, ironically, that describe Dante's hell.

Second, Ransom's negative expectations concerning outer space are naturally accompanied by apprehension concerning extraterrestrial beings, for the emotional correlative to darkness and death is fear, and its aesthetic correlative is hideousness: "He had read his H. G. Wells and others. . . . No insect-like, vermiculate or crustacean Abominable, no twitching feelers, rasping wings, slimy coils, curling tentacles . . . seemed to him anything but likely on an alien world" (*OSP* 35). In a universe that is the product of mindless evolution or of an amoral force that is indifferent to human beings, any number of grotesque things is possible. Once again, Ransom's preconceptions are exposed as misconceptions because although the three races on Malacandra have a somewhat alien appearance—the Séroni look like elongated men covered with feathers; the Hrossa are like tall, furry penguins; and the Pfifltriggi are like large grasshoppers—they do not fulfill his expectations of sheer hideousness.

More significantly, however, they do not fulfill Ransom's assumptions concerning their moral character. In his essay "De Futilitate," Lewis remarks that alien creatures in science fiction "are usually pictured as being wholly devoid of our moral standards but as accepting our scientific standards. The implication is, of course, that scientific thought, being objective, will be the same for all creatures that can reason at all, whereas moral thought, being merely a subjective thing like one's taste in food, might be expected to vary from species to species." In Ransom's case, "His whole imaginative training somehow encouraged him to associate superhuman intelligence with monstrosity of form and ruthlessness of will" (*OSP* 59). As he later tells the Oyarsa of Malacandra, "The tellers of tales in our world make us think that if there is any life beyond our own air it is evil" (*OSP* 121). In an ironic reversal, the only creatures on this planet who are amoral, ruthless, and hostile are the Earthmen. The Malacandrians, by contrast, live according to the ethical imperatives that are rooted in the nature of their benign creator, Maleldil, and thus bear only good will to their visitors, even after the Earthmen have killed some of the planet's inhabitants. Ransom's preconceptions about the morality of extraterrestrial beings are thus rectified by understanding the "Dantean" society on this planet.

One event for Ransom that recalls an important scene from the *Paradiso* occurs when he is with the Sorn Augray and is growing aware of the depth of humanity's moral failure. Ransom's situation echoes the scene in the eighth sphere of Fixed Stars in which Beatrice tells Dante's pilgrim to look down at Earth from his celestial vantage point (see *Par.* 22.128ff.). Viewing Earth from the perspective of a great height has precedents in Cicero and in Boethius (among others), but the emphasis for both those authors is on the diminutive size of Earth with respect to the whole universe and the humbling perspective that such a contrast brings. Dante's pilgrim likewise at first sees "this globe whose puny appearance made me smile" (*Par.* 22:134–135).

The vision of Dante's pilgrim, however, includes a moral element. As he looks down, he calls Earth "the little threshing-floor that makes people so ferocious" (*Par.* 22.151). He notes the size of Earth in contrast to the heavens ("little threshing-floor"), but he also indicates its moral and spiritual contrast to the heavens ("that makes people so ferocious"). When Augray asks Ransom to look down at Thulcandra from his current height in the universe through a telescope, Ransom's dual reaction is that of Dante's pilgrim. In "the bleakest moment in all his travels," Ransom identifies Earth as his planet: "It was all there in *that little disk*—London, Athens, Jerusalem, Shakespeare. There everyone had lived and *everything had happened*" (*OSP* 96; italics added). Like Dante's pilgrim, he sees Earth not just from a physical perspective but also from a moral one, and in both narratives this event immediately precedes further spiritual revelation and vision. (Ironically, Dante sees a round "globe" and Ransom sees a flat "disk," which inverts the common assumptions that Dante's age believed the world was flat, while Ransom's age knows it to be a globe.)

Ransom's time on Malacandra ends in a climax that parallels a significant feature of the conclusion to each of the three segments of the journey in *The Divine Comedy*. Each phase of the journey for Dante's pilgrim ends in a dramatic vision of (or encounter with) a single being who sums up the nature of each realm: Satan, the epitome of evil in the *Inferno*; Beatrice, the epitome of a purified human soul in the *Purgatorio*; and God, the epitome of good in the *Paradiso*. Likewise, Ransom's Malacandrian adventure ends with a significant encounter, in this case with the planet's Oyarsa, and that meeting sums up what he is learning about the spiritual dimensions of the universe.

Beatrice

Some scholars have noted a similarity between Ransom's meeting with the Oyarsa and Gulliver's interview with the Brobdingnagians and the Houyhnhnms in Jonathan Swift's *Gulliver's Travels*, primarily because these conversations shed a negative light on the customs and practices of the human race. Others have noted similarities with Cavor's interview with the Grand Lunar in Wells's *First Men in the Moon*. However, Lewis also structures this meeting to recall the encounter between Dante's pilgrim and Beatrice.

First, the settings are nearly identical. (1) Dante's pilgrim meets Beatrice at the summit of the mountain on the island of Purgatory. Similarly, Ransom's meeting occurs on the summit of the mountain on the island of Meldilorn. Lewis's description of it makes it similar in shape to Dante's purgatorial mountain with its garden and forest at the summit: "Amidst the lake there rose like a low and gently sloping pyramid . . . an island . . . , and on the summit a grove of . . . trees" (*OSP* 105). (2) Dante strolls "through the ancient forest" at the top of the mount (*Purg.* 28.23). Ransom sees on the summit "a grove of such trees as man had never seen" (*OSP* 105), which is also an "ancient forest" since this planet is very old. (3) Dante's pilgrim walks through the beautiful garden "very, very slowly" (*Purg.* 28.5), and Dante emphasizes that detail again a few verses later, mentioning the pilgrim's slow steps (see *Purg.* 28.22). As for Ransom, "All his movements became gentle and sedate" (*OSP* 108). (4) Dante's pilgrim is "eager to explore inside [the garden] and all around" (*Purg.* 28.1), and Ransom deliberately walks around the entire island to explore it (see *OSP* 109).

The similarity between the two settings is reinforced by the ensuing action. Just prior to Beatrice's arrival, Dante's pilgrim sees that "a light suddenly filled the large forest everywhere" (*Purg.* 29.16–17). Just prior to Oyarsa's arrival, Ransom "became conscious that the air above him was full of a far greater complexity of light than the sunrise could explain, and light of a different kind" (*OSP* 118). Beatrice's arrival is immediately preceded by a procession that has halted and is silent (see *Purg.* 29.151–154). Before the Oyarsa arrives, Ransom sees "that the monolithic avenue was full of Malacandrian creatures, and all silent . . . in two lines, one on each side" (*OSP* 118).

Ransom's initial physical reaction to Oyarsa is the same as that of the pilgrim's to Beatrice. Dante's pilgrim feels that "there is not a drop of blood in me that is not quivering" (*Purg.* 30.46–47); Ransom initially feels "a tingling of his blood" (*OSP* 119). Dante's pilgrim feels that "the ice that constricted my heart became breath and water" (*Purg.* 30.97–98); Ransom feels that "his heart and body seemed to him to be made of water" (*OSP* 119). Dante's pilgrim has difficulty speaking: "I was so confused that as my voice tried to come forth it spent itself before it could come out of my mouth" (*Purg.* 31.7–9). Ransom "wondered if he would be able to speak when speech was demanded of him" (*OSP* 119).

Oyarsa, like Beatrice, begins by addressing the pilgrim by name and asking him a question (see *Purg.* 30.55, 74–75; *OSP* 119), and the structure of his ensuing monologue follows the structure of Beatrice's monologue. (1) Dante's pilgrim is initially accused of his misdeeds by Beatrice, who is functioning as a heavenly judge. Ransom feels the Malacandrians and the eldils "were waiting for his trial to begin" (*OSP* 119). (2) Beatrice's accusation against the pilgrim is that he had turned away from her (see *Purg.* 30.129–131), and Oyarsa's accusation is that "you have spent all your time . . . in flying from me" (*OSP* 120). (3) Beatrice says that "neither did praying for inspiration to come to him through dreams and other means work to call him back" (*Purg.* 30.133–135). The Oyarsa tried various means as well: "I stirred up a *hnakra* to try if you would come to me of your own will," and although the Hrossa "told you to come to me, you would not. After that I sent my *eldil* to fetch you, but still you would not come" (*OSP* 120). (4) Beatrice frequently answers the pilgrim's unasked questions, and at one point, "Ransom was silent, but Oyarsa answered his unspoken questions" (*OSP* 120). (5) Dante's pilgrim is then given an account of the spiritual history of the Christian church by Beatrice; Ransom then hears an account of the spiritual history of the universe from the Oyarsa. (6) At the end, Beatrice prophesies the future deliverance of the church from various evils (see *Purg.* 33.43–45), and Oyarsa remarks, "The year we are now in . . . has long been prophesied as a year of stirrings and high changes and the siege of Thulcandra may be near its end" (*OSP* 143).

Although the conversation between the Oyarsa and Weston (which Ransom has to translate) recalls scenes in Swift and Wells, Lewis seems to have had Dante's garden scene in mind for Ransom's interaction with the Oyarsa. John's island in *The Pilgrim's Regress* is here replaced by a planetary eldil as the Beatrice figure, once again illustrating Lewis's idea that God can use anyone or anything as a channel of grace. As with all Beatrician experiences, Ransom is transformed by this meeting through the spiritual overview he now has of the universe.

Conclusion

Lewis once referred to Dante as "the lively 'scientifictionist,'" and according to him, "*The Divine Comedy* combines two literary undertakings which have long since been separated. On the one hand it is a high, imaginative interpretation of spiritual life; on the other it is a realistic travel-book about wanderings in places which no one had reached, but which every one believed to have a literal and local existence." In *Out of the Silent Planet*, Lewis likewise combines an imaginative presentation of a man's spiritual growth as he travels to a planet that no one had yet reached, and Lewis will again weave together those same two literary undertakings in his next science fiction novel, *Perelandra*.

Out of the Silent Planet, like *The Pilgrim's Regress*, recalls *The Divine Comedy* but in ways quite different from that first novel. Unlike the fictional geography in the *Pilgrim's Regress*, the universe in this novel is the modern cosmos, although imaginatively presented with features from Dante's cosmos. Lewis follows Dante's lead in ascribing spiritual significance to modern scientific constructs and in using Dante's syncretistic methodology for shaping his chief and lesser eldils.

Despite the ties between this novel and Wells's *First Men in the Moon* and despite calling David Lindsay "the real father of my planet books," Lewis opposes and contradicts the worldviews of both these authors in his spiritual configuration of the universe and through the experiences of his main character. To that extent, neither the content of Wells's story nor of Lindsay's can quite be said to have functioned as a "model" that Lewis "imitated"; they were instead stories that Lewis set out to "correct" concerning the moral quality of the universe and of alien beings. Science fiction historians Eric S. Rabkin and Robert Scholes state that Lewis was the first "example of combining Christian casuistry with science fiction" (although others later followed Lewis). Since Lewis's worldview accords with Dante's message that the Christian God rules the universe, Lewis looks back to Dante's universe in restoring a Christian character to the cosmos. The honor of being a "a model to imitate" goes to Dante here.

As for his main character, Lewis says that *Out of the Silent Planet* recounts "Ransom's *enfances*." *Enfances* is a genre of medieval literature that describes the birth and childhood of a hero. Although Ransom is "thirty-five to forty" years old during his journey, he is initially oblivious to the spiritual dimensions of the universe, so this novel recounts his *spiritual* childhood. In the sequence to this novel, Ransom will continue to recall his medieval kinsman, but he now understands, like Dante's pilgrim does after his journey in the *Inferno*, the source of evil (Satan, the Bent Eldil) and its presence in the universe.

CHAPTER FOUR

The Screwtape Letters

Introduction

Before being published as a book in 1942, *The Screwtape Letters* first appeared as weekly installments from May 2 to November 28, 1941, in *The Guardian*, an Anglican periodical in circulation until the early 1950s. This epistolary novel was published the same year as Lewis's *A Preface to "Paradise Lost"* and one year before his second science fiction novel, *Perelandra*. One of the things that these three works have in common is Lewis's discussion of Satan, hell, and temptation. In *A Preface to "Paradise Lost,"* Lewis analyzes John Milton's depiction of Satan and hell, and in *Perelandra* Lewis presents a new version of a Garden of Eden with temptations from Satan. Although Lewis's theology remains consistent on these theological issues in all three books, *The Screwtape Letters* is distinguished by its comical and satiric tone. The satire was perhaps too subtle for some readers. One clergyman cancelled his subscription to *The Guardian* "on the ground that 'much of the advice given in these letters seemed . . . not only erroneous but positively diabolical.'" This novel established Lewis's reputation on both sides of the Atlantic and was soon considered a classic. The popularity of *The Screwtape Letters* in the United States led to Lewis's appearance on the cover of *Time* magazine on September 8, 1947, with the grinning figure of a devil with horns and pitchfork behind Lewis's left shoulder and an angel behind his right shoulder; the cover inscription reads, "Oxford's C. S. Lewis, His Heresy: Christianity."

Lewis's novel records the correspondence from Screwtape, a senior devil, to Wormwood, his junior-tempter nephew. In thirty-one letters, the uncle writes advice concerning various spiritual matters, particularly concerning strategies for tempting a young man in England who is referred to only as "the patient." (In classical and medieval philosophy, an "agent" is someone/something that acts, while a "patient" is someone/something that is acted upon.) The novel is written entirely from the perspective of hell, and as such entails the consistent inversion of all normal standards and makes "the blacks all white and the whites all black." In *The Screwtape Letters*, the inversion is present even linguistically: The vast hierarchical network of hell, for instance, is called the "lowerarchy" and is ruled from the very bottom by "Our Father Below," with the "Miserific Vision" as its ultimate reward. The patient succumbs to a variety of temptations after his initial conversion but experiences a reconversion and makes progress in his spiritual life until he is killed during the war (World War II) and goes to heaven.

Although the major focus in this novel is temptation—its inner dynamic, the tempters, and those tempted—the novel includes Screwtape's commentary on hell and heaven, the devil and God, and sin and grace. Lewis's approach to these subjects creates the major connection between his novel and *The Divine Comedy*. The hell of *Screwtape Letters* and its various forms of devilry are presented comically, which differs from Dante's tone, and there is no literal journey by a pilgrim through the story. Nevertheless, *The Screwtape Letters* includes a host of theological and moral concepts from *The Divine Comedy*, presented with vocabulary from Dante. The subtext concerning the patient's spiritual development makes him resemble Dante's pilgrim, while the woman he loves is reminiscent of Beatrice.

Hell and Its Inhabitants

Because of Lewis's focus on temptation, this hell is not primarily depicted as an abode of punishment but as the headquarters for the war being waged against God and the human race. In his preface, Lewis says his "symbol for Hell is something like the bureaucracy of a police state or the offices of a thoroughly nasty business concern," and he chose that symbol "to picture an official society held together entirely by fear and greed."

Lewis emphasizes the psychology of hell's strategy rather than its geography, so no attention is paid to its layout. There is mention of a Training School for Tempters, a House of Correction for Incompetent Tempters, a Research Department, an Intelligence Department, and a Philological Arm (to determine the best use of language for hell's propaganda), but the exact location or description of these places remains vague. Unlike Dante's hell with its clearly delineated nine circles, no map can be made of this hell.

Nevertheless, there are several points of correspondence between Lewis's hell and Dante's that include the invention of devils' names and the nature of punishment for sinners.

Except for the name "Wormwood," Lewis's devils, like those in *Inferno* 21 and 22, do not have biblical or traditional names. Both authors invent names for them that are undignified and suggestive of their character. Lewis says he "aimed merely at making them nasty . . . by the sound," but names like Slubgose, Scabtree, Toadpipe, Slumtripit, Triptweeze, and Glubose sound ridiculous as well. These names are in the same vein as those Dante invents for his devils, collectively called Evil Claws (Malebranche), who are guarding souls in one ditch of the circle of fraud: Evil Tail (Malacoda), Wild Swine (Ciriatto), Dog Scratcher (Graffiacane), Nasty Dragon (Draghignazzo), Nasty Dog (Cagnazzo), and so forth (see *Inf.* 21.76ff.).

In both hells, God is referred to by souls and devils through circumlocution, and linguistic inversion occurs in Dante's *Inferno* when, for instance, Christ is called "the adverse judge" (*Inf.* 6.96). In Lewis's novel, the circumlocution always entails inversion, with God being referred to as "Our Oppressor," "the Enemy Above," or simply "the Enemy."

Unlike Dante's hell where sins are categorized according to their severity, Lewis's hell makes no distinction between sins. In Screwtape's view, "It does not matter how small the sins are, provided that their cumulative effect is to edge the man away from the Light and out into the Nothing. Murder is no better than cards if cards can do the trick" (Letter XII). Lewis is focusing on sin in general, on a person's choice to rebel against or be independent of God, so the particular manner in which this occurs is not the issue. As such, there is only one punishment in Lewis's hell applied to all souls regardless of their offenses: they are eaten by devils.

This punishment for souls, however, has traits in common with Dante's hell in two respects. First, Lewis's punishment echoes eating

images that reoccur in various places in Dante's hell. Hell's desire
to bite and consume is suggested through two guardians: Cerberus,
guarding the circle of gluttons, has three ravenous mouths, and
the Minotaur, who guards the circle of the violent and once fed
on human sacrifices, bites himself in rage when he sees Virgil and
the pilgrim (see *Inf*. 12.14). Hell is referred to in general as having
a "wide throat" (see *Purg*. 21.31). Two locations in Dante's hell are
personified as biting or eating. The first ditch of the circle of fraud
has "souls locked in its jaws" (*Inf*. 18.99), and the circle of traitors
is described as "the pit that devours Lucifer" (*Inf*. 31.142–143). In
addition, some souls are biting others or being bitten. In the circle
of the wrathful, they are "tearing off pieces of each other with their
teeth" (*Inf*. 7.114). When one sinner there (Filippo Argenti) is about
to be attacked by others, he bites himself in his fury (see *Inf*. 8.63).
In the circle of violence, "black she-dogs sank their fangs into [a
sinner] . . . and ripped him up piece by piece; then they carried off
his pitiful limbs" (*Inf*. 13.125–129). In the tenth ditch of the circle
of fraud, one of the souls in his attack on another "sank his teeth
into his neck" (*Inf*. 30. 28–29). In the icy circle of traitors, Count
Ugolino is feasting on a "horrendous meal" (*Inf*. 33.1); encased in
ice behind Archbishop Ruggieri (who had starved him and his innocent offspring in a locked tower), Ugolino eternally gnaws the
back of Ruggieri's neck (see *Inf*. 32.127–129). In the above examples,
however, the biting or being bitten is always incidental to a sinner's
primary punishment in his or her given circle.

On the other hand, there is one eternal torment in *The Divine
Comedy* that closely approximates the consumption of a sinner, and
it is administered by Satan himself in the very pit of hell in the
circle of treason. Dante's three-faced Satan, the prototype of all evil
and rebellion against God, is eternally gnawing three souls (see
Inf. 34.55–67). These three betrayed the most important historical leaders of the state and the church, the two institutions Dante
believed were appointed by God for the good of humanity and its
perfecting. By assassinating their friend Caesar, Brutus and Cassius
were treacherous to the state, and by turning Jesus over to those
who would kill him, Judas was treacherous to the church. For their
punishment, Satan is gnawing the upper part of Judas's body in his
central mouth and the lower half of Brutus's and Cassius's bodies
in his two lateral mouths.

Lewis, in choosing the punishment of consumption by devils, thus adapts the ultimate punishment in Dante's hell as the only punishment for his hell. Insofar as souls are food for devils, Lewis places all sinners in the circle of traitors, so to speak. In so doing, Lewis may be offering the commentary that all sinners, no matter the sin, are traitors because in rebelling against God, they are betraying their Creator, their chief benefactor.

The second way that the punishment in Lewis's hell echoes Dante's punishments is that it is a fresh instance of Dante's approach throughout the *Inferno*, in which each punishment involves a *contrapasso* ("counterpoint"), a punishment that reflects the essence of any given sin. For example, those who allowed sexual passion to rule their lives are now eternally tossed about and buffeted by winds—an outward manifestation of their choice to have the whirlwind of passion govern their lives. Flatterers are plunged in a ditch of human excrement because "dung" is what they offered others while feigning to offer truth. Those who were cold-heartedly treacherous are now partially or completely encased in ice, depending on the degree of their treachery. Dante only once spells out the moral connection between the sin and its punishment, leaving the reader to contemplate and discover all the other the links.

The punishment in *The Screwtape Letters*, like all the punishments in the *Inferno*, qualifies as a Dantean *contrapasso* because it vividly illustrates the essence and nature of sin—in this case, not of a particular sin but of sin in general. Unlike Dante, Lewis does spell out the connection. Screwtape explains that for devils, "a human is primarily food; our aim is the absorption of its will into ours, the increase of our own area of selfhood at its expense" (Letter VIII). In yielding to temptation and sin, human beings give their wills over to the will of hell, and having yielded their wills their identities are absorbed. The souls in Lewis's hell are, like their counterparts in the *Inferno*, rewarded for all eternity by being given precisely what they chose in life. Thus the spiritual cannibalism of this hell, "the sucking of will and freedom out of a weaker self into a stronger" (Letter XVIII), is Lewis's graphic representation of the consequence of sin in its essence. It is also Lewis's indirect commentary on what that punishment by Satan implies in Dante's ninth circle.

Absorption by consumption is hell's method of achieving unity in Lewis's novel. Screwtape discusses this—as he does many other facets of hell—with reference to its contrast in heaven: "Our war aim is a world in which Our Father Below has drawn all other beings into himself: the Enemy wants a world full of beings united to Him but still distinct" (Letter VIII). One of Dante's blessed souls says that God "wants all his court to be like himself" (*Par.* 3.45), and Screwtape repeats that idea, but in an inverted way, in describing the Enemy's goal as wanting "a lot of loathsome little replicas of Himself." However, Screwtape explains that this happens "not because He has absorbed them but because their wills freely conform to His" (Letter VIII). Hell's unity, then, is achieved at the price of individuality, while heaven's unity is grounded in the distinct individuality of each soul that has freely chosen to conform its will to God's will.

The same ideological contrast is present in Dante's poem. The souls of the uncommitted in hell's vestibule, "those who lived without dishonor and without praise" (*Inf.* 3.35–36), remain nameless because "the world does not allow a record of their lives" (*Inf.* 3.49). Souls in hell often prefer anonymity and display reluctance to discuss their identities or their past lives. When Dante's pilgrim attempts to recognize individual souls in the circle of the avaricious, for example, Virgil tells him that he cannot do so, because "the morally undiscerning life that sullied them now makes their identities hard to discern" (*Inf.* 7.53–54). In the ditch of panderers, a sinner (Venedico) unsuccessfully tries to hide his identity from Dante's pilgrim by lowering his face (*Inf.* 18.46–47). A sinner in the ditch of false counselors (Guido da Montefeltro) speaks to the pilgrim only because he assumes the pilgrim is dead and will not return to the world above (see *Inf.* 27.61–66). In the fourth subdivision of the circle of treason where souls are completely buried under the ice—the very last group the pilgrim sees—not one soul is named or identified. In contrast, the redeemed souls in the *Paradiso* are peacefully united to God, because, as one of them explains, "In his will is our peace" (*Par.* 3.85). They gladly reveal their identities and willingly share their stories. The same is true for the souls in purgatory who are bound for heaven who often eagerly ask for prayer and to be remembered to their loved ones. On the sixth ledge of the mount, when a soul reveals the identity of his companions who are unrecognizable because of their punishment of starvation for gluttony (see *Purg.* 24.17ff.), "all the souls seemed happy to be named" (*Purg.* 24.26). One of the results of sin in Dante's poem, reflected in Lewis's novel, is the diminishment or loss of self-identity and individuality.

All aspects of Lewis's hell—evil, sin, the devil—are presented as impotent, in contrast to God and grace, and this too is in line with concepts from Dante's poem. In the *Inferno*, no guardian, devil, or sinner has the power to impede Dante's pilgrim on his heaven-appointed journey. Virgil alludes to the impotence of this realm through the contrast he makes when he twice refers to heaven as "the place in which whatsoever is willed comes to pass" (*Inf.* 3.95–96; 5.23–24). When he uses this formula with Charon and Minos, who deny passage to the pilgrim because he is still alive, their resistance is quickly overcome because they must submit to the will of heaven. When the only angel who appears in the *Inferno* confronts the rebellious spirits at the gate of Dis, which separates upper and lower hell, he asks rhetorically, "Why are you resistant to that will whose goal can never be thwarted [?]" (*Inf.* 9.94–95). When the devils guarding a ditch in the eighth circle attempt to attack Virgil and the pilgrim, Virgil merely has to say to their leader, "It is willed by Heaven that I show him this savage path" (*Inf.* 21.83–84), and "then his arrogance was so deflated that he let his pitchfork drop to the ground" (*Inf.* 21.85–86). In fact, even the guardians, who ensure that sinners do not leave their appointed place of punishment, have their own movements restricted as well: "Divine Providence . . . removes from all of them the power to leave [the place they guard]" (*Inf.* 23.55–57).

All cases of hellish opposition in Dante's *Inferno* are easily neutralized and subdued because whatever heaven wills comes to pass. Hell, on the contrary, is the place of disjunction between power and will: That which is desired is not attained and that which is willed does not come to pass. The frustration of unfulfilled desire and impotence is part of these souls' eternal torment. Satan, the prototype of the entire realm, is immobilized, encased in ice up to the middle of his chest with uselessly flapping wings, and his depiction is Dante's visual—but nonverbal—commentary on the ultimate impotence of evil.

Lewis likewise depicts hell as impotent. Screwtape writes, "Our Research Department has not yet discovered (though success is hourly expected) how to produce *any* virtue" (Letter XXIX). Hell is impotent with regard not just to virtue but to pleasure as well: "It is His [God's] invention, not ours . . . : all our research so far has not enabled us to produce one" (Letter IX). That impotence is also reflected in some of hell's strategies for temptation. The tempters at times aim to suppress truth or block its entrance into people's minds: "It is funny how mortals always picture us as putting things into their minds: in reality our best work is done by keeping things out" (Letter IV). Hell's activity is at times reduced to a purely defensive reaction against the strength and power of truth: "Your task is purely negative," says Screwtape. "Don't let his thoughts come anywhere near it [truth]" (Letter XXI).

For both Dante and Lewis, the whole activity of hell, since it cannot create, is to spoil, to take something good and attempt to pervert it. Dante often uses the verb *torcere*, "to twist or bend," and its word derivatives in a moral sense. Dante's pilgrim is instructed that "the primal impulse [toward the good] is derailed if it is twisted by wrong desire" (*Par.* 1.134–135), and when someone "twists or bends" toward evil, sin begins (see *Purg.* 17.100–102). In Lewis's novel, if it is impossible to prevent the patient's spiritual growth, Screwtape says, "Very well, then; we must *corrupt* it" (Letter XXIII). If the patient "can't be cured of churchgoing," he should at least be led to church-shop constantly or be sent to a church where faith is watered down or the pastor is judgmental of others (Letter XVI). "If we can't use his sexuality to make him unchaste we must try to use it for the promotion of a desirable marriage" (Letter XX)—desirable from hell's point of view, of course. The entire issue of hell's negativity is summed up in Screwtape's lament that "everything has to be *twisted* before it's any use to us. We fight under cruel disadvantages. Nothing is naturally on our side" (Letter XXII).

Screwtape himself, in his function as a guide and mentor for Wormwood, can be considered as a corrupted version of Virgil. In this case the nature of the relationship between guide and pilgrim, between mentor and disciple, has been twisted. Just like Virgil who calls the pilgrim "dear son" (see *Purg.* 3.66, 17.91), Screwtape addresses his letters to "My dear Wormwood." Just like Virgil who has affection for the pilgrim (see *Inf.* 31.28), so Screwtape signs his letters, "Your affectionate uncle." In line with all the inversions in this novel, however, he is not affectionate toward the nephew he is guiding, and his nephew is not dear to him, as revealed in the last letter. Although he addresses his nephew there as "My dear, my very dear, Wormwood," he signs the last letter, "Your increasingly and ravenously affectionate uncle." Since Wormwood has failed in his task with the patient, Screwtape hopes he will be given to him as food—"As dainty a morsel as ever I grew fat on" (Letter XXXI).

Several of the guidelines for temptation in Lewis's novel have links with the discussion of spiritual principles in Dante's poem. Virgil's instruction on natural inclinations and impulses begins with the premise that people have natural instincts that draw them toward a perceived good (see *Purg.* 17.91–93), but these inclinations are neither good nor bad in themselves (see *Purg.* 18.59–60). Screwtape begins his instruction to Wormwood on this issue with the same premise: "The deepest likings and impulses of any man are the raw material, the starting point, with which the Enemy has furnished him" (Letter XIII). These impulses, then, are morally neutral; it is how a person deals with them that matters.

Screwtape's instruction regarding pleasure also echoes Dante's approach to that issue—inversely of course. Both Dante and Lewis posit that prosperity, food and drink, and sexual pleasure are all good things bestowed on the human race by God. Virgil, in describing these natural pleasures, says that when a person's desire or inclination is fixed on the ultimate good (God) and secondary goods are kept in subordination to him, then those pleasures do not lead to sin (see *Purg.* 17.97–99). In Letter IX, Screwtape warns that pleasure is very dangerous to work with because "when we are dealing with any pleasure in its healthy and normal and satisfying form, we are . . . on the Enemy's ground." In fact, providing pleasures as temptations is a "tiresome business" (Letter XII) because since all God-given pleasures are good in themselves, Screwtape complains that "no natural phenomenon is really in our favour" (Letter XV).

Pleasure can, however, lead to sin at times. Virgil warns that when a soul pursues a subordinate good "with too much zeal" or "with more focus than it should" (*Purg.* 17.96, 100), then that soul is acting against its Creator (see *Purg.* 17.102). In line with that concept, Screwtape counsels his nephew to tempt his patient with imbalanced pursuits: "All extremes except extreme devotion to the Enemy are to be encouraged" (Letter VII). Virgil explains that the misuse or abuse of these healthy pleasures—which leads to avarice, gluttony, and lust—occur when people abandon themselves to an excessive pursuit of a secondary good (see *Purg.* 17.136). Screwtape concludes that since pleasure "is His [God's] invention, not ours," then, "all we can do is to encourage the humans to take the pleasures which our Enemy has produced, at times, or in ways, or in degrees, which He has forbidden" (Letter IX).

The role of reason in spiritual life is paramount for both authors in helping lead a person to God. Dante's pilgrim is told that reason is "the light that is given to you to tell right from wrong" (*Purg.* 16.75), the faculty that distinguishes between good and evil inclinations (see *Purg.* 18.66). Dante describes the souls in the *Inferno* as those "who have lost the good of the intellect" (*Inf.* 3.18), meaning they have lost the purpose of the intellect, which is knowledge of God and truth. When souls have lost that "good of the intellect" and no longer have "healthy minds" (*Inf.* 9.61), they are bereft of the proper functioning of the accompanying attributes of light and reason, and their minds thus become darkened.

On one occasion, Screwtape uses this kind of terminology to describe an initial maneuver in temptation: "The way must be prepared for your moral assault by *darkening his intellect*" (Letter XXI; italics added). The initial goal in the assault is always to cloud the light and power of reason: "Do remember you are there to fuddle him" (Letter I), so "keep everything hazy in his mind" (Letter II), because "success . . . depends on confusing him" (Letter XXIV). In Letter V, Screwtape tells his nephew outright, "You may catch your man when his reason is temporarily suspended." The suppression of reason—which in Dante's terms results in a "darkened intellect"—is one of the vital prerequisites for hell to have victory over human beings. In a letter written a few years later, Lewis again connects a "darkened" mind to sin, saying that "the rebellion of the will is nearly always accompanied with *some* fogging of the intelligence." In recommending the darkening of the mind, Screwtape is countering the admonitions of Virgil, who wants his pilgrim to have a clear mind at all times and whose own reasoning and explanations are clear to Dante's pilgrim (see *Inf.* 11.67–68).

Another important rule in temptation involves leading people to focus on the past or the present, and what Lewis says helps clarify a puzzling situation among Dante's damned souls. In the *Inferno*, the damned remember their past and have the ability to see into the future as well, but they have no knowledge of the present (see *Inf.* 10.97–99). These souls can dimly see things that are remote from them, but when events are just about to happen or are presently occurring, their minds are blank (see *Inf.* 10.103). Dante gives no rationale for their inability to see the present, but Screwtape's discussion of the three modes of time for human beings sheds light on this situation. The senior devil urges his nephew to lead the patient into concentrating on the past or the future, emphasizing that "our business is to get them away from . . . the Present" (Letter XV) because "the Present is the point at which time touches eternity," and, therefore, "the Present is all lit up with eternal rays" (Letter XV). According to Screwtape, then, the Present is the only dangerous mode of time from hell's point of view, because it is only in the Present that God interacts with human beings and manifests himself. Given this theology of time, the souls in Dante's hell, who are cut off from God, are necessarily cut off from the one mode of time in which the eternal God is accessible.

According to both Dante and Lewis, the circumstances of life, like natural impulses, are neither good nor bad per se. Misfortunes, unexpected changes, good fortune—every event that is thrust upon a human being from without can lead to life or death but is in itself neutral; the crux of the matter is always how a person deals with these situations. Dante presents the example of two men who were both slandered at court, but one, Pier delle Vigne, killed himself and now finds himself in the Wood of Suicides (see *Inf.* 13.58–75), while the other, Romeo di Villeneuve, who bore his suffering silently and left the court, now finds himself in the sphere of just souls (see *Par.* 6.127–142). Dante's contrast is an example of the point that Screwtape makes when he says that "men are not angered by mere misfortune but by misfortune conceived as injury" (Letter XXI). Romeo rose above his circumstances; Pier did not. Screwtape tells his nephew that every event in life, even falling in love, is "simply an occasion which we and the Enemy are both trying to exploit. . . . It is, from the point of view of the spiritual life, mainly raw material" (Letter XIX).

For Screwtape, even war itself is ultimately a neutral event: "Of course a war is entertaining. The immediate fear and suffering of the humans is a legitimate and pleasing refreshment for our myriads of toiling workers. But what permanent good does it do us unless we make use of it for bringing souls to Our Father Below?" (Letter V). The same is true concerning the ravages of war in Italy during Dante's time. People involved in various wars are represented as damned or redeemed in *The Divine Comedy* but not because of the wars. In ante-purgatory, Ottokar of Bohemia is now comforting his bitter enemy, the emperor Rudolph (see *Purg.* 7.94–100). Charles I of Anjou killed Manfred, king of Sicily, at the battle of Benevento in 1266, but they are both in ante-purgatory now awaiting purification so they can join the redeemed. In fact, Charles is even singing a hymn alongside Peter III of Aragon, the man who wrested the kingdom of Sicily from him (see *Purg.* 7.112–114). Farinata and Bocca degli Abati were companions, not enemies, in battle at Montaperti in 1260, but they are both in hell, although for different reasons. For both Dante and Lewis, involvement in war itself or what side a person fought for is not what determines one's eternal state.

In Lewis's novel, as in Dante's poem, all of life's occurrences are secondary to the ultimate issue of people's choices that lead to the eternal destiny of their souls, for, as Screwtape sums up, "Nothing matters at all except the tendency of a given state of mind, in given circumstances, to move a particular patient at a particular moment nearer to the Enemy or nearer to us" (Letter XIX). In the end, what counts is the exercise of a human being's "innate liberty" (*Purg.* 18.68), which Dante calls "the noble faculty of free will" (*Purg.* 18.73–74).

An analysis of this novel is incomplete without briefly discussing Lewis's addendum. In 1961 Lewis added a new chapter at the end of the book, "Screwtape Proposes a Toast," in which Screwtape addresses the graduating class at the Tempters' Training College during a banquet. Screwtape expresses delight in the increase of tyrannical political regimes as a major way of destroying human beings' dignity and individuality. He also expounds on the distortions of the concept of equality in modern democracy—the idea that people should be the same without distinctive differences—that has led, in his view, to a wonderfully destructive mediocrity that penalizes excellence, especially in the area of education.

This addendum, like the rest of *The Screwtape Letters*, includes the ongoing presence of Dante. When Screwtape bemoans the insipid quality of the sinners they are feasting on, he exclaims, "Oh, to get one's teeth again into a Farinata" (p. 154), alluding to Dante's arrogant Ghibelline politician in hell's circle of heretics. Screwtape ascribes the poor quality of souls at the banquet to the fact that they are "so muddled in mind" (p. 156), recalling all of Dante's souls who have "lost the good of the intellect" and have darkened minds. Screwtape is delighted by the mediocre standards now entrenched in education because they will hold back the good student "who would be capable of tackling . . . Dante" (p. 167).

In the nearly twenty years between the novel's publication and this additional piece, Dante remained on Lewis's mind.

The Patient and His Journey

Within the context of infernal advice about temptation, the patient's spiritual development emerges as a distinct narrative thread, and specific details in his life cumulatively evoke the overall contours of the journey of Dante's pilgrim.

After the patient becomes a Christian, according to Letter II, Letters III to XII describe Wormwood's increasingly successful attempts at leading him away from his faith. Screwtape's description of that situation in Letter XII is expressed in terms that explicitly recall terminology and imagery from *The Divine Comedy*: "We know that we have introduced a change of direction in his course which is already carrying him out of *his orbit around the Enemy*. . . . [He] is now, however slowly, *heading right away from the sun* on a line which will carry him into *the cold and dark* [italics added]."

The phrase "his orbit around the Enemy" recalls the famous image of Dante's pilgrim at the conclusion of his journey when his union with God is described as his "orbiting" around God in the *Paradiso*: "Like a wheel moving in perfect balance, my desire and my will were already being revolved by the Love that moves the sun and the other stars" (*Par.* 33.143–145). For the patient to be carried out of "his orbit around the Enemy," then, means he is moving away from union with God. Screwtape's use of the "sun" as a metaphor for God duplicates its use in Dante's poem where the sun signifies God, so if the patient is "heading right away from the sun," he is increasingly moving away from God. Dante's hell, in which traditional hell-fire appears only occasionally, is both *dark*, since it is cut off from the sun, and *cold*, especially at its core in the ninth circle where ice encases treacherous souls and Satan.

Next, Letter XIII records a significant turning point in the patient's situation that Screwtape laments "is a defeat of the first order. It amounts to a second conversion," and it recalls the very beginning of the *Inferno* when Dante's pilgrim is undergoing his second conversion and a return to the path of righteousness.

(1) Dante's pilgrim, who once followed the path of truth, admits at the beginning of the poem that he "abandoned the true path" (*Inf.* 1.12). The Christian patient, who has been "heading right away from the sun," has also left the true path. (2) Dante's pilgrim is alone, walking away from a hill, when he is met by grace (Virgil has been recruited to help him) that will help set him back on the path to God. Lewis's patient is alone, walking away from an old mill in the country, when he is met by what Screwtape refers to as an "asphyxiating cloud"—namely, some kind of grace from heaven that devils cannot penetrate—that changes his direction and sets him back on the right path. (3) Dante's pilgrim, acknowledging his lost and confused state, says, "mi ritrovai per una selva oscura" (*Inf.* 1.2), which is most often translated as "I found myself in a dark wood," but the literal meaning of "mi ritrovai" is "I re-found / I recovered myself." Lewis's patient at this point feels "that he was . . . *recovering* [italics added] himself." (4) Dante's pilgrim says that Virgil is "taking me back home" (*Inf.* 15.54), and the patient now feels that "he was coming home."

Subsequent to this reconversion incident, Letters XIV to XXXI describe events that echo journey events in the *Purgatorio* and *Paradiso* and rely heavily on Dante's imagery and vocabulary.

(1) After his reconversion, the patient undergoes new assaults by Wormwood. He is initially tempted to pride (Letter XIV), and his period of testing ends with temptations to lust (Letter XX). This echoes the general pattern of an ascent from the first ledge of Dante's mount to its last ledge (from pride to lust).

(2) Dante's pilgrim, very shortly after passing beyond the ledge of lust, meets his beloved Beatrice in the garden. Soon after the patient's successful victory over lust, he meets a young Christian woman (Letter XXII), and Screwtape describes the patient as "under the influence of 'love'" (Letter XXIV).

(3) Dante's pilgrim, with Beatrice's help and guidance, is subsequently led up through the heavenly spheres where he encounters redeemed souls. According to Screwtape, the Enemy, through this

young woman's family and friends, "is *drawing* the young *barbarian up* to levels he could never otherwise have reached" (Letter XXIV; italics added)—spiritual levels of revelation and knowledge similar to the spiritual levels and heavenly spheres that Dante's pilgrim could not have reached without Beatrice.

(4) When Screwtape refers to the patient as a "young barbarian," that metaphor also connects him to Dante's pilgrim. In the *Paradiso* Dante's pilgrim compares himself to barbarians, saying that his astonishment at seeing God and the redeemed in the Empyrean is greater than the astonishment barbarians would have felt upon first seeing the wonders of Rome's splendid structures and monuments (see *Par.* 31.31–40). (Lewis mentions this Dantean simile twice in his other writings.)

The young man's spiritual journey on earth is concluded when he is killed in the war (Letter XXXI), and his initial visions of spiritual reality recall features of the visions of Dante's pilgrim in substance, detail, and wording. The patient is aware for the first time of the realities of the spiritual world and now sees devils and angels. Just as Dante's pilgrim was assisted on his journey by angels, so too the patient now realizes "what part each one of them [the angels] had played at many an hour in his life" (Letter XXXI).

When the patient next sees Christ, Screwtape describes that vision with images from Dante: "What is blinding, suffocating fire to you [Wormwood] is now cool *light* to him, . . . and *wears the form of a Man* [italics added]." His description condenses the vision of God as living light by Dante's pilgrim and his subsequent vision of how a human being's form now subsists in God because of the incarnation (see *Par.* 33.124–131).

After the patient's vision of God, Screwtape comments, "Pains he may still have to encounter, but [souls needing purification] *embrace* those pains." This mirrors the description of Dante's souls in purgatory as "those who are content in the [cleansing] fire" (*Inf.* 1.118–119). As one of Dante's souls says about purgatorial suffering, "I say punishment, but I should say solace" (*Purg.* 23.72). Like the souls on Dante's Mount Purgatory, the young man now avidly desires purification even though it means suffering.

Screwtape's subsequent comment describes the patient very specifically, but in a highly condensed way, as though he were Dante's pilgrim on his way to meeting Beatrice:

All the delights of sense or heart or intellect with which you [Wormwood] could once have tempted him . . . now seem to him in comparison but as *the half-nauseous attractions of a raddled harlot* would seem to a *man who hears that his true beloved whom he has loved all his life and whom he had believed to be dead is alive* and even now at his door. (Letter XXXI; italics added)

First, in one of his dreams as he ascends the mount, Dante's pilgrim sees a hideous hag-siren who is transformed into a beautiful woman (see *Purg.* 19.7–15), but when her garments are ripped away in the dream, stench pours out of her (see *Purg.* 19.32–33). The experience of the pilgrim who is first attracted but then repulsed by her is quite easily described as an encounter with "the half-nauseous attractions of a raddled harlot." Second, Dante's pilgrim in the poem indeed has heard that his true beloved, who had died, is indeed alive and will soon meet with him.

The overall narrative structure and sequence of events for the patient echo the threefold structure of the journey in *The Divine Comedy* in a generalized but quite distinct way. Letter I, like the first canto of the *Inferno*, sets the stage and introduces the patient. Letters II to XII recount the phase during which he succumbs to sin and temptation and moves away from God (recalling the state of sinners in the *Inferno*); Letters XIII to XXI describe his second conversion and the period during which he overcomes temptations, beginning with pride and ending with lust (recalling the structure of the mount in the *Purgatorio*); and Letters XXII to XXXI tell of the young Christian woman he loves, his spiritual growth because of her, and his eventual union with God (recalling the journey in the *Paradiso*). In *The Screwtape Letters*, as well as in his other novels, Lewis considers Dante's pilgrim an archetype of a person who undergoes spiritual growth, and thus even in a novel that does not focus directly on a character's spiritual journey, Lewis's young man still recalls that medieval pilgrim.

Beatrice

The young woman introduced in the last third of the novel as the object of the patient's affection in Letter XXII is a channel of grace for him. As such, she functions as this novel's Beatrice, and Lewis establishes several points of similarity between the two women.

Dante's pilgrim meets Beatrice in the *Purgatorio* shortly after he is purged of lust on the last ledge of the mount. Likewise, the patient meets this woman shortly after the point at which Screwtape says, "The Enemy has . . . put a forcible end to your direct attacks on the patient's chastity" (Letter XX). When Beatrice guides Dante's pilgrim through the heavens, he encounters an increasing number of saintly souls. When this Christian woman introduces the patient to her family and circle of friends, Screwtape laments that because of her, "the patient is now getting to know more Christians every day" (Letter XXIII) and, even worse, because of them he is daily "meeting Christian life of a quality he never before imagined" (Letter XXIV)—that is, mature Christians like those in Dante's *Paradiso*.

Screwtape, complaining about the effect this is having on the patient, has recourse to Dantean language and imagery when he says the patient is moving forward spiritually "by means of sexual love and of some . . . people far advanced in His service" (Letter XXIV). This also describes the love Dante's pilgrim has for his beloved Beatrice and its function for his spiritual growth, while the "people far advanced in His service" recall Dante's redeemed souls who help instruct him in the *Paradiso*. Beatrice is described as "the lovely lady who strengthens you for heaven" (*Par.* 10.93), and this young woman succeeds in helping the patient move forward spiritually so that at his untimely death he is prepared to join the community of the redeemed (or is at least prepared to be purified so he can join them).

Despite her minimal presence in the novel, this woman clearly fulfills a Beatrician function with regard to the patient and confirms his kinship to Dante's pilgrim. Of the many varieties of "Beatrice" that appear in Lewis's novels, this is the first one who is a young woman, but she is not the last.

Conclusion

The aim of *The Divine Comedy* is not to speculate on the afterlife but, according to Dante, "to remove those living in this life from a state of misery, and to bring them to a state of happiness." Similarly, Lewis's purpose in *The Screwtape Letters* is "not to speculate about diabolical life [or the afterlife] but to throw light from a new angle on the life of men." The Christian teachings about temptation, sin, and grace in this novel are not original to Dante or to Lewis, but Lewis's imagery and terminology tie him to Dante. The principles and guidelines set out by Screwtape repeat or expand teachings in *The Divine Comedy* in a psychologically inverted and satirical way that is nevertheless recognizable throughout. The patient's spiritual progress and the young woman who is a source of grace for him echo major features of Dante's narrative and demonstrate Lewis's agility at adapting and reworking material from *The Divine Comedy*—even in letters written by a devil.

CHAPTER FIVE

Perelandra

Introduction

Lewis says about *Perelandra* (1943) that the novel "can be read by itself but is also a sequel to *Out of the Silent Planet.*" In this second novel of the Ransom trilogy, Lewis returns to the framework of the fictional cosmos introduced in *Out of the Silent Planet* and retains the names invented for God, angels, and planets. However, he uses Christian terminology more freely here in addressing some of the same topics he did in *The Screwtape Letters*: temptation, sin, repentance, God, and the devil. Ransom has already become aware of the spiritual dimensions of the universe, so in this novel he learns that "it is not for nothing that you are named Ransom" (*Per.* 147), and he is called upon to participate in the cosmic battle between good and evil.

Sometime after his return from Malacandra (Mars), Ransom is sent on a mission by the Oyarsa of Malacandra (the planet's ruling spirit) to Perelandra (Venus) where the Bent Eldil (Satan) is planning some sort of attack. On this lovely planet of floating islands that includes the mythical Garden of Hesperides, Ransom at first encounters only one rational creature, the newly created Green Lady (Tinidril), the Eve of this world. Shortly after the scientist Edward Weston arrives in a spaceship, he calls into himself "the Life-Force" of the universe, which is actually a demonic spirit, and proceeds to tempt the Green Lady to disobey Maleldil's command not to sleep on the planet's Fixed Land. As the temptations continue relentlessly, Ransom realizes the only way to rid the planet of this evil force is to kill the body it is using. After a protracted physical battle that entails a sea chase, Weston, now called the Un-man, drags Ransom deep under the water near a cliff. When they emerge inside a cavern, Ransom eventually kills him and climbs up inside the cliff to the planet's surface. Ransom then explores this new area of the planet and ascends Perelandra's highest mountain. On the summit of that mountain he is reunited with Tinidril and meets the planet's Green Man (Tor). Having successfully rid the planet of evil and assisted that planet's first couple in remaining obedient to Maleldil, Ransom experiences a yearlong vision of ultimate reality, called the Great Dance, and returns home.

Given the theme of temptation for a sinless couple, scholars have naturally pointed to connections between this novel and John Milton's *Paradise Lost*. Some scholars also see connections with Edmund Spenser's *The Faerie Queene*, and others see links with H. G. Wells's science fiction novels. However, very few readers to this point have noted the many features of Lewis's narrative that recall Dante's Garden of Eden and Mount Purgatory. As is the case with Lewis's novels so far, this story and its setting draw on all three sections of Dante's poem, but again in new ways. It begins with a compressed journey that opens the book and recalls the *Inferno*. Next, Ransom continues to resemble Dante's pilgrim, but this time during the journey in the *Purgatorio* and at the end of the *Paradiso*. Although the Green Lady resembles Beatrice in many ways, Ransom's Beatrician experience is complete only when he meets Perelandra's royal couple together—in a garden at the top of a mountain of course.

The Narrator-Lewis's Journey

Perelandra begins with a short mini-journey by the novel's narrator, Lewis, as he walks from the Worchester train station to Ransom's cottage, where he has been invited to join Ransom on some sort of unexplained "Business" (*Per.* 9). Just as it is a Thursday when the story of Dante's pilgrim begins, so too narrator-Lewis has been summoned to "Come down Thursday" (*Per.* 9). This episode cannot be overlooked because it conflates several details of the journey of Dante's pilgrim through the *Inferno* in subtle but very distinct ways, thus introducing the journey that Ransom will take in the rest of the novel as reflective of the journey in the *Purgatorio*.

In *Perelandra*, narrator-Lewis sets out from the train station under a "gloomy five-o'clock sky" (*Per.* 9). As he goes forward, he has a "growing sense of *malaise*," and recognizes that his "emotion was . . . Fear" (*Per.* 10). Having left his pack on the train, he thinks, "It seemed perfectly obvious that I must retrace my step" (*Per.* 11), so the "only sensible course was to turn back at once and get safe home" (*Per.* 13). However, "*reason* . . . awoke and set me once more plodding forward" (*Per.* 11; italics added).

Dante's pilgrim descends into hell when "day was departing and it was getting dark" (*Inf.* 2.1). At the very outset, the pilgrim admits, "I fear my journey might turn out to be madness" (*Inf.* 2.35), and he remains fearful throughout his time in hell. At the gate of Dis when passage to the lower circles of hell seems blocked by rebellious sprits, the terrified pilgrim entreats his guide Virgil, "Let us retrace our steps together at once" (*Inf.* 8.102). Virgil, who often represents "reason" (among other things), manages to convince the protesting pilgrim to continue moving forward (see *Inf.* 8.104–105).

Narrator-Lewis's mental state during his short journey mirrors many details from characters, dialogue, and actions in cantos 29 and 30 of the *Inferno* (the ninth and tenth ditches of fraud), where the theme of madness and insanity in Dante's poem is most prominent. When Dante's pilgrim and his guide reach the edge of the tenth ditch, "always moving to the left," they "descended . . . [into] that dark valley" (*Inf.* 29.52–53, 65). Narrator-Lewis goes *down* a hill, turns *left* at a crossroads, and "staggered on into the . . . *dark*" (*Per.* 14; italics added). Dante begins *Inferno* 30 with three instances from classical literature of people going mad (see *Inf.* 30.1–23) and comments that two souls in that tenth ditch are even more insane. For narrator-Lewis, unnerved by swirling thoughts, the fear of madness becomes the main source of his discomfort. Earlier he "was wondering whether this might be the beginning of a nervous breakdown," and he was soon "already half convinced that I must be entering what is called Madness" (*Per.* 12, 14). One soul in Dante's ditch (Gianni Schicchi), who is described as a rabid shade (see *Inf.* 30.32–33), leaps onto another soul from behind and sinks his teeth in the nape of his neck (see *Inf.* 30.29). Some of narrator-Lewis's mental images echo that event: "Perhaps he [Ransom] would jump on me from behind," and "The impulse to retreat . . . leaped upon me with a sort of demoniac violence" (*Per.* 15, 16). Another soul in

Dante's tenth ditch (Griffolino of Arezzo), being punished for practicing sorcery, had told someone, "I know how to fly through the
air" (*Inf.* 29.113). Narrator-Lewis at one point feels that Ransom is
a "sorcerer" and later has the impulse to accuse Ransom of being a
"damned magician" (*Per.* 13, 20). (Ironically, unlike Griffolino who
lied about being able to fly, Ransom *will* fly through the air like a
magician when he goes to Perelandra).

Scenes from the *Inferno* at the gate of Dis and hell's next circle
are also recalled during the narrator's mini-journey. Despite the
forceful resistance of rebellious spirits on top of the wall at the gate
of Dis, Dante's pilgrim manages to pass through (see *Inf.* 9.104–106).
Similarly, arriving at the gate of Ransom's cottage, narrator-Lewis
comes up against "a sort of invisible wall of resistance that met me
in the face . . . [but I] managed to get through the gate" (*Per.* 15).
Immediately past the gate of Dis, Dante's pilgrim sees coffins that
house heretics (in the sixth circle), and "all the lids of the tombs
were opened" (*Inf.* 9.121). Narrator-Lewis, once past the gate and
inside the cottage, bumps into (what he later discovers) is a "large
coffin-shaped casket, open" (*Per.* 21).

Other details call to mind the last circle of Dante's hell where
traitors are encased in ice. Narrator-Lewis earlier feels, as he is
heading to Ransom's cottage, that he is "getting nearer to the one
enemy—the traitor" (*Per.* 13), and the coffin in Ransom's cottage is
twice described as being "like ice" (*Per.* 17, 21). Dante's pilgrim un-
expectedly stubs his foot hard against a face protruding from the ice
(see *Inf.* 32.78), and narrator-Lewis hits his "shin violently against
something"—in this case, against the coffin itself (*Per.* 16).

When Ransom finally arrives at the cottage, he confirms the
hellish nature of the narrator's short journey when he rhetorically
asks, "You got through the barrage without any damage?" He remarks that he expected Lewis would have encountered some difficulties getting there because "they [evil eldils] didn't want you
to get here" (*Per.* 21)—similar to the resistance Dante's pilgrim encounters from rebellious spirits at the gate of Dis and from others
elsewhere in hell. Ransom next gives the same two pieces of advice
the pilgrim receives in *Inferno* 29 and 30. Virgil advises the pilgrim,
who is staring at a soul (Geri del Bello) in the ninth ditch of fraud,
"don't focus your thoughts on him from now on; pay attention to
other things and leave him behind" (*Inf.* 29.22–24). Commenting

on Lewis's mental embattlement on his journey, Ransom says, "The best plan is to take no notice and keep straight on" (*Per.* 21). Ransom's second piece of advice—"Don't try to answer them. They like drawing you into an interminable argument" (*Per.* 21)—is also Virgilian. When Dante's pilgrim becomes absorbed in listening to an argument (between Master Adam and Sinon in the tenth ditch), Virgil rebukes him (see *Inf.* 30.130); at that point, Dante's pilgrim admits that he "was so full of shame that it is still now vivid in my memory" (*Inf.* 30.134–135). Narrator-Lewis likewise later regrets his earlier mental state, saying, "The state of mind I was in was one which I look back on with humiliation" (*Per.* 15).

Before the novel's publication, Lewis wrote to a friend, "The Venus book [*Perelandra*] is just finished, except that I now find the two first chapters need re-rewriting." Whatever those first two chapters looked like before their rewriting and whatever those changes involved, the beginning of the novel is now a neatly packaged descent into Dante's hell. This mini-journey at the beginning of the story with its condensed echoes of the *Inferno* illustrates the presence of evil forces in the universe, perhaps for someone who has not read the first novel of the trilogy, and functions as a prelude to Ransom's journey. It signals that the main journey that follows this "infernal" mini-journey will reflect the *Purgatorio*.

Perelandra and Its Inhabitants

In addition to the ongoing echoes of Dante's medieval cosmos in this novel, Lewis mirrors Dante's approach of reinterpreting classical mythology as a foreshadowing of Christian truth. In *The Discarded Image*, Lewis discusses the ways Christians have approached pagan material and notes that there has always been "a Christian 'left,' eager to detect and anxious to banish every Pagan element; but also a Christian 'right' who, like St. Augustine, could find the doctrine of the Trinity foreshadowed in the *Platonici* [Platonists and Neoplatonists]." Both Dante and Lewis are members of the Christian "right" with regard to classical philosophy, as the structures of their fictional universes demonstrate in their adaptations of classical notions, but they are also both members of the Christian "right" with regard to classical literature and mythology.

For Dante, classical philosophy may foreshadow truth in its *rational* quest for reality, while classical mythology may foreshadow truth in its *imaginative* quest for reality. Poetic vision may accurately see truth but fail to understand it fully, so it needs a true interpretation to be aligned with truth.

When Dante, for example, assigns classical mythological creatures as guardians of the circles in hell, he is reinterpreting them as poetic embodiments by pagan authors of what Christian doctrine calls sins. Three-headed Cerberus with his three ravenous mouths becomes a depiction for Dante of the gluttons he guards. The violent Minotaur, with his bull's head and human body, is only partly human; Dante's choice of the Minotaur as the guardian of the circle of the violent becomes his indirect commentary on the bestial and nonrational nature of sins of violence. In a subdivision of this circle, Centaurs, another half-human and half-animal species prone to violence, guard the sinners who shed the blood of others.

In another kind of instance, Lethe, the classical river of forgetfulness in Hades, appears in Dante's poem, but he relocates it from Hades to the Garden of Eden. Whereas the classical Lethe removes *all* memories, Dante's Lethe removes only the memories of repented sins and their accompanying guilt (see *Inf.* 14.136–138). For Dante, then, the ancients were correct about human beings' need to be released from the burden of their past, but they did not understand the spiritual aspect of that process, so his reinterpretation of Lethe is meant to demonstrate that truth. Insights from classical literature and myth, then, function in Dante's poem to foreshadow truth on the poetic level even if they need adjustments or corrections to be fully compatible with Christian truths.

Lewis's description of myth in *Miracles* as "a real though unfocused gleam of divine truth falling on human imagination" clearly echoes Dante's approach. The chief eldils of Malacandra and Perelandra, who are actually angelic beings, bear the characteristics of their mythical counterparts: the eldil of Mars is masculine and "shone with cold and morning colours, a little metallic. . . . [He] held in his hand something like a spear" (*Per.* 199–200). The eldil of Venus "glowed with a warm splendour, full of the suggestion of teeming vegetative life . . . [and her] hands . . . were open" (*Per.* 199–200). Ransom has the expected reaction of anyone who is familiar with classical mythology when he says, "My eyes have seen Mars and Venus. I have seen Ares and Aphrodite" (*Per.* 201). The ancients correctly intuited the distinct qualities of each of these planetary eldils but did not recognize them as angels and mistook them for gods. Lewis thus "corrects" the original myths about the classical gods. (Dante makes that very same correction when he speaks of "the ancient peoples in their ancient error" (*Par.* 8.6) who mistook the planets for gods to be worshipped.)

Lewis ties his approach to mythology explicitly to Dante's by echoing the connection Dante makes between the Garden of Eden and the Garden of Hesperides. The classical Garden of Hesperides was the ancients' version of an idyllic garden that was a parallel to the Garden of Eden. Dante's pilgrim, puzzled by the Garden of Eden's appearance at the top of Mount Purgatory, is told that "those who in ancient times wrote poetry about the Golden Age and its happy state [Garden of Hesperides] . . . were perhaps dreaming of this place [Eden]" (*Purg.* 33.139–141). Dante's allusion here to the Garden of Hesperides indicates he interprets that myth as a dim poetic vision of the real Eden by the ancients.

Lewis repeats, but inverts, this same dual-garden experience for Ransom, while making the same point as Dante. When Ransom comes upon the perplexing sight of a beautiful garden on Perelandra, "He recognized the garden of the Hesperides at once" (*Per.* 45). Ransom, in a counterpoint experience to that of Dante's pilgrim, sees the actual classical Garden of Hesperides, but its link in Dante to Earth's Garden of Eden implicitly suggests that this planet may be a new Eden. During the course of his adventures, Ransom finally concludes "that the triple distinction of truth from myth and of both from fact was purely terrestrial—was part and parcel of that unhappy division between soul and body which resulted from the Fall. . . . The Incarnation had been the beginning of its disappearance" (*Per.* 143–44). That division is healed for Ransom when truths from mythology and truths from Christian doctrine converge during the course of his journey, and his experience parallels that of Dante's pilgrim who witnesses that same convergence of truths during his journey.

From the very beginning of Ransom's adventures on Perelandra, Lewis's intimation that this planet may be a new Eden occurs primarily through distinct parallels with Dante's Garden of Eden. In Eden, Dante's pilgrim is told that "the holy land where you are . . . has fruit that is not plucked on earth" (*Purg.* 28.118–120). When Ransom tastes the yellow fruit on Perelandra, "It was like the discovery of a totally new *genus* of pleasures, something unheard of among men" (*Per.* 42), and this is true for other fruit he eats there as well (see *Per.* 103).

In Eden, the first person Dante's pilgrim sees is a lovely woman, Matilda, on the other side of a brook, "a lady all by herself, singing and gathering flowers" (*Purg.* 28.40–41). Lewis repeats that precise image when the first person Ransom sees is the Perelandrian Eve across the water as her island floats close to his: "There walking before him, *as if on the other side of a brook*, was the Lady herself— walking with her head a little bowed and . . . *plaiting together some* blue *flowers*. She was *singing* to herself in a low voice" (*Per.* 59; italics added).

In a 1944 letter, Lewis acknowledges that Tinidril "owes something to Matilda at the end of *Purgatorio*." Lewis reinforces the deliberate and unmistakable parallel through a variety of other narrative details. Matilda is about three paces away (see *Purg.* 28.70), and Lewis's lady is about five feet away (see *Per.* 59). When the pilgrim calls out to her, "she turned around toward me" (*Purg.* 28.55–56). When Ransom addresses the lady, she "turned as he hailed her" (*Per.* 59). Dante's pilgrim asks Matilda to come closer so he can hear the words she is singing (see *Purg.* 28.46–48), and Ransom asks the Green Lady "to repeat what she had been saying" (*Per.* 60) since he had not heard her words. Dante's lady and Lewis's are not identified by name until much later—Dante's Matilda is named five cantos later at the end of the *Purgatorio* (see *Purg.* 33.119), while Lewis's Tinidril remains nameless until the very end of the novel.

Lewis's lady as a mirror image of Dante's Matilda already subtly indicates that there may be trouble in Perelandra, because immediately after Dante's pilgrim sees Matilda, he comments that she reminds him of Proserpine (see *Purg.* 28.49–51). Proserpine, Ceres' daughter, was gathering flowers in a meadow when she was abducted by Pluto, the ruler of Hades. By specifically fashioning his lady to resemble Dante's Matilda, who is reminiscent of Proserpine, Lewis may obliquely be suggesting that she is in danger too, since "the ruler of hell" in his cosmic scheme (the Bent One) is trying to capture her as well.

The above narrative parallels hint that Perelandra is a new Garden of Eden, but Lewis also suggests that Perelandra will be the locale of temptation through other allusions to the *Purgatorio*. First, the colors in Lewis's Garden of Hesperides make it resemble Dante's only other garden on the island of Purgatory, which is located in ante-purgatory at the base of the mount. Dante describes the flowers in that garden as more brilliant than the colors that are found in gold, silver, red, and indigo-colored wood (see *Purg.* 7.73–74). The colors in the garden that Ransom sees include "*yellow . . . silver . . . indigo* [the stem of the tree] . . . and *red gold*" (*Per.* 45; italics added). Dante's valley-garden alludes to Edenic temptation because a serpent comes there nightly (see *Purg.* 8.38–39), "a serpent that is perhaps the one that gave Eve the bitter food" (*Purg.* 8.98–99). Dante's pilgrim sleeps and awakens in this valley-garden after his first night on the island of Purgatory (see *Purg.* 7.62ff.), and Ransom, after his first night in Perelandra, wakens to a visually similar garden. The colors and the context that make Lewis's garden resemble Dante's valley-garden, then, carry a subtle suggestion of future temptation.

In addition, Lewis's Perelandrian Eve, although entirely human in form, is bright green, and thus recalls the two instances of green characters in the *Purgatorio* and their significance. First, her coloring recalls the two angels who come each night to the valley-garden to protect souls against the serpent: "They had robes that were green like new leaves . . . [and they had] green wings" (*Purg.* 8.28–29). Her coloring, which brings these angels to mind, could be another oblique signal that temptation is coming to Perelandra. Second, Lewis's lady looks like the green woman who appears in Dante's Garden of Eden (at the side of Beatrice's chariot): "She looked as if her flesh and bones were made of emerald" (*Purg.* 29.124–125). To emphasize this similarity to Dante's emerald lady, Lewis says his lady looks like "a goddess carved apparently out of green stone" (*Per.* 54) and later describes her as shining like an emerald (see *Per.* 204). Dante's green lady in Eden represents the theological virtue of hope, and perhaps this is an indirect suggestion that there is hope for Lewis's Green Lady in this new Eden.

The hints from Lewis that this is a new Eden and that it will become a locus of temptation come mainly from Dante. The reader does not need to be aware of any of them to follow Lewis's story, but understanding the cues can help a reader be prepared for subsequent events.

Ransom and His Perelandrian Journey

In this new Garden of Eden, Ransom resembles Dante's pilgrim once again. Ransom's second cosmic adventure, like the second segment of the journey of Dante's pilgrim, marks his moral development: his growth in courage, his suffering, and his subsequent restoration and rejuvenation.

Just as the beginning of the journey in *Out of the Silent Planet* consists of several details that parallel the beginning of the journey in the *Inferno*, so too the beginning of this journey consists of several details that parallel the beginning of the journey in the *Purgatorio*.

(1) Dante's pilgrim freely undertakes the journey up Mount Purgatory, and Ransom freely undertakes his second journey (unlike his first journey when he was abducted). (2) The journey in the *Purgatorio* is part of the pilgrim's heaven-appointed journey. Ransom's journey is likewise heaven appointed. He has been summoned to Perelandra by someone "much higher up" than the Malacandrian Oyarsa (see *Per.* 23). (3) Dante's pilgrim begins the ascent of the mount very early in morning (see *Purg.* 9.13–14), and Ransom's journey begins "as soon as the sun is up" (*Per.* 27). (4) Dante's pilgrim is supernaturally transported up to the gate of the mount (which is inaccessible because of the high wall around its base) (see *Purg.* 9.19–33). Ransom is supernaturally transported from Earth to Perelandra (*Per.* 23, 27). (5) Both are transported through the agency of a heavenly being—Dante's pilgrim by one of the heavenly ladies assisting him on his journey, Lucia (see *Purg.* 9.55–57), and Ransom (in a white coffin) by the Malacandrian Oyarsa and angels (see *Per.* 23, 46, 193). (6) Dante is asleep when he is transported (see *Purg.* 9.52–53), and Ransom is "in some state of suspended animation" during his transport (*Per.* 27).

Ransom's initial adventures on Perelandra morally parallel an ascent of Dante's mount. The ascent by Dante's pilgrim simultaneously signifies cleansing from sinful inclinations, growth in their opposite virtues, and a shift from fear to courage as he undertakes that difficult journey. Similarly, the stages of Ransom's moral development unfold in a way that loosely parallel the ledges of Dante's mount, either by his resistance to one of the sinful inclinations purged there or by his demonstration of already having its opposite virtue.

The examples below follow Dante's categories of vices and virtues, but they are discussed in the sequence in which they appear in Lewis's novel. Dante makes use of the traditional sequence of the seven capital sins in his construction of Mount Purgatory, but Lewis is not bound by that. As is always the case, Lewis's imitation of Dante (and others) is not rigid or slavish. Although Lewis at times follows the general contours of the pattern on Dante's Mount Purgatory (from pride to lust) in some of his fictive journeys, this time he creatively recombines and transforms those elements from Dante's poem into a new unity.

Sloth/Zeal

After struggling in the water upon arrival in Perelandra and successfully gaining access to a floating island, "It seems that he must have remained lying on his face, doing nothing and thinking nothing for a very long time" (*Per*. 39). However, Ransom never again remains inactive on the planet during his time with the Green Lady except for times of needed rest as he tirelessly tries to assist and protect her.

Gluttony/Temperance

When he is about to reach for a second delicious yellow gourd, even though he is no longer hungry or thirsty, "It appeared to him better not to taste again" (*Per*. 43). He later resists that same temptation with a red-centered berry, always obeying "that same inner adviser" (*Per*. 50), thus displaying temperance.

Avarice/Generosity

Enjoying the refreshment from the water globes on the bubble trees, he thinks about wanting to gratify the "itch to have things over again" and wonders if that desire—rather than the love of money—might be "possibly the root of all evil" (*Per*. 48). He realizes that money is a means to ensure control over the repetition of pleasure, so he implicitly understands the folly of amassing and hoarding wealth.

Pride/Humility

He could allow his pride to be stung when the Green Lady laughs uproariously at his half-white, half-sunburned body, an appearance acquired during his journey (*Per*. 55–56). No one enjoys being laughed at, and he had not been prepared "to be . . . an absurdity" (*Per*. 56). However, he chooses the path of humility: "He felt a momentary impatience. . . . Then he smiled in spite of himself at the very undistinguished career he was having on Perelandra" (*Per*. 56).

Lust/Chastity

Although Weston later accuses him of lust with the "naked savage woman" because they are both unclothed (*Per*. 87), from early on during Ransom's encounters with the Green Lady, "Embarrassment and desire were both a thousand miles away from his experience" (*Per*. 59).

Anger/Meekness

At one point he is "stunned by some measureless anger in the very air" (*Per*. 70) when he tells a lie, and another time he has "a feeling of angry frustration" (*Per*. 97), even losing his temper once (*Per*. 132). His impatience and anger are generally due to the difficulty of his initial communications with the innocent Perelandrian Eve, but he succeeds in dealing with her patiently and meekly for the rest of his time there.

Envy/Kindness

Ransom does not have to deal with envy since Weston and the Green Lady are the only people on the planet, and neither provokes him to envy. He does, however, manifest the virtue of kindness in showing brotherly love and concern for her, especially when she comes under attack from Weston.

In the first part of the story, Ransom develops and/or demonstrates his moral rectitude, being led and strengthened at times to resist temptation by grace from Maleldil, the "inner adviser." At this point he is now qualified to be of assistance to the Green Lady in *her* time of temptation, since only the person who has trod a certain path is in a position to guide and assist another on it.

The Green Lady's temptation to disobey Maleldil's command not to sleep on the Fixed Land has no parallel with any temptation in Dante's poem, but *The Divine Comedy* sheds light on the manner in which that temptation is carried out. Lewis's Eve is tempted by the Bent Eldil through the agency of Weston in a way that Dante illuminates in the *Inferno*. In the ninth circle of traitors, Alberigo, explaining the presence of his soul in hell while he appears to be alive on earth, tells Dante's pilgrim that "as soon as a soul commits a betrayal the way I did, his body is taken over from him by a demon who controls it from then on until [that body's] allotted time has ended" (*Inf.* 33.129–132). This friar's situation, although irregular, is not uncommon; Alberigo points out Branca d'Oria with him in the ninth circle who likewise "left a devil in his stead in his body" (*Inf.* 33.145–146).

On Perelandra, Weston's body is taken over by Earth's Bent Eldil—and for a similar transgression to that of Dante's souls. Both Alberigo and Branca were traitors to their kinfolk, and Lewis may be suggesting that Weston has likewise betrayed his kindred—in this case, all of humanity. Weston has abandoned his previous devotion to human beings—he was at least committed to the perpetuation of his species in *Out of the Silent Planet*—but he is now "a convinced believer in emergent evolution" (*Per.* 90) and committed to a life force, which he describes as the "blind, inarticulate purposiveness thrusting its way upward and ever upward in an endless unity of differentiated achievements" (*Per.* 91). (Any normal person would already know something is wrong here.) Weston summarizes his spiritual progression as first working for himself, then for science, then for humanity, but "now at last for Spirit itself," so now, "To spread spirituality, not to spread the human race, is henceforth my mission" (*Per.* 91).

Despite Ransom's insistence to Weston that "there's nothing specially fine about simply being a spirit. The Devil is a spirit" (*Per.* 93), Weston yields himself up totally to this life force and becomes, in theological terms, possessed. Lewis purposely refers to Weston as "Weston's voice," Weston's body," "it," and, most significantly, as the "Un-man" from this point on to indicate that Weston has disappeared and that his body is now merely a vessel used by an entirely different personality. Whether his body was taken over by "the Bent One, or one of his lesser followers, made no difference" (*Per.* 111–12) because the Un-man is now either "Satan, or one whom Satan has digested" (*Per.* 173)—an image reminiscent of the fate of sinners in *The Screwtape Letters*.

To underscore that Weston's condition is indeed demonic, Lewis has recourse to images and details from *Inferno* 22, which describes the fifth ditch of the circle of fraud in Dante's hell. This is one place where devils guard sinners, in this case corrupt civil servants who are submerged in boiling pitch. Dante compares the sinners in that ditch to frogs (see *Inf.* 22.26), and one of the devils (Rubicante) is urged by the others, "Dig your claws into [that soul's] back so that you can skin it off" (*Inf.* 22.40–41). Lewis echoes both the frog image and that devil's action when Ransom discovers a frog whose "whole back had been ripped open" (*Per.* 108) and then sees the Un-man "tearing a frog . . . almost surgically inserting his forefinger, with its long sharp nail, under the skin behind the creature's head and ripping it open" (*Per.* 109–110). Ransom's physical struggle with the Un-man later on also brings to mind the devils in this scene because the Un-man's "fingers [were] arched like claws . . . [and he] wanted to grapple" (*Per.* 154), reminiscent of the devils' claws and the grappling hooks used against Dante's souls (see *Inf.* 22.69, 137). During his struggle with Ransom, in fact, the Un-man's "nails were ripping great strips off his [Ransom's] back" (*Per.* 153). Lewis obliquely compares the Un-man to Satan himself through this detail of a person's back being ripped open, because Dante's three-faced Satan is eternally gnawing the top part of Judas in one of his three mouths, with the result that "sometimes the skin on [Judas'] back was all stripped off" (*Inf.* 34.59–60).

Just as Dante's difficult ascent of Mount Purgatory includes actual physical suffering as he passes through the fire on the ledge of lust, so too Ransom undergoes physical suffering—in his case, because of physical combat with the Un-man. His combat with the Un-man corresponds to no event in *The Divine Comedy*, but Lewis combines echoes from the *Inferno* and the *Paradiso* to describe that long ordeal.

During the battle that involves a sea chase, Ransom eats seaweed and "felt his mind oddly changed" (*Per.* 162). This recalls Dante's pilgrim in the *Paradiso* when he first rises up into the heavens and compares himself to Glaucus who was transformed into a sea god by eating a sea herb (see *Par.* 1.67–69). The pilgrim feels that he has similarly undergone an inner change but cannot explain it: "'Trans-humanize' cannot be signified by words" (*Par.* 1.70–71). On Perelandra, Ransom's eating of seaweed "gave knowledge . . . though *not a knowledge that can be reduced to words*" (*Per.* 162; italics added).

After Ransom kills the Un-man in the cliff's cavern and ascends the cliff from inside, his experience recalls several features of the journey through the *Inferno*. Although he is climbing up inside a mountain on the planet's surface, Ransom refers to his movement as "a subterranean journey" (*Per*. 183) and calls his location "this prison" (*Per*. 175)—Dante refers to hell as a "prison" four times. Ransom's "slow uphill trek through darkness lasted so long that he began to fear he was going round in a circle" (*Per*. 176), which is of course consistent with the path of Dante's pilgrim through hell's circles (although in an opposite direction). At one point Ransom looks up and "perceived that he was looking up a funnel" (*Per*. 178), the very shape of Dante's hell. Ransom emerges from the mountain when a river current propels him forward through a cave opening, and Dante's pilgrim emerges from hell through a round opening at the end of a tunnel (see *Inf*. 34.138). Ransom's first sight is of "*sweet blue* turf" (*Per*. 185; italics added). The first sight of Dante's pilgrim when he emerges from hell is the sky with its "*sweet* color of oriental *sapphire*" (*Purg*. 1.13; italics added). The color blue in the similar context of reemerging from under the earth could be too tenuous to tie Lewis to Dante here, but there seems to be no reason to describe the Perelandrian turf—of all things!—as "*sweet* blue" unless he is thinking of the "*sweet* sapphire" color Dante's pilgrim sees as he emerges from hell.

After climbing Perelandra's highest mountain, Ransom finds at its summit a beautiful garden in a small valley that has links to features in both the *Purgatorio* and the *Paradiso*. First, as the meeting place between Ransom and Perelandra's king and queen, it recalls the meeting in the Garden of Eden between the pilgrim and Beatrice (which will be discussed in the next section). Second, it is the location of Ransom's vision of ultimate reality, referred to as the Great Dance, which condenses and mirrors various visions of Dante's pilgrim in the *Paradiso*.

Ransom's vision of the Great Dance, a traditional metaphor for the harmonious motion of the universe, is another instance of the synthesizing procedure Lewis used to construct the cosmos as first seen in *Out of the Silent Planet*. Here he combines the various interpretations of the dance metaphor by Plato, Plotinus, and Dante. Plato applies the metaphor to the movement of planets and stars, while Plotinus applies it to the movement of all creation.

Dante, on the other hand, uses dance imagery only in relation to the redeemed and other heavenly beings, so dance for him signifies a form of praising God and is an expression of heavenly joy. Although Lewis takes on Plato's and Plotinus's interpretations by applying his dance metaphor to the movement of heavenly bodies as well as to the rest of creation, he follows Dante's interpretation of that heavenly dance with its qualities of praise and joy. His Great Dance thus becomes a metaphor not only for the harmony of the universe but also for joy in and the praise of God.

The concluding details of Ransom's vision combine and condense certain details of what Dante's pilgrim sees in the heavenly spheres and in the Empyrean.

(1) During the course of his heavenly journey, Dante's pilgrim sees lights moving at various speeds (see *Par.* 8.19–21) and in a variety of directions (see *Par.* 14.109–111). He describes seeing shooting sparks (see *Par.* 7.8), flashes of lights (see *Par.* 10.64), rings of lights (see *Par.* 14.74–75), ribbons of light (see *Par.* 15.22), and circling lights (see *Par.* 12.20; 18.75) His blessed souls are most often seen in groups of wheeling circles and are frequently compared to dancers. Lewis blends Dante's multiple images into one overarching image of light for his Great Dance that consists of "the intertwining undulation of many *cords* or *bands* of light . . . *ribbons* [of light] . . . and inter-animated *circlings*" (*Per.* 218–19; italics added).

(2) In Dante's poem all of creation reflects God's light. Beatrice shines by reflecting his rays (see *Par.* 11.19); one redeemed soul is called a "holy mirror" (see *Par.* 18.2; also *Par.* 17.123); and Dante's angels are described as countless mirrors in which God is reflected (see *Par.* 29.143–144). Ransom is similarly told that "Each thing . . . is . . . the *mirror* in which the beam of His brightness comes to rest and so return to Him" (*Per.* 217; italics added).

(3) Dante's pilgrim first receives instruction and revelation about God and creation from heavenly beings and then sees ultimate reality for himself. Ransom is instructed about creation by unnamed voices on the mountain (*Per.* 214–18), and then sees ultimate reality, the dance, for himself: "What had begun as speech turned into sight" (*Per.* 218).

(4) The metaphor Dante uses for his pilgrim's final vision of the heavenly court is his famous "white rose" image (*Par.* 31.1: "candida rosa"). As if to signal that Ransom is near the end his journey

and in the appropriate location for heavenly visions, the flowers that cover the summit of Lewis's mountain seem to reverse Dante's image because of his phrasing of their description: "like a lily but tinted like a rose" (*Per.* 193)—the inverse of Dante's image that could be described as "like a rose but tinted like a lily."

(5) During their visions, their mode of perception is identical. For Dante's pilgrim, "From this point my seeing was greater than our language, which gave way before such a sight, and my memory gave way before such overabundance" (*Par.* 33.55–57). Similarly, for Ransom, "that part of him which could reason [language] and remember [memory] was dropped farther and farther behind that part of him which saw" (*Per.* 219).

Both heavenly visions express a unity-in-diversity of all creation, but the emphasis in the experience of Dante's pilgrim is on unity, while the emphasis in Ransom's is on diversity. In fact, Lewis structures Ransom's vision in a contrapuntal fashion to the one in the *Paradiso*. Dante's pilgrim sees all of creation as a whole at rest in God (see *Par.* 33.85–87), while Ransom sees creation as a vast ensemble of bands and sparks of light in motion. The vision for Dante's pilgrim proceeds in tranquil simplicity (see *Par.* 33.91), whereas Ransom's vision expands into further movement and complexity (see *Per.* 219). The *Paradiso* vision, however, ends on a note of implied movement when, for Dante's pilgrim, "like a wheel moving in perfect balance, my desire and my will were being revolved by the Love that moves the sun and the other stars" (*Par.* 33.143–145). Ransom's vision, on the other hand, ends in rest: "A simplicity beyond all comprehension, ancient and young as spring, illimitable, pellucid, drew him with cords of infinite desire into its own stillness" (*Per.* 219).

Although Lewis adapts many of Dante's images for his Great Dance, he is not replicating that vision. He is presenting a variation, as Dante is, on a theme that was invented by neither of them. When Ransom sees complexity, diversity, and increased movement, the other sees simplicity, unity, and increased brightness; when Ransom is led to stillness, the other is led to movement. The difference in the outward shape of the two visions, however, does not eliminate the essential parallel that exists between them, for each vision signifies total union with God and signals the conclusion of a long, arduous journey by a pilgrim.

Ransom's journey to Perelandra begins with details that echo the beginning of the journey in the *Purgatorio* and ends with a vision that echoes the journey in the *Paradiso*. One could say that in this novel, Ransom has the benefit of two Dantean journeys "rolled into one." For both pilgrims, however, their heavenly visions complete their intellectual, moral, and spiritual transformation and prepare them for the tasks they will each be assigned in the future once they have returned to Earth.

Beatrice

Although Ransom's mission on this planet ends with his victorious battle against the Un-man, his Perelandrian adventure concludes in the garden on the summit of a mountain. Lewis structures Ransom's meeting with Tor and Tinidril, Perelandra's Adam and Eve, to parallel several features of the pilgrim's meeting with Beatrice in the garden.

Even before this point, however, apart from the Green Lady's initial appearance recalling Dante's Matilda, there are many instances of her resemblance to Beatrice throughout the story. Right before Dante's pilgrim meets Beatrice in the garden, "a gentle, steady breeze brushed [his] forehead" (*Purg.* 28.7–8). The day before Ransom meets the Green Lady, "a light wind, full of sweetness, lifted the hair on his forehead" (*Per.* 43). When Beatrice tells Dante's pilgrim at the beginning of their meeting to look at her, he lowers his head and looks down, embarrassed about his past transgressions (see *Purg.* 30.76). When Ransom is at first with the Green Lady, he "found it was difficult to look higher than her feet" (*Per.* 62), in his case because he is embarrassed about all of humanity's need for a redeemer. Dante's pilgrim speaks of the regal bearing of Beatrice's look (see *Purg.* 30.70), and the Green Lady likewise carries "in her face an authority" (*Per.* 65). Beatrice expresses the inequality between herself and Dante's pilgrim by employing the familiar "tu" used by superiors to those under them (see *Purg.* 30.55ff.) while the pilgrim uses the honorific "voi" for her (see *Purg.* 31.36ff.). When the Green Lady realizes Ransom is not the king and father of his world, "She knew now at last that she was not addressing an equal" and then relates to him differently, although "her manner to him was henceforth more gracious" (*Per.* 67). These echoes of Beatrice, however, are only foreshadows of Ransom's more complete Beatrician experience on the summit of the mountain.

The Perelandrian mountain of meeting is referred to as "the Holy Mountain" (*Per.* 196, 206, 221), echoing Dante's descriptions for Mount Purgatory as "the holy mountain" (see *Purg.* 28.12) and "the sacred mountain" (see *Purg.* 19.37). Lewis's description of the meeting in a valley at the top of the mountain repeats some familiar features from his earlier novels that echo the pilgrim-Beatrice dynamic in the garden, but, as always, he introduces new parallels too.

(1) Before meeting Beatrice, Dante's pilgrim experiences a strange new light filling the garden whose source he does not understand (see *Purg.* 29.16–17). Ransom perceives "an oddity in the light" at the top of the mountain (*Per.* 194) and "a pure daylight that seemed to come from nowhere in particular" (*Per.* 204). (2) Dante's pilgrim is first greeted in the garden by Matilda singing, "Blessed are those whose sins are taken away" (*Purg.* 29.3), and the Malacandrian Oyarsa announces that "[Ransom's] sins are forgiven" (*Per.* 195). (3) In Dante's garden, the procession that precedes Beatrice's arrival has, among other participants, twenty-four elders in pairs followed by four creatures (see *Purg.* 29.83, 92). On Perelandra, the procession preceding the King and Queen's arrival consists of creatures "mostly *in their pairs*" followed by the sound of "*four* singing beasts" (*Per.* 203; italics added). (4) Dante's twenty-four elders are crowned with white lilies (see *Purg.* 29.84), and the seven men at the end of the procession are crowned with "with roses and other red flowers" (*Purg.* 129.148). Perhaps as an echo of these flower details, the "red lilies" that cover Lewis's garden area could represent a conflation of these flowers in Dante's garden procession. (5) Angels precede Beatrice's arrival, and the chief eldils (angels) of Malacandra and Perelandra are already present with Ransom in this garden. Lewis's description of their faces—"Pure, spiritual, intellectual love shot from their faces" (*Per.* 199)—is his paraphrase of Dante's description of the heavenly Empyrean as "pure light, intellectual light, full of love" (*Par.* 30.39–40). (6) Dante's pilgrim feels that "hardly a drop of blood in me is not quivering" (*Purg.* 30.46–47), and for Ransom, "the blood pricked his veins" (*Per.* 194). (7) Dante's pilgrim is

called by name only once in the poem—by Beatrice in the garden (see *Purg.* 30.55). Ransom is referred to in this garden by his first name "Elwin"—by the Malacandrian Oyarsa (*Per.* 195) and the Perelandrian Oyarsa (*Per.* 197).

This kind of stage setting naturally calls for a new Beatrice, and this time it is not one but two people: the Perelandrian couple. When Ransom first sees them, he refers to them as a single entity: "The holy *thing*, Paradise itself in *its two Persons*, Paradise walking hand in hand, *its two bodies* shining in the light . . . *its male right hand* uplifted" (*Per.* 204; italics added). Tor also refers to himself and his wife as two halves of one single entity. Speaking in the third person about his test to obey Maleldil while his wife was being tested elsewhere, he says, "Though half of him turned into earth [if Tinidril had disobeyed and died] . . . the living half [himself] must still follow Maleldil" (*Per.* 210). Even the shared titles that the Oyarsa of Perelandra confers on them reflect this concept since the titles are in the singular: "Oyarsa-Perelendri [because they now co-rule the planet], the Adam, the Crown" (*Per.* 206).

Lewis compares the appearance of "this living Paradise" (*Per.* 207) to one particular aspect of Beatrice's appearance in a stunningly creative way. When Dante's pilgrim is told in the garden, "Do not hold back your gaze from the emeralds we have placed you in front of" (*Purg.* 31.115–116), he is being told to look at Beatrice's two green eyes. Ransom likewise looks at two emeralds in this garden, but what he sees are the two royal Perelandrians who are "shining . . . like *emeralds*" (*Per.* 204; italics added).

Details of Ransom's interaction with them also reflect the pilgrim's interaction with Beatrice. (1) Dante's pilgrim has to cross the river Lethe to reach Beatrice (see *Purg.* 31.94–96), and Ransom has to wade through the pool in the middle of the garden to reach Tor and Tinidril (see *Per.* 208). (2) Dante's pilgrim, who had used the respectful "voi" for Beatrice, uses the familiar form of "tu" with her when he becomes her spiritual equal in the Empyrean (see *Par.* 30.79–90). When Ransom, at first treated as an inferior by the Green Lady, wades through the pool, Tor and Tinidril "rose to meet him and both kissed him . . . as *equals* embrace" (*Per.* 208; italics added). (3) Beatrice, at the end of an allegorical presentation of church history in the garden, prophesies the future deliverance of the church from evil (see *Purg.* 33.34–45). Likewise, Tor ends his speech by prophetically alluding to the siege of Thulcandra, the end of the rule of the Bent One, and other apocalyptic events (see *Per.* 212–13).

In making the Beatrice of this novel a married couple, Lewis underscores the Christian teaching on marriage that the two become one—a theme that will reappear in the final novel of the trilogy. He is also reiterating his belief that God can use any created being—or in this case, *two beings together*—as channels of grace. Lewis will not use two people to function simultaneously as one Beatrice again, but he will continue to borrow and adapt details from Dante's garden scene to narrate yet more Beatrician experiences.

Conclusion

Lewis calls Dante's poem "both a mimesis of the whole spiritual life and first-class science fiction." For both of his science fiction novels, Lewis draws from the wellspring of *The Divine Comedy* in combining an imaginative interpretation of the entire cosmos, fantastic journeys, and the presentation of Christian truths—all clear characteristics of *The Divine Comedy*.

Although he draws primarily on Dante's *Purgatorio* to help establish the atmosphere of a new Eden for Ransom's adventures in *Perelandra*, Lewis incorporates several features from the *Inferno* and *Paradiso* in his story as well—the narrator's short *Inferno* journey introducing Ransom's purgatorial journey, with the Great Dance closing it. One Dante scholar refers to Dante's pilgrim as "spectator [*Inferno*], participant [*Purgatorio*], and pupil [*Paradiso*] as he goes from world to world," and this pattern applies equally well to Ransom. He is primarily a spectator on Malacandra, a participant during his adventures in Perelandra, and a pupil during the yearlong vision of the Great Dance as he comes to understand the interconnectedness between all created things and their relationship to God.

Perhaps because of the book's beautiful descriptions of this planet, its hopeful message, and the cosmic hymn of praise at the end, Lewis says that of his novels penned up to this time, "What I enjoyed [writing] most was *Perelandra*." Although he later considered *Till We Have Faces* his best novel, he earlier states that "*Perelandra* is much the best book I have written." "Best," however, is not the same as "favorite," and one month before his death, he writes to a correspondent, "*Perelandra* is *my* favourite too."

CHAPTER SIX

That Hideous Strength

Introduction

That Hideous Strength (1945), Lewis's longest story, is the third and last novel of what Lewis calls "the Ransom trilogy." It has no space journeys and takes place entirely on earth. Lewis subtitles it "A Modern Fairy-Tale for Grown-Ups," calling it "a 'tall story' of devilry" because it deals with spiritual forces attempting to take over England. Nevertheless, this book is linked to the first two as the concluding novel of Lewis's silent planet myth. Ransom appears once again, as do Dick Devine (now Lord Feverstone) and the chief eldils that were introduced in *Out of the Silent Planet* and *Perelandra*.

Ransom's new mission is to thwart the attempt of a take-over of England by the scientific institute, the National Institute for Coordinated Experiments (N.I.C.E.), temporarily headquartered at Belbury south of Edgestow. The "head" of the N.I.C.E. is ostensibly the severed head of a scientist kept alive by technology, but in fact the earth's Bent Eldil (Satan) is the guiding force behind the whole enterprise. Ransom is assisted in this endeavor by a small group of Christians living in his manor at St. Anne's-on-the-Hill located east of town, as well as by Merlin (awakened after centuries of sleep) and by planetary eldils from Deep Heaven. The narrative tracks the movements, in alternating sections, of a young married couple, Mark and Jane Studdock. Mark, a sociologist at Bracton College, becomes more and more involved with the N.I.C.E. while Jane, who is experiencing unwanted visionary power, eventually becomes part of the community at St. Anne's. During a celebratory banquet at the N.I.C.E. toward the end of the novel, its experimental laboratories are destroyed and its leaders are killed in a variety of ways. Mark and Jane, each having undergone spiritual awakening and character transformation, are then reunited at St. Anne's, and Ransom returns to Perelandra for the healing of the wound in his heel that previously occurred there.

Lewis's silent planet myth provides the framework in this novel for the incorporation of yet another myth: the legends of King Arthur. Ransom is now also called Mr. Fisher-King (of the Grail myth) as well as the Pendragon (Arthur's successor), and a reawakened Merlin joins forces with Ransom's group. The ongoing battle between secular Britain and Logres (spiritual Britain) that has continued since Arthur's time functions as a localized example of the cosmic battle between good and evil in Lewis's silent planet myth.

Along with the addition of Arthurian material, Lewis continues to make use of many features of *The Divine Comedy*. His contrast between the N.I.C.E. and the community at St. Anne's draws on elements from the *Inferno* for his depiction of the hellish community at Belbury and from the *Purgatorio* and *Paradiso* for the Christian community at St. Anne's. Ransom, who no longer travels, continues to resemble Dante's pilgrim but in quite an unusual way. Mark's spiritual journey is shaped by patterns in the *Inferno* while Jane's is shaped by patterns in the *Purgatorio*, and each of their journeys involves a Beatrice figure.

The Inhabitants of Belbury and St. Anne's

Since he is dealing with historical characters, Dante is not free to invent his characters' names. However, he does invent names for the devils who guard one ditch of the circle of fraud that are designed to convey their personalities. They are collectively called Evil Claws (Malebranche), and individual devils have names like Evil Tail (Malacoda), Wild Swine (Ciriatto), Dog Scratcher (Graffiacane), and so forth (see *Inf.* 21.76ff.).

Lewis is free to invent names for all the characters in this novel, and many of the names of the members of the N.I.C.E. at Belbury help set the tone for his depiction of that group. Its two main leaders are John Wither (the Deputy Director) whose name bespeaks the slow death of something living, and Augustus Frost (the second-in-command), whose name brings to mind ice—perhaps as ice encases the cold-hearted sinners in Dante's lowest circle in hell. In terms of their characteristics, Wither's speech is rambling and purposefully ambiguous, while Frost's speech is terse, cold, and precise. Wither is described as "a shapeless ruin" and Frost as a "hard, bright, little needle" (*THS* 299). Despite these distinctive differences, they are similar in being "two birds of prey" (*THS* 327). Their hellish embrace at one point—"with sudden swift convulsive movement, the two old men lurched forward toward each other and sat swaying to and fro, locked in an embrace from which each seemed to be struggling to escape" (*THS* 243)—recalls the scene in Dante's ninth circle of the two brothers (who killed each other over their inheritance) who are locked in a tight embrace "like two enraged goats, butting at each other" (*Inf.* 32.50–51).

Lord Feverstone, the entrepreneur who supports the N.I.C.E.'s programs and has "'crook' written all over him" (*THS* 245), is interested in money, just as he was in *Out of the Silent Planet*. Devine's new name could suggest fever for gold or precious stones. Fairy Hardcastle, the sadistic police chief for the N.I.C.E., has a name that recalls images from children's stories of fairies and castles, but the syllable "hard" between those two words neutralizes any pleasant associations.

The group is held together by its shared purpose to "take over the human race and re-condition it" (*THS* 41), employing "sterilization of the unfit, liquidation of backward races, . . . [and] selective breeding" as needed (*THS* 42). Although Wither twice describes this community as "a very happy family" (*THS* 53, 54) and "as being so many brothers and—er sisters" (*THS* 206), the Italian physiologist Filostrato tells Mark, "You will find frictions and impertinences among this *canaglia*, this rabble" (*THS* 60). Personal ambition is the hallmark of Belbury: the sociologist Cosser hopes "to get Steele [another sociologist] out of the department altogether" (*THS* 86), and Hardcastle promises Mark, "If you hold on you'll come out above them [Steele and Cosser]" (*THS* 97). The members of Belbury disrespect and belittle one another behind their backs. Although Steele tells Mark not "to take much notice of what Lord Feverstone says" (*THS* 59), Filostrato tells him, "these Steeles . . . are of no consequence" (*THS* 60). Frost, Wither, and Hardcastle agree that if public sentiment rises against the N.I.C.E., Feverstone, as one of its public representatives, "could be sacrificed" (*THS* 169). Belbury, as Mark eventually discovers, is a "world of plot within plot, crossing and double-crossing, of lies and graft and stabbing in the back, of murder" (*THS* 245).

Belbury is also characterized by its lack of respect for the dignity and freedom of individual human beings. Wither describes the group at Belbury as being "like a family, or even, perhaps, like a single personality" (*THS* 120). He comments about Mark's joining Belbury, "I would welcome an *interpenetration of personalities* so close . . . that it almost transcends individuality. . . . I would open my arms to receive—to *absorb*—*to assimilate* this young man" (*THS* 243; italics added). This is the same concept and wording that Wormwood's uncle uses in *The Screwtape Letters* to describe hell's punishment for sinners, which involves being consumed by devils (see Letters VIII and XVIII).

Dante's hell is called a "prison" four times because souls can never leave there, and Belbury likewise functions like a prison. The apostate clergyman Straik tells Mark, "No one goes *out* of the N.I.C.E." (*THS* 80), and Hardcastle's chief officer, Captain O'Hara, tells him, "No one leaves the Institute" (*THS* 125). When William Hingest, the Bracton College scientist, discovers that the N.I.C.E. is not a legitimate scientific enterprise and tries to leave, he is murdered. When Wither refers to Mark's "temporary captivity" at Belbury, he says he means it in "a metaphorical sense" (*THS* 212), but when Mark is falsely accused of Hingest's death, Belbury literally becomes his prison.

At the Belbury banquet meant to celebrate the success of the N.I.C.E. at the end of the novel, the members of the N.I.C.E. and their supporters are punished—in line with Dante's concept of *contrapasso*—in ways that fit their offense. First, Merlin invokes the "curse of Babel" (*THS* 350) on the attendees, confusing their speech as he proclaims in Latin, "They that have despised the word of God, from them shall the word of man also be taken away" (*THS* 351, n. 1). They abused language in deceiving the general populace about their true intentions and methods, so now the gift of language is taken away from them.

Next, since Merlin freed the animals that were being abused by the N.I.C.E.'s laboratory experiments, many attendees at the banquet are killed by various animals. Steele, for instance, who had trampled on the truth in his written articles on behalf of the N.I.C.E., is trampled by an elephant (*THS* 348).

Death comes to some of the N.I.C.E.'s leaders in ways that echo specific punishments in *The Divine Comedy*. The deaths of Filostrato and Straik, for example, echo scenes from *Inferno* 28. In the ditch of the circle of fraud where sinners who sowed division have various body parts cut off or lanced by a devil's sword, one soul (Bertran de Born) is seen carrying his own severed head (see *Inf.* 28.121). Filostrato, who planned to remove all organic life from the earth's surface—"One day we shave the planet" (*THS* 172)—and thus to cut off Nature's head, so to speak, has his head cut off by Wither and Straik. Lewis echoes the image of Betran when Wither then walks off carrying Filostrato's severed head (see *THS* 355). Another soul in Dante's ditch has a slit throat (see *Inf.* 28.64). Lewis echoes this image as well when Wither slits Straik's throat several times because he is not strong enough to behead him (see *THS* 355). The clergyman who severed quotes in the Bible from their true meaning now has the vocal cords that preached apostasy severed.

As for Wither, Lewis twice directly applies verses from *The Divine Comedy* to him. In the first instance, Lewis describes Wither—using Dante's characterization in *Inferno* 3.18 of all the souls in hell—as being like "the souls who have lost the intellectual good" (*THS* 213). Right before Wither commits violent murders at the end of the novel, Lewis describes him as being like those who are "so full of sleep . . . when they leave the right way" (*THS* 353), a paraphrase of *Inferno* 1.11–12, in which Dante's pilgrim says, "I was so full of sleep at the point when I abandoned the true path." Wither perishes when he is mauled by a bear that was released from the laboratory, and is so mentally muddled and undiscerning of truth that he wonders if Straik has returned as a bear to revenge himself.

Fairy Hardcastle and her demise incorporate Dante's entire circle of violence. The seventh circle of Dante's hell punishes violence against others, against God, against nature, and against self: murder, blasphemy, sodomy, and suicide. Fairy Hardcastle—who has committed murder (Hingest and Horace Jules), frequently swears, and is a lesbian—is guilty of the sins punished in this circle.

Her manner of death under a dining room table at the banquet is ambiguous: She either shoots herself or shoots at an escaped tiger that mauls her. Whichever kind of death Lewis intended—and perhaps it is intentionally ambiguous—she commits either the sin of suicide or receives the punishment similar to that of the profligate sinners in the circle of violence who are mauled by vicious dogs (see *Inf.* 13.125–128). In either case she brings to full circle the sins of this circle.

Augustus Frost locks himself inside Belbury's "Objective Room"—the training room designed to release new members psychologically from traditional values and any sense of decency and normalcy—and sets himself and the room on fire (see *THS* 358). The manner of his demise corresponds to the traditional image of hell-fire punishment, but more significantly, it specifically recalls the fate of Dante's heretics in the sixth circle. The souls there, primarily those who denied the existence of the soul, are in coffins with flames around them because they believed life ended at death. Frost is likewise someone who denied the soul's existence and who even at the moment of death "refused the knowledge . . . that he had been wrong from the beginning" (*THS* 358). Because of the heresy he deliberately chooses even at the moment of death, he is now burning in a locked room that Lewis describes as a "long, high *coffin* of a room" (*THS* 299; italics added).

When Lord Feverstone drives away from the chaos at Belbury and his car ends up in a ditch upside down (see *THS* 364), his physical position is at first visually reminiscent of the simoniacs in the circle of fraud who are buried head first upside down because their love of money made them fix their eyes on earth (see *Inf.* 19.22–30). Escaping from the wreck and walking into town, he is swallowed up during an earthquake and covered with dirt (see *THS* 367). The earth he wanted to conquer has now conquered him.

Each member of the N.I.C.E. who, knowing or unknowingly, labored on behalf of the Bent Eldil, encounters a terrible end because, as Ransom remarks, bad masters "break their tools" (see *THS* 316). When Kath Filmer objects to Lewis's "nasty and inhumane" portrayal of the various deaths at the N.I.C.E. banquet, her complaint might be more properly leveled at Dante, since so many of the Belbury punishments either come directly from the *Inferno* or are in line with its *contrapasso* principle.

By contrast, the community at St. Anne's is characterized by kindness, love, mutual respect, and free association. As with the names at Belbury, Lewis chooses some of the names to convey a certain tone, in this case, a homey, simple, and traditional tone: Cecil and Margaret Dimble (Jane's former professor and his wife), Ivy Maggs (a former domestic servant for the Dimbles and the Studdocks), and Andrew MacPhee (the skeptical Ulsterman scientist). Other names have symbolic meaning. Grace Ironwood (Ransom's personal physician) reflects the strong nature of grace. The surnames of the Dennistons evoke noble warriors: Arthur (a professor and Mark's former classmate) recalls King Arthur, and his wife Camilla recalls the tall female general in Book 11 of Virgil's *Aeneid* who rode into battle on her horse and was called "divine Camilla" (11.893). Lewis describes Camilla Denniston in Virgilian terms as "so valiant, so fit to be mounted on a horse, and so divinely tall" (*THS* 63).

Greatly outnumbered by Belbury's minions, the group consists of seven people under Ransom's leadership (eight when Jane joins them). Ransom, although the group's head, is not the organizer of the group. Because he did not bring the group together, he cannot dissolve it or dismiss anyone: "You never chose me. I never chose you. . . . You and I have not started or devised this: it has descended on us" (*THS* 198). However, unlike the situation at Belbury, each "must come in freely" (*THS* 115), and no one is forced to stay.

Equality in the midst of diversity and hierarchy is the hallmark of Dante's souls in the *Paradiso*, and there is great diversity at St. Anne's in terms of age, profession, and marital status, and yet there is equality among them. Ivy Maggs is still a maid but "no more than anyone else" (*THS* 168). Margaret Dimble explains, "There are no servants here . . . and we all do the work"; in fact, "The women do [the work] one day and the men the next" (*THS* 167). One of Dante's souls in paradise explains the source of their unity: "It is essential to this blessed state that we keep ourselves within the divine will" (*Par.* 3.79–78). Similarly, what Ransom tells Dimble applies to all the members of the group: "Keep your will fixed in the will of Maleldil" (*THS* 229).

The company at St. Anne's, however, primarily recalls the souls in Dante's *Purgatorio* who are still in the process of purification and at various stages of spiritual development. Cecil Dimble struggles with charity toward Mark Studdock (see *THS* 219); MacPhee and Dr. Ironwood quarrel at times (*THS* 197, 200). Ransom describes the whole group when he says of Jane, "She is doubtless *like all of us a sinner*" (*THS* 278; italics added). When Dimble wonders to himself, "Is there a whole Belbury inside you too?" (*THS* 224), the answer is yes, for every human being has a fallen nature that needs purifying.

Dante's Mount Purgatory, however, is not just for purification; its equally important purpose is a soul's growth in virtue. Humility, generosity, meekness, zeal for the good, liberality, temperance, and chastity are the seven corresponding virtues to the capital sins purged on Dante's mount, and they are often on display at St Anne's in the group's interactions with one another. Like Dante's souls in purgatory (and in paradise), the residents at St. Anne's are united in their obedience to God (Maleldil) and submitted to his will. However, just as the initial obedience of Dante's pilgrim is given to Beatrice (see *Purg.* 31.106–108), obedience to Ransom temporarily counts as obedience to Maleldil for those who are in the earlier stages of their development: MacPhee, who is not yet a believer; Merlin, who obeys Ransom because he is Arthur's successor; and Jane, who eventually commits herself to obey Ransom.

Resisting the N.I.C.E. means engaging in warfare. Feverstone tells Mark it is "a real war with real casualties" (*THS* 41), and Hardcastle tells Mark, "We're an army" (*THS* 99). At St. Anne's, Ransom tells Jane, "We had hoped you would . . . become one of our army" (*THS* 144). In this conflict that has only two sides, Camilla tells Jane, "You can't be neutral" (*THS* 115). This is a spiritual war, however, and the residents of St. Anne's, who do not have a battle plan, do not win the victory by their efforts. When Ransom sends Cecil, Arthur, and Jane out to find Merlin and bring him back—their *only* reconnoitering mission—the men take revolvers that they never use, and their mission fails (although Merlin later comes to Ransom on his own). Even the minimal action and effort they put forth comes to nothing.

What wins the day is the power of Deep Heaven that comes to Belbury to wage the war through Merlin and the power of Nature unleashed at Belbury and in Edgestow. When the chief eldils of five planets descend to St. Anne's to bring judgment, the song they are singing—"the *Gloria* which those five excellent Natures perpetually sing" (*THS* 327)—is reminiscent of the *Gloria* sung in the *Paradiso* by the heavenly host right before St. Peter pronounces judgment on church evils (see *Par.* 27.1, 22–63). When Ransom says, "I have become a bridge" (*THS* 291), he means he is a connecting point for Maleldil's supernatural power that comes down through heavenly agents, who then work through Merlin to destroy the enemy. He and the community of St. Anne's, not having succeeded in doing anything battle-worthy, provide the access point for heavenly grace to come fight the battle. St. Anne's is an illustration of the concept that "being"—who they are—is far more important than "doing" and that their fellowship and love for one another is a powerful force that opens a space for the arrival of these heavenly presences on earth.

Although Ransom has no journey in this novel, spiritual or otherwise, he continues to recall Dante's pilgrim but on a new level. In *Out of the Silent Planet* he resembles Dante's pilgrim in the *Inferno*, and in *Perelandra*, he resembles that pilgrim both in the *Purgatorio* and the *Paradiso*. Dante's pilgrim attains the stature of a *king* and *priest* once his moral rectification is completed by his ascent of the mount and Virgil announces, "I *crown* and *miter* you over yourself" (*Purg.* 27.142; italics added). In a similar way, Ransom has been transformed from being a timid linguistic professor to a man of authority who now, with similar stature to Dante's pilgrim, evokes the "word *King* itself with all the linked associations of battle, marriage, priesthood, mercy, and power" (*THS* 143). In fact, Ransom now eats only bread and wine (see *THS* 149), an echo of the king-priest Melchizedek in Genesis 14.

There are several parallels between the poem's narrator and Director Ransom at this point. After their transformative journeys, they each must fulfill a mission assigned by heavenly beings when they return to earth, although their tasks are quite different. Dante's pilgrim is commissioned six times by redeemed souls to report either all or part of what he has seen and heard in the afterlife. Ransom is commissioned by the Malacandrian Oyarsa to thwart the Bent Eldil's plans for England. And each divine mission, although carried out in different ways, has spiritual ramifications for others.

The task assigned to Dante's pilgrim during his journey is now carried out by the poem's narrator who, like the pilgrim, is a character in the poem and should not be confused with the historical poet Dante. The narrator has completed a weeklong journey that has radically changed him, so rather than merely recounting the journey, his character now at times "assumes the role of a moralist, educator, preacher, or even prophet." Similarly, Ransom, after his otherworldly journeys, is now Director Ransom, a spiritual leader for the members of St Anne's. There is no traveling for *The Divine Comedy's* narrator after he returns from the afterlife and recounts the pilgrim's story. Similarly, there is no traveling for Ransom now that he has returned from the heavens—Ransom, in fact, never leaves his manor at St. Anne's until the end of the novel when he returns to Perelandra. *The Divine Comedy's* narrator recedes into the background for the most part since the action focuses on the pilgrim's experiences in the afterlife. Ransom, although directing the action of his group at St. Anne's, likewise recedes into the background as the action focuses on the experiences of Mark and Jane. In fact, Ransom is not introduced until chapter seven and appears in only fourteen of the eighty-five subsections of the novel's seventeen chapters.

Although both journeys into the heavens have been for the benefit of each pilgrim, they have also been for the benefit of others. *The Divine Comedy's* narrator and Ransom, who have already undergone their transformations, are now instruments for the transformation of others. As with most Christian visionaries, "divine fecundity is to be their last state." As one Dante scholar notes, the purpose of the epic journey "is to cleanse [the hero's] soul so that . . . he can return to earth and attempt to aid others in finding the divine." The narrator in Dante's poem, as he carries out his mission of writing "the sacred poem that both heaven and earth have set their hand to" (*Par.* 25.1–2), will thereby give people "vital nourishment when it is digested" (*Par.* 17.131–132). He is to tell what he saw in the afterlife "for the good of the world that lives unrighteously" (*Purg.* 32.103). Dante intends readers to ponder the issues of sin and grace, eternal rewards and punishments, and to benefit spiritually from the poem. Similarly, Ransom, as the leader of St. Anne's, becomes a catalyst for the transformation of the members of the group under his charge, which is particularly evident in Jane's case, and his transformative presence extends even to the animals (see *THS* 164)!

The parallels between Ransom and Dante's pilgrim have been carried to their ultimate limit. Similarities because of their otherworld journeys, spiritual transformations, and heavenly visions now continue as they fulfill their assigned tasks on earth. In the context of the trilogy's presentation of a modern version of Dante's cosmos, it seems fitting that a modern version of Dante's pilgrim— and even of Dante's narrator—should appear.

Mark's Journey

David C. Downing's excellent analysis in *Planets in Peril* has clearly identified Mark's time with college colleagues and members of the N.I.C.E. as reflective of a journey through the nine circles of the *Inferno*. He points out parallels between sinners in each of hell's nine circles and either the characters Mark meets or Mark himself. Curry, the opportunistic subwarden at Bracton College, like the uncommitted souls outside Dante's hell, stands for neither good nor evil. Some of the scholars at the college recall the righteous pagans in Dante's Limbo. Mark's interest in his marriage seems limited to its sexual aspect; Feverstone and the college officials discussing the N.I.C.E.'s cost and salaries at a sumptuous dinner represent the circle of gluttony as well as the circle of avarice/prodigality. The wrathful and sullen are well represented by the sociologists Steele and Cosser, and Reverend Straik belongs with the circle of heretics. Violence is part of Belbury's modus operandi (the murder of Hingest and Fairy Hardcastle's predilection for torture), while fraud (against the public and inside Belbury with one another) is an activity in which all the members of that group participate. And finally, all of Belbury's members are traitors to the human race because of their plans.

In addition to Downing's insights, however, there is a way to track each circle of hell through Mark's own sin. Unlike Dante's pilgrim who is a mere observer of the nine circles of hell, Mark is himself guilty of participating in the sins of all nine circles to varying degrees—and in the exact sequence in which those sins appear in Dante's hell.

Lust: The newlywed Mark, as Downing points out, is an absentee husband who seems mainly interested in the sexual side of marriage (see *THS* 13–14).

Gluttony: He drinks heavily during dinner with Feverstone and college officials as they discuss the N.I.C.E. (see *THS* 37–40, 46), and that activity becomes increasingly habitual during his time at Belbury.

Avarice: When he is offered a job at the N.I.C.E. that has no clear specifications, Mark dismisses his ongoing uneasiness about accepting the position only because of the promise of a good salary (see *THS* 43, 55, 104).

Anger: He loses his temper when Steele and Cosser summarily dismiss a report he has written and is frustrated when he cannot get a clear job description from Wither, so he almost goes home for good (see *THS* 94–97).

Up to this point, Mark's sins are only the sins of the upper circles of Dante's hell, the sins of the flesh, the sins of incontinence. However, once he decides to stay at Belbury—in the chapter aptly titled "Fog" (see *THS* 119)—he consciously chooses to be part of a group whose goals involve social engineering for the populace and the destruction of nature under the guise of research. When he agrees to write an article for the newspapers about riots before they happen, it is the first thing he consciously does at Belbury that he "clearly knew to be criminal" even "before he did it" (*THS* 130). At this point he crosses over spiritually from Dante's upper hell into the four lower circles of hell where *premeditated* sins of the mind, heart, and will are punished. When he makes this decision, "the moment of his consent almost escaped his notice; certainly, there was no struggle, no sense of turning a corner" (*THS* 130). Mark's conscience begins to be seared, and he becomes "more and more reconciled to the job the longer he worked at it" (*THS* 135).

During his downward spiritual spiral, Mark can also be linked to the sins of the lower circles of hell in the City of Dis. *Heresy*, circle 6: He thinks "Christianity was nonsense" (*THS* 336) and "had never believed in it at all" (*THS* 334). In fact, "in Mark's mind hardly one rag of noble thought, either Christian or Pagan, had a secure lodging" (*THS* 185). *Violence*, circle 7: Although he commits no acts of physical violence personally, he tolerates and is complicit with the violence perpetrated by the N.I.C.E. when it stages riots in Edgestow. *Fraud*, circle 8: His primary job consists in writing false news reports from a variety of viewpoints for different newspapers to deceive the public and manipulate public opinion.

It is only when he is confronted with the sin of Dante's last circle, *Treason*—in this case betrayal of all that is good and decent—that

Mark begins to recoil and finally rejects evil. After he is wrongly arrested for the murder of Hingest, he is taken to the "Objective Room" where its visual perversions "withered the mind" (*THS* 298, a nice pun on John Wither's effect on people). When he is asked to trample on a crucifix and realizes the figure on the cross "had lived and had been executed thus by the Belbury of those days" (*THS* 336), Mark refuses. He makes the moral choice not to align himself with the hell of Belbury and rejects its values: "He was choosing a side: the Normal" (*THS* 299). Mark has to hit bottom—the circle of betrayal—before this moral awakening. This is not the path for everyone, but it is the necessary path for Mark, just as it was for Dante's pilgrim. Beatrice says about the pilgrim, "He sank so low that the only means for his salvation was showing him the damned in hell" (*Purg.* 30.136–138). Ironically, the Objective Room, which Lewis describes as coffin-shaped (see *THS* 299), is, as one Lewis scholar aptly notes, "the intended tomb for Mark as a moral human being," but it "becomes the site of his rebirth."

During Mark's time at Belbury, Fairy Hardcastle functions in some ways as a perverse version of Virgil, the guide for Dante's pilgrim through hell. Like Virgil, who often calls the pilgrim "son," Fairy most often calls Mark "Sonny." Like Virgil who guides the pilgrim into unknown regions, Fairy takes Mark under her wing and instructs him about the lay of the land at Belbury and how to maneuver it. At first he feels uncomfortable as an outsider, but "that feeling completely disappeared while Miss Hardcastle was talking to him" (*THS* 69) because "what had reassured him most of all was his conversation with the Fairy" (*THS* 68). Just as Virgil counsels the pilgrim in hell about what and what not to worry about, she informs Mark, "You needn't bother your head about all the Steeles and Cossers" (*THS* 97), but warns him to be cautious about Wither and Frost (see *THS* 70). She encourages him when Wither is annoyed that he "will thaw in time" (*THS* 127) and advises him twice, "Do what you're told" (*THS* 98, 121). She instructs Mark, "Don't believe everything you're told" (*THS* 70), but also, "Don't put your nose outside Belbury" (*THS* 212). Like Virgil who always assuages the pilgrim's fears, "She had laughed at his fears in general" (*THS* 70). Like Virgil who is always looking out for the pilgrim, she insists, "I'm speaking for your own good" (*THS* 99), and "I'm doing all I can for you" (*THS* 186). However, her seeming marks of friendship have an ulterior motive (to get Jane to Belbury because of her visionary gifts), and, as a counterfeit of Virgil, she was never a true friend or guide. As with the other people at Belbury, Mark slowly perceives the truth about her and in the end tells her, "Go to the devil" (*THS* 187).

When Mark is taken to the Belbury banquet, during the chaos he loses consciousness (see *THS* 350)—generally a signal in Dante, which Lewis follows, to indicate that a spiritual transition is forthcoming. For example, Dante's swoon before he crosses the Acheron river in hell (see *Inf.* 3.136) is the first of many such instances in *The Divine Comedy* that indicate a spiritual transition. Similarly, prominent instances in Lewis's novels that point to a spiritual transition include Ransom's loss of consciousness when he leaves earth to wake up on the spaceship headed for Malacandra in *Out of the Silent Planet* (*OSP* 20), and his state of suspension when he is transported to and from Perelandra in a coffin (*Per.* 27, 222).

After Mark faints, Merlin wakens him, saying, "'*Surge, miselle* (Get up, wretched boy)'" (*THS* 352), releasing him from the spell that Belbury represented and sending him off to meet his wife at St. Anne's. This scene recalls Virgil's waking of the pilgrim in the *Purgatorio* to release him from the hag-siren's spell in his dream, saying, "Surgi e vieni" (*Purg.* 19.35: "Get up and come along"), so that they can move ahead to meet Beatrice at the top of the mount. Right after this hag-siren dream, Dante's pilgrim visits the upper ledges of purgatory where disordered love of the good is purified and transformed, and Mark is at a similar moral crossroad at this point.

Through his ordeal with the N.I.C.E., Mark has become conscious of his sinfulness, and his new awareness marks the beginning of his spiritual transformation. Similar to the souls who are ferried to Mount Purgatory, Mark is transported by a lorry to within a few miles of the hill at St. Anne's (see *THS* 359). Like Dante's pilgrim facing Beatrice in the garden and comparing himself to those who feel a paralyzing awe in the presence of their betters (see *Purg.* 33.25–26), Mark feels "a sort of shyness" (*THS* 359) because, like the pilgrim who climbed the mount to see Beatrice in Eden, Mark will climb St. Anne's "to see Jane in what he felt to be her proper world" (*THS* 360).

Mark's Beatrice

Jane, despite having abandoned church attendance since her school days (see *THS* 1), nevertheless functions as a "Beatrice" for Mark. She is a beacon to him, a standard by which to judge right and wrong and to discern reality from illusion. Trying to picture her at Belbury, Mark realizes that "what he now regarded as common prudence would seem to her, and through her to himself, mere flattery [and] back-biting" (*THS* 171). Knowing now that Feverstone is not to be trusted, he is aware that "Jane . . . would have seen through him at once" (*THS* 245). When the leaders at Belbury insist that he bring her there because of her visionary powers, he decides to protect Jane from them: "For almost the first time in his life a gleam of something like disinterested love came into his mind" (*THS* 185–86). The mere thought of her begins to crack his shallow, self-centered core, and he becomes "devoured with a longing for Jane which was . . . [not] at all sensual," and he wants "to get back to Jane" (*THS* 189).

As his standing at Belbury becomes increasingly precarious and he thinks of Jane, she "seemed to him . . . to have in herself deep wells and knee-deep meadows of happiness, rivers of freshness, enchanted gardens of leisure" (*THS* 247). Mark's description recalls several features of Dante's Garden of Eden, and the thought of Jane now conjures up a similar reality to him. As Mark begins to reject the values of Belbury, "already he was with Jane and *with all she symbolised*" (*THS* 268; italics added). When Mark is in the Objective Room, repulsed by the "sour and crooked," he has "some kind of vision of the sweet and straight. . . . It was all mixed up with Jane" (*THS* 299). Despite being still somewhat muddled, Mark realizes that Belbury is evil and that with regard to Jane he needs "the humility of a lover" (*THS* 380).

After Merlin sends him away from the chaotic aftermath of the carnage at the Belbury banquet, Mark is reunited with Jane at a cottage at St Anne's—located at the summit of a steep hill in a lovely garden, of course. Lewis does not describe their meeting at the cottage, but the essence of that reunion echoes the reunion of Dante's pilgrim with the woman who had been a channel of grace for him. Before that meeting Virgil tells Dante's pilgrim, "You will see her [Beatrice] above at the top of this mount smiling and happy" (*Purg.* 6.47–48). In a similar setting, Mark will meet a Jane who now has a similar disposition. Jane is the third woman to be a Beatrice figure so far in Lewis's novels, but she has the distinction of being the only one who is the wife of the protagonist she inspires. She also holds a unique position in Lewis's novels in that she both functions as a Beatrice and is in need of a Beatrice herself. And in an instance of Lewis's frequent gender reversal, her "Beatrice" will be a male.

Jane's Journey

Jane's spiritual journey begins with several emotional parallels to those at the beginning of the pilgrim's journey in the *Inferno*. Dante's pilgrim is lost and confused in "that wood that pierced my heart with fear" (see *Inf*. 1.14–15), and Dante uses the word *fear* (*paura*) five times in forty-seven lines (see *Inf*. 1.6–53). Jane is likewise in "extreme confusion" and "was frightened" (*THS* 44, 45) because of an earlier nightmarish dream, and Lewis repeats the words *frightened* or *fear* nine times on those two pages. When Dante's pilgrim attempts to escape the dark wood by climbing a hill and is blocked by three beasts, the sight of the third beast "so overwhelmed me with fear . . . that I lost hope" (*Inf* 1.52–54) and he rushes back down the hill (see *Inf*. 1.61). Jane attempts to escape her fear by phoning the Dimbles for comfort, but when no comfort is forthcoming, "terror, as if insulted by her futile attempt to escape it, rushed back on her" (*THS* 45).

Despite the beginning of Jane's journey recalling the *Inferno*, her story primarily echoes the *Purgatorio*. Although it is true, as Downing says, that Lewis used the *Inferno* "as his structural subtext," that applies only to Mark's spiritual journey and some aspects of Belbury. No one seems to have accounted for the novel's other equally compelling subtext, the *Purgatorio*, in terms of Jane's concurrent journey. In a similar vein, another Lewis scholar remarks that "the struggle for Mark's redemption is the central element of the story." However, given the contrapuntal fashion in which Lewis presents Mark's moral descent at Belbury and Jane's moral ascent at St. Anne's, her story of repentance and redemption is just as central to the story. In fact, one could even make the case that her story is more important, because without her Mark's story might not have ended well.

Jane's trip to St. Anne's to consult Dr. Grace Ironwood for help about her visionary nightmares is the first of two visits before she joins that company. The details of her first visit parallel those of Dante's pilgrim at the beginning of his journey up Mount Purgatory. (1) Before his arrival at the gate of Mount Purgatory, Dante's pilgrim has a dream in which he is on fire, "and the fire in the dream was so intense it woke me from sleep" (*Purg.* 9.32–33). Prior to her trip to St. Anne's, Jane's dream of a head being screwed off and a head being dug up "frightened Jane so badly that she woke up" (*THS* 15). (2) Dante's pilgrim climbs upward in a heavenly direction. Jane takes the train east, which in Lewis's novels generally indicates a heavenward direction. (3) Dante's pilgrim must climb a steep mount. Since St. Anne's is on a hilltop at some distance from the train station, Jane too must climb up a steep hill. (4) As he approaches the ledges of the mount, Dante's pilgrim follows a path "through a crevice in a rock that wound one way and then another" (*Purg.* 10.7–8). Jane has to walk along a "winding road between high banks" (*THS* 51). (5) Dante's pilgrim sees the high wall that surrounds the entire mount with a small entrance in it (see *Purg.* 9.50–51). Jane comes "to a high wall . . . that seemed to run on for a great way: there was a door in it" (*THS* 51). (6) The angel guarding the gate blocks the pilgrim's entrance until Virgil explains that a heavenly lady has sent them there (see *Purg.* 9.88–93). Camilla Denniston blocks Jane's entrance until she discovers that Dr. Dimble has sent her (see *THS* 61). (7) As they approach Mount Purgatory, Virgil, "my leader . . . moved ahead . . . and I followed behind" (*Purg.* 9.68–69). As they approach the manor, Camilla leads the way, telling Jane, "There's not room for two on this path so . . . I [will] go first" (*THS* 61).

During her first visit, Jane experiences three reactions that correspond to the sinful dispositions purged on the first three ledges of Mount Purgatory: pride, envy, and anger.

Pride: Various details connect Jane directly and indirectly to souls on Dante's ledge of pride. First, she is in some ways a female version of Dante's Tuscan nobleman, Omberto. He confesses that "my ancient lineage and the gallant deeds of my ancestors made me very arrogant" (*Purg.* 11.61–62). Meeting with Dr. Grace Ironwood, Jane "was anxious not to be supposed vain of her ancient [Tudor] ancestry" (*THS* 65). Omberto admits, "I held everyone in great disdain" (*Purg.* 11.64), and disdain is what Jane feels for a wide range of people. Very early on in the novel, she is described as having "contempt for the kind of woman who buys hats as . . . a consolation" (*THS* 28) and for women "of the chocolate-box variety" (*THS* 28–29); with Mrs. Dimble she preserves "a certain sense of superiority" (*THS* 30); and she has contempt for Mark since she considers him "so easily taken in" (*THS* 30). Omberto, like many proud people, uses the pronoun "I" ten times in twenty lines (see *Purg.* 11.52–72). Jane makes twenty-one "I" statements on two pages in her discussion with Ironwood that focus on herself and wanting things her way (see *THS* 66–68). Of the examples of pride carved on that ledge for souls to meditate on, one includes Michal, King David's wife (see *Purg.* 10.67–69), who scorned him as he danced before the Lord and was punished by being barren (see 2 Samuel 6). Jane, who scorns her husband and has "resentment . . . against Mark" (*THS* 72) and a "grudge against Mark" (*THS* 143) is also barren, although in her case it is by choice.

Envy: With genuine admiration for Camilla's beauty but a tinge of envy for her character, Jane thinks, "It would be nice . . . to be like that—so straight, so forthright, so valiant" (*THS* 63)—all moral qualities that Jane is far from possessing at this point.

Anger: In response to Grace's assessment that Jane's dreams do not point to illness but to visionary power, "red, undisguised anger rushed back into her face" (*THS* 67). Jane's emotions circle back to pride at the end of her first visit as "all her repugnance came over her again—all her wounded vanity, all her resentment" (*THS* 68), so she decides to turn her back on St. Anne's.

Dante's pilgrim is warned not to look back after he goes through the gate of purgatory because it would indicate an inexcusable lack of resolve to be purged (see *Purg.* 10.6). Jane's leaving demonstrates her unwillingness to lose her fierce independence and be transformed. Her departure at this point is fitting because entrance to purgatory is denied "to souls whose wrong kind of love . . . makes their twisted path seem straight" (*Purg.* 10.2–3). The invective against pride by Dante's narrator can be applied to Jane: "Be proud, then, and go forth with a haughty look . . . and do not bend your head down lest you see your wrong path" (*Purg.* 12.70–72).

Jane's second visit is precipitated by seeing Frost in town, whom she had seen only in a dream. What resolves her to return to St. Anne's "was something different from fear. . . . It was a total rejection of, or revulsion from, this man on all levels of her being at once" (*THS* 137). The journey of Dante's pilgrim through and out of hell signifies his rejection of sin and evil and necessarily precedes his ability (and worthiness) to ascend the mount. Jane's rejection of Frost, who represents the hell of Belbury that he carries within him, signifies she too is now rejecting evil.

Jane's decision to join St. Anne's occurs on the last page of the chapter called "Fog," the same chapter in which Mark decides on its first page to take the job at Belbury (see *THS* 119). On the train, "the slow journey through the fog almost sent her to sleep" (*THS* 137)—suggesting, as it did for Mark, a spiritual transition point for Jane. When she emerges from the fog that completely enshrouds the landscape below and approaches the hilltop manor bathed in sunlight, Jane is "looking down on a *sea* of white fog" and "saw that she was standing *on the shore of a little green sunlit island*" (*THS* 138; italics added). The description here recalls Dante's island of Purgatory, the island-mountain rising out of the sea. Ironically, Jane is emerging from fog literally and spiritually just as Mark is choosing to remain in the literal and spiritual fog at Belbury, which for Mark later "continued and grew denser" (*THS* 121).

Now that Jane chooses to meet the director and stay at St. Anne's, she is let in this time "not by that door [in the wall] but by the main gate" (*THS* 139). The next scene recalls a scene not from the *Purgatorio* but from the *Paradiso*. Like Dante's pilgrim who is questioned by three apostles to determine if he is sufficiently prepared to enter the Empyrean (see *Par.* 24.22–26.66), Jane is questioned by three people (Ironwood and the Dennistons) to see if she is prepared to meet Ransom. Dante's pilgrim compares himself to a student at an oral exam (see *Par.* 24.46–48, 25.66), and Jane "felt as if she were the candidate in a *viva voce* [oral] examination" (*THS* 139). Dante's pilgrim is asked about the three theological virtues, and Jane is asked three questions: about her dreams, her identification of Frost, and her readiness to meet Ransom (see *THS* 140). During the questioning of Dante's pilgrim, a fourth soul (Adam) joins the group but is silent (see *Par.* 26.81). At Jane's interview, a fourth person, Ivy Maggs, is also present, but she too is silent and does not ask questions (see *THS* 139).

The scene as Jane approaches the room to meet Ransom echoes the scene when Dante's pilgrim arrives at the gate of Mount Purgatory. In Dante's poem, three steps lead up to the gate (see *Purg.* 9.76); at St. Anne's—in a variation of Dante's preferred number scheme of three and its multiples—there are six steps that lead up to Ransom's door (see *THS* 141). At the top of the steps to the gate of purgatory sits a silent angel-guardian (see *Purg.* 9.78–80). At the top of the steps to Ransom's room, "Camilla quiet and alert sat waiting" (*THS* 141). Dante's gate-angel is dressed in gray robes (see *Purg.* 9.115–116), and the only clothing ever described for Camilla (which occurs later) is a dress that "looked like steel in colour" (*THS* 362).

Jane determines to stay at St. Anne's after her meeting with Ransom, but in an ironic twist, Ransom turns her away for the time being (because her husband is at the N.I.C.E.). In Dante's *Purgatorio*, souls who delayed repentance must wait before ascending the mount and remain in the area of ante-purgatory "where [wasted] time is compensated for by [delayed] time" (*Purg.* 23.84). Jane experiences the same *contrapasso*, a situation that fits her offense. What she chose is what she is given: having delayed in joining the group, her membership is now further delayed.

Jane once more finds herself back in Edgestow at square one. As she wanders through the town overrun by the N.I.C.E. police, she once again recalls Dante's pilgrim at the very beginning of his journey in the *Inferno*. Lewis's earlier parallels were mainly emotional (fear, confusion), but now they become physical as well. Dante's pilgrim mentions his weary body (see *Inf.* 1.28); Jane is "tired to death" (*THS* 153). Dante's pilgrim had wandered away from familiar paths and does not know where he is (see *Inf.* 1.2–3). Similarly, Jane "had been driven out of her natural route" and "found herself in a street she did not even know" (*THS* 153). When Dante's pilgrim looks back at the dark wood he just escaped, he compares himself to a panting swimmer who finally arrives safely on shore (see *Inf.* 1.22–23). Lewis echoes Dante's simile in describing Jane's course as being "like that of a man trying to get home along the beach when the tide is coming in" (*THS* 253). Although many of Lewis's characters find themselves in a real or metaphoric "dark wood" before their journeys begin—whether it be physical disorientation, mental confusion, or spiritual darkness—Jane is the only one of Lewis's characters who experiences a "dark wood" twice, and in both cases, Lewis uses details that parallel the beginning of the *Inferno* to describe it.

Unlike Mark, whose confusion leads him to endure a passage through an inferno, Jane's path leads straight to a purgatorial experience. When she returns to town and is arrested by Hardcastle, circumstances free her from that detention, and an unnamed married couple offers to drive Jane home. For the first time she identifies her home as "the Manor at St. Anne's" (*THS* 159), and her choice to join the community at St. Anne's, her "ascent of the mount," begins in earnest this time. Dante's pilgrim is asleep when he is transported from ante-purgatory to the gate of Mount Purgatory (see *Purg.* 9.56–57), and Jane falls asleep in the car on the way to St. Anne's. Dante's pilgrim wakes to his new location dazed and disoriented (see *Purg.* 9.34–40), and Jane wakes to find herself at St. Anne's "too tired to remember how or where she got to bed" (*THS* 159).

Once at St. Anne's the process of Jane's purification begins. She must first acknowledge and then repent of the sins that need to be purged—the pride, envy, and anger she exhibited during her first visit.

Pride. During her first meeting with Ransom, she begins to see her own part in the deterioration of her marriage: "A novel sense of her own injustice and even of pity for her husband arose in her mind" (*THS* 147). Mrs. Dimble corrects her about seeming to think herself superior to the maid Ivy Maggs (see *THS* 161). Ransom frankly tells her, "Mrs. Dimble is a Christian wife and you are not" (*THS* 314), and he specifies, "Your trouble has been . . . Pride" (*THS* 315). As she begins to recognize her own failings, Jane learns obedience and humility, first by obeying Ransom, next by submitting to Maleldil, and finally by accepting Mark with humility when they are reunited.

Envy. Toward the end of the novel when she sees Arthur and Camilla (whom she had earlier envied), Jane could "hardly bear to look on them: *not through envy (that thought was far away)* but because a sort of brightness flowed from them that dazzled her" (*THS* 322; italics added).

Anger. When Jane first sees Ransom, she momentarily "forgot . . . her faint grudge against Grace Ironwood, and her more obscure grudge against Mark" (*THS* 143). When Ransom tells her she "lost

love because you never attempted obedience," Jane would generally have reacted angrily to such a remark, but now "anger . . . was
banished to a remote distance" (*THS* 147). During her time at St.
Anne's, Jane develops meekness in her dealings with the others and
in her attitude toward Mark.

Jane's transformation occurs partly through her interactions
with the members of St. Anne's, but Ransom is its main catalyst.
Her transformation from a prideful woman, unwilling to yield
her independence, to a humble Christian woman who can now
become a Christian wife, has begun. Like Dante's souls who have
climbed Mount Purgatory, she too can be said to have been on the
"the mountain that cures souls" (*Par.* 17.20); she too has undergone
the rectification of her love from its disordered state to its right
order through divine love.

Jane's Beatrice

Lewis scholar Joe R. Christopher calls Jane's meeting with
Ransom a "Beatrician experience," and that is precisely the case. In
yet another creative variation on Lewis's part, a man now plays the
role of a Beatrice for a female pilgrim.

Unlike the garden meetings for the variety of Beatrices in
Lewis's novels so far (and hereafter), the parallel details are restricted here to the psychological and emotional levels. There are
no rivers or forest descriptions, no change in light, no singing, no
presence of heavenly spirits, and no procession as a prelude to the
appearance of this Beatrice. Focusing on the inner nature of this
experience, Lewis uses an enclosed space this time—Ransom's
room at the manor—as the setting. The only immediate prelude
to this meeting is Grace Ironwood's introduction of Jane into the
room, and on one level it can be said that "grace" has finally brought
Jane to this room. Dante's pilgrim reaches the meeting place with
Beatrice after a long journey descending into hell and ascending
the mount. In a highly condensed brief echo, the area of the manor
that leads to Ransom's room could only "be reached by descending
to a landing and ascending again" (*THS* 165).

Jane's meeting includes several parallels to the pilgrim's meeting with Beatrice. (1) Beatrice is slightly raised off the ground in a

chariot looking down at the pilgrim (see *Purg.* 30.61). Ransom is on a sofa on a slightly raised dais looking down at Jane. (2) At the first sight of Beatrice, Dante's pilgrim trembles in her presence (see *Purg.* 30.34–36). On first seeing Ransom, Jane "was shaken: she was even shaking" (*THS* 143). (3) Dante's pilgrim "broke under that heavy load [of emotion]" (*Purg.* 31.19), and Jane's first response in seeing Ransom is that "instantly her world was unmade"—a reaction that Lewis repeats three times (*THS* 142–43). (4) For Dante's pilgrim, "with tears and sighs bursting forth, my voice failed" (*Purg.* 31.20–21). Jane, approximating the pilgrim's emotional condition, "hoped intensely that she was not going to cry, or be unable to speak" (*THS* 143). (5) Dante's pilgrim, when he admits his failings, "had so much shame on my face" (*Purg.* 30.78), and Jane, newly aware of some of her failings, is "wishing that she did not keep on being red" (*THS* 144). (6) Dante's pilgrim stares at Beatrice so intently that "all my other senses were not functioning" (*Purg.* 32.3). Jane "had been staring rudely" (*THS* 143) at Ransom so intently that she "hardly took in what the Director was saying" (*THS* 144). (7) Beatrice, the reader is later told, has laughing eyes (see *Par.* 3.42; 10.62; 15.34). Ransom "looked at her with laughter in his eyes" (*THS* 149). (8) Dante's pilgrim, after his conversation with Beatrice, describes her as "the one who closed my mind off to anything but herself" (*Purg.* 32.93). After her interview with Ransom, "Whatever she tried to think of led back to the Director himself" (*THS* 152). (9) The pilgrim says that his soul is now joyful (see *Purg.* 31.127–128), and Jane "was simply in the state of joy" (*THS* 151). (10) Dante's pilgrim becomes "completely devoted to her [Beatrice's] commands" (*Purg.* 32.106–107). For Jane, "the word Obedience . . . came over her" (*THS* 147), later telling Ransom, "I place myself in obedience to you" (*THS* 229).

Dante makes clear that Beatrice never was the ultimate goal but the mediator of the true goal, God, and Lewis makes that point clear here just as he does in his earlier novels. Ransom's acceptance of Jane's obedience, loyalty, and love is on a temporary basis, because, as he tells her, Maleldil (God) "will have you for no one but Himself in the end" (*THS* 230). After Beatrice leads Dante's pilgrim into the Empyrean, she shifts her gaze from the pilgrim, and "then she turned back to the eternal fountain [God]" (*Par.* 31.93), and it is only then that the pilgrim has direct visions of God.

Similarly, it is only after Jane has left a meeting with Ransom that she has a direct experience of God—this time in a garden setting. Like Dante's pilgrim who crosses over from the physical universe into the spiritual realm to see God, for Jane, "A *boundary had been crossed . . . into another world,* or into a Person, or into the presence of a Person" (*THS* 318; italics added). It is because of her experience with Ransom that Jane comes to understand that she is "made to please Another and in Him to please all others" (*THS* 319).

Conclusion

Apart from married couples among the species of Hrossa in *Out of the Silent Planet*, the only married couple in Lewis's novels so far has been Tor and Tinidril in *Perelandra*, whose marriage is just beginning. The theme of marital unity briefly presented there continues here more prominently. The first word of this novel is "Matrimony," and the story ends with Mark and Jane's reunion. The different spiritual journeys they undergo are meant to transform them and equip them so that they *can* function as a married couple in the right way with the appropriate virtues of humility, kindness, and generosity in dealing with each other and with an openness to receiving offspring from God.

In addition to the other kinds of contrasts he makes between the two groups, Lewis is also contrasting the sterility of the members of Belbury, who are serving the Bent Eldil, with the promise of fruitfulness in the members St. Anne's, who are serving Maleldil. Significantly, there are no married couples at Belbury—or even any mention of the men having wives or children—and the only woman introduced to the reader there is a lesbian. In contrast, St. Anne's company includes two married couples, the Dimbles and the Dennistons, and another woman, Ivy Maggs, who, like Jane, is reunited with her husband at the end. Even the animals mate when Venus is over St. Anne's (see *THS* 375–79)! Fruitfulness for the members of St. Anne's, however, is not restricted to bearing offspring. The Dimbles are childless but take genuine concern for his students, and St. Anne's includes two single people, Ironwood and MacPhee, who are both fruitful, respectively, in caring for the medical needs of others and in tending the garden and the animals.

The basis for potential fruitfulness of many kinds at St. Anne's lies in their love for God, for one another, and for God's creation—and all of those features are antithetical to Belbury's ideals.

In this context, the journey of Dante's pilgrim is once again a model for a spiritual journey—this time for two characters on separate journeys. Mark and Jane have separate character defects and weaknesses, thus calling for different changes and therefore different kinds of journeys: a hellish one for Mark and a purgatorial one for Jane. However, their spiritual paths converge at the end now that they have begun their relationships with God, which leads to their reconciliation with each other. Like Ransom before them, they too have become aware of the heavenly and demonic dimensions of the universe. The fact that the two Beatrice-like characters of this novel include a wife who is a lapsed Christian and an unmarried, male, interplanetary traveler is a striking example of Lewis's belief that God can use any part of his creation to lead people to himself.

Dante's pilgrim is once again recalled in this novel, but he is recalled in creative new ways by three separate characters: Mark as Dante's pilgrim in the *Inferno*; Jane as Dante's pilgrim in the *Purgatorio*; and Ransom as Dante's pilgrim-turned-narrator subsequent to the journey through the afterlife.

The growing complexity of Lewis's use of Dante's poem that is demonstrated in this novel foreshadows the intensity—and new kinds of complexity—of the presence of *The Divine Comedy* in his next novel, *The Great Divorce*.

CHAPTER SEVEN

The Great Divorce

Introduction

In contrast to *The Screwtape Letters* in which he depicts hell's attempt to lure human beings into its kingdom, Lewis depicts heaven's attempt to draw human beings into *its* kingdom in *The Great Divorce: A Dream* (1946). Similar to the publication for *The Screwtape Letters*, this novel was published earlier in weekly installments in the church magazine *The Guardian* from November 10, 1944, to April 13, 1945.

In this dream-vision narrative of the afterlife, an unnamed narrator accompanies souls from Grey Town (hell) who arrive at the Plain (the outer limit of heaven) where they are each invited by a Mountain-Dweller to journey to the Mountains in the east (heaven). Most of the story takes place on the Plain and consists of episodes the narrator witnesses in which the visitors from Grey Town decide whether to go to the Mountains or return home. Halfway through his time on Plain, the narrator is joined by a guide, George MacDonald, a fictional representation of the nineteenth-century Scottish minister and author, who gives him instruction about what he sees and hears. The story ends when the narrator wakes up.

Many readers and scholars have noted a fundamental similarity between *The Divine Comedy* and *The Great Divorce* because each story is set in the afterlife and deals with the state of souls after death. Lewis's novel has also been compared more narrowly to the *Inferno*, to the *Purgatorio*, and to the *Paradiso*. Some have compared the guide MacDonald to Virgil, to Beatrice, or to both. The relationship between *The Great Divorce* and *The Divine Comedy*, however, is much more complex and profound than these surface correspondences, which have usually been noted without much elaboration, if any. In fact, Lewis's story is comprised in large part of settings, characters, episodes, and teachings from Dante's poem that are reworked to produce a highly condensed version of *The Divine Comedy.*

Although Lewis's short novel (less than 120 pages) cannot be compared in its breadth and depth to Dante's lengthy poem (14,233 verses), it does succeed in evoking the key elements of *The Divine Comedy* through a composite approach: two or more settings from Dante's poem are blended into a new setting; two or more Dantean characters are fused into a single character; two or more episodes from Dante's poem are condensed into one. Through this technique, Lewis is able to refer simultaneously to all three realms of Dante's afterlife simply through the presence of a single setting, character, or event. In addition, more than half of *The Great Divorce* and *The Divine Comedy* consists of dialogue, and Lewis echoes dialogues in Dante's poem, often using Dante's vocabulary.

The very premise of Lewis's story that Ghosts can go to the Mountains is partly based on an example from Dante. When the narrator of *The Great Divorce* asks how Ghosts are allowed to come to the Plain, MacDonald refers to the idea of excursions for the damned found in the writing of Jeremy Taylor, a seventeenth century English churchman, and Prudentius, a fourth-century Latin poet. However, in response to whether or not Ghosts can actually *stay*, MacDonald responds, "Aye. Ye'll have heard that the emperor Trajan did." In referring to that pagan emperor who left hell and is among the blessed in Dante's paradise (see *Par.* 20.106–117), Lewis is pointing to Dante as the authoritative source for that possibility to occur for the characters in his story as well.

A further link between these two works is their core message. Dante states that the theme of his *Divine Comedy* is to show how a person "by his merits or demerits in the exercise of his free will . . . is deserving of reward or punishment by justice." Similarly, the central teaching of *The Great Divorce* is that people freely choose either hell or heaven as their eternal abode: "All that are in Hell, choose it. . . . No soul that seriously and constantly desires joy will ever miss it" (*GD* 72–73). Partly because of Lewis's central focus, this novel includes explicit discussions of Christian theology on heaven, hell, and free will.

Lewis's focus on the afterlife, however, is different from Dante's. Dante's poem highlights the *effects* of free will, the working out in eternity of a person's choices, so the action of his story is divided equally among the three realms that correspond to the three basic choices people can make: rejection of God, growth toward God through purification, and union with God. In *The Great Divorce*, where the last judgment has not yet occurred, the focus is on the *exercise* of a person's free will, on the act of choosing. The narrator is told by his guide about the Grey Towners, "What concerns you is the nature of the choice itself: and that ye can watch them making" (*GD* 69). Because of this focus, Lewis's story is divided into several episodes that revolve around a Grey Towner's decision to choose hell or heaven, and Lewis draws primarily on Dante's *Purgatorio* for the major features of this story.

Lewis's World of the Afterlife and Its Inhabitants

Just as Dante fashions three realms in the afterlife, Lewis designates three distinct areas in his afterlife: Grey Town, the Plain, and the Mountains. Strictly speaking, however, the Plain, unlike Dante's purgatory, is not a geographically distinct area that represents a particular state of souls. It is the outer limit of heaven, the place from which a journey to the Mountains can begin. In the preface to this novel, Lewis says that "[William] Blake wrote the Marriage of Heaven and Hell [*sic*] . . . [and] in some sense or other the attempt to make that marriage is perennial." He states that he has "written of their Divorce" because, in his view, there is no way of embracing both alternatives: it is an either/or situation. The "great divorce" is between two regions, not three.

However, the idea of only two realms in the afterlife applies equally well to Dante's fictive universe. Although Dante's purgatory is geographically distinct, he describes it as the realm "where the human soul purifies itself and becomes worthy to ascend to heaven" (*Purg.* 1.5–6). It can thus in some sense be called the outer limit of heaven, heaven's vestibule, because each soul there is destined for heaven. After the last soul completes its purification, Dante's purgatory will no longer be inhabited since all souls will be either in heaven or hell.

Lewis makes room for the concept of some kind of purgatory in *The Great Divorce*, not by making it a spatial area but a relative one. One of the Grey Towners is told, "You have been in Hell: though if you don't go back you may call it Purgatory" (*GD* 39). In a similar relative way, the Plain can be called "the Valley of the Shadow of Life," but for those who go on to the Mountains, this area where souls undergo purification, "will have been Heaven from the first" (*GD* 67).

Lewis's Plain, as the ante-chamber of heaven, functions as a moral equivalent of Dante's purgatory because it is the place of preparation for heaven. In Dante's purgatory, "the ascent is always difficult at the beginning, but the more one climbs the less it hurts" (*Purg.* 4.89–90). Similarly, in Lewis's "purgatorial" Plain, "the first step is a hard one" (*GD* 91), and the journey "will hurt at first" (*GD* 42), but "it will hurt less at every step" (*GD* 60).

Lewis's approach to the concept of purification is a deliberate reaffirmation of Dante's concept of purgatory. In *Letters to Malcolm: Chiefly on Prayer*, Lewis's narrator objects to the concept of purgatory as primarily retributive punishment. He points to Dante's *Purgatorio*, in which suffering and pain are remedial, as a far more accurate interpretation of the theological concept of purgatory. Lewis maintains that although the process of purification will normally involve suffering, "I don't think suffering is the purpose of purgation." Cleansing and remediation, not punitive suffering, is the purpose of purgatory for Lewis, and his narrative, like Dante's, depicts that viewpoint.

The Plain also functions as the setting for Lewis's moral contrast of the essence of heaven and hell. Although Lewis's heaven and hell are geographically distinct areas, he relies primarily on visual imagery rather than on spatial distinction for his presentation of the spiritual contrast between these two realms. Following Dante's approach in *The Divine Comedy*, he bases his imagery on a pair of physical characteristics that signify spiritual reality.

Throughout *The Divine Comedy*, "light and dark" function to communicate the spiritual contrast between the three realms of Dante's afterlife. The moral quality of each realm is immediately signaled by its relative degree of light contingent on its location with respect to the sun (God): hell is cut off from the sun, purgatory involves an upward climb toward the sun, and the heavens are the sun's location. In *The Great Divorce*, Lewis relies on this imagery to some extent. There is perpetual twilight in Grey Town, which will become total darkness on judgment day; there is perpetual dawn on the Plain, which will become blazing light on the last day; and the Mountains in the distant east are continuously bathed in light.

Lewis's chief imagery, however, is based on the opposition between "solid and shadow" or, in philosophical terms, between "substance and lack of substance." In classical and medieval philosophy, substance is a characteristic of being and is associated with goodness. Lack of substance, on the other hand, is a characteristic of nonbeing and is associated with evil. The combined association of these elements—being/substance/goodness and non-being/lack of substance/evil—is part of a long tradition that can be found in Augustine, Boethius, Thomas Aquinas, and others. Basing his imagery on those philosophical associations, Lewis depicts heaven and its souls as solid and substantial, while Grey Town and its souls are portrayed as shadowy and insubstantial. Like Dante's "light and dark," Lewis's "solid and shadow" represent moral categories and function as visual indications of the spiritual quality of each realm and the state of each soul.

The Plain—as the outer limit of heaven—is full of flowers, trees, streams, and even animals. (There are at least birds, lions, horses, panthers, deer, dogs, cats, and unicorns here.) Everything on the Plain is solid, physical, and definite, for here begins what could be called the "Kingdom of Being." By contrast, Grey Town, briefly presented at the beginning of the novel, has no flora, no fauna, no presence of any life-forms apart from the shadowy souls who dwell there. In this realm from which even color is absent, the rows and rows of transparent houses do not protect souls from the perpetually drizzling rain. MacDonald explains that "the whole difficulty of understanding Hell is that the thing to be understood is so nearly Nothing" (*GD* 75). That point is made clear near the end of Lewis's story when MacDonald reveals that hell is actually located in a small crack in the ground of the Plain and "is smaller than one atom of *this* world, the Real World" (*GD* 122). He describes a soul from hell in a similar way: "A damned soul is nearly nothing: it is shrunk, shut up in itself" (*GD* 123). Grey Town and its inhabitants come as close to representing the "Kingdom of Non-Being" as possible without disappearing altogether.

Lewis sustains his presentation of the characteristics of heaven and hell primarily through the contrasts between the physical qualities of the two categories of characters who meet on the Plain. Lewis's Mountain-Dwellers, at times called the "Solid People" and the "Bright People," are so substantial that when they come down to the Plain, the "earth shook under their tread" (*GD* 30). By contrast, the visitors to the Plain from Grey Town discover that "in the light, they were transparent . . . , smudgy and imperfectly opaque. . . . They were in fact ghosts: man-shaped stains on the brightness of that air" (*GD* 27). The Plain is physically uncomfortable for these visitors: the light is too bright, the grass cuts their feet, and the gentlest breeze can knock them down.

Lewis initially connects his Plain to Dante's purgatory by constructing several parallels between the souls' arrival at Dante's island and the Grey Towners' arrival at their new location. (1) Souls are transported to Dante's purgatory in a boat full of light (see *Purg.* 2.16ff.). Souls are transported to the Plain in a flying omnibus "blazing with golden light" (*GD* 13). (2) Dante's transported souls arrive very early in the morning at a grassy region on the shores of the mount (see *Purg.* 1.102; 2.55–56). On Lewis's Plain, it is a bright, early morning when the souls arrive at a lovely, grassy region with beautiful flowers. (3) In the *Purgatorio* "the crowd that remained here [on the shore] seemed unfamiliar with this place, looking all around, like people assessing something new" (*Purg.* 2.52–54). The newcomers to Lewis's Plain, unsure of their direction in this new environment, strike the same pose: they "were still grouped about in the neighbourhood of the omnibus, though beginning, some of them, to walk forward into the landscape with hesitating steps" (*GD* 27).

Another important detail in this scene concerns the character that transports the souls from Grey Town to the Plain. Lewis's Bus-Driver seems to be a fusion of two of Dante's angels whose functions together help reveal the identity of the newcomers and the significance of the Plain. First, Lewis's Driver, waving one of his hands "before his face as if to fan away the greasy steam of the rain [in Grey Town]" (*GD* 13), recalls the only angel who appears in the *Inferno*, the angel at the gate of Dis, who "often waved the putrid air away from his face with his left hand" (*Inf.* 9.82–83). Lewis responds to a reader's query that "The bus-driver in the Divorce [*sic*] is certainly, and consciously, modeled on the angel at the gates of Dis." This angel, who has the authority to open the gate to lower hell for Virgil and the pilgrim, is unaffected by the rebellious spirits there and "had the look of someone focused on concerns other than the one that is before him" (*Inf.* 9.101–103). Similarly, Lewis's Driver, oblivious to the Grey Towners' critical and cynical remarks about him, "had a look of authority and seemed intent on carrying out his job" (*GD* 14). The reminiscence of this angel recalls the *Inferno* and is an initial indication about the place from which these souls are being transported.

However, Lewis's Driver also recalls the angel who transports souls to Dante's purgatory in a swift-moving boat (see *Purg.* 2.41). Lewis's driver of the fast moving bus "seemed full of light," and light is the primary characteristic of Dante's boat-angel (see *Purg.* 2.17ff.). Because Lewis's Driver "used only one hand to drive with" (*GD* 13), his casual style conveys the same impression of effortless ease with which Dante's angel pilots his vessel merely by using his wings (see *Purg.* 2.32–33). By combining an echo of both these Dantean angels in himself, Lewis's Driver becomes an indirect suggestion that the Grey Towners are coming from a new hell and are being transported to a new purgatory.

There is some indication that Lewis's Driver may also represent Christ, because MacDonald tells the narrator at the end of the story that "only the Greatest of all can make Himself small enough to enter Hell. . . . Only One has descended into Hell" (*GD* 123–24). In that case the Driver, who is able to enter Grey Town, would also recall Christ, and he would thus be a composite of three characters.

Although the setting of Lewis's scene initially recalls the shore area at the base of Mount Purgatory, other details about Lewis's Plain recall Dante's purgatorial mount as well. In one area of the Plain, the narrator comes upon a tree near a waterfall that combines the two different trees on Dante's mount where gluttony is purged. Dante's first tree is near a high rock with a waterfall, and "clear water sprayed over the leaves below" (*Purg.* 22.137–138). Lewis's tree is also near a waterfall and is likewise described as "wet with spray" (*GD* 49). Dante's second tree with its lush, verdant branches—most probably an apple tree (see *Purg.* 24.103–104)—is reflected in the shape of Lewis's tree with its "billowy foliage" and its "apples of gold gleam[ing] through the leaves" (*GD* 49). In the

Purgatorio, a voice issues forth from each tree with prohibitions to the gluttons: "You are denied this food," and then, "Move away without drawing closer" (*Purg.* 22.141, 24.115). In Lewis's story, the voice comes from the waterfall next to the tree, but it also issues a prohibition to a Grey Towner who is attempting to steal a gold apple: "Put it down. You cannot take it back" (*GD* 51–52).

Although this episode recalls the setting on the sixth ledge of gluttony, its moral significance recalls the fifth ledge where avarice is purged. The Grey Towner is trying to steal as many golden apples as possible to take home, and it is only his lack of substance and the weight of the apples that prevent him from stealing all but the smallest gold apple. Lewis, through the setting and the action, thus combines echoes of two ledges from Dante's mount in one scene.

Lewis also alludes to Dante's Garden of Eden at the top of Mount Purgatory when he mentions a fountain located in the Mountains that is "a little like Lethe" (*GD* 82), the classical river of forgetfulness in Hades. Dante, referring to it once as a *fountain* (see *Purg.* 28.124), relocates Lethe to his Garden of Eden, and all souls are submerged in it before their entrance into heaven. Dante's Lethe is perpetually shaded by trees and is thus *cold*, and its waters are *clearer* than any water on earth (see *Purg.* 28.33, 28.28ff.). Lewis uses only two adjectives to describe his Lethe-fountain—"Very cold and clear" (*GD* 82). The classical Lethe removes all memories, good and bad, but souls submerged in Dante's Lethe are purged only of their bitter memories sin and guilt (see *Purg.* 31.11–12). Lewis's Lethe-fountain makes a person "forget forever" the ownership of one's works (*GD* 82), but, like Dante's purgatorial stream, it also performs a purifying function because "if there is any . . . inflammation [of selfishness] left it will be cured when you come to the fountain" (*GD* 81–82). Because of its moral significance and its relocation from hell, Lewis's fountain is meant to echo Dante's Lethe rather than the classical Lethe.

In addition to parallels in the overall setting, many of Lewis's characters are fashioned as composites of several characters from Dante's poem, as is the case with his Bus-Driver. Lewis's Mountain-Dwellers resemble the redeemed souls in Dante's *Paradiso* who radiate love, joy, and blinding light. One of them appears "almost blindingly white" (*GD* 38); another was "shining with laughter"

(*GD* 83); another, as he speaks, was "shining with love and mirth so that my eyes were dazzled" (*GD* 94).

However, these characters also include a simultaneous reference to Virgil and Beatrice because their roles blend some distinctive characteristics of those two guides. Like Virgil who offers to lead Dante's pilgrim on a spiritual journey, each Bright Person offers to lead a Grey Towner on a spiritual journey. Virgil offers the pilgrim encouragement, instruction, guidance, and even at times physical support. The Mountain-Dwellers likewise encourage, give instruction, answer questions, and even offer physical support: "You can lean on me all the way" (*GD* 60), one of them says, and when MacDonald invites the narrator for a walk, he too offers, "Lean on my arm" (*GD* 75)—in both cases, this offer comes because of the Ghosts' physical difficulty in maneuvering in this environment.

Like Beatrice who left her seat in the heavenly Empyrean to help initiate a lost soul's journey (see *Inf.* 2.83–84), each of the Bright People has left the Mountains and has "retraced immeasurable distances to come down today on the mere chance of saving some Ghosts" (*GD* 72). After Beatrice meets the pilgrim at the top of Mount Purgatory, she then personally accompanies him to heaven; likewise, each Mountain-Dweller has come to the Plain to accompany a particular Ghost to heaven personally. Just as Beatrice is the channel through which grace is given to the pilgrim for his journey to heaven, so too each Bright One is a similar channel. One of them tells a Grey Towner that God "is in me, for you, with that power" (*GD* 42). Beatrice is also the mediator between God and the pilgrim, and when one of the Ghosts says he is not sure what he believes in, the Bright Person, acting as a mediator, asks as a first step, "Will you believe in *me*? . . . Will you come with me to the mountains?" (*GD* 42).

In *The Divine Comedy* there is some level of prior acquaintance between Dante's pilgrim and his two main guides: he has studied Virgil's poetry, and he has known Beatrice in Florence. Likewise, each Solid Person is already connected in some capacity to the Grey Towner he or she comes to greet: an employee greets his employer; an artist greets another artist; a wife greets her husband, and so forth. The Mountain-Dwellers, in fulfilling the roles of both Virgil and Beatrice, thus continuously serve as subtle reminders of all three realms of Dante's afterlife.

The narrator's guide, MacDonald, resembles Virgil and Beatrice in the same ways the other Bright People do—and in even more specific ways that will be discussed later—but he also plays the role of three other Dantean characters: Cato, the guardian of purgatory; the angel at the gate of purgatory; and Cacciaguida, a distant ancestor of Dante's pilgrim.

MacDonald's similarity to Cato on the shore of the island of Purgatory is achieved through a number of close parallels: (1) Cato is the first one to accost Virgil and Dante's pilgrim when they reach the shores of Mount Purgatory; MacDonald is the first Mountain-Dweller to accost Lewis's narrator in this "purgatorial" setting. (2) Cato's greeting challenges the presence of the two pilgrims arriving from hell: "Who are you to have escaped from the eternal prison?" (*Purg* 1.40–41). MacDonald's startling and unexpected greeting to the narrator, who has just arrived from hell, seems to take the form of an apparent challenge: "Where are ye going?" (*GD* 64). (3) The contextual parallel is strengthened by the appearance of both men. Cato, an old man with a long beard, is alone (see *Purg.* 1.31–36). MacDonald, described as "an old weather-beaten man" with "a flowing beard" (GD 64), is also alone. (4) Cato's face seems to reflect the shining sun (see *Purg.* 1:38–39), and his "countenance was worthy of much reverence" (*Purg.* 1.32). MacDonald, in his overall bearing, seems to be "an enthroned and shining god" (*GD* 64).

Second, MacDonald resembles the angel guarding the gate of Mount Purgatory. Dante's angel is seated on a stone step (see *Purg.* 9.103), and MacDonald is at first seated on a rock. The angel asks the pilgrim, "What do you want?" (*Purg.* 9.85), and MacDonald likewise begins by asking the narrator where he is going. The angel grants the pilgrim access to purgatory, and it is MacDonald's explanations that introduce the narrator to the significance of the Plain and the souls there.

MacDonald's final conversation with the narrator recalls yet a third character, this time from the *Paradiso*. At the end of the novel, MacDonald briefly assumes the role and even the language of the pilgrim's ancestor, Cacciaguida. (1) Cacciaguida calls the pilgrim "son" because he is one of his descendants. Although there is no family relationship between MacDonald and Lewis's narrator, he calls him "Son" during this final discussion (*GD* 127). (2) Cacciaguida charges his progeny to report his vision of the afterlife accurately and without lies (see *Par.* 17.127). MacDonald likewise charges the narrator that he must be truthful and clear (that this is a dream): "And if ye come to tell of what ye have seen, make it plain. . . . See ye make it very plain" (*GD* 127). His insistence on "very plain" speech is itself an echo of Cacciaguida's manner of speaking that is described as "clear words in plain speech" (*Par.* 17.34–35). Cacciaguida's plain speech is specifically contrasted to "dark oracles" (see *Par.* 17.31) that are hard to interpret and understand. Similarly, MacDonald wants the narrator's speech to be plain because "I'll have no Swedenborgs and no Vale Owens among my children" (*GD* 127), referring to an eighteenth-century scientist who became a visionary and a twentieth-century spiritualist. (4) Dante's pilgrim is concerned about the reception he might get since "I have learned things that would leave a very bitter taste for many if I retell them" (*Par.* 17.116–117). Lewis's narrator, concerned about sharing what MacDonald says (about natural loves needing to die and rise again), objects, "I don't know that I dare repeat this on Earth, Sir. . . . They'd say I was inhuman" (*GD* 97). (5) Cacciaguida reassures the pilgrim that even if his truthful words seem harsh at first, they need to be said and will become nourishment (see *Par.* 17.130–132). MacDonald likewise tells the narrator that "someone must say in general what's been unsaid among you this many a year. . . . It's cruel not to say it" (*GD* 97). (6) Cacciaguida informs his descendant about the *bitter* difficulties that lie ahead for him (see *Par.* 17.55ff.), and MacDonald tells the narrator, "The bitter drink of death is still before you" (*GD* 127). (7) Cacciaguida explains that God's foreknowledge does not abrogate free will (see *Par.* 17.37–42), and MacDonald is the one who explains that same point (see *GD* 125). In the explanations by both characters, the emphasis is that God's act of "seeing" all things in his eternal present does not *cause* events to happen or choices to be made. (8) Near the end of the dialogue with his descendant, Cacciaguida "became even more resplendent, like a golden mirror reflecting sunlight" (*Par.* 17.122–123). In MacDonald's final appearance in the novel as he faces the rising sun, "His face flushed with a new light" (*GD* 128).

MacDonald, as a detailed composite of five characters from *The Divine Comedy*, is one of the most vivid examples of the technique Lewis uses throughout this novel to create continuous, multilayered echoes of Dante's poem.

In addition to the setting on the Plain and characters who meet there, the narrative structure and specific episodes in *The Great Divorce* evoke Dante's poem, in particular the *Purgatorio*. The sequence of episodes in Lewis's narrative can be divided into successive encounters between Mountain-Dwellers and Grey Towners that function somewhat like the separate ledges on Dante's Mount. Those encounters reveal the presence of specific attitudes on the part of Grey Towners that must be purged in order for them to move forward toward the Mountains, and those attitudes, like the sinful dispositions on Dante's ledges, are each unique.

Although Lewis does not use the seven capital sins for his framework, his narrative pattern follows the basic organizing principle of Dante's mount by adapting its underlying philosophy of natural loves gone wrong in a variety of ways. The general division of Dante's Mount, elaborated in *Purgatorio* 17.113–139, is based on the distinction between perverted loves and disordered loves needing to be set in right order (see especially *Purg*. 17.95–96, 100–102). Perverted love involves love for the wrong object, while disordered love involves a disproportionate love for something good. Virgil describes the souls on the three lower ledges of the mount as needing to be purged of perverted love (pride, envy, and anger), and souls on the upper ledges as needing to be purged of disordered love (sloth, avarice, gluttony, and lust).

Lewis approximates this general division for his ten main episodes—episodes that consist of three or more pages. The first five are illustrations of some kind of perverted love, while the next five episodes are illustrations of disordered love. The first group of Grey Towners can be classified as displaying perverted love through instances of (1) pride or self-righteousness (the Big Ghost), (2) heresy (the apostate bishop), (3) avarice (the gold-loving Ghost, Ikey), (4) cynicism or lack of faith in goodness (the Tall Ghost), and (5) vanity (a lady Ghost). The second group of five can be classified as instances of disordered love: (6) love of art for art's sake (the artist Ghost), (7) excessive, smothering love (Robert's wife), (8) possessive love (the mother Pam), (9) lust (the young man with the lizard), and (10) the use of love to manipulate and control (Sarah's husband, Frank). Lewis's illustrations of sin do not duplicate Dante's medieval categories of sin, but his illustrations present modern attitudes that are readily recognizable by today's reader—just as Dante's categories were readily recognizable by his contemporaries.

The lower ledges of Dante's mount represent more serious sin than the ledges that are farther up, but Lewis presents no such classification for the sinful attitudes of the Grey Towners. In *The Great Divorce*, each of their wrong attitudes is on the same level spiritually in terms of blocking or hindering the journey to the Mountains and can only be removed by a Ghost's free-will decision to relinquish it. Lewis's focus is not on categorizing the specific reasons for a Grey Towner's resistance to journey to the Mountains, but on analyzing them in their essence.

On the surface, each Grey Towner has a different motive for not immediately undertaking (or for never undertaking) the journey, but the common denominator in each motive is self-focus. Every refusal to journey essentially flows from the choice of oneself over God, and that choice for independence from God is a manifestation of pride. In that sense, all of Lewis's Grey Towners could be said to be examples of souls who belong on the ledge of pride on Dante's mount because there can be no spiritual growth unless there is the humility to acknowledge one's sin and weakness. Unless the Grey Towners relinquish their sinful attitudes and accept the necessary correction for the perversion or the disorder in their love, they cannot move ahead.

Although each Ghost is afforded the same opportunity to journey to the Mountains, the offer is received in a variety of ways. Several characters decide to return to Grey Town; one character vanishes (*GD* 89); one Ghost decides to journey to the Mountains; and the choice of some is left in doubt when the narrator does not witness the conclusion of some conversations. The outcome of any particular encounter, however, is a secondary focus for Lewis. The narrator's attention is on the power and process of choice and the exercise of free will.

In addition to the overall structure of his narrative, Lewis makes use of the *Purgatorio* for the content of three episodes concerning disordered love. In particular, episodes six, nine, and ten consist of material from the *Purgatorio* that Lewis taps into, but he does so in different ways: (1) the sixth episode *echoes* two conversations in Dante's *Purgatorio*; (2) the ninth episode closely *duplicates* the details of an event on Dante's mount; (3) and the tenth episode *parallels but inverts* the main event in Dante's garden.

The sixth episode, a dialogue between two artists, is Lewis's illustration of the "disordered love" of art for art's sake. Lewis combines dialogues from two scenes in the *Purgatorio* that reveal Dante's position on the relationship of art to spiritual life into one scene for his own similar teaching on art.

Lewis's episode initially recalls the meeting between Dante's pilgrim and his musician friend Casella who has just arrived at the shore of purgatory (see *Purg.* 2.76ff.). When Cato, the guardian of purgatory, rebukes the group of souls lingering on the shore to listen to Casella sing the melody he wrote for one of Dante's poems—thus delaying their ascent of the mount to be purified (see *Purg.* 2.120–123)—Dante is not implying that art has no place in the spiritual life but rather that nothing, not even art, should be allowed to hinder the soul's pursuit of holiness.

Lewis begins the dialogue of his sixth episode with that very point. When the Grey Towner artist wishes to remain on the Plain only to paint it, he is told by the Mountain-Dweller to put art aside temporarily to attend to matters of graver significance: "At present your business is to see. Come and see. He [God] is endless" (*GD* 80). As in *The Divine Comedy*, art is not condemned, for the Grey Towner is told that later, when "you've grown into a Person ... there'll be some things which you'll see better than anyone else. One of the things you'll want to do will be to tell us about them" (*GD* 80). Although art is not inconsistent with or contrary to spiritual life and can even communicate that life, when it no longer maintains a secondary, subordinate position and ceases to be a means of expressing reality and becomes an end in itself, it is no longer in "right order." When love of art is in that "disordered" state, it effectively eclipses the reality that art has the potential to communicate. The Mountain-Dweller tells the artist, "If you are interested in the country only for the sake of painting it, you'll never learn to see the country" (*GD* 81). When the Mountain-Dweller explains that here, "Glory flows into everyone, and back from everyone: like light and mirrors" (*GD* 82–83), Lewis is echoing light and mirror images from the *Paradiso*, as well as adapting the *Paradiso*'s famous opening line: "The glory of the One Who moves all things permeates the universe and shines in some parts more and in some less" (*Par.* 1.1–3).

The dialogue then moves on to echo the conversation on the ledge of pride between Dante's pilgrim and the artist Oderisi of

Gubbio, a thirteenth-century illuminator of manuscripts. Oderisi, describing a link that can occur between art and pride, begins his discussion with the variations that occur in style and tastes in the art world, and the displacements that ensue: "Cimabue thought he led the field in painting; but now Giotto is the favorite and obscures the other's fame" (*Purg.* 11.94–96). In Lewis's episode, a similar displacement has occurred. The Mountain-Dweller tells the artist Ghost, "You and I are already completely forgotten on the Earth. . . . We're dead out of fashion" (*GD* 83). Oderisi, however, has wisely learned that "earthly fame is like the color of grass that comes and goes" (*Purg.* 11.115–116), and he is now content to be purged of his pride and concern for his reputation. Lewis's Grey Towner, on the other hand, is unwilling to have his love of art set in right order. His refusal leads him back to Grey Town because "one has one's duty to the future of Art. . . . I must write an article. There must be a manifesto. We must start a periodical" (*GD* 83). Heaven has been put aside, ostensibly for the sake of art, but the Grey Towner is actually going back to defend *his* ideas and *his* reputation. His attitude is, of course, contrary to that of Dante's prideful souls in the *Purgatorio*, but Lewis is here echoing Dante's artist-dialogue and making the same points, although the outcome is different.

The ninth episode in *The Great Divorce*, which involves a young man with a red lizard on his shoulder, recapitulates the scene of Dante's pilgrim on the ledge of the lustful, closely paralleling its prototype in the *Purgatorio*.

This episode is the only instance in Lewis's novel where an angel comes to greet a Grey Towner, and, like Lewis's Bus-Driver and MacDonald, this angel is a composite of several characters from the *Purgatorio*. First, his appearance recalls that of all of Dante's angels who typically have "radiance" that overcomes sight (*Purg.* 27.59–60). Lewis's angel was "so bright that I could hardly look at him" (*GD* 98). Second, he echoes the angel of Dis who "left off singing alleluia [in heaven]" (*Inf.* 12.88) to come down to hell in order to assist Dante's pilgrim to continue his journey. Lewis's angel likewise comes down from his heavenly place in the Mountains to assist this Grey Towner on his journey. Third, he is particularly reminiscent of the angel on the stairs leading up to the seventh ledge of lust who is the only fiery angel in Dante's poem: "No one has ever seen glass or metals in a furnace burning so bright and red as the one I saw" (*Purg.* 24.137–139). Lewis calls his angel the "Burning One" and "the flaming Spirit" (*GD* 101, 99) because "there was heat coming from him as well as light" (*GD* 98). Fourth, he is functionally reminiscent of the seven angels guarding the stairs between the ledges who remove one of the seven P's (*Peccatum*, "sin") inscribed on the pilgrim's forehead that represent the seven capital sins. Lewis's angel here fulfills a similar task by removing the visible sign of the Grey Towner's sin—in this case, a red lizard on his shoulder. And fifth, this angel is reminiscent of Virgil because his conversation with the young man replays Virgil's dialogue with the pilgrim at this juncture in Dante's story.

Just as Dante's pilgrim must willingly pass through the wall of fire to be purged of lust, so this Grey Towner must allow the fiery angel to kill the red lizard of lust on his shoulder that is continually whining and whispering to him.

(1) Dante's pilgrim halts adamantly before the wall of fire on the ledge of lust, resisting Virgil's prodding, and remains "very firm and unyielding and a bit embarrassed" (*Purg.* 27.34–35). Similarly, Lewis's young man, firmly and at length, resists the angel's multiple offers to remove the lizard, calling his situation "damned embarrassing" (*GD* 99).

(2) Virgil informs Dante's pilgrim that "this may cause pain but not death" (*Purg.* 27.21). Lewis's burning angel informs the young man, "I never said it wouldn't hurt you. I said it wouldn't kill you" (*GD* 100).

(3) As Dante's pilgrim moves forward into the fire, the pain is so intense that "I would have flung myself into boiling hot glass to cool myself" (*Purg.* 27.49–50). The pain is so great for Lewis's young man at the lizard's removal by the angel with "burning hands" (*GD* 99) that he "gave a scream of agony such as I never heard on Earth" (*GD* 101).

(4) Passage through the wall of fire in the *Purgatorio* effects a growth in the desire of Dante's pilgrim that is now rightly ordered: "Waves of desire came over me to be up there [in the Garden of Eden] so that with every step I felt my wings growing for flight" (*Purg.* 27.121–123). The purification for Lewis's Ghost also effects a growth—in this case, not metaphoric wings but a visible, physical metamorphosis. The Ghost grows "every moment solider . . . brighter still and stronger" (*GD* 102). Transformation also occurs

in the lizard that the angel had flung to the ground, and he becomes a silvery white stallion for the young man to ride up to the Mountains. The commentary by the narrator's guide on the lizard's metamorphosis is an apt explanation for the similar new energy that Dante's pilgrim describes in his own situation: "Lust is a poor, weak, whimpering whispering thing compared with that richness and energy of desire which will arise when lust has been killed" (*GD* 104–5).

Lewis continues with more parallels after these transformations. The successful passage through the ledge of fire by Dante's pilgrim is followed by Virgil's solemn pronouncement to the pilgrim, "I crown and miter you over yourself" (*Purg.* 27.142). These are Virgil's final words to the pilgrim indicating that he has now spiritually attained the status of a king and a priest; he is now master of himself and is no longer in need of Virgil's guidance. As Lewis's young man rides off, Nature sings a hymn, the last line of which repeats the significance of Virgil's pronouncement and expands it: "*Master, your Master has appointed you for ever: to be our King of Justice and our high Priest*" (*GD* 104). Although Dante's pilgrim is pronounced master of himself, Lewis's young man is pronounced master of himself *and* of Nature, for whoever is able to rule over himself is worthy to rule over creation. The hymn sung by Nature is Lewis's poetic paraphrase of verses from Psalm 110, and it reflects Dante's procedure of poetically paraphrasing a scriptural prayer (for one example, see Dante's expanded version of the "Lord's Prayer" recited by the souls on the ledge of the prideful in *Purg.* 11.1–24).

The conclusion of this episode concerning the young man includes still more echoes of the *Purgatorio*. First, whenever Dante's mount shakes or trembles, it is a sign that a soul has completed its purgation on a given ledge and is currently advancing to the next one (see *Purg.* 21.58–60). When the young man, now purged of lust, rides off toward the Mountains, "the whole plain and forest were shaking" (*GD* 103). The second sign of a soul's advancement on Dante's mount is a loud shout by the souls on the mount who praise God for that soul's advancement and sing the *Gloria* (see *Purg.* 20.132–136). As Lewis's young man rides off, the shaking of the earth is accompanied by a hymn sung by "the Nature or Archnature of that land," that produces "a sound which in our world would be too large to hear" (*GD* 103). In both stories, all creation trembles, rejoicing to see the manifestation of the sons of God, and God is praised in song.

Unlike the ninth episode that closely mirrors the events in Dante's poem, Lewis's tenth episode begins to mimic but then inverses its counterpart in *The Divine Comedy*. Since it involves yet another, but more distinct, Beatrice in this novel, it will be discussed in that section. Lewis's setting, dialogues, and characters, which recall the three realms of Dante's afterlife though various details—and Dante's purgatory in particular—form a solid backdrop for the appearance of a new protagonist resembling Dante's pilgrim.

The Narrator and His Journey

Although the narrator's journeying is limited to his trip from Grey Town and to walking around the Plain, his time on the Plain constitutes a spiritual journey. His instruction occurs in ways that parallel the three modes of instruction for Dante's pilgrim. First, in both stories the physical universe and its characters carry spiritual meaning visually—through the metaphors of Dante's "light and dark" and Lewis's "solid and shadow"—so Dante's pilgrim and Lewis's narrator can learn much simply by looking around and listening. Second, each of them is instructed by the redeemed. Dante's pilgrim learns from the heaven-bound souls in the *Purgatorio* and the blessed souls in the *Paradiso,* while the narrator learns from the Mountain–Dwellers who likewise bring forth spiritual truths and principles as he overhears their conversations with the Grey Towners. Third and most important, both pilgrims have guides who offer major doctrinal instruction. Through the combination of these three modes, there is a sequential unfolding of instruction for Lewis's narrator about the nature of hell, heaven, repentance, purification, and grace.

This is the first of Lewis's novels that has a first-person narrator as the main protagonist. Although he is never named, cues from things he says indicate that, unlike Lewis's other chief protagonists so far, he bears some intentional similarity to the historical Lewis. For instance, this narrator happens to be a teacher like Lewis, and details of his conversion mirror the experience of the historical

Lewis (*GD* 65). MacDonald, who says he is well acquainted with the narrator's biographical details, tells him not to think of the Plain yet as Heaven: "'Not *Deep Heaven*, ye understand.' (Here he smiled at me)" (*GD* 67)—a bit of an inside joke about the phrase that Lewis had invented to describe outer space for his recently published Ransom trilogy.

However, Lewis's first-person narrator both is and is not C. S. Lewis in the same way that the first-person narrator of *The Divine Comedy* is and is not Dante Alighieri the poet. Just as Dante the poet at times transposes some of his own experiences into his poem and ascribes them to his fictional pilgrim—and readers often mistakenly identify the poem's pilgrim with the historical Dante—so too Lewis ascribes some of his own life events to the narrator. This occurs primarily during the first interchange between the narrator and MacDonald.

The narrator's personal connection to MacDonald vividly mirrors the personal connection that Dante's pilgrim has not just to one but to both of his guides. Lewis combines the initial encounters of Dante's pilgrim with Virgil and with Beatrice into one scene. When Virgil reveals his identity to Dante's pilgrim, the pilgrim immediately responds by saying, "You are my teacher and my [most esteemed] author" (*Inf.* 1.85), indicating his great respect and admiration for Virgil as a literary master. He mentions his long study and great love of Virgil's poetry (see *Inf.* 1.83–84), and in fact, he knows every line of Virgil's *Aeneid* (see *Inf.* 20.114). Likewise, when the Scottish author introduces himself, Lewis's narrator immediately tries "to tell this man all that his writings had done for me" (*GD* 65). Historically, as the author of sermons and Christian fantasy stories, MacDonald had given Lewis inspiration and insight for his writings. (Lewis, in his introduction to *George MacDonald: An Anthology*, which consists of quotes Lewis gathered from MacDonald's writings, says, "I fancy I have never written a book in which I did not quote from him.")

MacDonald, in addition to being this narrator's Virgil by influencing the narrator's writings, simultaneously functions as this narrator's Beatrice, a channel for revelation and grace. In the same scene, Lewis's narrator tells MacDonald that his novel *Phantastes* "had been to me what the first sight of Beatrice had been to Dante: *Here begins the New Life*" (*GD* 65). The dual reference here is that

Dante's first sight of Beatrice had awakened him to new life, the spiritual life; afterward he wrote a collection of poems about her actually called *The New Life* (*La Vita Nuova*). MacDonald, as the author of the novel *Phantastes*, had awakened Lewis to spiritual life and was thus influential in his later conversion. (Lewis says that after reading this novel, "I knew I had crossed a great frontier," and it was "as if I had died in the old country and could never remember how I came alive in the new.")

After these initial acknowledgements to MacDonald by the narrator, the ensuing dialogue next recalls the confession of Dante's pilgrim during his meeting with Beatrice in the Garden of Eden. Dante's pilgrim admits that for many years after she died he was guilty of turning aside from the right path that Beatrice had shown him when she was alive (see *Purg.* 31.34–36). Lewis's narrator likewise acknowledges his guilt before this "Beatrice" of not moving ahead for many years into the right path that he had showed him: "I started to confess how long that Life had delayed in the region of imagination merely: how slowly and reluctantly I had come to admit that his Christendom had more than an accidental connexion with it, how hard I had tried not to see that the true name of the quality which first met me in his books is Holiness" (*GD* 65). (There was a fifteen-year gap between Lewis's reading of *Phantastes* and his conversion from atheism to theism and then to Christianity.)

Another factor that connects MacDonald to Virgil and Beatrice concerns Lewis's literary characterization of him not only as a historical character but as a special kind of character called "figura" that is specific to Dante's poem. Historical characters in fiction do not necessarily have to represent themselves or their ideas—depending on an author's purpose for including them—but a "figura" in literature is a historical character who continues to speak, act, and function in a fictional story in the same way that he or she did on earth. Virgil, whose poetry was a guide for the historical Dante in his writing, continues to act as a guide for him in Dante's fictional afterlife, and Beatrice Potinari, who was a channel of God's grace in Florence for the historical Dante, continues to act as a channel of grace in his poem as she leads him to God in the Empyrean. Lewis likewise shapes MacDonald as a "figura." As the author of sermons, MacDonald gave the historical Lewis inspiration and guidance for his writings, and as the author of the novel that was influential in Lewis's conversion, he was also a channel of grace for him. As a "figura" in this novel, he continues to fulfill the role of teacher, guide, and channel of grace that he played for Lewis on earth, and thus the manner in which Lewis shapes his character echoes even the literary status of both Dante's guides.

Although MacDonald functions as both Virgil and Beatrice, his relationship to the narrator primarily mirrors that of Virgil. Virgil never addresses the pilgrim by name but calls him "son" multiple times; MacDonald never addresses the narrator by name but calls him "Son." Dante's pilgrim never addresses Virgil by name and most often calls him "teacher" and "sir"; the narrator never calls MacDonald by name and refers to him as "my Teacher" and addressing him as "Sir."

MacDonald provides three major teachings to the narrator. In Dante's poem, issues such as free will and the nature of virtue, vice, hell, and sin are presented for the most part by the pilgrim's guides: Virgil gives *philosophical* and *moral* instruction to the pilgrim, while Beatrice gives him *theological* instruction on these issues. The bulk of the content of the teaching that Lewis's narrator receives, however, echoes teaching from the *Purgatorio*—which Lewis said was perhaps his favorite part of *The Divine Comedy*—because most of Dante's exposition on the doctrine of free will occurs there.

There are two instances of major exposition by MacDonald that approximate teachings from Virgil. MacDonald's first major instruction, on free will and divine justice, is the central teaching of *The Great Divorce* as it is in Dante's poem. Virgil's teaching on free will and natural loves in the *Purgatorio* occurs when they are on the stone stairs between two ledges and have stopped their walking for the day (see *Purg.* 17.76–78). MacDonald's discourse on free will occurs when he and the narrator are seated on a rock (see *GD* 65). Dante's core teaching on free will is that people have the power to control their natural loves or inclinations because of the noble faculty of free will (see *Purg.* 18.71–74). Once reason distinguishes between good and bad inclinations or loves, free will governs a person's assent and is therefore the principle whereby someone deserves praise or blame for what he or she chooses (see *Purg.* 18.62–66). Dante's conclusion, and the premise of his poem, is that the justice of God gives every soul precisely what he or she has chosen.

Lewis approaches the relationship between free will and divine justice in precisely the same way. MacDonald tells the narrator, "All that are in Hell, choose it. Without that self-choice there could be no Hell" (*GD* 72). People are given either heaven or hell, according to their desire, because God respects the exercise of that free will. Souls are damned not because God condemns them but because heaven is not forced on anyone: "There is always something they insist on keeping, even at the price of misery. There is always something they prefer to joy—that is, to reality" (*GD* 69). There are, in the end, only citizens of hell and of heaven in Dante's afterlife, and Lewis's souls are likewise classified into two categories: "There are only two kinds of people in the end: those who say to God, 'Thy will be done,' and those to whom God says, in the end, 'Thy will be done'" (*GD* 72).

The second major Virgil-like teaching deals with the primacy of love for God and the place of natural loves, and it makes use of concepts and vocabulary from the *Purgatorio*. It begins with remarks by a Mountain-Dweller to a mother, who refuses to go to the Mountains unless she is first reunited with her deceased son, and concludes with remarks by MacDonald. Virgil's discussion of love is based on the premise that love—an attraction to a good or a perceived good—is the cause of all virtue and sin (see *Purg.* 17.104–105). In itself, however, "natural [love] is always blameless" (*Purg.* 17.94). The Mountain-Dweller echoes, "No natural feelings are high or low, holy or unholy, in themselves" (*GD* 93). Virgil tells Dante's pilgrim that "when it [love] is directed to the primary Good and keeps secondary goods in their place, it cannot be the cause of sinful joy" (*Purg.* 17.97–99). The Mountain-Dweller follows up with the point that natural loves "are all holy when God's hand is on the rein" (*GD* 93). However, natural loves, like the mother's love for her son, are good only insofar as they are properly related to and subordinated to love for God. MacDonald begins his comments at this point, "There's something in natural affection which will lead it on to eternal love. . . . But there's also something in it which make it easier to stop at the natural level and mistake it for the heavenly." (*GD* 96–97). Virgil warns, "But when the soul turns to evil or pursues some good with too much or too little zeal, then the creature is working against the Creator" (*Purg.* 17.100–102). MacDonald echoes that concept, saying, "There is but one good;

that is God. Everything else is good when it looks to Him and bad when it turns from Him" (*GD* 97–98).

There are two ways that natural loves can lead to sin, and MacDonald repeats Virgil's teaching about this. Virgil points out that love "may err through having a wrong object" (*Purg.* 17.95), for instance, desiring a neighbor's harm, and that kind of error leads to *perverted love*. The second way that love can err is "through excessive or defective intensity" (*Purg.* 17.96), and that leads to *disordered love*. MacDonald's analysis of the mother's attitude is according to Dante's categories: "Excess of love, did ye say? There was no *excess*, there was *defect*. She loved her son too little, not too much" (*GD* 105; italics added). Although her love for her son appears excessive, it is in fact defective because her chief desire is to have her son with her, and "it may well be that at this moment she's demanding to have him down with her in Hell" (*GD* 105).

At the end of the episodes on the Plain, MacDonald presents his last major teaching, but this time it is reminiscent of Beatrice's instruction in the *Paradiso* on free will and the necessity of the incarnation. Beatrice says about free will, "The greatest gift God gave through his bounty in creating man, the one most conformed to his own goodness and that he most values, was the freedom of the will" (*Par.* 5.19–22). In MacDonald's version, free will is "the gift whereby ye most resemble your Maker and are yourselves parts of eternal reality" (*GD* 125). In their explanations of the incarnation, both guides use the contrast of "descent and ascent." Beatrice says that "given his limitations, man could never make amends because he could not descend in humble obedience as far as he intended to ascend in disobedience" (*Par.* 7.97–100). MacDonald expands this concept: "Only the Greatest of all can make Himself small enough to enter into Hell. For the higher a thing is, the lower it can descend. . . . Only One has descended into Hell" (*GD* 123–24). These particular theological points are not something Virgil would have known, since he has no Christian revelation, so it has to be Beatrice who explains them.

One additional parallel that Lewis sets up between Virgil and MacDonald involves their "self-correction." Dante, in *The Divine Comedy*, attempts to distance Virgil from his medieval reputation in some quarters as a magician or a diviner. Although in ancient times people often obtained the name of a new city through sorcery, and Virgil's *Aeneid* indicates his city was named after the pagan prophetess Manto (see *Aeneid* 10.198–200), Dante has Virgil explicitly say that Mantua was named without recourse to sorcery (see *Inf.* 20.93) and warns the pilgrim not to believe any other explanation (*Inf.* 20.97–99). In a similar way, Lewis attempts to defend MacDonald against the charge of universalism, traditionally considered a heretical notion, by directly confronting the issue. When the narrator is confused about people being able to choose to remain in Grey Town (hell), he says to his guide, "In your own books, Sir, . . . you were a Universalist. You talked as if all men would be saved" (*GD* 124). Lewis has MacDonald reply, "Ye can know nothing of the end of all things. . . . It's ill talking of such questions" (*GD* 124). In both cases, the authors are rehabilitating their fictional guides in light of the historical accusations or suspicions against them.

In contrast to the main characters in Lewis's other novels so far, the protagonist of *The Great Divorce* approximates Dante's pilgrim in several unique ways: there is an overlap between the historical author and the fictional first-person narrator; there is a "teacher-son" relationship between the protagonist and his guide reflected in the author's history; and the same instruction on the nature of free will and on people's choice of their eternal abode occurs in a "purgatorial" setting. These particular similarities to Dante's pilgrim in *The Great Divorce* are not repeated elsewhere by Lewis because only here does Lewis follow Dante's use of "figura" for both his protagonist and guide.

Beatrice

Each Mountain-Dweller, and MacDonald in very specific ways, echoes Beatrice in coming come down to the Plain from heaven to try to help rescue a soul from hell. However, Lewis presents an even more distinctive Beatrice in this novel, who is not a composite of several characters but is meant to parallel Dante's Beatrice more specifically. In *The Divine Comedy*, passage through the fire on the ledge of lust is immediately followed by the pilgrim's entrance into Eden for his meeting with Beatrice. Lewis, in line with this narrative sequence, presents another version of Beatrice immediately following the ninth episode of the young man with the lizard of lust. However, unlike the continually close parallels in the episode of the young man, Lewis inverts the dialogue in Dante's scene.

For this last major episode of *The Great Divorce*, Lewis follows some of Dante's stage directions for the arrival of this Beatrice, as he does in other novels. (1) In *The Divine Comedy* Dante's pilgrim is alongside a river in the forest. Lewis's narrator in the forest *wonders* if there is a river nearby (see *GD* 106). (2) For Dante's pilgrim, a sudden light floods the forest and "the air under the green boughs seemed lit up as though by fire" (*Purg.* 29.34–35). Lewis's narrator sees in the forest that "the under-sides of the leafy branches had begun to tremble with dancing light" (*GD* 106). (3) In Dante's garden "a sweet melody was floating through the luminous air" (*Purg.* 29.22–23). In Lewis's story, the sudden, unexplained light is also accompanied by singing (see *GD* 106–7). (4) As Dante's pilgrim is about to meet Beatrice, he hears the hymn *"Asperges me"* sung "so sweetly that my mind cannot recall it or write it down" (*Purg.* 31.98–99). The song that accompanies the entrance and exit of Lewis's lady is too sublime to describe or even recall: "If I could remember their singing and write down the notes, no man who read that score would ever grow sick or old" (*GD* 106–7). (5) In Dante's poem the new light and singing set the stage for a procession preceding Beatrice's arrival. In Lewis's story, these signs likewise indicate that a "kind of procession was approaching us" (*GD* 106). (6) Beatrice is immediately preceded by "ministers and messengers of eternal life . . . scattering flowers into the air and all around" (*Purg.* 30.18, 20). Lewis's lady is preceded by "bright Spirits . . . who danced and scattered flowers—soundlessly falling, lightly drifting flowers" (*GD* 106). (7) One of the dancing ladies accompanying Beatrice "looked as if her flesh and bones were made of emerald" (*Purg.* 29.124–125). Lewis's narrator notes that all the Spirits dancing and throwing flowers are "like emeralds" (*GD* 107).

After such a specific kind of prelude, Lewis's narrator naturally has to ask his guide, "Is it? . . . is it?" (*GD* 107), meaning, of course, "Is it . . . is it Dante's Beatrice?" The question need not have been repeated twice, but perhaps Lewis had in mind Beatrice's repetition in her initial greeting when she first appears in the garden: "Ben son, ben son Beatrice" (*Purg* 30.73), meaning, "I really am, I really am Beatrice."

Lewis's lady is initially reminiscent of Beatrice because of her appearance. Love increasingly emanates from Beatrice throughout the journey, and as for Lewis's lady, "Love shone not from her face

only, but from all her limbs" (*GD* 109-110). Beatrice increasingly
shines with blinding light as well; when Lewis's lady speaks, "Her
beauty brightened so that I could hardly see anything else" (*GD* 111).

These parallels between the arrivals of Dante's Beatrice and
Lewis's lady and their appearances only serve to highlight the contrast that ensues. Although Lewis's "Beatrice" has also come to
meet a man who loved her—in this case, her husband, Frank, also
called the "Tragedian"—the dialogue differs from its prototype in
the *Purgatorio* because Lewis structures it as a complete inversion
of its pattern in Dante's poem.

Dante's Beatrice not only is but always has been a channel of
grace, and thus the atmosphere of sublimity and grandeur surrounding her entrance is consistently maintained throughout
Dante's garden scene. Lewis, on the other hand, momentarily
breaks the sublime atmosphere in his scene by the manner in
which this lady's identity is revealed. In a curt, no-nonsense style,
MacDonald tells the baffled narrator that this important person is
"someone ye'll never have heard of. Her name on earth was Sarah
Smith and she lived at Golders Green" (*GD* 107). The change in
tone serves to emphasize the fact that this heavenly lady (like all
of Lewis's Bright People) was once an ordinary, imperfect, sinful
woman. Lewis quickly resumes the sublime through the charity
and graciousness that flow forth from Sarah, but the distinction
established between this lady and Dante's Beatrice sets the stage for
the different content in the ensuing dialogue. Lewis writes in a letter that "the meeting of the 'Tragedian' with his wife is consciously
modeled on that of Dante & Beatrice at the end of the *Purgatorio*,
i.e., it is the same predicament, only going wrong. I intended readers to spot these resemblances."

In *The Divine Comedy*, Beatrice gives a severe, ironic greeting
to Dante's pilgrim: "How did you dare to climb the mount? Don't
you know that this is the place where happiness is found?" (*Purg.*
30.74–75). In contrast, Sarah's first words to her Grey Towner husband, Frank, are "Darling! At last!" (*GD* 109). Rather than challenge the newcomer's presence in this region as Beatrice does,
Sarah warmly welcomes him: "Here is all joy. Everything bids you
stay" (*GD* 116). Rather than insisting on a confession from the newcomer of his wrongdoing as Beatrice does (see *Purg.* 31.34–36), it is
Sarah who asks, "Before anything else, forgive me. For all I ever did

wrong and for all I did not do right since the first day we met, I ask your pardon" (*GD* 110). Both ladies speak as God's representatives, but Beatrice's words flow from divine justice and Sarah's words flow from divine charity.

In the course of her conversation with her husband, Sarah recapitulates and clarifies a statement made by Beatrice in the *Inferno* about being impervious to hell. Beatrice tells Virgil, "God has made me in such a way, by his grace, that your misery does not affect me" (*Inf.* 2.91–92). Sarah, in terms of her husband, is likewise "untouched by his misery" (*GD* 120). However, neither in her case nor in Beatrice's does this attitude represent cold-heartedness or lack of pity. Sarah tells her husband, "You made yourself really wretched. That you can still do. But you can no longer communicate your wretchedness. . . . Our light can swallow up your darkness: but your darkness cannot now infect our light" (*GD* 118). In the end, Beatrice succeeds in her mission of rescuing the lost pilgrim while Sarah does not. The reason Sarah and Beatrice, however, can remain unmoved by hell's misery is that the ultimate condition of human beings, as both Lewis and Dante firmly insist, is the result of the deliberately conscious choices they make.

Beatrice and the participants in the garden procession walk away to the sounds of a heavenly song (see *Purg.* 32.33). As Sarah moves away with the Bright Spirits, they sing a paraphrase of Psalm 91 that is applied to and personalized for Sarah (see *GD* 119–20).

Sarah is clearly shaped to recall Beatrice, but in a much more specific way than the Mountain-Dwellers and MacDonald. In *The Great Divorce*, Lewis offers the most complex and multidimensional presentation of some of the many ways a Beatrician figure can function.

Conclusion

One commentator on *The Great Divorce* says that the novel's "connections with Dante are rather remote and tenuous." That statement can be challenged on several levels, and most Lewis scholars at least acknowledge the obvious direct allusions. However, the connection goes far beyond the surface links. Lewis adapts the setting, the teachings, the narrative structure, and some episodes and characters primarily from Dante's *Purgatorio*, while the composite characters of the Bus-Driver, the Mountain-Dwellers, the burning angel, and MacDonald create echoes from all three parts of Dante's poem.

Lewis's novel recaptures the heart of Dante's poem through its focus on free will, which they both underscore by two similar narrative techniques. First, the teaching in Dante's poem on love and free will occurs when the pilgrim is on the stairs that separate the ledges of perverted love and disordered love; similarly, the teaching on free will in Lewis's novel occurs between the first group of episodes of perverted love and the second group of episodes of disordered love. Second, Dante's presentation on free will occurs in cantos 16–18 of the *Purgatorio*, which are numerically the central cantos of the whole poem. Likewise, Lewis's teaching on free will is strategically located in the middle pages of the novel at the heart of his story. For both authors, these narrative techniques are often-unnoticed structural articulations, in addition to their verbalizations, of their central message on free will.

As is the case with Lewis's hell in *The Screwtape Letters*, the spiritual world in this novel is not meant to be his speculation about the afterlife: MacDonald warns the narrator at the end, "Give no poor fool the pretext to think ye are claiming knowledge of what no mortal knows" (*GD* 127). Lewis's imaginary afterlife, like Dante's, is meant to illuminate what occurs in *this* world.

Although *The Divine Comedy* is present in all of Lewis's fiction, Dante's poem does indeed come to the fore more obviously in this work than in Lewis's other novels. On this basis, scholars have called this novel Lewis's *Divine Comedy*, with one scholar even calling it "a miniature replica" of Dante's poem. It is true that his use of Dante's poem is more visible in this novel: it is the only novel that takes place in the afterlife; the biographical details of the protagonist, who has a Virgil-like guide, overlap with those of Lewis; it has several Beatrice figures, and its main message is free will and its implications for a person's eternal state. Lewis uses Dante's poem in a wide variety of ways here that are not duplicated in his other novels, but, conversely, his other novels make use of Dante's poem in other ways not seen here. For that reason I maintain that it is *all* of his fiction, and not just this novel, that constitutes Lewis's *Divine Comedy*.

CHAPTER EIGHT

The Chronicles of Narnia

Introduction

When Lewis published his adult fantasy novel, *The Great Divorce*, no one could have anticipated—including Lewis himself—that he, at that time an unmarried scholar of medieval and Renaissance literature, would ever write anything for children, but the next books he published were The Chronicles of Narnia (1950–1956). In addition, Lewis never had any intention of writing a series. In a 1957 letter to a young fan, Lewis notes, "When I wrote *The Lion* I did not know I was going to write any more. Then I wrote *P. Caspian* as a sequel and still didn't think there would be any more, and when I had done the *Voyage* I felt quite sure it would be the last. But I found I was wrong."

In an essay in *Of Other Worlds*, Lewis writes, "All my seven Narnian books . . . began with seeing pictures in my head." These pictures included a faun with an umbrella, a queen on a sledge, and other characters and scenes that are now familiar to readers of the series. As "these images sorted themselves into events (that is, became a story) they seemed to demand no love interest and no close psychology," which led Lewis to note that "the Form which excludes these things is the fairy tale." The images Lewis discusses in the essay all found expression in the first book of the series, *The Lion, the Witch and the Wardrobe*, so on one level there was no need for more Narnia stories. According to Lewis, however, the series came about because Aslan, the integrating factor for the first novel, "pulled the six other Narnian stories in after Him." Somehow, after Lewis had written the first story, The Chronicles of Narnia seemed to take on a life of their own.

In this series, a total of eight different children (in a variety of combinations) are magically transported from Earth to Narnia, a land of talking animals ruled by the lion Aslan (the Narnian deity), whose inhabitants include traditional fairy-tale characters such as giants, witches, and dwarfs. Because of its courtly, chivalrous atmosphere, many scholars have noted connections between The Chronicles of Narnia and Edmund Spenser's *Faerie Queene* (1590–1596). There are also echoes of Thomas Malory's *Le Morte d'Arthur* (1485) whose atmosphere Lewis describes as "aristocratic" and "noble." A more recent, innovative approach has been to read the Narnia Chronicles as based on the seven heavens of the Ptolemaic universe. At first glance, Lewis's fairy tales would seem unlikely to have any connection to *The Divine Comedy*, a complex medieval poem about the afterlife filled with philosophical and theological discourse. However, the parallels to biblical events in Lewis's stories are narrated according to the same typological approach used by Dante, and two of the novels in this series include journey patterns and scenes taken directly from *The Divine Comedy*.

Narnia and Its Inhabitants

Lewis's imaginary world differs from most fairy-tale worlds in three respects: its location, its time frame, and the quality of its magic phenomena. In most fairy tales, as the genre is generally understood, the setting is Earth, and the story is distanced imaginatively through the indefiniteness of time and place; for example, "Once upon a time, there lived a king. . . ." Lewis's Narnia, on the other hand, is a country in a world that exists alongside our own universe in another dimension as a separate cosmos.

Second, the time frame in most fairy tales is generally restricted to particular events in the lives of the major characters, but Lewis's stories span 2,555 years of Narnian time. Due to the time disparity between Earth and Narnia—a month or 1,000 years may pass in Narnia during a single year on Earth—the entire history of the Narnian universe is able to unfold during the course of the 52 years that span the children's visits.

Third, the supernatural phenomena in Narnia differ fundamentally from the magic in most fairy tales in which magic is fanciful or arbitrary; for example, a frog becomes a prince or vice versa, and the power at work is never explained. In contrast, the magic that appears in Lewis's imaginary cosmos, like other aspects of Lewis's story, is grounded in the Christian theological system that underlies his fictive world.

Lewis's handling of the magic in Narnia parallels the approach Dante uses for handling supernatural phenomena in *The Divine Comedy*. In addition to the obvious supernatural framework of the afterlife in Dante's poem, the supernatural incidents there are always designed to reflect Christian principles and truths. When the angel in *Inferno* 9, for instance, comes to open the gate of Dis that leads to lower hell and is blocked by rebellious spirits, it is not the small wand he holds that overpowers hell's resistance but the authority and power of heaven (see *Inf.* 9.89–90). When Dante's pilgrim is mysteriously transported from the purgatorial plain to the inaccessible gate of Mount Purgatory as he sleeps (see *Purg.* 9.55–57), it is Lucia, representing grace, who carries him and not some arbitrary magical power. As Dante's pilgrim flies effortlessly up through the heavens, it is not magic but "the innate and perpetual thirst for God's realm [that] carried us upward" (*Par.* 2.19–20), or the law of "spiritual gravity," so to speak, that draws him up toward God.

Similarly, the supernatural phenomena in Narnia also have spiritual and moral significance. Narnian magic is shaped to be consistent with the invisible spiritual forces that fill our own world, according to Christian doctrine. Susan's horn to summon help in times of national crisis or Lucy's healing vial—unlike golden keys, magic stones, and so forth—are not primarily for the benefit of their owners. The magical objects given to the children—like talents given to human beings—are intended for the good of others. When the creature-statues are restored to life in *The Lion, the Witch and the Wardrobe*, it is not by magic incantations but by the breath of the Narnian deity as he breathes on each one, reminiscent of the manner of God's creation of Adam in Genesis. The occasional physical transformations that occur in this series are not due to arbitrary spells or tricks, but are instead manifestations of spiritual reality. The insolent students in a classroom in *Prince Caspian* are turned into pigs because they are brutish at heart; Eustace becomes a dragon in *The Voyage of the "Dawn Treader"* because he is a greedy little boy; Rabadash becomes a donkey in *The Horse and His Boy* because he is a stubborn, unrepentant fool. Their transformations are in line with Dante's *contrapasso* for sinners, a punishment that fits the sin, and reflect exactly who they have chosen to be.

The "evil magic" in Narnia is likewise an analogue for spiritual reality. The White Queen in *The Lion, the Witch and the Wardrobe* can turn living creatures into statues—evil can rob creatures of their vital life force—but she cannot change a man into a frog or a faun into a bird. When at one point in that story she turns herself into a stump and a dwarf into a boulder, the narrator states that "it was part of her magic that she could *make things look like what they weren't*" (italics added). Her power is purely negative, not creative; she can spoil and plunder what exists or create false impressions, but she cannot recreate or change the fundamental essences of things. When she brings cold, snow, and ice to Narnia, she deprives the land of warmth. Like the good phenomena in Narnia, evil supernatural phenomena are structured to reflect the spiritual and moral forces operative in our universe, and, as such, there is a philosophical and theological cohesiveness to such occurrences in Narnia, just as there is in Dante's poem.

The Chronicles of Narnia also recall *The Divine Comedy* in the way Lewis makes use of biblical material. Unlike Milton, for example, who in *Paradise Lost* imaginatively dramatizes and expands the biblical story of humanity's fall but adheres to the specific narrative details recorded in Genesis, Dante does not retell or dramatize biblical events. Instead, he follows the typological approach of biblical narratives that prefigures or repeats the central significance of a biblical event but under different circumstances.

The *New Bible Dictionary* defines "typology" as "a way of setting forth the biblical history of salvation so that some of its earlier phases are seen as anticipations of later phases, or some later phase as the recapitulation or fulfillment of an earlier one." According to this approach, which was used primarily by church fathers and some medieval writers, events and biblical personages in salvation history are interrelated in terms of *prefigurement, fulfillment,* and *reenactment.* Moses, as he leads the people from Egypt to the Promised Land, *prefigures* Christ who leads people to spiritual freedom; the New Testament disciple Stephen *reenacts* Christ's death as he forgives those who unjustly put him to death (see Acts 7:54–60).

In both cases, the *spiritual* significance of a major event is repeated, although the circumstances and details are new, and the narration is designed to recall its prototype.

In *The Divine Comedy*, Dante presents his pilgrim's journey as a *reenactment* of the Israelites' Exodus journey from slavery to freedom. Beatrice explains the pilgrim's otherworldly journey by saying, "It has been granted to him to come *from Egypt to see Jerusalem*" (*Par.* 25.55–56; italics added). For medieval exegetes, the concept of the Exodus was applicable not only to the history of Moses leading the Israelites out of bondage, but also to any soul as it forsakes its bondage to sin for the free salvation offered by Christ. Near the end of the poem, Dante's pilgrim acknowledges to Beatrice that through her guidance, "you have led me from bondage to freedom" (*Par.* 31.85). Dante likewise structures the arrival of souls at the shore of Mount Purgatory as a *reenactment* of the Exodus. They are all singing Psalm 114—"When Israel went forth from Egypt" (see *Purg.* 2.46)—a psalm of praise to God for deliverance during the Exodus. In a spiritual reenactment of the Israelites' journey, these souls have spiritually left the corruption and bondage of this world and are now journeying to the Promised Land of the heavenly Jerusalem. In another fascinating example, when Dante's pilgrim journeys up to the heavens and sees heavenly visions, he is *reenacting* the journey of St. Paul into the heavens (see 2 Cor. 12.2–4) and the purpose of his visions is similar.

Dante's poem also imaginatively *prefigures* an event referred to in John's Revelation: the Last Judgment. His fictive afterlife could be called a "preliminary look," so to speak, at the eternal state of souls after the event that John speaks about occurs. When human beings, according to John, are given their rewards or punishments at time of judgment, things will of course not look like the afterlife in *The Divine Comedy*, but Dante is projecting a possible scenario of the bliss of heaven and the pains of hell that John prophesies will occur.

Lewis uses this same narrative technique in recounting the overall pattern of Narnia's history whenever it reflects events in Earth's biblical salvation history. *The Magician's Nephew* (1955) recounts the creation of Narnia; *The Horse and His Boy* (1954) recounts an Exodus story of a young boy's escape from servitude to freedom; *The Lion, the Witch and the Wardrobe* (1950) presents the death and resurrection of the Creator-King of Narnia; *The Last*

Battle (1956) tells of the apocalyptic end of the Narnian universe. The other three novels in the series—*Prince Caspian* (1951), *The Voyage of the "Dawn Treader"* (1952), *The Silver Chair* (1953)— recount adventures that occur between the resurrection of Narnia's Creator and the destruction of Narnia and contain allusions to other biblical events.

Lewis, like Dante, reenacts and prefigures Narnian events in a way that is meant to recall their particular biblical prototypes. Lewis's *reenactments* of the essence of biblical events are not to be confused with allegories of those events—and Lewis continually protested that they were not allegories. Allegories would entail a strict one-to-one correspondence with the details from the original event, but Lewis's reenactments, in line with typological narratives, include new or different details that do not correspond with the biblical details. Narnia, for instance, is created *ex nihilo* by a pre-existent Creator—the essence of the creation event in Genesis—but Narnia is sung, not spoken, into existence, in less than one day, not six, and Narnian creation culminates with the appearance of Talking Beasts rather than human beings. In *The Horse and His Boy*, the Narnian deity reveals his identity as "Myself" to a young boy on the top of a mountain. Lewis's story here reenacts the substance of God's self-revelation to Moses as "I AM" on top of Mount Sinai (see Exod. 3:14), but this is a new instance of God's self-revelation with different details. Although the young boy Shasta helps rescue his people from an attack, he is not their leader, and Aslan repeats his identifying name as "Myself" three times in succession, perhaps to reflect the Christian Trinity and as an echo of the Old Testament "I AM" said three times.

Lewis likewise imaginatively *prefigures* certain future events recorded in John's Revelation. This occurs primarily in *The Last Battle*, in which the appearance of a false Aslan near the end of Narnian history is an imaginary prefigurement, a fictional version, of the appearance of an Antichrist figure foretold in Revelation 13. In a letter, Lewis explains that "the Ape and Puzzle, just before the last Judgment (in the *Last Battle*) are like the coming of Antichrist before the end of our world." Lewis also presents a variation on Christ's parable of the Last Judgment recorded in Matthew 25:33 foretelling that he will place the sheep (the righteous) at his right hand and the goats (evildoers) at his left. When, at the end of Narnian history, all creatures appear before Aslan and gaze into his face, good creatures move to Aslan's right and enter into his kingdom, while wicked creatures move to Aslan's left and go into the outer darkness. This echoes the essence of the event in the parable but with different details. This same narrative procedure applies to some characters in *The Divine Comedy*. Beatrice is the character who is shaped to reenact Christ in the poem. Like Christ, she can descend into hell to effect salvation for a lost soul (see *Inf.* 2.53–74; *Par.* 31.80–81). Like Christ who will judge each soul, she can judge the pilgrim for his sin (see *Purg.* 31.34–36). She can quote Jesus' words at the Last Supper (Jn. 16:16) about soon not seeing her any longer and apply it to herself (see *Purg.* 33.10–12). Like Christ, in whose face shines "the light of the knowledge of the glory of God" (2 Cor. 4:6), her face shines and dispenses that same knowledge to Dante's pilgrim throughout the *Paradiso*.

Now we come to Lewis's significant exception in this whole scheme. Aslan is *not* a typological reenactment of Christ. He is not an allegory of Christ, or a symbol of Christ, or a Christ-figure, or a representative of Christ, or a mirror of Christ, or an echo of Christ. Lewis describes Aslan in one of his letters as "an invention giving an imaginary answer to the question, 'What might Christ become like if there really were a world like Narnia and He chose to be incarnate and die and rise again in *that* world as He actually has done in ours?'" The direct identification between Aslan and Christ is made clear in *The Voyage of the "Dawn Treader"*—which Lewis thought would be the last book in the series—when Aslan reveals that on Earth, "I have another name. You must learn to know me by that name" (*VDT* 273). The conclusion to all this is that Christ—God and man on Earth—now becomes God and lion in Narnia; the fictional character Aslan speaks and acts like the historical Jesus because he *is* Christ under different circumstances. In fact, Lewis relates that in writing *The Lion, the Witch and the Wardrobe*, "I don't think I foresaw what Aslan was going to do. . . . I think He just insisted on behaving . . . in His own way . . . and the whole series became Christian." (Note that Lewis capitalizes "He" and "His" in that statement.) And indeed, as Lewis states elsewhere, "The whole Narnian story is about Christ."

On the other hand, Lewis does narrate some of Aslan's *actions* as reenactments of Christ's actions in the typological mode. Christ comes to earth from his Father in Heaven, and Aslan comes to Narnia from his Father in the Utter East. When Aslan offers himself as a substitute sacrifice, dies, and is resurrected in *The Lion, the Witch and the Wardrobe*, he is put to death by a witch and her cohorts, not by a Roman governor and soldiers; he is killed with a knife, rather than being crucified, and he dies for the sake of a single person rather than for all human beings. Just as Christ descended into hell to set the captives free (see 1 Pet. 3:19, 4:6), so too, after his resurrection, Aslan invades the White Queen's dwelling and sets her captives free, causing the destruction of her castle's gates as he exits and demonstrating that her gates cannot prevail or hold out against him (see Matt. 16:18). Lewis's narration of these and many other actions is meant to recall their biblical prototypes, but these new events with different details are not reproducing the original event in an allegorical fashion.

Despite the exception of his unique characterization of Aslan, Lewis's use of the typological narrative technique produces fairy tales that avoid being either a literal retelling or an allegorical presentation of the biblical stories. Like Dante's poem, Lewis's stories include events that become other examples, in time and space, of God's saving action in history (although in the history of a fictional universe) that find their prototypes in the Bible.

Dantean Journeys in Narnia

All seven novels in Lewis's series involve journey stories with children traveling to Narnia or within Narnia. Occasional echoes of Dante's poem are found throughout the series, but the most significant echoes occur mainly in two particular stories. *The Voyage of the "Dawn Treader"* (1952) adapts material from both the *Purgatorio* and the *Paradiso*, while *The Silver Chair* (1953) contains frequent parallels to scenes in the *Inferno*.

The Voyage of the "Dawn Treader": A Dantean Journey to Narnia's Utter East

In *The Voyage of the "Dawn Treader,"* King Caspian and his Narnian crew are joined by Lucy, Edmund, and Eustace as they sail east in search of seven lords who were exiled during the reign of wicked King Miraz. East is the location of Aslan's country, Narnia's equivalent of heaven, so an eastern journey in this context equates a journey toward heaven. First, the Narnians sail to three charted islands that belong to Narnia and then to six uncharted islands. In the second part of the journey, they sail beyond the last island to the Utter East, where no one has sailed before. At the end, the valiant mouse Reepicheep enters into Aslan's country, Lucy and Eustace are sent back to Earth by Aslan, and the rest of the Narnian crew sails home.

Certain parallels can be made to other adventurous sea journeys that explore unknown regions—like the journeys of Jason, Odysseus, Aeneas, and many medieval seafarers. The hero of the *Odyssey* is mentioned once by his Roman name, Ulysses (see *VDT* 264), but the overall structure of Lewis's novel is not Homeric. *The Voyage of the "Dawn Treader"* is linear, while much of the *Odyssey* is told through flashbacks, and the episodes of Lewis's novel do not clearly correspond to or recall the episodes of Homer's epic. Instead, the first part of this Narnian journey recalls the journey in the *Purgatorio*, while the second part creatively replicates journey events in the *Paradiso*.

Once the Earth children join the Narnian ship already en route, the geographical scheme of the islands that remain to be visited—three Narnian islands and six uncharted islands—generally parallels the division and structure of Dante's purgatory. The first three islands, the Lone Islands, evoke ante-purgatory, the area surrounding the base of Mount Purgatory that is reserved for those who repented late. One section of ante-purgatory is set aside for negligent or failed rulers (see *Purg.* 7.90–136), and it is on one of the Lone Islands that the travelers come upon a negligent ruler, Governor Gumpas, under whose watch "everything in the islands was done in a slovenly, slouching manner" (*VDT* 54).

Each of the next six islands is located farther and farther east, thus recalling on a horizontal level the vertical design of Dante's mountain ledges located higher and higher up. Forward movement in each respective journey means increasing proximity to heaven. Just as Dante's pilgrim is purified of one particular evil inclination on each ledge, so the Narnian crew generally overcomes some kind of evil on each island, be it evil from within or from without. Although

Lewis does not duplicate Dante's purgatorial scheme of the seven cardinal sins in this children's book, three instances overlap. On Deathwater Island, where the water turns everything to gold, the entire scouting party temporarily comes under an overwhelming temptation to avarice (Dante's fifth ledge on Mount Purgatory), and on the Island of the Voices, Lucy, as she is reading the Magician's Book, is tempted to pride and envy (Dante's first and second ledges).

The stars in this new region constitute another echo of Dante's purgatory. When Dante's pilgrim first looks up at the sky on the island of Mount Purgatory, he "saw four stars never seen before" (*Purg.* 1.23–24). Similarly, for the Narnians, "There rose in the east new constellations which no one had ever seen in Narnia and perhaps . . . no living eye had seen at all" (*VDT* 206).

The correspondence between the *Purgatorio* and the first half of this Narnian journey is made more explicit through the major episode involving Eustace's physical and moral transformation, because it condenses several experiences of Dante's pilgrim on the mount.

The island in this episode, which they later name Dragon Island, visually recalls Dante's Island of Purgatory with its lofty mountain in Earth's *southern* hemisphere. Lewis's Dragon Island has "a *very high mountain* . . . off to the *southeast*" (*VDT* 79; italics added). When Dante's pilgrim first looks at Mount Purgatory, "its summit was so high it could not be seen" (*Purg.* 4.40); as for the mountain ridge with its "steep ascent" on Lewis's Dragon Island, "you could not see their tops" (*VDT* 80).

Up to this point, Eustace has consistently acted spoiled and self-centered. Attempting to escape from doing his share of the work with the rest of the crew, he climbs a mountain and falls asleep in a dead dragon's cave, but he wakes up to an unexpected change: "Sleeping on a dragon's hoard with greedy, dragonish thoughts in his heart, he had become a dragon himself" (*VDT* 96).

Eustace's adventures after this transformation parallel the purification experience of Dante's pilgrim during the ascent of the mount. In *The Divine Comedy* the seven P's (*peccatum*, "sin") inscribed on the pilgrim's forehead at the gate of Mount Purgatory are the outward signs of the seven sinful inclinations in his—and every person's—heart. In Lewis's story, Eustace likewise now has a visible outward sign of the sin in his heart, his dragon body.

The reversal of Eustace's condition is accomplished when Aslan leads him to the top of a mountain where "there was a garden—trees and fruit and everything. In the middle of it there was a well" (*VDT* 114). Although Eustace describes it in children's vocabulary, the area evokes the Garden of Eden at the summit of Dante's mount with its trees, fruit, and streams. It is in this setting that Eustace is purged or cleansed. First, the outward sign of Eustace's sin, his dragon skin, is removed. That procedure parallels the pattern of the repeated removal of the visible sign of sin in the *Purgatorio*: Dante's pilgrim experiences the removal of a "P" each time he leaves a ledge to ascend a new one. Eustace repeatedly strips off his dragon skin—in his case, only to find another dragon skin underneath. For Dante's pilgrim, the removal of the last "P" is for the first time accompanied by extreme pain (see *Purg.* 27.49–51). In a similar way, the removal of Eustace's last dragon skin by Aslan "hurt worse than anything I've ever felt" (*VDT* 116).

Eustace's restoration also occurs in a manner similar to that of Dante's pilgrim, a point that has been noticed by some scholars. A heavenly agent, Matilda, immerses Dante's pilgrim in the waters at the top of the Mount (see *Purg.* 31.94–102 and *Purg.* 33.124–138). Similarly, a heavenly agent, Aslan, immerses Eustace in the pool at the top of a mountain. Dante's pilgrim emerges from the stream of Eunoë "remade" (*Purg.* 33.142: "rifatto"). Eustace likewise emerges from this mountain pool literally "remade," because the water "turned [him] into a boy again" (*VDT* 117). In Dante's poem, physical cleansing signifies inner cleansing and restoration, and similarly, for Eustace, from this point on he "began to be a different boy. . . . The cure had begun" (*VDT* 120). Lewis's use of the word *cure* here echoes Dante's description of the effects of sin as "wounds" ("piaghe") that need healing and of Mount Purgatory as "the mountain that heals souls" (*Par.* 17.20).

In addition to clear links with the *Purgatorio* so far, two distinct echoes from the *Inferno* occur as the first phase of this journey concludes. In a situational parallel, as the Narnians arrive at the *ninth* and *last* island, Ramandu's island, their experience is similar to that of Dante's pilgrim as he arrives at the *ninth* and *last* circle of hell. In the *Inferno*, Dante's pilgrim thinks he sees *towers* when he is actually looking at *giants*, and *trees* are obliquely referenced when one of the giant's faces (Nimrod) is compared to a large pine-cone sculpture (see *Inf*. 31.58–59). As the Narnian scouting party approaches this ninth island and sees tall perpendicular shapes in the distance, Caspian asks if they are *trees*, Eustace thinks they are *towers*, and Edmund says they might be *giants* (see *VDT* 208–9). The mysterious objects are actually huge pillars around an open-air banquet table, but their misperception of distant objects as well as the combination of *trees, towers*, and *giants* hardly seems random on Lewis's part given the similar narrative context. As one Lewis scholar has remarked, "Randomness is not a characteristic feature of [Lewis's mind]."

The second clear echo from the *Inferno* occurs when the Narnians come upon three sleeping lords at the banquet table on this island. The island is called the World's End because no one has ever sailed beyond this point, and this recalls the situation of Dante's Ulysses in the *Inferno*. Dante's story of Ulysses' last journey and his death by drowning, recounted in *Inferno* 26.90–142, seems to have no literary or historical precedent and to have been Dante's invention. Dante gives over the narration of these events to the character of Ulysses himself, and it includes the speech he gave to stir up his elderly crew to explore uncharted waters: "During this short time that remains to our senses, do not deny yourselves the experience of seeing the unpeopled world behind the sun. Consider your origin: you were not meant to live like brutes but to seek after virtue and knowledge" (*Inf*. 26.114–120).

Lewis's sleepers paraphrase that very speech. When Caspian tries to shake the sleeping lords awake, one of the lords mumbles in truncated phrases, "Weren't born to live like animals. Get to the east while you've a chance—lands behind the sun" (*VDT* 212). Ramandu's daughter later quotes one lord's speech more fully: "We are men and Telmarines, not brutes. What should we do but seek adventure after adventure? We have not long to live in any event. Let us spend what is left in seeking the unpeopled world behind the sunrise" (*VDT* 218).

Lewis inserts this last echo from the *Inferno* at the precise point in his story when the Narnians are themselves about to travel to unpeopled regions. In the *Inferno*, Ulysses recounts that he and his crew sailed past the pillars of Hercules, which the ancients believed were the boundaries set by the gods beyond which no ships were meant to sail (see *Inf*. 26.107–109). Sailing south, they saw the

Island of Purgatory in the distance, but since the only legitimate access to purgatory is through repentance before death, they and their ship were destroyed by a whirlpool that sank them. In contrast, the Narnian crew will also sail "beyond the world," but not because of their curiosity and willful desires like Ulysses did. They too will pass the pillars on the island of the World's End—Lewis mentions "pillars" here four times (*VDT* 209–10, 216, 257)—but they will sail by the will of heaven, because one of Aslan's servants, Ramandu, assigns them that task (see *VDT* 225–26).

With reminiscences of the *Inferno* and the *Purgatorio* now behind, the second phase of the Narnian sea voyage shifts to a duplication of many features of the journey in the *Paradiso*. Its goal is the Utter East—the Narnian heaven—and it too concludes with visions of the deity. In adapting events in the *Paradiso* to shape this phase of the Narnian journey, Lewis uses a procedure that I would call "transpositional" or "incarnational": Lewis takes what is metaphoric and symbolic in Dante's *Paradiso* and makes it literal in his story.

This procedure is already somewhat in play from the beginning of the story when the entire Narnian sea voyage makes literal Dante's ship metaphors in *The Divine Comedy*. Dante uses ship metaphors to refer to his spiritual journey (and to the process of writing the poem). At the beginning of the *Purgatorio*, Dante tells his readers that "the small ship of my wit now hoists her sails" (*Purg.* 1.1–2), as he is about to recount his pilgrim's ascent of the mount. The Narnians are literally sailing into territory that reflects a horizontal layout of Mount Purgatory. In the *Paradiso*, Dante warns those who continue to follow that "the water I now sail has never been sailed before" (*Par.* 2.7). As the *Dawn Treader* begins the second phase of its journey, the Narnian ship is, of course, similarly headed into uncharted waters that have never been sailed before. Dante's pilgrim now travels into the heavens beyond this world, and the Narnian crew members likewise "began to feel that they had already sailed beyond the world" (*VDT* 238).

Lewis narrates much of the rest of the journey for the *Dawn Treader* crew "incarnating" journey patterns in *Paradiso*.

(1) Dante's pilgrim travels effortlessly up into the heavens, drawn upward by the *spiritual* force of his desire for the heavenly kingdom (see *Par.* 2.19–20). The Narnian crew also travels effortlessly because

they are caught in a strong current, so that "without wind . . . the *Dawn Treader* glided smoothly east" (*VDT* 257). As they get closer to the Utter East in a smaller boat, "There was no need to row, for the current drifted them steadily" (*VDT* 267).

(2) When Dante's pilgrim first rises up from the earth, the light increases so that it seems "as though God had adorned heaven with another sun" (*Par*. 1.63), and it continues to increase thereafter. The increase of light for the Narnians is due to the sun's *literal* increase in size: "The sun when it came up each morning looked twice, if not three times, its usual size" (*VDT* 238), and by the end of the journey the sun is actually "now five or six times its old size" (*VDT* 252). In both stories, the increasing light indicates an increasing proximity to the deity's location.

(3) Since Beatrice has the ability to stare at the sun as they rise from sphere to sphere, the pilgrim compares her to an eagle (see *Par*. 1.47–48). As for the Narnians' ability to stare at the sun, "Their eyes had . . . by now grown as strong as eagles' [eyes]" (*VDT* 260).

(4) Beatrice's appearance becomes brighter and brighter as she moves up through the spheres. Likewise, as the Narnians sail farther east, "their own faces and bodies became brighter and brighter" (*VDT* 251–52).

(5) When Dante's pilgrim sees light in the form of a river in the Empyrean, Beatrice tells him to drink from it (see *Par*. 30.73), so "the eaves of my eyelids drank it in" (*Par*. 30.88–89). This finds its parallel in Lewis's story when the Narnians actually drink the water they are sailing through, water that is "like light more than anything else. . . . Drinkable light" (*VDT* 251).

(6) The increasing light strengthens the capacity of Dante's pilgrim to withstand even more light from sphere to sphere. The capacity of Lewis's travelers to withstand more light increases as they drink this water, so that when "the light grew no less—if anything, it increased . . . they could bear it" (*VDT* 251).

(7) Dante's pilgrim, gazing upon a symbolic river of light in the Empyrean, is strengthened for the true vision of the court of heaven. He compares that assembly to a white rose (see *Par*. 30.1) with a golden center because the redeemed, wearing white robes, are seated in circular rows gazing at the golden point of light representing God. The Narnian crew, having drunk the water for a number of days, sail through an area that recalls Dante's flower image,

because the water here is completely covered by flowers with white petals: "Whiteness, shot with faintest colour of gold, spread round them on every side" (*VDT* 260). When Dante's pilgrim looks at the entire assembly of the redeemed, he exclaims, "How vast that gathering in white robes is" (*Par.* 30.129) and "How vast is this rose to its outer petals!" (*Par.* 30.116–117). Similarly for the Narnians, as they look around, "there seemed no end" to the white flowers (*VDT* 261).

(8) Dante uses lilies as a metaphor for the apostles he sees in the sphere of Fixed Stars (see *Par.* 23.75), and the Narnian crew compares the unnamed flowers they are sailing through to lilies (see *VDT* 259–61).

(9) When the pilgrim seems to see all of creation in God (see *Par.* 33.85–87), Dante's narrator notes the difficulty of remembering what he saw and compares that moment to "the very moment . . . that made Neptune wonder in amazement at the shadow of the *Argo*" (*Par.* 33.94, 96). (Dante is referring to Jason's *Argo*, the first ship ever built, and he invents the notion that Neptune was startled by the shadow it cast in the water.) Dante's allusion becomes literal in Lewis's novel, when Lucy observes Sea People "coming up to find out the meaning of this big, black thing which had come between them and the sun" (*VDT* 245). The Sea Ladies' faces "were filled with astonishment. Lucy felt sure they had never seen a ship or a human before" (*VDT* 246).

(10) Dante's pilgrim sees God as "living light" (*Par.* 33.109). In Lewis's story, in which water often parallels Dante's light, the scouting party comes upon what could be called living water: "a long tall wave—a wave endlessly fixed in one place" (*VDT* 267) through which they can gaze at Aslan's country, which lies behind it.

(11) Dante's pilgrim sees three circles of different colors in that living light and describes the interrelationship of the first two circles with a rainbow simile (see *Par.* 33.116–119). Lewis's travelers, gazing at the upright wave, watch as it "turned into wonderful rainbow colors" (*VDT* 267).

(12) Dante's pilgrim attempts to understand how the image of man can dwell in the Godhead, but is suddenly halted because his mind is no longer adequate to take in the vision (see *Par.* 33.139). The Narnian voyagers, gazing beyond the living water, are also halted, for "at that moment, with a crunch, the boat ran aground. The water was too shallow now for it" (*VDT* 269). What is too deep

for the mind of Dante's pilgrim is, in a converse parallel, too shallow even for the smaller Narnian scouting boat.

(13) Dante's symbolic vision of the three circles representing the Trinity is followed by a mystical understanding of the incarnation when he seems to see a human form united to the Godhead (see *Par.* 33.129–131). Lucy and Edmund likewise see a symbolic vision of the Narnian deity when Aslan appears first as a Lamb, and—like the pattern in all of Dante's symbolic visions—this first vision prepares the pilgrims for the true vision that follows. The Lamb's "snowy white flushed into tawny gold and his size changed and he was Aslan himself" (*VDT* 271–72).

(14) The journey of Dante's pilgrim ends with his union with God, and he will return to Earth to live a wiser life than he had before. The children's final vision of the Narnian deity likewise signals the culmination of their adventures, and they also return to Earth, now better prepared to live life here because of their experiences there.

There is almost no invention of material on Lewis's part here. The invention lies in his embodiment or conversion of Dantean material in the *Paradiso* onto a literal and physical level for a children's story. In one of his essays, Lewis quotes and agrees with T. S. Eliot that "the last canto of the *Paradiso* . . . is the highest point that poetry has ever reached." More than half of the fourteen points listed above come from the very last canto of *The Divine Comedy*.

Lewis states that *The Voyage of the "Dawn Treader"* represents "the spiritual life," so with its clear echoes of Dante's *Purgatorio* and *Paradiso*, Lewis is paying high tribute to Dante as having laid out a literary pattern for depicting spiritual life. Since Lewis thought that this story would be the last in the series, it is here that Aslan, who at the end appears first as a lamb and then as a lion, identifies himself as the Jesus of this world. However, had it indeed been the last story, it is significant that Lewis made sure to incorporate solid echoes of Dante in what he thought would be the end of a much shorter series.

The Silver Chair: A Dantean Journey to the Underworld

Oddly enough—or perhaps not—the very next story in the series that Lewis thought was already completed has multiple echoes of the *Inferno*, which had enjoyed only brief echoes in *The*

Voyage of the "Dawn Treader." The Silver Chair, unlike any other of the Narnian stories, involves a journey to the underworld. A reader might be reminded of earlier heroes who had contact with or journeyed through the underworld (Ulysses, Aeneas, and so on), and the book's title brings to mind the enchanted silver chairs that hold heroes captive in Circe's home (*Odyssey,* 10.353–355) or in Proserpina's garden in Spenser's *Faerie Queene* (2.7.53). Nevertheless, this story also bears several similarities to the journey in Dante's *Inferno,* since it involves a journey to an underworld kingdom with an evil ruler.

In this story, Jill, Eustace, and their Marshwiggle guide, Puddleglum, are assigned by Aslan to rescue the missing Narnian Prince Rilian, who disappeared in his quest for the serpent who poisoned and killed his mother. Their mission leads them first to the north of Narnia and then down into the underworld, where the Green Lady, the Queen of Underland (also called the Deep Realm), is keeping the prince captive through deceptive enchantment. They succeed in rescuing Rilian from the queen's spell, after which he kills the queen, and in bringing Rilian home to Narnia as its rightful heir.

The first unmistakable reminiscence of Dante's poem occurs when the children, during the beginning of their northward journey, come upon giants in a rocky gorge. Lewis again uses the scene from *Inferno* 31 when Dante's pilgrim comes upon the giant guardians of the ninth circle that he briefly echoes in *The Voyage of the "Dawn Treader"* when the Narnians approach the ninth island. Lewis parallels that scene more fully here. (1) Dante's pilgrim first has a mistaken perception of the giants: "They seemed to me like many high towers" (*Inf.* 31.20). Lewis's travelers likewise initially perceive the objects on the edge of the gorge as "little towers of rocks." (2) Dante's giants, buried upright in the bank that surrounds the ninth circle of hell, are visible only from the waist up. Lewis's giants, like their Dantean counterparts, are similarly visible from the mid-chest up as they lean their elbows on the gorge (see *SC* 80). (3) Dante's raging Ephialtes, chained up but trying to move, shakes the ground like an earthquake (see *Inf.* 31.106–108). Lewis mirrors this image when his giants, who are playing a game with rocks, "jumped in their rage, and each jump shook the earth" (*SC* 82). (4) Dante's Nimrod shouts out nonsense syllables that cannot be understood (see *Inf.* 31.67). Likewise, Lewis's giants "stormed and jeered at one another in long meaningless words" (*SC* 82). (5) Virgil calls Nimrod "Stupid fool" (*Inf.* 31.70), and the Narnian giants are referred to as "stupid' (*SC* 82), partly because their rock-throwing is "about the only game they're clever enough to understand" (*SC* 81), and partly because despite hurting their fingers when they hit each other on the head with hammers, they "would do so the same thing a minute later" (*SC* 82).

When Lewis's travelers next come upon an ancient bridge and road, the scene recalls details from an episode in *Inferno* 21. The ten circular ditches where various sins of fraud are punished in the eighth circle of Dante's hell are connected by stone bridges, and the bridge between the fifth and sixth ditches is broken. In Lewis's story, the ancient bridge the children come upon is broken, for in "many places the great stones had dropped out, leaving horrible gaps" (*SC* 86). Virgil and the pilgrim are greeted by a demon guardian, Malacoda (Evil Tail), who tells the truth about the broken bridge ahead but lies about the condition of the next bridge that is also broken (see *Inf.* 21.106–111). Lewis's three travelers are met by a new Malacoda, the Green Lady. She likewise speaks a half-truth and a half-lie about the path ahead: she truthfully indicates that the ancient road "leads to the burgh and castle of Harfang," but she says the castle is the dwelling of "the gentle giants" (*SC* 89). However, since these "gentle giants" consider humans to be a gastronomic delight, the queen is deceiving the children by sending them there as appetizers for the giants' Autumn Feast.

After the Narnians discover this deception, the scene of their escape from the castle recalls the escape of Dante's pilgrim from Malacoda and his demon companions. As Dante's pilgrim leaves the company of devils behind, he fears they will pursue him like a hunting hound pursues a rabbit (see *Inf.* 23.17–18). The Narnians are pursued by *real* hounds as the king returns from a hunt and sees them trying to escape: his "hounds were much nearer. . . . [Jill] was like a hunted animal now" (*SC* 135–36). Dante's pilgrim keeps looking back over his shoulder as he moves away from the devils (see *Inf.* 23.20), and "Jill couldn't help glancing over her shoulder" (*SC* 134). Virgil grabs the pilgrim and slides on his back down a stony bank that walls off the next ditch below (see *Inf.* 23.43–45). After the Narnians escape into the underground through a hole, Jill soon after finds herself "sliding, sliding, hopelessly sliding . . .

down . . . a slope of small stones and rubbish," and she too slides down on her back, for during her descent she "was more lying than standing" (*SC* 138). In both cases, the downward slides extricate the characters from their pursuers. When Lewis's travelers subsequently enter the Deep Realm under the earth, they successively pass through caves that parallel the trajectory of the journey through the circles of Dante's hell, because "always they were going downhill and each cave was lower than the last" (*SC* 146). After passing through the first five circles of hell, Dante's pilgrim is taken by boat across the river Styx to the city of Dis with its high walls, where he sees more than a thousand spirits at its entrance (see *Inf.* 8.78, 82). After passing through several caves, Lewis's travelers are taken by boat across the Sunless Sea and arrive at "wall, towers, and moving crowds," at which point Eustace exclaims, "A city!" (*SC* 149). The city of Dis is the dwelling of the evil ruler in Dante's hell, and Lewis's underworld city contains the castle dwelling of the Queen of Underland.

When they meet with the Queen of Underland and she fails in her attempt to bewitch the travelers, she undergoes a transformation that echoes the transformation of the thieves in *Inferno* 25. In the seventh ditch of fraud in Dante's hell, thieves are punished either by fusing with serpents to form new entities or by being completely transformed into serpents themselves. In *The Silver Chair*, the queen's transformation reflects both of these punishments as her body first fuses with her green dress to create a new shape, and then that new shape is transformed into a serpent. Among her other evil deeds, theft is at issue here since she is responsible for the fact that Caspian's "only son [Rilian] was *stolen* from him" (*SC* 25; italics added). Her transformations are thus in line with Dante's punishment for thieves.

In becoming a serpent, the evil queen of course recalls the lying and deceptive serpent in the Garden of Eden in the Bible. Lewis chooses the word *worm* more often than *serpent*, however, to describe the green snake that fatally stung Rilian's mother: Rilian "saw the worm gliding away . . . that venomous worm" (*SC* 58), and Lord Drinian, concerned about Rilian's obsession with the snake, tells him he "must soon give over seeking the worm" (*SC* 59). When the queen is transformed into a serpent in the underworld and Rilian kills her, he remarks, "This is undoubtedly the same worm I pursued in vain . . . so many years ago" (*SC* 185). Lewis says in a letter, "From reading Beowulf and the Edda the word 'Worm' in the sense of 'dragon' has become . . . familiar to me," so the word *worm* can be used to describe other harmful creatures. Although Dante refers to Satan once as a "serpent" in *Purgatorio* 32.32, in the *Inferno* he calls him instead "the evil *worm* that stings the world" (*Inf.* 34.108; italics added). Lewis's use of the word *worm*, in addition to coming from other sources, could be an echo of Dante's vocabulary, especially since the emphasis in Dante's phrase is not on deception or temptation but on "stinging"—which is what Lewis's "worm" does to Rilian's mother.

After the three travelers rescue the prince and the serpent-queen is killed, they do not leave the underworld by retracing their steps. Neither do Virgil and Dante's pilgrim; instead they travel *south* away from hell through a long tunnel that reaches the earth's surface. Similarly, Rilian and company travel *south* through a long tunnel that opens up into Narnia. Dante's pilgrim emerges from under the earth through a small round opening (see *Inf.* 34.138), and Jill pokes her head through a small round hole from which she will eventually emerge (see *SC* 215). Dante's pilgrim emerges at dawn when the sky is a lovely soft blue color (see *Purg.* 1.13), and when Jill looks up from the small opening, she sees that "the light was pale and blue" (*SC* 216)—although in this case, the pale blue light is moonlight (see *SC* 217). The last line in the *Inferno* tells the reader that Dante's pilgrim emerges from hell "once more to see the stars" (*Inf.* 34.139), and since it is midnight when Jill looks up from the small opening as she is about to emerge from the underworld, she sees "of course! There were the *stars*" (*SC* 217; italics added).

Echoes from the *Inferno* are less pronounced in this novel than the echoes of the *Purgatorio* and the *Paradiso* in *The Voyage of the "Dawn Treader,"* but Lewis clearly succeeds in introducing parallels to all three segments of *The Divine Comedy* into Narnian history.

Beatrice

Since Beatrice is a channel of grace and a guide to God, there is no need for her in Lewis's fairy tales because the Narnian deity Aslan relates directly to the characters and uses no intermediaries. Nevertheless, there is a brief echo of Beatrice in *The Silver Chair*.

Like Beatrice who is sent from heaven and returns there, Jill is sent from the Mountain when the story opens and returns there when her task is finished. More specifically, just as Lewis's three travelers are about to descend into the underworld, Jill evokes a distinct image of Beatrice. Although Beatrice, like all the redeemed, wears a white robe when she is in the court of heaven, she is dressed otherwise when she meets the pilgrim in the garden. She is wearing a white veil, a green cloak, and a red robe (see *Purg.* 30.31–33), the three colors traditionally associated with faith (white), hope (green), and love (red). When Jill is at Harfang, just before her escape, the giants clothe her in "a vivid green robe, . . . and over that a scarlet mantle fringed with white fur" (*SC* 133). Although the colors of Jill's robe and mantle reverse the order of colors in Beatrice's clothing, the color scheme of white, green, and red is identical, and Jill is dressed this way just as she is about to perform a Beatrician function. Beatrice is commissioned by heavenly ladies to help rescue the pilgrim (see *Inf.* 2.93–108), and Jill has been commissioned by Aslan to "seek this lost prince" (*SC* 25). Beatrice elicits the help of Virgil for the rescue (see *Inf.* 2.52–75), and Jill is assisted by Eustace and Puddleglum. Beatrice has to go under the earth and enter hell to initiate the rescue of the pilgrim who has lost his way; Jill will also go under the earth into an evil realm to rescue a confused and lost soul. It is fitting that in this instance she should be dressed in a manner generally reminiscent of Beatrice.

Conclusion

Contrasting *The Divine Comedy* and *Paradise Lost*, Lewis says that Dante "is telling the story of a spiritual pilgrimage. . . . Milton is giving us the story of the universe itself." Lewis combines both kinds of stories in The Chronicles of Narnia by presenting spiritual journeys for children, as well as telling the story of that universe. Although the knightly adventures and atmosphere throughout Lewis's stories have clear affiliations with Spenser's *Faerie Queene* and other such stories, Dante's story nevertheless has a solid presence in Narnia.

Lewis's parallel universe with talking animals and other fairy-tale characters may have an initial appeal to many children, but "the child reader," he says, "is neither to be patronized nor idolized; we talk to him as man to man." That being the case, Lewis believes, "We must meet children as equals in that area of our nature where we are their equals," and "in the moral sphere they are probably at least as wise as we." Lewis draws on *The Divine Comedy* for his Narnia stories because if, as Lewis believed, that poem is indeed an archetype for the spiritual journey and a model for the imaginative presentation of perennial truths, then Dante's story is just as relevant and important for children as it is for adults.

Using Dante's typological approach to biblical material, Lewis takes the opportunity to retell the substance of major events in biblical history in the context of a fairy-tale world, with complete freedom to change and invent the accompanying details. In his essay about fairy tales, Lewis says that "by casting all these things into an imaginary world, stripping them of their stained-glass and Sunday school associations, one could make them for the first time appear in their real potency"—and the effect of this approach applies equally to children and adults.

In his essay "On Three Ways of Writing for Children," Lewis says that "everything in the story should arise from the whole cast of the author's mind" and that "the matter of our story should be part of the habitual furniture of our minds." Given that Dante's poem was part of the "habitual furniture" of Lewis's mind, it could be expected that Dante's poem would surface somehow in Narnia. With clear echoes from the *Inferno* (*SC*), the *Purgatorio*, and the *Paradiso* (*VDT*)—and brief flashes of Dante's story in other Narnian tales—*The Divine Comedy* makes its appearance in this series to become a permanent part of Narnian history.

CHAPTER NINE

Till We Have Faces

Introduction

Lewis's last novel, *Till We Have Faces: A Myth Retold* (1956), retells the myth of Cupid and Psyche from Apuleius's *Golden Ass* (also called *Metamorphoses*). Unlike any of Lewis's other novels, it has a first-person female narrator (Orual, an ugly queen in ancient times), and the story concerns her pre-conversion state as a pagan who resents the gods until she comes to faith. This seemingly pagan story, however, is a Christian story told within the framework of a classical myth.

In the original myth (which Lewis retells in the "Note" at the end of the novel), when Psyche, the youngest of three sisters, is worshipped by the people, a jealous Venus sends her son Cupid to punish her. He falls in love with her instead and takes her to his palace, forbidding her ever to look upon his face. When her two unnamed sisters visit her, they insist that she uncover her mysterious lover's true appearance and identity, but when Psyche lights a lamp to see Cupid's face as he sleeps, she is banished from their home. As penance for her disobedience, Venus assigns Psyche seemingly impossible tasks that she is nevertheless able to complete with the help of others. In the end Jupiter makes her a goddess and Cupid marries her. This myth has generally been interpreted as an allegory of the union of a soul (*psyche* in Greek) with God.

Part I of Lewis's two-part novel is Orual's autobiography up to her retirement. As the former queen of Glome, a city-state in the pre-Christian Hellenistic age, her story covers her childhood to the end of her reign as queen and is written as a complaint about the cruelty of the gods. When Orual's beautiful half-sister Psyche is given as a sacrifice to the monster Shadowbrute of Grey Mountain to save her people (as commanded by the stone fertility goddess Ungit), Orual begins to distrust and resent the gods. When she later tries to find Psyche's body in the mountains, she discovers Psyche living joyously with an unseen husband in a lovely palace that Orual cannot see (except for an ambiguous momentary glimpse). Orual threatens to kill herself if Psyche does not agree to light a lamp to see her husband's true appearance, and when Psyche does so she is banished by her husband. Orual realizes that she is responsible for her sister's loss of happiness and blames the gods not only for taking Psyche away but also for tricking her about whether Psyche's palace was real or not. At this point Orual begins to cover her face with a veil that she wears for the rest of her life. After she retires as queen, she visits a shrine where the priest tells the story of Psyche (as the myth of Istra), but in the priest's version the older sister destroys her sister's happiness out of envy. Orual angrily decides to "correct" the story and records her self-justifications and accusations against the gods.

Part II, which is only one-fifth as long as the first part, is her record of the events that follow the writing of her autobiography—events that contradict her original memory of things and lead to a different perspective of her experiences. Through a series of conversations, dreams, and visions, she gradually sees that she has been self-centered all her life, and she turns from hatred of the gods to faith in Psyche's god (a pagan version of Christ).

The pagan setting and atmosphere in this novel might seem to have fewer affiliations with *The Divine Comedy* than Lewis's other novels do, but there are several parallels nonetheless. Lewis's changes to Apulieus's myth reflect the procedure Dante uses to make adjustments to the myths he incorporates in his poem, and Lewis's moral assessment of Orual as a pagan parallels Dante's treatment of some pagan and classical characters in his poem. Whether or not Lewis consciously had any of Dante's characters in mind when depicting Orual's failings, her attitudes at times echo those of some souls in the *Inferno* and *Purgatorio*. In Part II of the novel, which describes her spiritual journey to the truth, Orual begins to resemble Dante's pilgrim as she goes through a kind of mini-journey that one Lewis scholar calls "a condensed version of Dante's journey in *The Divine Comedy*."

Glome and Its Inhabitants

Both Dante and Lewis make adjustments to classical myths by changing details to conform to the specific Christian messages in their stories. As described in chapter 5 on *Perelandra*, since Lewis believed that pagan stories contain a mix of truth and error, the factors that contradict or do not support Christian truth are corrected or adapted. Believing that ancient stories are imperfect revelations of truth but that "all truth is God's truth," both Lewis and Dante regularly incorporate and allude to pagan and classical insights in their works.

Dante's adjustments to classical myths in *The Divine Comedy* are based on his premise that all human beings are to be judged by the God revealed in the Bible. Since there is no heaven or purgatory for human beings in the classical afterlife, Dante's changes apply primarily to the ancient underworld. He identifies the Roman God of the underworld, Dis (another name for Pluto), as Satan (see *Inf.* 11.65; 34.20), indicating that the ancients intuited there was a ruler of the underworld but did not know his true name or nature. The ancients believed the City of Dis encompassed all of the dead in the underworld, but Dante adjusts this concept in two ways. The realm under the earth is only for unrepentant sinners now, and his City of Dis encompasses only the lower circles of hell where premeditated sins of mind and will are punished. Dante leaves the classical river Acheron unchanged as the stream that one must cross to gain access to the underworld, but he qualifies it by making its crossing give access only to hell now. Dante adds moral qualities to the other classical rivers in hell: the river Styx is now the muddy swamp for the punishment of the wrathful and sullen; Phlegethon, the river of fire, is now a river of boiling blood that punishes those who shed the blood of others; Cocytus, the river of wailing, becomes a frozen lake in the ninth circle where traitors are punished. Although Dante includes and adapts these classical rivers for his hell, he relocates Lethe, the classical river of forgetfulness in the underworld, to his Garden of Eden where it becomes a spiritually purgative stream that removes not *all* memories but only memories of the guilt and shame attached to sin. Other adjustments include his reinterpretation of some classical creatures as symbols of sins for the circles they guard in hell. Three-headed Cerberus, for instance, who guarded the entire ancient underworld, now guards only the circle of gluttony because he has three ravenous mouths (see *Inf.* 6.13–22). Dante subordinates pagan concepts to Christian truth, preserving truths that can be included in his presentation of the afterlife but openly correcting them as he sees fit. In the case of Venus and her son, for instance—which is relevant to Lewis's story—Dante notes that "ancient peoples in their ancient error" (*Par.* 8.6) believed that Venus brought love to the earth. She and her son were honored and were offered sacrifices (see *Par.* 8.3–7) because people were ignorant of the true identity of the God of love.

Lewis's changes to the Cupid and Psyche myth also derive from his story's focus, which in this case is a human being's resistance to union with God. Lewis shifts the focus from Psyche to Orual's perspective of events and says his "central alteration . . . consists in making Psyche's palace invisible to normal, mortal eyes" (*TWHF* 313). That modification turns the ancient myth into a story about a person's struggle of faith and surrender to God.

With Orual as the central character now, Lewis adjusts several features of the original myth to suit that change. He invents Orual's kingdom of Glome as its setting; Venus becomes Ungit, a dark stone goddess rather than a lovely goddess of classical mythology; and Cupid becomes the Shadowbrute. Major characters are added around Orual: Lysias (the Fox), a Greek slave purchased by her father (King Trom) as a tutor for his three daughters; Bardia, the captain of Glome's troops; and minor characters that include the priests at the temple of Ungit, personnel at the palace, and rulers and warriors of political entities in the surrounding area.

Some scholars have noted that Orual's mentor, the Fox, is reminiscent of Dante's Virgil. The Fox is the voice of reason, classical philosophy, and poetry in the novel. Like Virgil who admits, "I will show [the pilgrim] things insofar as my own learning will permit" (*Purg.* 21.32–33), the Fox teaches Orual only what philosophy can discover about virtue and vice. His instruction includes the concept that "the god within you is the god you should obey: reason, calmness, self-discipline" (*TWHF* 303). He therefore explains everything, including religious matters, as having natural or reasonable causes, which leads Psyche to her assessment that "the Fox hasn't the whole truth" (*TWHF* 70). Given her strained relationship with her father, Orual considers the Fox "the central pillar of my whole life" (*TWHF* 209) and relates to him as a father. Similar to the pilgrim who addresses or refers to Virgil at times as "father" and whom Virgil addresses as "son," Orual most often calls the Fox "Grandfather," and he most often calls her "Daughter." At the end, in Orual's dream-vision of her trial before the gods, the Fox recognizes the shortcomings of his strictly rational approach to life: "I made her [Orual] think that a prattle of maxims would do. . . . I fed her on words" (*TWHF* 295). He also acknowledges his limitation in understanding the divine, confessing, "Why the people got something from the shapeless stone [Ungit] . . . I didn't know; but I never told her I didn't know" (*TWHF* 295).

Bardia is also reminiscent of Virgil, but for different reasons. Just as Virgil protects the pilgrim and helps him maneuver the journey, Bardia safeguards and protects Orual and helps her maneuver the practical and governmental side of her life. Like Virgil who believes God exists but does not know him, Bardia is a "god-fearing man" (*TWHF* 99) and "an honest man, . . . and (in his own way) wise" (*TWHF* 134), who respects the gods but keeps his distance from them.

In some respects, it is the two of them together who comprise the "Virgil" of this novel. Each cares deeply for Orual and is a loyal guide and mentor. Bardia understands war and politics, while "the Fox understood what Bardia did not," but they are very much alike in that "neither cared a straw for his own dignity or advancement when my needs were in question" (*TWHF* 227–28). It is together, she says, that "these two very good counselors" are one of her main strengths (*TWHF* 227). Each of them fulfills a Virgilian function in leading Orual to a significant meeting with Psyche when she is acting as a Beatrice figure: Bardia is Orual's guide up to Grey Mountain for her first meeting with Psyche, and the Fox is Orual's guide to her second meeting with Psyche in her final vision.

In the end, however, it is the Fox who is most like Virgil since he is the one in Orual's last vision who meets her in an infernal setting, which has clear parallels to Dante's hell, and leads her from there into an area that recalls features of Mount Purgatory and its Garden of Eden. However, despite his assistance to her, the Fox, like Virgil, cannot lead Orual to fullness of truth—a "Beatrice" is needed for that.

Orual's Journey

This novel has what is called an "unreliable narrator," a narrator who does not always tell the truth or who twists the truth, leaving the reader to read between the lines. Partly because of this complexity, it is initially easy for readers to sympathize with Orual's character and to overlook or minimize her many serious wrongdoings.

Orual's journey is not that of a person who, like Dante's pilgrim, returns to the path of righteousness and then grows in virtue and in knowledge of the truth. Her journey is primarily a journey from willful self-deception to truth, from distrust and hatred for the gods to faith in Psyche's god. As such, in Part I her character recalls specific attitudes—and sometimes the vocabulary—of certain characters in the *Inferno* and the *Purgatorio*.

Her long-standing perspective of the gods as unjust and of herself as wronged makes her similar to Dante's souls in hell, who are all described as those "who have lost the good of the intellect" (*Inf.* 3.18). They are unable to perceive the truth about God's nature or to admit the truth about themselves. Dante's souls, who are waiting for Charon to ferry them across the river Acheron into hell, blame and curse God (and others) for their misery (see *Inf.* 3.103–105). Orual likewise lays blame on the gods for her misery, claiming that "the gods deal very unrightly with us" (*TWHF* 249). God is thus seen as an enemy by Dante's souls and by Orual. In Dante's hell, Christ is referred to as "the adverse judge" (*Inf.* 6.96), and Orual believes not only that "the god of the Grey Mountain . . . hates [her]" (*TWHF* 4) but also that "the gods . . . hated [her]" (*TWHF* 175). Francesca, in the circle of lust, sees God as her enemy (see *Inf.* 5.91) and believes it is "love" that led her to hell (see *Inf.* 5.106), ignoring the fact that she was committing adultery with her brother-in-law when she died. Orual believes it is her love for Psyche that leads her to do what she does, ignoring the fact that her love is self-focused and possessive, so she too feels justified in considering the gods hostile to her and justified in her hate for them.

Orual's hatred of the gods leads to attitudes and actions that Dante classifies as premeditated and deliberate sins of mind and heart—sins that he distinguishes from sins of the flesh by placing them in the lower circles of hell. Like some of Dante's sinners, this pagan queen is guilty of heresy, violence, fraud, and treason.

Heresy. Orual's hatred perverts her perspective about the nature of the gods, so she does not speak the truth about them and their relationship to her. She insists that they are "cruel gods" (*TWHF* 200) who engage in "divine mockery" (*TWHF* 134), and that they "accuse and mock and punish" her (*TWHF* 150). Her hostility to them is summed up in her resentment of their very existence: "That there should be gods at all, there's our misery and bitter wrong" (*TWHF* 291), especially since "the gods . . . are viler than the vilest men" (*TWHF* 71).

Violence. Dante's circle of violence includes the sins of blasphemy, suicide, and murder, and Orual is guilty here too. Dante's blasphemers "despise God in their hearts and through their speech" (*Inf.* 11.51). Orual likewise hates and reviles the gods for many decades after Psyche's sacrifice to the Shadowbrute: "There is no creature (toad, scorpion, or serpent) so noxious to man as the gods" (*TWHF* 249). With respect to Psyche's god, her reaction is, "I hate it. Hate it, hate it, hate it" (*TWHF* 124).

Orual in this instance recalls Dante's most prominent blasphemer, Capaneus. A classical warrior king during the siege of Thebes, Capaneus cursed Jupiter for killing him with a thunderbolt, so Dante places him in hell with the blasphemers against the true God (see *Inf.* 14.52ff.). (Capaneus was mistaken about who the supreme God is, just as Orual is, but he still knowingly rebelled against the heavenly deity, just as Orual does.) Capaneus is described as sullen and disdainful (see *Inf.* 14.47), and even in the midst of his punishment and suffering, he "scorned and still seemed to scorn God and seemed to hold him in little esteem" (*Inf.* 14.69–70). Orual holds on to her lifelong "sullen bitterness" (*TWHF* 282), and in the midst of her suffering she too scorns the gods in an ongoing way. Virgil tells Capaneus, "no torment except your fury could punish you more fittingly for your rage" (*Inf.* 14.65–66). Orual's long-standing "old rage [and] resentment" (*TWHF* 282) against the gods for taking Psyche is likewise its own torment. Capaneus's recalcitrance is so entrenched that he does not care if God "shoots [his bolts] at me with all his strength; he would not get vengeance so easily from doing that" (*Inf.* 14.59–60). Orual likewise does not care if the gods punish her and even expects them to: "I believed that some sudden stroke of the gods would fall on me very soon" (*TWHF* 183). Like Capaneus, she too hopes she can somehow avoid

giving them any satisfaction: "If Orual could vanish altogether into
the Queen, the gods would almost be cheated" (*TWHF* 201). After
her betrayal of Psyche, she in fact follows through on this and says,
"I locked Orual up . . . deep down inside me" (*TWHF* 226).

Orual is guilty of blasphemy in another way that Dante describes. Virgil explains that hating God and cursing him are not the
only ways to blaspheme, because a person "can be violent against
the deity . . . by *despising his goodness in nature*" (*Inf.* 11.46–48; italics added). God is reflected in the creation that proceeds from him,
so rejection of God can entail rejection of his creation as well. On
the other hand, a correct belief about God brings with it a view of
nature that is reflective of his love. As one Dante scholar notes, in
The Divine Comedy "the whole created universe is contemplated . . .
as a book written by God's love."

Dante expresses this perspective through his recurring personification of the sky and the planets as "smiling." When his
pilgrim emerges from hell and sees the morning star, "the lovely
planet made the whole eastern horizon *smile*" (*Purg.* 1.19–20; italics added). After a breeze dissolves the mist from the sky, "the sky
smiles in its loveliness" (*Par.* 28.83–84; italics added). When Dante's
pilgrim rises to the planet of Mercury, "the star changed and *smiled*"
(*Par.* 5.97; italics added), and having risen to Mars, he notices "the
fiery-red *smile* of that star" (*Par.* 14.86; italics added). When he
hears the heavenly host singing praise to the Trinity, he says, "What
I was seeing seemed to me to be the *universe smiling*" (*Par.* 27.4–5;
italics added). A joyful universe is the creation of joyful God, and
Dante even refers to him once as the "joyful creator" (*Purg.* 16.89).

Unlike Dante's pilgrim who is attuned to the love and joy in the
universe, Orual has a different experience, because her hatred of
the gods leads her to scorn the goodness in nature. Before meeting
Psyche on the mountain, Orual is surrounded by such beauty in nature that she says it "made me feel that I had misjudged the world;
it seemed kind, and laughing, as if its heart also danced"; however,
she quickly struggles against "this fool-happy mood" (*TWHF* 96).
In direct contrast to Dante's pilgrim—and in an echo of Dante's
vocabulary—Orual is convinced that she "knew the world too well
to believe this sudden *smiling*" (*TWHF* 97; italics added). She intuits the connection between a beautiful creation and the goodness of
the gods, so "the nearest thing we have to a defence against them . . .

is . . . never to look at earth or sky" (*TWHF* 80–81). In deliberately rejecting Psyche's husband-god, she rejects creation as well: "It is a strange . . . thing, to look round on earth and grass and the sky and say in one's heart to each, 'You are all my enemies now. . . . I see now only executioners'" (*TWHF* 175–76). As Dorothy L. Sayers points out in her first book on Dante, "If we rebel against the nature of things and choose to think that what we . . . want is the centre of the universe, . . . the first effect in us will be that the whole universe will seem to be filled with an implacable and inexplicable hostility." (Lewis had read and praised Sayers's book before his composition of this novel, in which she quotes *Paradiso* 27.4–5 in Italian and then refers to the "rejoicing universe.")

As for the violence of suicide and murder, Orual is prepared to commit both those acts in a premeditated way. During her first meeting with Psyche on the mountain, she stabs herself in the arm to prove her intentions of suicide if Psyche does not come away with her. If she does not leave her husband-god, Orual's rationale for then killing Psyche—to rescue her from the Shadowbrute— surely comes from a "darkened intellect" when she says, "There is a love deeper than theirs who seek only the happiness of their beloved" (*TWHF* 138). According to Orual's logic, killing Psyche indicates her "deeper love" for her (see *TWHF* 165). Just as Dante's Pier delle Vigne, a minister at the court of Frederick II, blames others for making him kill himself because his reputation was vilified at court (see *Inf.* 13.70–72), so too Orual blames the gods for not showing her whether Psyche's palace was real or not and thus for leading her to consider committing suicide and killing Psyche.

Fraud. Orual's fraud involves deceiving others, giving fraudulent counsel, and deceiving herself. On her first night on Grey Mountain, when she drinks from the stream in the sacred valley— ironically, in a kneeling position!—she sees a glimpse of the god's palace (see *TWHF* 132–33). She subsequently misleads Bardia, the Fox, and Psyche by not admitting that she briefly saw the palace. When she glimpses Psyche's god after Psyche is banished and sees "the beauty this face wore" (*TWHF* 173), she determines not to inform Bardia and the Fox about that experience either. Second, Orual gives fraudulent counsel to her sister when she tells Psyche that she must disobey her husband. Even after Orual experiences a "fear . . . that I had advised her wrongly," she "governed it" (*TWHF*

169). She deliberately chooses to insist that her counsel is correct. Her greatest deception, though, is against herself. From this point on, she decides to veil her face permanently, a visible sign of the veil covering her heart and her deliberate covering over of the truth that the gods are good. Having seen Psyche's beautiful god and having heard his "sweet" voice (*TWHF* 173), she nevertheless deliberately suppresses that truth: "The memory of his voice and face was kept in one of those rooms of my soul that I didn't lightly unlock" (*TWHF* 244–45).

Treason is classified as the worst kind of fraud by Dante, because it is performed against someone who should have been able to trust the betrayer (see *Inf.* 11.54). Orual is treacherous to Psyche by forcing her to choose between obedience to her husband and preventing her own threatened suicide. When Orual first sees that Psyche is happy, she considers leaving her in that situation, but says "my heart did not conquer me" (*TWHF* 138) and "I hardened my resolution" (*TWHF* 152). When she makes the deliberate choice to blackmail Psyche emotionally, her self-description recalls Dante's souls encased in ice for their cold-hearted, premeditated betrayal: "My heart was still as *ice*, heavy as lead, *cold* as earth" (*TWHF* 157; italics added). In describing her heart as being "heavy as lead," she is also reminiscent of Dante's hypocrites who are wearing heavy golden-looking cloaks made of lead (see *Inf.* 23.100–101). In her treachery against Psyche, Orual is also a hypocrite since deep down she knows the truth.

The fact that Orual is a pagan without the benefit of Christian revelation does not absolve her from her attitudes and actions, and Dante likewise does not absolve pagans in his hell because of their lack of Christian truth. Although Dante places righteous pagans in Limbo (where they are cut off from God's presence but do not otherwise suffer), he places other classical figures in various circles of hell for punishment, since they disobeyed or acted contrary to the light and truth they did have. In *The Divine Comedy*, Dante holds pagans to the standards that they had because the intent of the heart is of paramount importance, and Lewis follows that approach with Orual. She should have, and could have, known better. Instead she has chosen hell, which Dante aptly describes, and which Orual experiences, as "the world of endless bitterness" (*Par.* 17.112).

Orual, however, is not wholly evil—she is generally regarded as a good queen who cared for her people and ruled her kingdom well. She is, like all humans, a mix of good and bad, and as such she displays the sins common to all fallen human beings, that is, dispositions that focus on self and that need purging on Dante's mount. Dante categorizes the ways love can go wrong into perverted love and disordered love (see *Purg.* 17.91ff.), and Orual displays both kinds. Perverted love focuses on self to the detriment of others and leads to *pride*, *envy*, and *anger*, the dispositions purged on the first three ledges of Dante's mount (see *Purg.* 17.115–123). Orual demonstrates those three vices regularly, often with regard to Psyche. When she tells the Fox about possibly killing Psyche, he rightly identifies that there is "one part love in your heart, and five parts *anger*, and seven parts *pride*" (*TWHF* 148; italics added). Behind Orual's reasonable-sounding arguments about rescuing Psyche lurk pride and anger about not getting her way and, like Virgil, the Fox can easily recognize wrong dispositions. After Orual's sword fight with Argan, her pride and envy of Psyche show themselves. Orual imagines that had she been fearful, the Fox and Bardia would have contrasted her lack of courage to how bravely Psyche sacrificed herself, and so Psyche "would be far above me in everything: in courage as well as in beauty. . . . 'She shall not,' I said with my whole soul" (*TWHF* 200). In the *Purgatorio* one of the examples on the ledge of envy for souls to meditate on is Aglauros (see *Purg.* 14.139). This daughter of the king of Athens tried to prevent the union of her youngest sister with the god Mercury. Orual, in actually preventing her younger sister Psyche from remaining united with her husband-god, has succeeded in doing what Aglauros only tried to do, and in both cases the action was from envy of a youngest sister. Orual is also envious of Bardia's wife, Ansit, and displays her jealousy, saying she wanted Bardia "clear of that wife of his. . . . I was fretted by the thought of . . . this petted thing" (*TWHF* 153). As for Orual's anger, it is perpetually directed at the gods but is also displayed against her father, her sister Redival, and even Psyche.

The second way love can go amiss, according to Dante, occurs when a natural or normal love becomes disordered because it is not subordinated to the love of the supreme good, God, and this disorder can occur through excess and defect (see *Purg.* 17.96–102, 126). As Virgil remarks, "Oh, how the truth is concealed from people who assert that every love is a laudable thing in itself" (*Purg.* 18.34–36). In Part I it becomes clear that Orual's love for the three most important people in her life—Psyche, the Fox, and Bardia—can be categorized as disordered love. Her love for Psyche is so excessive that any kind of interference with it is considered cruel and evil. The "gods . . . had stolen her. They would leave us nothing" (*TWHF* 120–21), accusing them of sadistic intentions because "those we love best . . . are the very ones you'll pick out" (*TWHF* 290). When it is Psyche herself who interferes with that love by insisting that she must obey her husband rather than Orual, "I learned then how one can hate those one loves" (*TWHF* 127).

Her love for the Fox is defective because it does not focus on what is best for him. When she gives the Fox his freedom and he considers returning to Greece, "It embittered me that the Fox should even desire to leave me" (*TWHF* 209). She mentally accuses him, "It was Psyche he loved. Never me." Although she says, "*I knew while I said it that was false,*" she persists in her self-pity: "yet I would not . . . put it out of my head" (*TWHF* 209; italics added). This is one more instance of her willful rejection and twisting of the truth. Only much later during the vision of her trial at the court does she openly admit to the Fox, "I knew you stayed only in pity and love for me" (*TWHF* 296).

Her love for Bardia is likewise defective because it too is self-centered. Despite knowing that Bardia is married, she keeps him with her at the court as much as she can because she is in love with him. Because of the long hours Orual keeps him away from his family, Ansit complains, "Your queenship drank up his blood year by year and ate out his life" (*TWHF* 264). She rightly accuses Orual, "When you had used him, . . . I had what you left of him" (*TWHF* 262). In the end Orual acknowledges that her so-called love for Bardia was "a gnawing greed for one . . . of whom I craved all" (*TWHF* 267).

Despite her protestations about her love for others to herself and to the reader, Orual does not understand the nature of selfless love, and what she thinks is love for the three main people in her life is obviously possessive in various degrees. She clearly articulates that possessiveness about Psyche when she states, "Psyche was mine and no one else had any right to her" (*TWHF* 291–92). She drains those around her and in the end comes to see herself, accurately, as "the swollen spider . . . gorged with men's stolen lives" (*TWHF* 276). With the use of the spider metaphor here, Lewis may be alluding to Arachne and Dante's choice of her as one of the negative examples on the ledge of pride for souls to contemplate (see *Purg.* 12.43–45). Arachne defied and scorned the gods (by challenging Athena to a weaving contest) and was turned into a spider for her pride, so it is perhaps appropriate that Orual, who likewise defied and scorned the gods, now refers to herself a "spider."

Although she cannot be blamed for being subject to the sinful dispositions common to fallen human nature, Orual still has little excuse for her choices. Paul says that although the unrighteous "knew God, they glorified him not as God, neither were thankful; but became vain in their imaginations, and their foolish heart was darkened" (Rom. 1:21)—a very clear description of Orual. Psyche, who is raised in the same environment, has the same education and the same rudimentary and incomplete knowledge about the gods that Orual does, is nevertheless able to long for and love the mysterious mountain god that Orual distrusts and hates. Psyche intuits that sacrifice is part of life and that death brings life: "How can I be a ransom for all of Glome," she asks Orual, "unless I die?" (*TWHF* 72). Despite her fears she joyfully gives herself in sacrificial marriage to that God, considering herself "a god's bride more than a Brute's prey" (*TWHF* 72). In contrast to Psyche, Orual sees sacrifice as a cruel demand on the part of the gods and believes that Psyche's love for her god means that she will love Orual less. Psyche, however, understands that loving her mysterious mountain-husband does not in any way diminish her love for others, including Orual, and in fact, she says that loving her husband "makes me love everyone and everything—more" (*TWHF* 159). Her statement reflects the attitude of Dante's redeemed souls in the *Paradiso* who joyfully greet any new soul in heaven precisely because "here comes someone who will increase our love" (*Par.* 5.105). In the words of one Lewis scholar, Orual "encounters the Good, the Beautiful, the True, embodied in Psyche"—but she definitively rejects Psyche's example.

In the Fox, Orual has an example that using love as a weapon the way she does with Psyche is wrong. After the Fox tries to dissuade her from single combat with Argan, he apologizes, saying, "I was wrong to weep and beg and try to force you by your love. Love is not a thing to be so used" (*TWHF* 204). Orual is surrounded by examples of good behavior and good teaching that she refuses to learn from and willfully ignores.

Nor can it be said about Orual that she makes a wrong choice once or twice. She has a choice at several points along the way between the truth and a refusal of the truth. When she sees Psyche happy and well in the mountain valley, she wavers at first: "If this is all true, I've been wrong all my life. Everything has to be begun over again" (*TWHF* 115). She in fact admits that she came close to faith at this point—"I came almost to a full belief" (*TWHF* 120). However, when Psyche says that everything will turn out right, Orual makes her choice again: "I don't want it. I hate . . . [this] thing that comes to you in the darkness" (*TWHF* 124). Even when Orual sees Psyche's god on the mountain after Psyche is banished and hears her weeping, she still does not acknowledge the truth. She is resentful that Psyche's god "made it to be as if . . . all [her] doubtings . . . had been trumped-up foolery, dust blown in [her] own eyes" (*TWHF* 173), but the god was right because this is what she has done. Orual's betrayal of Psyche, according to her, though, is still not her fault but the gods' fault for not making things clearer, and she persists in adhering to that untruthful perspective throughout her years as queen. Dante says that the exercise of one's free will is what determines if a person is "deserving of reward or punishment," and as Lewis writes, "it is by his *will* that man is bad or good." Orual has exercised her free will over and over and over again.

In Part II, Orual begins the journey out of the hell of herself, and in this section echoes of *The Divine Comedy* are more pronounced. A series of conversations with people begins to crack her self-contained and self-focused mind-set. Tarin, a former soldier in Glome, points out that he pitied Redival as a young girl for her loneliness because Orual ignored her, fixed her affection on the Fox, and then became obsessed with Psyche. Conversations with Ansit after Bardia's death begin to shine a different light on her so-called love for Bardia. Dante's pilgrim prays for the souls on the ledge of envy in the *Purgatorio*, "May God's grace soon wash away the film clouding your consciousness so that *the stream of memory may flow through you clearly*" (*Purg.* 13.88–90; italics added). This describes the very process Orual is going through as her memory of the past is being adjusted and cleansed. She begins to make the crucial acknowledgement that "those divine Surgeons [the gods] had me tied down and were at work" (*TWHF* 266).

These conversations are followed by a series of dreams and visions that bring her more and more truth. On the ledge of anger, Dante's pilgrim says the thick smoke there acts as "a veil" to his face (see *Purg.* 16.4–5). Orual, with her face still veiled, is dealing with an "anger [that] protected me only for a short time" (*TWHF* 266). On this ledge, Dante's pilgrim has ecstatic visions of examples of anger and meekness (see *Purg.* 15.85ff.). Similarly, Orual is now "drenched . . . with seeings" (*TWHF* 276) that begin to purge her anger and lead her to grow in meekness.

Her first vision involves her father as they dig through the center of the Pillar Room only to find a smaller Pillar Room in a black hole below, and then another smaller room below that one, reminiscent of Dante's descending circles in a funnel-shaped hell. In the last room, as she sees herself in a mirror, she realizes, "I am Ungit" (*TWHF* 276), someone who demands blood sacrifice. Recognizing her misdeeds, she rejects her sinful attitudes and selfishness. She removes the veil from her face—because she is now removing it from her mind and heart—and, when she is too feeble to kill herself with a heavy old sword, she tries to drown herself in a river as the way to reject the evil she has discovered in her heart.

Although her attempt at killing herself represents a misunderstanding of *how* to reject evil, it nonetheless represents a deliberate rejection of sin on her part, and this opens the way to grace for her. The voice of a god quickly rescues her by holding her back from killing herself, saying, "You cannot escape Ungit by going to the deadlands, for she is there also. Die before you die" (*TWHF* 279). There is no opportunity to choose the good after that. Dante describes his hell as the place "from which a person can never go back to having the will to do good" (*Par.* 20.106–107). When the blasphemer Capaneus says, "What I was when I was alive I still am now that I am dead" (*Inf.* 14.51), he is a reminder that repentance and change must occur before death.

Orual, in contrast to earlier times, now obeys the god's voice because "there was no rebel in me now" (*TWHF* 280). Her trajectory at this point echoes that of Dante's Sapia of Sienna on Mount Purgatory. When Sapia had been gladdened by the defeat of her townspeople in battle because of her envy, she had "lifted up an emboldened face, crying to God, "Now I no longer fear you!'" (*Purg.* 13.121–122), but afterwards, "I sought peace with God at the end of my life" (*Purg.* 13.123–124). Orual too is in the process of moving from defiance of the gods to approaching reconciliation with them.

Understanding that being Ungit means her soul is brutish, Orual tries to "change my ugly soul into a fair one" by practicing "true philosophy, as Socrates meant it" (*TWHF* 282). She desires to be purified and cleansed, like the souls on Mount Purgatory, only to discover—as Eustace did with his last dragon skin and as Dante's pilgrim did with the seven P's on his forehead—that outside assistance is needed for purification. She realizes, "I could mend my soul no more than my face. Unless the gods helped" (*TWHF* 282). As in Dante's poem, good philosophy and good intentions are not enough, and Orual's outside help comes to her in the form of further dreams and visions.

Like the layers of an onion, her sins are exposed and peeled away, but her misperception of her love for Psyche remains as the last layer of her self-deception: "However I might have devoured Bardia, I had at least loved Psyche truly. There if nowhere else, I had the right of it and *the gods were in the wrong*" (*TWHF* 285; italics added). The path of purification and knowledge of the truth is a progressive one as a person moves forward, and the truth often has to unfold in stages. Despite her growth in self-awareness, she still insists on blaming the gods when it comes to her loss of Psyche. Like one of the souls in Dante's ante-purgatory, whose "excessive love I had for my family is being refined here" (*Purg.* 8.120), she still needs to have her love for half-sister Psyche purified. This last layer of self-deceit is removed during her trial before the gods.

On her journey to the mountain where her trial will take place, Lewis implies that justice will occur through an echo of Dante's eagle image in the *Paradiso*. As Orual approaches the mountain, she is accosted by an eagle—"an eagle from the gods. . . . It was a divine creature" (*TWHF* 287)—who tells her, "Come into court. Your case is to be heard" (*TWHF* 287). In *Paradiso* 19 and 20, the speaking figure of an eagle, comprised of the souls of righteous kings and other rulers, is the one who explains divine justice to the pilgrim (see *Par.* 19.13ff.).

Lewis presents Orual's last vision and her trial in a hellish set-ting that has several Dantean features. As she reaches the mountain, "a great black hole yawned before me" and she is then led "into the dark innards of a mountain and then further and further in" (*TWHF* 288). Lewis's image here reflects the dark mountain of Dante's hell that goes farther and farther down.

When she is brought to the court in the deadlands, she at first sees "so vast a concourse"—which includes the servant Batta, her father, the priest Argan, and the Fox—that it startles her: "In my foolishness I had not thought before how many dead there must be" (*TWHF* 289). This directly echoes the description of the long train of uncommitted people in the vestibule of Dante's hell whose sight prompts the pilgrim to say, "I could not have imagined that death could have undone so many" (*Inf.* 3.56–57).

Echoes of Dante's hell continue in this setting. Although Orual's judge is veiled and unknown to her, the Fox addresses the judge as "Minos . . . [or] whatever name you are called" (*TWHF* 295). In confessing his part in Orual's scorn for the gods and offering to be punished in her stead, he uses that name again, saying, "Send me away, Minos" (*TWHF* 295). It is not surprising that the Fox assumes this judge to be Minos, since he is the judge in the ancient classical underworld (see *Aeneid* 6.432). However, there are two details that make him more similar to Dante's Minos in the *Inferno*. First, in the ancient underworld Minos judges and assigns all the souls—good and bad—to their appropriate places, but Dante's Minos judges only sinners: "When the *evil soul* comes to stand before him, it confesses all" (*Inf.* 5.7–8; italics added). Orual's complaint to the gathered court ironically is a confession her evil and wrongdoing. Second, Dante's Minos, "leaving aside the performance of his official role" (*Inf.* 5.18) in the pilgrim's case, does not judge him or assign him to a circle in hell. So too Lewis's Minos does not judge Orual. At the end he calls her "a plaintiff, not a prisoner," saying, "If the gods in turn accuse her, a greater judge and a more excellent court must try her case" (*TWHF* 296).

Orual's complaint-confession brings the final light she needs. Stripped of her veil and clothes by others and standing on a platform in that dark cave inside the mountain, she reads her "vile scribble" (*TWHF* 290), "the book full of my poison" (*TWHF* 300), and issues her chief complaint: "She [Psyche] was mine. *Mine.* . . . Mine! You're thieves, seducers" (*TWHF* 292). In the end, hearing herself say what had been at the core of her soul for years, she understands that "till that word can be dug out of us, why should they [the gods] hear the babble that we think we mean? How can they meet us face to face till we have faces?" (*TWHF* 294).

The Fox, Virgil-like, then leads Orual out of this infernal setting and accompanies her to her final meeting with Psyche. Lewis combines into one scene the meeting with Beatrice in the garden and the pilgrim's vision of God in the *Paradiso*. Dante's pilgrim confesses his sin to Beatrice, and this time Orual finally confesses to Psyche her sin of possessiveness in their relationship: "Never again will I call you mine; but all there is of me shall be yours" (*TWHF* 305). Dante's pilgrim describes one of the souls on Mount Purgatory as one "who cleanses yourself to return beautiful to the One who made you" (*Purg.* 16.31–32). By assisting Psyche in her punitive tasks and surrendering to the truth about Psyche's god, Orual has unknowingly participated in making herself beautiful too. Orual next hears the voice of Psyche's god and surrenders herself to him. Orual acquires a pure soul, and she is given Psyche's beauty as well.

Four days after she wakes from that dream vision, Orual says, "I know now, Lord,"—notice it is no longer "gods" but the singular "Lord"—"why you utter no answer. You are yourself the answer" (*TWHF* 308). The god she hated she now knows is a loving, gracious, and forgiving God. She can now say, with Dante's pilgrim, that God "has rescued me from the sea of twisted love and has placed me on the shore of righteous love" (*Par.* 26.62–63).

Beatrice

There are two incidents involving Psyche in a garden setting that recall Beatrice in her role as mediator between the human and the divine. The first incident occurs when Bardia leads Orual up Grey Mountain to find what she expects will be Psyche's body.

Virgil and Dante's pilgrim travel up Mount Purgatory's "holy road" (*Purg.* 20.142) that neither has traveled before. Likewise, Bardia and Orual journey up the mountain on "the sacred road" (*TWHF* 98) that she has never traveled before. Their trip "gently and steadily upward" (*TWHF* 95) is reminiscent in a general way of the ascent of Dante's mount. For Dante's pilgrim, the mountain's summit was so high he could not see it (see *Purg.* 4.40), and for Orual the mountain is "far greater . . . than I expected" (*TWHF* 95). When they come to a garden valley at the top of the mountain— "a small valley bright as a gem" that has green turf, groves of tress, and water (*TWHF* 101)—they see Psyche across a stream just as Dante's pilgrim initially sees Beatrice across a stream in Eden's lovely garden. In order to meet with Beatrice, however, Dante's pilgrim must first pass through a wall of fire on the ledge of lust (see *Purg.* 27.49–51), and Orual, before she crosses the stream to meet Psyche, exclaims, "I'd go if the river *flowed with fire* instead of water" (*TWHF* 103; italics added). Virgil disappears when Beatrice arrives, and Bardia, who is not invited to cross the stream, is likewise not a party to this meeting.

Like Lewis's Green Lady in *Perelandra*, Psyche on this occasion combines echoes of both Matilda and Beatrice as they first appear across a small stream. Matilda is three paces away (see *Purg.* 28.70) and Psyche is less than six feet way (see *TWHF* 101). Matilda takes the pilgrim's hand to help him across Eunoë (see *Purg.* 33.133), and Psyche stretches out her hand to help Orual across the stream (see *TWHF* 103). Beatrice is said to have "eyes [that] were shining more brightly than a star" (*Inf.* 2.55), and Psyche's "eyes [were] like two stars" (*TWHF* 102).

In this encounter, Psyche is a potentially transformative Beatrice, a channel of grace and truth and a mediator of faith, but Orual does not see the palace or Psyche's beautiful clothes. Although Psyche encourages Orual that her husband-god will make her able to see, Orual makes her choice: "I saw in a flash that I must choose one opinion or the other; and in the same flash I knew which I had chosen" (*TWHF* 126). When she returns a few days later to conclude that meeting, she reprises her substitute-mother role and is resolved to take Psyche away: "You cannot go your own way. You will let me rule and guide you" (*TWHF* 159). Because of Orual's deliberately unbelieving attitude, this meeting ends as a "failed Beatrician experience," so to speak, and recalls the dynamic of the conversation between Sarah Smith and her husband in *The Great Divorce*. Orual makes a choice at this point for hate and misery and against love and joy.

The second Beatrice scene occurs after Orual's trial when she is reunited with the Fox. When Virgil leads the pilgrim to the garden,

Beatrice first appears as the pilgrim's judge (see *Purg.* 30.106–145), and when the Fox takes Orual to Psyche, he announces, "We must go to your true judges now" (*TWHF* 297)—in this case, Psyche and, next, Psyche's husband-god.

They come to a garden area that has a chamber with walls on three sides with paintings that come alive showing Psyche fulfilling various punitive tasks. This recalls the white marble carvings of three examples of humility on Dante's ledge of pride in which "the dead seemed dead and the living seemed alive" (*Purg.* 12.67). Dante's pilgrim comments that the angel Gabriel who came to Mary, "seemed so lifelike to us that he did not seem to be a silent image" (*Purg.* 10.37–39). Next, the engravings of King David dancing before the Lord with the people looking on (see 2 Sam. 6:16–23) seem so real that the pilgrim cannot tell if he is smelling the incense and hearing the people singing or not (see *Purg.* 10.59–63). In the third scene, the pilgrim seems to hear the dialogue between the Roman emperor Trajan and a widow pleading for justice (see *Purg.* 10.83–93) and describes the carving as "visible speech" (*Purg.* 10.95). Orual can see the characters' movements depicted in the paintings on the chamber walls and hear the singing and dialogue as well. Dante, who does not repeat himself without purpose, uses the phrase "I saw" ("vidi") eight times for emphasis in fewer than forty lines as his pilgrim gazes at these carved examples; in a stylistic parallel Lewis uses "I saw" or "I could see" eight times as Orual is gazing at the living pictures.

It is significant that these paintings parallel the engravings on the ledge of pride, because that is the place where a soul grows in humility. It requires humility on Orual's part as she sees herself helping Psyche with some of her tasks, demonstrating her willingness to serve her and give of herself. In so doing, she is the one who has carried some of the burden for Psyche and endured some of the suffering.

The open end of this chamber with paintings leads to a grassy court with a bath of clear water, recalling Dante's Garden of Eden with its cleansing streams. Before Beatrice's arrival, there is a burst of incandescence in the forest "and its radiance, as it continued, increased more and more" (*Purg.* 29.20). As the Fox is leading Orual there, "the light was strengthening as we went" (*TWHF* 297). Before Beatrice's arrival, a hundred spirits rose up (see *Purg.* 30.17–18), and before Psyche arrives, Orual hears "a moving and rustling of invisible people, and more voices" (*TWHF* 305). Beatrice's arrival is announced by the participants in the allegorical procession that precedes her (see *Purg.* 30.11–12, 19), and Psyche's arrival is announced by "many voices" saying, "Our lady returns to her house" (*TWHF* 305). Virgil's disappearance at Beatrice's arrival is echoed by the Fox's disappearance at Psyche's arrival. When the pilgrim sees Beatrice, "she seemed to me to surpass her former self [in beauty]" (*Purg.* 31.83). When Orual sees Psyche on one of the painted walls of the chamber, she says, "no words I have would serve enough then, to tell you how beautiful she was. It was as though I had never seen her before" (*TWHF* 298). Just as Dante acknowledges his sin against Beatrice to her in the garden (see *Purg.* 31.34–36), so too Orual confesses her sin against Psyche: "I never wished you well, never had one selfless thought of you. I was a craver" (*TWHF* 305). However, there is no condemnation from this "judge." Psyche instead repeats her earlier prophecy on the mountain that they would be together and happy in her god's house.

Just as the pilgrim's meeting with Beatrice is preparation for his ultimate vision of God, so too Orual "knew that all this [meeting with Psyche] had been only a preparation" (*TWHF* 307). Just as Beatrice is not the ultimate goal of the journey, so too for Orual, "it was not, not now, she [Psyche] that really counted. Or if she counted . . . it was for another's sake" (*TWHF* 307).

The arrival of Psyche's husband-god likewise echoes elements of the encounter with Beatrice. For Dante's pilgrim, "The air became transformed into a *fiery light*" (*Purg.* 29.34–35; italics added), and for Orual, "The air was growing brighter and brighter . . . as if something had *set it on fire*" (*TWHF* 307; italics added). After Beatrice tells the pilgrim to look at her, "I lowered my eyes and looked down at the clear stream, but seeing myself reflected there I looked down on the grass" (*Purg.* 30.76–78). In a variation of this action, Orual looks down as Psyche's god approaches, and sees her reflection and Psyche's in the pool (see *TWHF* 307).

When Orual faces her final judge, the first words of Psyche's god, unlike those of Beatrice, do not condemn or upbraid Orual for her past sin. She hears a voice that says, "You also are Psyche" (*TWHF* 308), meaning, she who was formerly a bitter, ugly woman is now beautiful within and without, fulfilling the prophecy he spoke in a gentle way without anger when she first saw him on the mountain so long ago (see *TWHF* 174).

Like Beatrice, Psyche in the end successfully fulfills the role of leading a pilgrim to union with God.

Conclusion

Lewis said in 1946 that "*Perelandra* is much the best book I have written," but he later ended by saying, "I think it [*Till We Have Faces*] far and away my best book." It is certainly his most atypical novel since it has no Christian characters and its narrator is an untruthful female. Although this novel involves a pagan myth and pagan characters, Lewis's story about a human being who resists union with God—and about God's grace in rescuing such a person—depicts a dynamic that transcends time. As the Fox says, "All, even Psyche, are born into the house of Ungit [with fallen human nature]. And all must get free from her" (*TWHF* 301). For Lewis, a myth can be used to convey such a message because myths can foreshadow the truths of Christianity: "Pagan stories . . . are mere beginning—the first, faint whisper of the world from beyond the world—while Christianity is the thing itself." In his autobiography, Lewis states it this way: "Paganism has been only the childhood of religion, or only a prophetic dream."

Lewis in fact describes the novel's two main characters in Christian terms in one of his letters: "Psyche has a vocation and becomes a saint. Orual lives the practical life and is, after many sins, saved." Lewis is not saying that these women in pre-Christian times are Christians, but that people honestly seeking the one true God will find Christ, the Son of God, and will find him to be a loving, beautiful, and forgiving God even if they have an imperfect understanding of him and do not know his true name. Lewis remarks in a letter, "I think that every prayer which is sincerely made even to a false God or to a v. [*sic*] imperfectly conceived true God, is accepted by the true God and that Christ saves many who do not think they know him."

Lewis's approach on this point is consistent with that of Dante in cantos 19 and 20 of the *Paradiso* in which Dante's speaking eagle, shaped by lights representing just rulers, discusses the issue of salvation and God's justice concerning nonbelievers. Virgil had earlier explained that "I lost heaven through no other fault than not having faith" (*Purg.* 7.7–8) and that, regarding righteous pagans, "the merit they had was not enough; they did not have baptism, the doorway to faith" (*Inf.* 4.34–36). The question raised in this canto for the pilgrim concerns the justice of God in condemning a righteous man in a far-off place who, through no fault of his own, has not heard the gospel and dies without baptism (see *Par.* 19.70–78). The answer the pilgrim receives is that God's eternal judgment is too deep for people to comprehend but that God's will is always good (*Par.* 19.58–60, 98–99). In line with this theological principle, Dante's righteous pagans are found in Limbo.

However, the matter is far from settled because in the very next canto, Dante presents two exceptions of pagan souls who *are* in heaven: the Roman emperor Trajan, who lived in Christian times but died a pagan (see *Par.* 20.45–48), and Rhipeus, a hero in pre-Christian times during the Trojan War (see *Par.* 20.67–69). In the case of Trajan, according to medieval legend, when Pope Gregory prayed for his redemption, Trajan was raised from the dead and came back from hell "so that he could exercise his free will" (*Par.* 20.111)—always a major motif for Dante. Having returned to life, "he believed in the One who could help him [Christ]" (*Par.* 20.114) and was then baptized. Trajan's case is a highly unusual and unique exception, but having been baptized, he has access to heaven.

The second example of Rhipeus is the more mysterious exception, since he was not baptized and there are no spectacular miracles to account for his presence in heaven. His case is the one that has bearing on the situation for Psyche and Orual. He is described in the *Aeneid* as a man zealous for justice and righteousness. Dante's eagle explains Rhipeus's presence among the blessed by saying that he devoted himself to righteousness "through grace from a fountain so deep that no creature has ever plumbed its depth" (*Par.* 20.119–120), and God then "opened his eyes to our future redemption and he believed in it" (*Par.* 20.122–124). This clarifies the eagle's somewhat mysterious statement in the previous canto that "no one ever rose to this realm [heaven] who did not have faith in Christ, whether it was *before or after* he was nailed to the wood" (*Par.* 19.103–105; italics added), indicating that faith in Christ *before* the crucifixion is somehow possible.

In terms of the required baptism that Rhipeus was lacking, the eagle declares that his faith, hope, and charity "functioned as baptism for him . . . more than a thousand years before baptism was" (*Par.* 127–129). Dante's example of Rhipeus is a fictional application of the theological concept of "baptism by desire," one of the three kinds of baptism described by church fathers. Dante ends by warning his readers not to judge hastily about who is not redeemed and who is, because no one fully knows or understands the mysterious working of grace and providence (see *Par.* 20.133–135).

Lewis was aware of Dante's two pagan examples and made reference to them more than once in his writings. According to Walter Hooper, "Lewis came to believe that . . . pagans could be saved through Christ." Emeth, in *The Last Battle*, is Lewis's first fictional demonstration of this concept, and Lewis demonstrates it again through Psyche and Orual.

In this novel, in which Orual is most often reminiscent of sinners in Dante's hell and purgatory, she becomes in the end yet one more of Lewis's characters who recall Dante's pilgrim on the journey to union with God despite their pagan status. Psyche, in her role as a Beatrice figure, is unique among Lewis's multiple Beatrices: she plays that role for a woman, and she is the only "Beatrice" who has to play it twice—once in a failed attempt and then in a successful one. In all of Lewis's novels, as in Dante's poem, free will is the rudder that charts a person's course, and this story underscores that concept by being the case even for pagans.

CHAPTER TEN

Conclusion: In the Footsteps of Dante

Ongoing research remains to be done on Lewis's relationship to several other major authors, such as Chaucer, Milton, and Spenser. Lewis's narratives are multilayered in terms of allusions to great literary works, and some of those echoes may still have gone unnoticed. Even so, it is clear that Dante is a major presence, if not the major presence, in Lewis's work. David C. Downing writes, "By studying his use of predecessor texts, one sees the kind of literary art Lewis valued most highly in other writers and discovers also his own literary art in shaping such a variety of allusions into a coherent narrative." An overview of the links between Lewis and Dante indicates that what he valued most in Dante's art were his techniques for transposing Christian teaching into accessible literary forms as well as his narrative depictions of the Christian pilgrim and the Christian journey. Lewis's art reflects an astonishing depth of creativity in shaping his allusions to Dante's poem.

Examples of Lewis's use of *The Divine Comedy* cover the entire gamut of ways that an author can make use of a predecessor's text: direct or paraphrased quotes; modes of constructing fictional worlds; and a wide range of parallels, adaptations, and echoes of Dante's journey narrative and of his major characters. None of Lewis's individual novels retells the whole of Dante's story, but in none of Lewis's novels is Dante's story absent.

Lewis directly quotes Dante in Italian in two epitaphs and a chapter heading in *The Pilgrim's Regress*. He paraphrases a verse in the *Paradiso* describing the Empyrean to characterize the faces of the two eldils in *Perelandra*, and he paraphrases two verses from Dante's *Inferno* in *That Hideous Strength* to describe John Wither. A reader can find many quotes from Dante in all of Lewis's nonfiction, including his letters, but after his first novel, Lewis never again quotes Dante's poem directly in his longer fiction. *The Divine*

Comedy recedes from a kind of facile visibility to be woven into the fabric of Lewis's stories in subtle, powerful ways.

Lewis's construction of fictional worlds follows techniques from Dante's poem that vary depending on the quality of a given world. The allegorical landscape in *The Pilgrim's Regress* has moral parallels to the geography of Dante's hell and purgatory. In the Ransom trilogy, Lewis presents a medieval-modern cosmos with clear echoes of Dante's Christian interpretation of the Ptolemaic universe. Lewis shapes a world of the afterlife in *The Great Divorce* whose physical significance is a metaphor for spiritual reality, as is the case in Dante's afterlife. In *The Voyage of the "Dawn Treader,"* Lewis lays out a geography that is horizontally patterned after that of Dante's Mountain Purgatory and his heavens. During Orual's dreams and visions, the ancient kingdom in *Till We Have Faces* gives way to a spiritual landscape that echoes features of Dante's hell and purgatory.

Lewis's main pilgrims include both men and women. There are wide-ranging reasons for these pilgrims' journeys, and the pilgrims are in need of different kinds of spiritual development. With regard to his male pilgrims, John is seeking the truth about his island; Ransom never seeks or initiates his adventures; the patient tempted by Wormwood is perhaps even unaware he is on a journey; Mark's decisions lead him farther into a spiritual hell; an unnamed narrator has a dream about the afterlife; and the Narnians are in search of missing lords (*VDT*) and of a missing prince (*SC*). Lewis's main female pilgrims include a lapsed Christian wife, young girls from England, and a pagan queen. There are no clones, no "stock" characters here; each is unique with distinct strengths and weaknesses, but one common thread that links them together is their advancement in their knowledge of God and union with God.

The journeys of Lewis's pilgrims are structured to recall at least one stage of the three-phase Dantean journey. Definitive parallels to a journey in the *Inferno* emerge during John's journey west (*PR*), Ransom's journey to Malacandra (*OPS*), the narrator-Lewis's mini-journey (*Per.*), Mark Studdock's time at Belbury (*THS*), the journey to the underworld for Jill and Eustace (*SC*), and Orual's court trial before the gods (*TWHF*).

Parallels with the *Purgatorio* journey appear during John's journey east (*PR*), Ransom's adventures on Venus (*Per.*), the narrator's time on the Plain (GD), Jane Studdock's spiritual development (THS), the first part of the Narnian sea voyage (VDT), and the last part of Orual's dream-visions (TWHF).

Echoes of the Paradiso journey (or of direct encounters with God) can be brief and fleeting, as is the case for the patient (SL), Jane in the garden (THS), and Orual (TWHF). However, pronounced allusions of that journey occur during Ransom's Great Dance vision (Per.) and in the second part of the Dawn Treader's voyage (VDT).

Although some journeys are primarily connected to a specific stage of the Dantean journey, others reflect all three stages whether fleetingly (the patient in SL, Orual in her dream-visions) or in more detailed ways (Ransom in OSP and Per.). When a pilgrim's journey focuses on a single stage, Lewis always incorporates allusions to other segments of Dante's poem through specific characters, events, or dialogue.

In some of Lewis's stories, echoes of Virgil emerge briefly or at length. The female knight Reason helps John at critical junctions (PR), George MacDonald guides the narrator for half of his time on the Plain (GD); the Fox teaches Orual what he knows throughout her life (TWHF). Lewis even depicts a perverse Virgil in Screwtape's guidance of Wormwood and in Fairy Hardcastle as she takes special concern for Mark Studdock (THS).

Although Lewis's variety of pilgrims is very broad, his "Beatrices" perhaps best demonstrate Lewis's creativity in his imitation of The Divine Comedy. He reconfigures Dante's Beatrice and the "Beatrician encounter" in ways that grow increasingly varied and complex but are never repetitive. First, there is the "island-Beatrice" for John (PR) followed by the Malacandrian Oyarsa for Ransom (OSP). Subsequently, all of Lewis's Beatrices are human beings—perhaps to demonstrate that this experience generally occurs through human relationships rather than objects and that it is potentially available to every person, and not just to special people who encounter planetary angels.

Next, in The Screwtape Letters, Lewis's Beatrice is a young unmarried woman who fulfills that role for a young unmarried man (SL). This is the closest parallel Lewis has to the Beatrice-Dante relationship in The Divine Comedy, and it is the only time that Lewis presents that encounter as occurring between a couple that is single. In *Perelandra*, Lewis begins to expand the Beatrician horizon in having an extraterrestrial married couple fill that role. *That Hideous Strength* is the first (and only) novel to have two main characters on separate spiritual journeys, and Lewis provides two Beatrices for them: a man for a woman (Ransom for Jane) and a woman for a man (Jane for Mark). Up to this point, Ransom has the unique distinction, in Lewis's panoply of characters, of having had *two* journeys (to Mars and Venus) that represent multiple spiritual stages and of having *two* Beatrician encounters. Furthermore, in this novel he now becomes a Beatrice himself—for a woman! Jane is Lewis's only other character who is in need of a Beatrician encounter but who also plays the role of Beatrice herself (unknowingly, in this case, as Mark's inner standard).

Lewis's next novel, *The Great Divorce*, explodes in a multiplicity of Beatrice figures: each Mountain–Dweller fulfills that function for a Ghost in a very basic way; MacDonald plays that role in a much more detailed manner for the narrator; and Sarah Smith is the "Beatrice" to her husband, Frank. This is also the first Lewis novel in which a Beatrician encounter fails to produce the desired result when Sarah's husband refuses heaven.

The last two Beatrices in Lewis's novels continue to be uniquely distinct from their earlier counterparts. In *The Silver Chair,* there is a brief flash of Beatrice in Jill—the only Lewis-Beatrice who travels into an underworld to help rescue someone and the only one who echoes any kind of physical resemblance to Dante's Beatrice (because of her clothes). The Beatrice of *Till We Have Faces* has three unique characteristics. A woman, Psyche, fulfills that role for another woman; their relationship is that of siblings; and she is the only character in Lewis's novels who plays that role twice (once unsuccessfully and then successfully).

Except for two instances of a wife and husband (Jane and Mark, Sarah and Frank), Lewis does not repeat the specific relationship between a Beatrice and a given pilgrim. There are mountain-top experiences for this encounter (*OSP, Per., TWHF*), garden settings (*PR, Per., GD, TWHF*), and interior spaces (*THS*). The common element that runs through all of Lewis's widely differing Beatrician encounters is the importation of details from Dante's Garden of Eden scene, whether it be the setting, the dialogue, or emotional reactions. Despite the differences in relationships and settings, Lewis ties the core of that encounter solidly to Dante's narration of the encounter with Beatrice in the garden.

The particular links between any given novel and Dante's poem vary depending on the novel genre Lewis is using. Chad Walsh remarks that Lewis has "written a small library, offering half a dozen literary roads to Jerusalem." Jerusalem is the metaphor that Beatrice uses to describe heaven when Dante's pilgrim finally reaches it (see *Par.* 25.56). Even though Lewis did not preplan the corpus of his novels, he offers several literary paths to that destination: an allegorical novel, science fiction, an epistolary novel, adult fantasy, children's fantasy, and a mythological novel. Readers who may not like science fiction may enjoy children's fantasy, so they may choose from many "literary roads" that Lewis supplies. By Lewis's own accounting, the genesis of each of his novels is tied to certain ideas he wanted to express, to popular ideas he wanted to correct, and/or to pictures in his head that required a specific genre. Once a specific genre was chosen, Lewis's use of Dante was necessarily tailored to that genre.

Lewis's twentieth-century novels obviously differ on many levels from Dante's medieval poem, yet they clearly bear the stamp of that predecessor's text. However, as Downing notes, "Lewis often illuminates his predecessors' texts more than those texts illuminate our reading of Lewis." Knowledge of Lewis's novels is in many ways a preparation for reading Dante, just as knowledge of Dante's poem paves the way for a rich reading of Lewis. Lewis's discussion of Matthew Arnold's *Sohrab and Rustrum* and the *Iliad* is to the point here:

> Parrot critics say that *Sohrab* is a poem . . . to be enjoyed only by those who recognize the Homeric echoes. But I . . . knew nothing of Homer. For me the relation between Arnold and Homer worked the other way; when I came, years later, to read the *Iliad* I liked it partly because it was for me reminiscent of *Sohrab*. Plainly, it does not matter at what point you first break into the system of European poetry [literature]. Only keep your ears open and your mouth shut and everything will lead you to everything else in the end—*ogni parte ad ogni parte splende.*

Lewis does not translate this last phrase, but it comes from the *Inferno* (7.75): "every part shines light on every other part."

Applying Lewis's dictum here to his own work, his link with Dante can work both ways: a reader who already knows Dante will recognize the literary tradition to which Lewis belongs, but by the same token, a reader who already knows Lewis will not find Dante entirely unfamiliar. The reader who breaks into the system of European literature through Lewis—whose fiction is buttressed by many authors but perhaps primarily by the poet he admired the most—will eventually be led to Dante.

The relationship between Lewis and Dante, however, is not a slavish sort of "imitation." As Northrop Frye remarks in his *Anatomy of Criticism*, "The real difference between the original and the imitative poet is simply that the former is more profoundly imitative." The fact that the depth of Lewis's relationship and debt to Dante has for the most part been fleetingly referred to without many examples by most scholars is itself evidence that Lewis's adaptations and transformations of Dante's material is so profoundly creative that much of it has gone unseen. However, as Michael Ward notes, "No artist is obliged to unveil his every strategy," and as Walter Hooper points out, "It is part of the success of a great author that the sense of his book not depend on the reader's knowing the original source of its ingredients."

Clearly, Lewis approached *The Divine Comedy* as a literary archetype for presenting the Christian message and the Christian pilgrim. For this reason, Lewis appropriates Dante's poem as an important template for his novels. As Lewis once described him, "In some matters, 'the phoenix Dante is a vast species alone.'" Using the bones of Dante's story, so to speak, to fashion his own stories, Lewis repeats Dante's messages and updates them in modern vernacular with modern images. One scholar calls Dante "a champion of imaginative truth," and the same can appropriately and easily be said about Lewis. His remark in a letter describing his Ransom stories can be applied to all his novels: "They may be regarded as imaginative hypotheses illustrating what I believe to be theological truths."

In an essay describing imagery in Dante's last part of the *Paradiso*, Lewis says his goal there is to examine "the imagination of the poet in its most secret workings, to disengage that incessant orchestration which accompanies his drama and which, though it may escape notice while our attention is fixed on the stage, probably contributes in the highest degree to the total effect." The goal of this book has been to examine Lewis's "imagination . . . in its most secret workings" insofar as Dante's *Divine Comedy* is concerned. Because of the myriad of different ways in which *The Divine Comedy* and its messages are recast and reflected in Lewis's novels, I believe that Dante's poem has been given renewed life in the modern imagination—whether readers are aware of it or not—and that Lewis, in his own right, can be called "a Dante for the modern age."

Notes

Introduction

1 {books about Lewis}   Only a brief sampling of authors (some of whom have written several books on Lewis) can be given here on topics that cover a wide range: Lewis's life (Roger Lancelyn Green and Walter Hooper, A. N. Wilson, Alan Jacobs, Alister E. McGrath); his theological themes (Chad Walsh, Leanne Payne, John Randolph Willis); his literary artistry (Joe R. Christopher, Donald E. Glover, Thomas Howard, Colin N. Manlove); his personality (Owen Barfield, James T. Como); the interplay of reason and imagination in his work (Peter J. Schakel, Leland Ryken), his faith (Richard B. Cunningham, Paul Holmer, David C. Downing); his fiction in general (Clyde S. Kilby, Evan K. Gibson, Doris T. Myers); specific novels (Peter J. Schakel, David C. Downing, Michael Ward, Thomas Williams); his poetry (Don W. King); his use of myth (Mark Edwards Freshwater); his cultural insights (Peter Kreeft, Gilbert Meilander); his relationship with friends and their influence on him (Humphrey Carpenter, Diana Pavlac Glyer); his presentation of gender (Monika B. Hilder); and even his approach to environmental issues (Matthew Dickerson and David O'Hara)!

1 {Lewis's "novels"}   Although most people refer to Lewis's long fiction as "novels," Joe R. Christopher, basing his remarks on categories in Northrop Frye's *Anatomy of Criticism*, maintains that Lewis's fiction "consists of romances, not novels, . . . although often, outside of the Narnia books, . . . a hybrid between the romances and other forms." *C. S. Lewis* (New York: Twayne, 1987), 89. Lewis himself, for example, refers to his science fiction novels as "planetary romances." *Surprised by Joy: The Shape of My Early Life* (New York: Harcourt, Brace & World, 1955), 36. For purposes of simplicity, I will refer to his book-length fiction as "novels" in the chapter discussions.

1 {no book on significant role} *Reading the Classics with C. S. Lewis*, ed. Thomas L. Martin (Grand Rapids, MI: Baker Academic, 2000) has essays on Lewis and Shakespeare, Spenser, Milton, etc., but none on Dante. Conversely, Stuart Y. McDougal's book *Dante among the Moderns* (Chapel Hill: University of North Carolina Press, 1985) includes chapters on William B. Yeats, Ezra Pound, T. S. Eliot, etc., but nothing on Lewis.

1 {model for his fiction} Wayne Martindale says Dante's *Divine Comedy* "is a major literary backdrop for much of Lewis's fiction," which I heartily agree with, but he supports that declaration with only the one example that a resurrected Caspian in *Prince Caspian*, who does not want wrong things anymore, is like Dante's pilgrim whose will has been rectified after his ascent of the mount. *Beyond the Shadowlands: C. S. Lewis on Heaven and Hell* (Wheaton, IL: Crossway, 2005), 113.

1 {"a Source . . . in a certain way"} C. S. Lewis, "The Literary Impact of the Authorized Version," in *Selected Literary Essays*, ed. Walter Hooper (Cambridge: Cambridge University Press, 1969), 133.

2 {linguistic treatise} *On the Eloquence of the Vernacular* (*De vulgari eloquentia*) is an unfinished treatise that argues for the use of vernacular language for literature at a time when Latin was considered the formal language for writing.

2 {political treatise} *On Monarchy* (*De monarchia*) deals with the distinctions between the roles of church and state.

2 {philosophical treatise} *The Banquet* (*Convivio*), an unfinished treatise, includes some of his poems with a commentary on their allegorical meaning.

3 {transcend denominations} Dante was a member of the pre-Reformation Roman church and Lewis was Anglican.

4 {Garden of Eden details} In drawing on details in the setting, action, dialogue, emotional reactions, etc., from the meeting scene in Dante's garden, Lewis signals that a significant transformative encounter will be taking place through a new Beatrice figure. The one exception is *The Screwtape Letters* because it does not describe the young man's initial meeting with the woman he loves.

6 {conscious on Lewis's part?} For an excellent discussion of the procedure—and the pitfalls—in determining literary influence on a writer, see Diana Pavlac Glyer, *The Company They Keep: C. S. Lewis and J. R. R. Tolkien as Writers in Community* (Kent, OH: Kent State University Press, 2007), especially pp. 33–45. As Christopher

points out, however, "no number of parallels can prove an indebtedness," so more is required than just the presence of parallels. *C. S. Lewis*, 118.

6 {asked him more questions}   However, as Michael Ward points out, "No artist is obliged to unveil his every strategy." *Planet Narnia: The Seven Heavens in the Imagination of C. S. Lewis* (Oxford: Oxford University Press, 2008), 7. As time goes on, it is my expectation that more and more of Lewis's literary strategies will be uncovered.

7 {"Lewis was deeply . . . only begun"}   Alister E. McGrath, *The Intellectual World of C. S. Lewis* (Malden, MA: John Wiley and Sons, 2014), 5.

7 {Italian quotations}   Italian quotes are from *La Divina Commedia*, Scartazziniano edition, ed. Giuseppe Vandelli (Milan: Ulrico Hoepli, 1965). The English translations, which are mine, aim at being literal. Although there are many good translations that convey Dante's concepts accurately in good, flowing English, they often depart significantly from the precise Italian wording that Lewis might have had in mind when he was composing his own works.

Chapter 1: Lewis, Dante, and Literary Predecessors

9 {"monuments" of previous writers}   T. S. Eliot, "Tradition and Individual Talent," in *Selected Prose of T. S. Eliot*, ed. and intro. Frank Kermode (London: Faber and Faber, 1975), 38.

9 {"involves . . . presence"}   Ibid.

9 {"not only . . . vigorously"}   Ibid.

9 {". . . prose or verse"}   C. S. Lewis and E. M. W. Tillyard, *The Personal Heresy: A Controversy* (Oxford: Oxford University Press, 1939), 107.

9 {literary criticism}   See, for instance, *The Personal Heresy* (1939), a series of literary debates with E. M. W. Tillyard; *An Experiment in Criticism* (1961), a discussion of literature in particular and of good and bad approaches to criticism; and *Of Other Worlds* (1966), a series of essays and lectures that describe the genesis of some of his fiction and discuss some of the genres he used.

10 {"old critics . . . profit"}   Lewis and Tillyard, *The Personal Heresy*, 119.

10 {"healthy . . . entertainment"}   "Letter to Dom Bede Griffiths," April 16, 1940, in *The Collected Letters of C. S. Lewis*, vol. 2, *Books, Broadcasts, and the War 1931–1949*, ed. Walter Hooper (New York: HarperCollins, 2004), 390–91.

10 {challenged in modern times} The postmodern concept that "truth is relative" makes it a tenuous proposition for any authors to be considered as "teaching" since they can express only "their own truth."

10 {"Until . . . appreciate the bard"} C. S. Lewis, "Good Works and Good Work," in *"The World's Last Night" and Other Essays* (New York: Harcourt Jovanovich, 1960), 78–79.

10 {"a separate . . . mahatmas"} Lewis and Tillyard, *The Personal Heresy*, 104.

10 {"the end . . . poet's soul"} Ibid., 1.

10 {". . . pair of spectacles"} Ibid., 12.

10 {"a man of genius . . . undisciplined coxcombs"} Eliot, *"Ulysses, Order, and Myth,"* in *Selected Prose of T. S. Eliot*, 176. In all fairness to Eliot, it should be noted that he later admitted, in his essay "To Criticize the Critic" (1961), that upon rereading many of his earlier essays, "There are . . . statements with which I no longer agree. . . . There are errors . . . of tone: the occasional note of arrogance, of vehemence, of cocksureness or rudeness" (*"To Criticize the Critic" and Other Writings* [London: Faber and Faber, 1965], 14). His statement here about Joyce would seem to qualify as one of those errors that have a "note of arrogance."

11 {"is not . . . incompetence"} Lewis, "Good Works and Good Work," 80.

11 {"Literature . . . delightful things"} C. S. Lewis, *The Discarded Image: An Introduction to Medieval and Renaissance Literature* (Cambridge: Cambridge University Press, 1964), 214. Lewis is echoing Paul's admonition in Philippians 4:8: "Whatever is true, whatever is honorable, whatever is just, whatever is pure, whatever is lovely, whatever is gracious, if there is anything worthy of praise, think on these things" (Revised Standard Version).

11 {"Our whole . . . Wisdom"} C. S. Lewis, "Christianity and Literature," in *Christian Reflections*, ed. Walter Hooper (Grand Rapids, MI: Eerdmans, 1967), 7. Reprinted by permission of the publisher; all rights reserved.

11 {superior truths} In Lewis's scheme—where literature is not the highest value, and indeed, should be in service to higher values—there is, therefore, no room for any art-for-art's-sake theory. Nor is there any room for a concept of literature as the self-expression of the poet, no matter how superior an individual he or she might be, because the proper subject matter of literature lies outside the poet.

11 {adding layers of meaning}   Concerning the possibility that some-
one might write letters that imitate those in *The Screwtape Letters*,
Lewis says, "My own feeling is that a literary idea ought to belong to
anyone who can use it and that literary property is a sort of Simony."
"Letter to Sister Penelope," December 30, 1950, *The Collected Letters of
C. S. Lewis*, vol. 3, *Narnia, Cambridge, and Joy 1950–1963*, ed. Walter
Hooper (New York: HarperCollins, 2007), 79.

12 {"In the New Testament . . . 'spontaneous'"}   Lewis, "Christianity
and Literature," 8.

12 {until the modern period}   Most criticism and literary theory written since the 1970s is likewise critical of the modernist writers who
emphasized originality over imitation and claimed singular genius
for themselves. Among recent schools of criticism it is generally acknowledged that all writing is in some way imitative, as writers can
only work using the models they have received from past writers. At
the very least, all writers, no matter how creative, necessarily work
with idioms and conventions they have learned from others.

12 {"We . . . men of genius"}   Lewis, "Christianity and Literature," 3.

12 {not exclusive terms}   As Doris T. Myers points out, Lewis "consciously followed the masters of ancient and medieval literature by
never aspiring to originality." *Bareface: A Guide to C. S. Lewis's Last
Novel* (Columbia: University of Missouri Press, 2004), 145.

12 {recent theories}   In the second half of the twentieth century, one
approach sets forth the view that the relationship between authors
and predecessors is primarily an Oedipal struggle in which predecessors become obstacles for new authors to overcome rather than men-
tors and helpers. See, for instance, Walter Jackson Bate, *The Burden of
the Past and the English Poet* (1970), and Harold Bloom, *The Anxiety
of Influence: A Theory of Poetry* (1973).

12 {"In literature . . . noticed it"}   C. S. Lewis, *Mere Christianity* (New
York: Macmillan, 1952), 190.

13 {affinity with European Literature}   Judged by the standards set by
T. S. Eliot in his essay "Tradition and Individual Talent," Lewis's literary theory, and his fiction that is shaped by that theory, clearly links
him to the Western literary heritage. "Intertextuality" is one of the
more common terms currently in use to address this interweaving of
sources into any creative composition.

13 {reading *Inferno*}   "Letter to His Father," February 8, 1917, *The
Collected Letters of C. S. Lewis*, vol. 1, *Family Letters 1905–1931*, ed.
Walter Hooper (New York: HarperCollins, 2004), 275.

13 {reading *Purgatorio*}   "Letter to Arthur Greeves," October 13, 1918, *The Collected Letters of C. S. Lewis*, vol. 1, 406. See also his "Letter to Greeves" on October [?], 1918, 403, in which he says he is reading the *Purgatorio* in the Temple Classics edition.

13 {acquire edition}   "Letter to His Brother," July 1, 1921, *The Collected Letters of C. S. Lewis*, vol. 1, 559.

13 {*Paradiso* "more important"}   "Letter to Arthur Greeves," January [13?], 1930, *The Collected Letters of C. S. Lewis*, vol. 1, 193. Unless otherwise indicated, all italicized material is original to the quotation.

13 {*Paradiso* "heights of poetry"}   "Letter to Arthur Greeves," July 8, 1930, *The Collected Letters of C. S. Lewis*, vol. 1, 915.

13 {*Paradiso* with Barfield}   "Letter to Arthur Greeves," January 3, 1930, *The Collected Letters of C. S. Lewis*, vol. 1, 856–57.

13 {finish *Paradiso* with Barfield}   "Letter to Arthur Greeves," July 8, 1930, *The Collected Letters of C. S. Lewis*, vol. 1, 915.

13 {read Dante with Barfield}   "Letter to Arthur Greeves," June 26[?], 1931, *The Collected Letters of C. S. Lewis*, vol. 1, 963.

13 {join Dante Society}   He became a member on February 16, 1937, according to *Centenary Essays on Dante*, ed. Colin Hardie (Oxford: Clarendon Press, 1965), 147.

13 {read Dante with Hardie}   Humphrey Carpenter, *The Inklings: C. S. Lewis, J. R. R. Tolkien, Charles Williams, and Their Friends* (Boston: Houghton Mifflin, 1979), 194. See "Letter to His Brother," November 11, 1939, *The Collected Letters of C. S. Lewis*, vol. 2, 288, and "Letter to His Brother," November 19, 1939, in which Lewis reports meeting Hardie on Monday evenings for their readings. *The Collected Letters of C. S. Lewis*, vol. 2, 292.

14 {feedback to Sayers}   See his letters to Dorothy L. Sayers on her translation of the *Inferno* on November 11, 1949, November 15, 1949, and November 21, 1949, in *The Collected Letters of C. S. Lewis*, vol. 2, 995–97, 999–1001. His comments on her translation of the *Purgatorio*, which he says is even better than her translation of the *Inferno*, appear in a letter to her on July 31, 1955, *The Collected Letters of C. S. Lewis*, vol. 3, 633–35. He also praises her book *Introductory Papers on Dante* (1954), calling it "a regular feast" and "a lovely book" and offering occasional suggestions or adjustments in a letter to her on November 14, 1954, *The Collected Letters of C. S. Lewis*, vol. 3, 523–27. See also his letter to her about her book *Further Papers on Dante* (1957) on June 25, 1957, which he says is even better than her first book on Dante. *The Collected Letters of C. S. Lewis*, vol. 3, 860–61.

14 {"supreme poetical honours"}   C. S. Lewis, *The Allegory of Love: A Study in Medieval Tradition* (1936; repr., New York: Oxford University Press, 1969), 155.

14 {"greatest of all poetry"}   C. S. Lewis, "Dante's Similes," in *Studies in Medieval and Renaissance Literature*, coll. Walter Hooper (Cambridge: Cambridge University Press, 1966), 76.

14 {Dante, favorite poet}   George Sayer, "Jack on Holiday," in *"C. S. Lewis at the Breakfast Table" and Other Reminiscences*, ed. James T. Como (New York: Macmillan, 1979), 203. Michael Ward also refers to Dante as "Lewis's favourite poet." *Planet Narnia: The Seven Heavens in the Imagination of C. S. Lewis* (Oxford: Oxford University Press, 2008), 41.

14 {lifelong love of Dante}   George Sayer, *Jack: A Life of C. S. Lewis* (Wheaton, IL: Crossway, 1988), 116.

14 {remembered all he read}   William Empson, quoted in James T. Como, ed., *"C. S. Lewis at the Breakfast Table" and Other Reminiscences* (New York: Macmillan, 1979), xxi.

14 {"verbatim memory"}   George Sayer, *Jack: C. S. Lewis and His Times* (San Francisco: Harper and Row, 1988), 47.

14 {multiple references to Dante}   Lewis makes fourteen references to Dante or his poem in *Selected Literary Essays* (1969), essays on a variety of authors and topics; thirteen in *Experiment on Criticism* (1965), a book on how to appreciate art and literature; nine in *English Literature in the Sixteenth Century Excluding Drama* (1954); six in *The Preface to "Paradise Lost"* (1942); five in *Christian Reflections* (1971); four in his autobiography *Surprised by Joy* (1955); three in *Studies in Words* (1966), which traces the evolution of the meaning of seven words; and three in *The Personal Heresy* (1939), a book on literary theory.

14 {necessary reading}   See, for example, "Letter to Sister Madeleva," June 7, 1934, *The Collected Letters of C. S. Lewis*, vol. 2, 142; "Letter to Mary Neylan," October 2, 1941, *The Collected Letters of C. S. Lewis*, vol. 2, 492. See "Letter to Mary van Duesen," November 6, 1951, *The Collected Letters of C. S. Lewis*, vol. 3, 126, in which he recommends *The Divine Comedy* in a short list of "good religious works."

15 {*Commedia*'s title}   Dante called it simply the *Commedia* partly because, according to Aristotle's *Poetics*, a comedy is a story that ends well. Beginning in 1555, more than two hundred years after Dante wrote his poem, publishers added the adjective *"Divina"* to the title, and it has persisted since then.

15 {fourteenth-century composition}   Critics dispute the exact dates, but they range from 1305 to 1320.

16 {"by his merits ... by justice"}   Dante, "Letter to Can Grande," *Dantis Alagherii Epistolae*, 8, trans. Paget Toynbee, 2nd ed. (Oxford: Clarendon Press, 1966), 200. This letter presents his dedication of the *Paradiso* to his patron, an Italian nobleman.

16 {"to remove ... happiness"}   Ibid., 15, 202.

16 {basic doctrines of all denominations}   As Robert Hollander points out, "No one would dispute the fact that the Bible is the central text which shaped Dante's *Commedia.*" *Dante and Paul's Five Words with Understanding* (Binghamton, NY: Medieval and Renaissance Texts and Studies, 1992), 3. This is true for Dante's other works as well: "When Dante's writings are considered as a whole, the Christian Scriptures turn out to be the source of more reference and allusion than any other work: by one count ... 575 citations of the Bible." Peter S. Hawkins, *Dante's Testaments: Essays in Scriptural Imagination* (Stanford, CA: Stanford University Press, 1999), 36.

16 {Dante's *Purgatorio*}   Despite the doctrine of purgatory being chiefly a Catholic doctrine, the activities of the souls in Dante's *Purgatorio* are meant to demonstrate how all Christians should live their lives *on earth* to prepare for heaven: repent of sinful attitudes, grow in virtue, sing hymns, pray. On each ledge, souls recite a particular prayer, generally from the Psalms, so this is perhaps the reason George Holmes refers to the "liturgical atmosphere" of the *Purgatorio* in his book *Dante* (New York: Hill & Wang, 1980), 73. Lewis himself says the *Purgatorio* "is perhaps my favourite part of the Comedy [*sic*]," probably because it does indeed have so many practical applications to daily Christian life. "Letter to Dorothy L. Sayers," December 16, 1953, *The Collected Letters of C. S. Lewis*, vol. 3, 2007), 387. As Wayne Martindale explains, the *Purgatorio* "is many readers' favorite part of *The Divine Comedy*, including mine—because it says so much about human nature and the role of discipline and sanctification in our earthly lives." *Beyond the Shadowlands: C. S. Lewis on Heaven and Hell* (Wheaton, IL: Crossway, 2005), 202.

17 {reflects the particular sin}   Each *contrapasso* "is calculated to provoke rational thought concerning the nature of the sin, that is, the way in which it deviates from the divine." Erich Auerbach, *Dante: Poet of the Secular World*, trans. Ralph Manheim (Chicago: University of Chicago Press, 1961), 111. As Marguerite Mills Chiarenza explains, the punishments are "concrete versions of their [sinners'] choices in life,

not just arbitrary consequences of their sins." *"The Divine Comedy":
Tracing God's Art* (Boston: Twayne, 1989), 28.

17 {premeditated sin}   Chiarenza notes the distinction that "When
passion [upper circles] passes away the will to sin passes with it, while
malice [lower circles] becomes a habit." *"The Divine Comedy,"* 32.

18 {seven capital sins}   Although Dante was free to structure his hell,
the church's long tradition of the seven deadly sins is the basis for the
structure of his Mount Purgatory.

18 {eyes cast down}   As with many scenes in Dante's poem, this punishment is a visual demonstration of a Scripture verse, in this case,
Isaiah 2:11: "The lofty looks of man shall be humbled, and the haugh-
tiness of men shall be bowed down."

18 {humility and pride examples}   According to Richard Lansing, "The
ritual of purgation requires reinforcement of virtue as the first step
towards confession, an act that enables the true penitent to confront
vice later with strength and equanimity." "Narrative Design in Dante's
Earthy Paradise," in *Dante: Contemporary Perspectives*, ed. Amilcare
A. Iannucci (Toronto: University of Toronto Press, 1997), 138.

19 {Ptolemaic universe}   See Lewis's description of the Ptolemaic
model in *The Discarded Image*, 96.

21 {readers' difficulties}   Lewis admits that it "was my first religious
book and I didn't know how to make things easy." "Letter to Belle
Allen," January 19, 1953, *The Collected Letters of C. S. Lewis*, vol. 3,
Narnia, Cambridge, and Joy 1950–1963, ed. Walter Hooper (New
York: HarperCollins, 2007), 282. Blaming himself rather than the
reader, he tells Joan Bockelmann in a letter on May 29, 1959, "I was a
very inexperienced writer when I wrote *The P's Regress* [sic] and that
is why it is so difficult." *The Collected Letters of C. S. Lewis*, vol. 3, 1054.

Chapter 2: *The Pilgrim's Regress*

21 {desire for island's beauty}   Lewis describes some childhood experiences of objects or stories that aroused this longing in his autobiography, *Surprised by Joy: The Shape of My Early Life* (New York: Harcourt,
Brace & World, 1955), 16–17.

22 {compared to *Pilgrim's Progress*}   Colin Duriez, like many Lewis
scholars, calls it "an early twentieth-century version of John Bunyan's
great allegory." *The C. S. Lewis Handbook* (Eastbourne, UK: Monarch,
1990), 163. For an interesting alternative comparison, see Jeffrey L.
Bilbro who sees closer links with George MacDonald's *Phantastes*.

"Phantastical Regress: The Return of Desire and Deed in *Phantastes* and *The Pilgrim's Regress*," *Mythlore* 28, nos. 3–4 (Spring/Summer 2010): 21–37.

22 {secular vs. religious allegory}   See Lewis's *Allegory of Love: A Study in Medieval Tradition* (London: Oxford University Press, 1936; repr., New York: Oxford University Press, 1969), 48, n. 2. Commenting that he is focused on secular allegory, Lewis does not elaborate on the differences between these two kinds of allegory.

23 {"scriptural allegory"}   Various adjectives are used in the discussion about this kind of allegory. Some Dante scholars, like Charles S. Singleton, call this style "scriptural allegory." See his *Dante Studies*, 2 vols. (Cambridge, MA: Harvard University Press, 1954–1958). For an in-depth discussion of Dante's allegory and its precedents, see the entry "Allegory" in *The Dante Encyclopedia*, ed. Richard Lansing (New York: Routledge, 2010), 224–34. For a history of allegory see *Cambridge Companion to Allegory*, eds. Rita Copeland and Peter T. Struck (Cambridge: Cambridge University Press, 2010), especially chapter 10, "Medieval Secular Allegory: French and English," 136–47, and chapter 11, "Medieval Religious Allegory: French and English," 148–61. Prue Shaw adds yet another adjective to describe this kind of allegory, saying it "is sometimes called 'historical allegory' because the people in it really lived." *Reading Dante: From Here to Eternity* (New York: Norton, 2014), 79.

23 {Dante's mode of allegory}   It is widely accepted by Dante critics that "the poet's style and his allegory both find their unique model in . . . Holy Scripture." Charles S. Singleton, *Dante Studies*, vol. 1, *"Commedia": Elements of Structure* (Cambridge, MA: Harvard University Press, 1954), 58.

23 {significance on literal level}   The events and characters of scriptural allegory, in the words of Dante critic Erich Auerbach, differ from most allegorical forms "by the historicity both of the sign and what it signifies." "Figura," in *Scenes from the Drama of European Literature* (New York: Meridian, 1959), 54. For a full discussion of this issue, see Auerbach's whole chapter (pp. 11–76) and Robert Hollander, "Dante 'Theologus-Poeta,'" *Dante Studies*, ed. Christopher Kleinhenz (Albany: State University of New York Press, 1976), 91–136.

23 {interpretations not restricted}   In terms of the Bible, St. Thomas Aquinas in his *Summa Theologica* 1.1.10 outlines four simultaneous levels of meaning that occur in Scripture: first, the literal, and next the three spiritual senses based on the literal, i.e., the allegorical, moral, and anagogical.

23 {Williams on Virgil}   Charles Williams, *The Figure of Beatrice* (London: Faber & Faber, 1943), 70.

23 {Sayers on Virgil}   Dorothy L. Sayers, *Further Papers on Dante* (London: Methuen, 1957), 56–57.

23 {"from 'popular realism' . . . to Christianity"}   C. S. Lewis, preface, *The Pilgrim's Regress: An Allegorical Apology for Christianity, Reason, and Romanticism*, 3rd ed. rev., with new pref. (London: Geoffrey Bles, 1944), 5. Reprinted by permission of the publisher; all rights reserved. All quotes from Lewis's text will be indicated by book and chapter number.

24 {"Lewis's emulation . . . Bunyan well"}   Jared C. Lobdell, *The Scientifiction Novels of C. S. Lewis: Space and Time in the Ransom Stories* (Jefferson, NC: McFarland, 2004), 93.

25 {sun represents God}   See Psalm 84:11: "The Lord God is a sun."

26 {departures from Truth}   Insofar as any metaphysical or philosophical system contains "Northern" as well as "Southern" elements in Lewis's view, that shire is located on both sides of the Main Road, i.e., the shires of Pagus and Puritania, for example.

26 {"Southerners . . . Northerners"}   Lewis, preface, *The Pilgrim's Regress*, 11–12.

26 {Lewis's North and South}   North and South, according to Lewis, are not inventions of his own but are in fact archetypes that "enter our experience on many different levels." Lewis, preface, *The Pilgrim's Regress*, 11. As archetypes, North and South have reference not just to the contrast of head and heart, but to any pair of opposites. Lewis goes on to posit a North and South in soil (too barren, too fertile), in eating (too bitter, too sweet), in art (too purist, too uncritical), etc.

27 {Bunyan's locations and characters}   The experience of Bunyan's hero in the Slough of Despond is, on one level, in the same category as his experience with Mr. Worldly Wiseman because both represent hindrances to his journey that must be overcome, so the function of characters and locations is interchangeable in his allegory.

28 {". . . in desire to dwell"}   This is Lewis's translation for the verses in *Inf.* 4.40–42: "Per tal difetti, non per altro rio, / semo perduti, e sol di tanto offesi, / che sanza speme vivemo in disio."

28 {*Inf.* 4.68–69}   *Inf.* 4.68–69: ". . . un foco / ch'emisperio di tenebre vincìa."

28 {*Inf.* 4.131–132}   *Inf.* 4.131–132: ". . . 'l maestro di color che sanno / seder tra filosofica famiglia."

28 {*Inf.* 4.112–114}   *Inf.* 4.112–114: "... occhi tardi e gravi, / ... / parlavan rado, con voci soavi."

29 {*Inf.* 4.26}   *Inf.* 4.26: "... mai che di sospiri." See also *Purg.* 7.30.

29 {"... desire without hope"}   James Collins comments that the souls in Limbo are receiving the same justice, or *contrapasso*, as other souls in hell because "they receive only what they freely chose—a purely natural bliss." *Pilgrim in Love: An Introduction to Dante and His Spirituality* (Chicago: Loyola University Press, 1984), 87.

29 {*Inf.* 4.34–36}   *Inf.* 4.34–36: "... s'elli hanno mercedi, / non basta, perchè non ebber battesmo, / ch' è porta della fede. ..." Virgil says of himself, "I lost heaven through no other fault than not having faith" (*Purg.* 7.7–8: "... per null' altro rio / lo ciel perdei che per non aver fè"). He goes on to say, "I am there with those who are not clothed in the three holy virtues [faith, hope, and charity], and without having any vices, they were aware of the other virtues and practiced all of them" (*Purg.* 7.33–35: "quivi sto io con quei che le tre sante / virtù non si vestiro, e sanza vizio / conobber l'altre e seguir tutte quante").

29 {*Inf.* 4.38}   *Inf.* 4.38: "non adorar debitamente a Dio." Virgil himself confesses, he "was rebellious to His [God's] law" (*Inf.* 1.125: "... io fu' ribellante alla sua legge"). Sayers says, "Faith is imagination actualised by the will. What was lacking in the heathen philosophers was precisely the imagination of [heavenly] bliss. They had not, so to speak, sufficient faith in the good intentions of the universe." *Further Papers on Dante*, 48. John's guide makes the same point: "The Landlord does not condemn them to lack of hope: They have done that to themselves" (Book X, 3).

29 {*Purg.* 7.25–26}   *Purg.* 7.25–26: "Non per far, ma per non fare ho perduto / a veder l'alto sol che tu desiri."

30 {"If there are ... know nothing"}   Joseph Anthony Mazzeo, "Dante's Three Communities: Mediation and Order," in *The World of Dante: Six Studies in Language and Thought*, eds. S. Bernard Chandler and J. A. Molinaro (Toronto: University of Toronto Press, 1966), 71.

30 {map of truth and error}   I would therefore strongly disagree with scholars who restrict the map's meaning only to the soul or psyche. Duriez believes that Lewis's "*Mappa Mundi*" (world map) in this novel is a map "in which the human soul is divided into north and south." *The C. S. Lewis Handbook*, 163. Similarly, Colin Manlove believes that this novel is "a psychomachia, in which the landscapes and characters met were in part extensions of the spirit of the central character." "'Caught Up into the Larger Pattern': Images and

Narrative Structures in C. S. Lewis's Fiction," in *Word and Story in C. S. Lewis*, eds. Peter J. Schakel and Charles A. Huttar (Columbia: University of Missouri Press, 1991), 274. John D. Haigh also believes that the allegorical landscapes represent "'inner space,' or the individual psyche." "C. S. Lewis and the Tradition of Visionary Romances," in *Word and Story in C. S. Lewis*, eds. Peter J. Schakel and Charles A. Huttar (Columbia: University of Missouri Press, 1991), 193. In all three cases these scholars seem to overlook the objective quality of Lewis's landscape as philosophies, theologies, and schools of thought that John encounters but that are certainly not equal to or representative of his soul or anyone else's soul. The fact that there are areas on the map that John never even visits seems proof of that.

31 {journey west, journey down}   Wisland, the shire of wisdom in the far west, does not at first seem to fit this scheme, but it lies in a valley at the southern end of the canyon, so it is quite separate from the areas that lie north and south of the Main Road.

31 {kinship of hell and purgatory}   Dante's hell and purgatory also have similar moral structures: Hell is an inverted mountain with circles proceeding downward, with its last circle (treason) representing the most serious sin in Dante's view, while purgatory is a mountain with ledges proceeding upward with its last ledge (lust) representing the least serious capital sin being purged.

32 {*Par.* 3.85}   *Par.* 3.85: "E 'n la sua volontade è nostra pace." Lewis references the idea in this verse but not its exact wording, and he spells "volontade" as "voluntade."

32 {sees differently, is different}   The theme of someone seeing the same thing differently after an inner change is a recurring one for Lewis. It is perhaps best articulated in one of the Narnia Chronicles when the narrator says, "What you see and hear depends a good deal on where you are standing: it also depends on what sort of person you are." *The Magician's Nephew* (New York: Macmillan, 1955), 125.

33 {*Inf.* 3.18}   *Inf.* 3.18: "c'hanno perduto il ben dell'intelletto."

33 {"return journey … simple"}   Lewis, "Letter to Mary Neylan," October 2, 1941, *The Collected Letters of C. S. Lewis*, vol. 2, *Books, Broadcasts, and the War 1931–1949*, ed. Walter Hooper (New York: HarperCollins, 2004), 492.

34 {*Purgatorio* as "heart" of poem}   "Letter to His Brother W.," July 1, 1921, *The Collected Letters of C. S. Lewis*, vol. 1, *Family Letters 1905–1931* (New York: HarperCollins, 2001), 560.

34 {"Beatrician experience"} C. S. Lewis, "A Commentary on the Arthurian Poems of Charles Williams," in *Arthurian Torso: Containing the Posthumous Fragment of "The Figure of Arthur" by Charles Williams* (Oxford: Oxford University Press, 1948), 116.

34 {"joy . . . awakens desire"} "Letter to Dom Bede Griffiths," November 5, 1954, *The Collected Letters of C. S. Lewis*, vol. 3, 523.

34 {". . . inconsolable longing"} Lewis, *Surprised by Joy*, 72. Joy arouses "an unsatisfied desire which is itself more desirable than any other satisfaction," 17–18.

34 {"recurrent experience . . . delight"} Lewis, preface, *The Pilgrim's Regress*, 7.

35 {constant thought of Beatrice} Beatrice is "the name that always springs up in my mind" (*Purg.* 27.41–42: ". . . il nome / che nella mente sempre mi rampolla").

35 {*Purg.* 27.36} *Purg.* 27.36: "tra Beatrice e te è questo muro."

35 {glimpses in night visions} In Book VII, 7, John and one of Wisdom's daughters, Contemplation, fly westward and glimpse the island. In John's second dream-vision (Book IX, 1) when another lady, also named Contemplation, and John fly westward, they fly "in a sphere of light," and the "drop of light in which they had journeyed entered into an ocean of light and was swallowed up." Kathryn Lindskoog notes that this is "reminiscent of the ocean of light in *Paradise*." *Surprised by C. S. Lewis, George MacDonald & Dante: An Array of Original Discoveries* (Macon, GA: Mercer University Press, 2001), 40. Commenting on John's vision of "the light [that] ran down as a river in the midst of the fields . . . too bright to look at" (Book IX, 1), Lindskoog states, "This journey is obviously composed of images from *Paradise*," 40. However, she fails to note that this is an exact parallel to the event in which Dante's pilgrim sees a light in the shape of a river flowing between two banks of flowers that is very bright (see *Par.* 30.61–63).

35 {*Purg.* 30.121–123} *Purg.* 30.121–123: "Alcun tempo il sostenni col mio volto: / mostrando li occhi giovanetti a lui / meco il menava in dritta parte volto."

35 {*Purg.* 30.126} *Purg.* 30.126: ". . . si tolse a me, e diessi altrui."

35 {*Purg.* 31.34–36} *Purg.* 31.34–36: ". . . Le presenti cose / col falso lor piacer volser miei passi, / tosto che 'l vostro viso si nascose."

35 {*Purg.* 30.131–132} *Purg.* 30.131–132: "imagini di ben seguendo false, / che nulla promission rendono intera."

35 {hermit Mr. History} Kathryn Lindskoog believes that readers
of the *Purgatorio* "are apt to notice a resemblance between Lewis's
ancient hermit and the ancient man [Cato] who greeted and advised Dante when he began his ascent toward heaven." *Finding
the Landlord: A Guidebook to C. S. Lewis's "The Pilgrim's Regress"*
(Chicago: Cornerstone, 1995), 87. It is unclear to me where the resemblance might lie. The hermit's appearance is not like Cato's, and Cato
rebukes the pilgrim first for seeming to escape from hell and then for
lingering on the shore and delaying his ascent up the mount—hardly
on a par with the nice, long, friendly explanations that the hermit
gives John.

36 {". . . all false paths"} Lewis, preface, *The Pilgrim's Regress*, 10.

37 {*Purg.* 28.33} *Purg.* 28.23: "dentro alla selva antica. . . ." See *Purg.*
28.3–30 for the pilgrim's initial time in the garden.

38 {all of creation to attract} In his commentary on Charles Williams's
Arthurian Torso, Lewis states, "Every created thing is, in its degree, an
image of God, and the ordinate and faithful appreciation of that thing
a clue which, truly followed, will lead back to Him." "A Commentary
on the Arthurian Poems of Charles Williams," 151.

38 {"Beatrician experience"} Lewis says that "the Beatrician experience may be defined as the recovery . . . of that vision of reality which
would have been common to all men in respect to all things if Man
had never fallen." Ibid., 116.

38 {"reading allegory . . . revival"} Lewis, *The Allegory of Love*, 116.

38 {images for abstractions} For example, the sharp, icy crags of the
North accurately reflect—in landscape terms—cold, dogmatic philosophies, etc.

39 {"motifs . . . reappear"} Joe R. Christopher, *C. S. Lewis* (New York:
Twayne, 1987), 14.

Chapter 3: *Out of the Silent Planet*

41 {Ransom Trilogy} The third novel of the trilogy is now generally
categorized as adult fantasy rather than science fiction, so the description "Ransom trilogy" for these three books is more accurate
than calling it "the science fiction trilogy" or "the cosmic trilogy,"
which many scholars still do.

41 {"thriller . . . Mars"} "Letter to Charles Williams," September 23,
1937, *The Collected Letters of C. S. Lewis*, vol. 2, *Books, Broadcasts,*

and the War 1931–1949, ed. Walter Hooper (New York: HarperCollins, 2004), 219–20. Lewis also describes this book as a "thriller" in his "Letter to Owen Barfield," September 2, 1937. Ibid., 218.

41 {variety of purposes}   Lewis points out that some science fiction writers "are primarily interested in technology. Some use [science fiction] . . . simply for literary fantasy and produce what is essentially *Märchen* or myth. A great many use it for satire." *An Experiment in Criticism* (Cambridge: Cambridge University Press, 1965), 109.

42 {"filled by spiritual experience"}   "Letter to William L. Kinter," March 28, 1953, *The Collected Letters of C. S. Lewis*, vol. 3, *Narnia, Cambridge, and Joy 1950–1963*, ed. Walter Hooper (New York: HarperCollins, 2007), 314.

42 {"What . . . opposite side"}   "Letter to Roger Lancelyn Green," December 28, 1938, *The Collected Letters of C. S. Lewis*, vol. 2, 236–37.

42 {challenge to science fiction}   Eric S. Rabkin and Robert Scholes credit Lewis with being the "most vigorous champion" of the "anti-science-fiction movement." *Science Fiction: History, Science, Vision* (New York: Oxford University Press, 1977), 15. In that capacity, however, Lewis was also the first "example of combining Christian casuistry with science fiction," 16.

42 {"Lewis's imitation"}   Joe R. Christopher, *C. S. Lewis* (Boston: Twayne, 1987), 33.

42 {"creative alteration"}   Robert Boenig says that Lewis is adapting Wells. "Critical and Fictional Pairing in C. S. Lewis," in *The Taste of the Pineapple: Essays on C. S. Lewis as Reader, Critic, and Imaginative Writer*, ed. Bruce L. Edwards (Bowling Green, OH: Bowling Green State University Press, 1988), 138. Doris T. Myers says that Lewis added "philosophical depth to his reworking of Wells's story." *C. S. Lewis in Context* (Kent, OH: Kent State University Press, 1994), 41. Both these comments understate the fact that Lewis was intentionally contradicting and correcting Wells's worldview about the universe. In a later book, Myers calls this novel "a virtual rewriting" of Wells's story, which is more accurate. See *Bareface: A Guide to C. S. Lewis's Last Novel* (Columbia: University of Missouri Press, 2004), 145.

42 {polemic against Wells}   David C. Downing accurately comments that this novel "is fundamentally anti-Wellsian." *Planets in Peril: A Critical Study of C. S. Lewis's Ransom Trilogy* (Amherst: University of Massachusetts Press, 1992), 124. He says in a later essay that despite the similarities in plot it is "very nearly opposite in its themes." "Science Fiction," in *Reading the Classics with C. S. Lewis*, ed. Thomas

L. Martin (Grand Rapids, MI: Baker Academic, 2000), 303. I would go further and say that it is not just "nearly opposite" but completely and purposefully opposite in theme due to Lewis's polemical intention.

42 {counter Wells's viewpoint}   Brian Murphy's comment that this novel is "one more indication of Lewis' [*sic*] contentiousness that he elected to write one of these pulpy and absurd things, to model it on H. G. Wells' space stories . . . and to give it the rather lurid title *Out of the Silent Planet*" seems to indicate that he did not quite understand Lewis's purpose or procedure in this novel. *C. S. Lewis* (Mercer Island, WA: Stormont, 1983), 14.

42 {main characters intact}   I would disagree with Myers who believes that Lewis "darkens[s] their characters, by making them despicable where Bedford and Cavor are simply funny." *C. S. Lewis in Context*, 42. In the second chapter of Wells's book, Cavor destroys homes and properties for twenty miles around through one of his experiments, showing no compunction whatsoever for the damage and claiming that scientists have to take risks, and Bedford deceitfully agrees to blame the event on a cyclone so that Cavor can fraudulently collect insurance for his destroyed home. Unsure if his three assistants perished in the blast, Cavor nonchalantly considers it no great loss if that had happened. It seems to me that Wells's Cavor and Bedford show themselves to be callous and amoral rather than funny from the start, and Lewis re-portrays them quite accurately in his Weston and Devine.

43 {"real model"}   "Letter to William L. Kinter," March 28, 1953, *The Collected Letters of C. S. Lewis*, vol. 3, 314.

43 {"what . . . good for"}   C. S. Lewis, *Of Other Worlds: Essays and Stories*, ed. Walter Hooper (New York: Harcourt Brace Jovanovich, 1966), 12.

43 {"scientifiction" and "supernatural" appeal}   "Letter to Charles A. Brady," October 29, 1944, *The Collected Letters of C. S. Lewis*, vol. 2, 630.

43 {"spiritual outlook . . . crude style"}   Ibid.

43 {eldils}   Although Lewis says that "*Eldila* is the true plural," he does allow that "you can Anglicise it as *eldils*." "Letter to Mary Willis Shelburne," March 4, 1953, *The Collected Letters of C. S. Lewis*, vol. 3, 301.

43 {Oyarsa}   In Pseudo-Apuleius's *Asclepius*, 14, there is a being called an *Ousiarch* in the sphere of Fixed Stars who is described as one "who makes diverse forms from diverse images" (*qui diversis speciebus*

diversas formas facit). The Greek root *ousia* means "substance or essence," and *arch* is the root for "ruler." Later in Bernardus Silvestris's twelfth-century poem *De Mundi Universitate*, a being in the sphere of fixed stars is described as "Oyarses, the guardian spirit dedicated to the skill and work of a painter and shaper" (*Oyarses et genius in artem et officium pictoris et figurantis addictus*). Lewis adapts the names and the functions of these beings for his own purposes. Each Oyarsa is a blend of the *Ousiarch* and the *Oyarses*: each rules its own substance and shapes the matter of a specific planet.

44 {theological foundation not understood}   As John Killinger notes, "Our age no longer lives under the unification of the great mythological structure which Dante and Spenser and Milton and Bunyan inherited. . . . In Dante's world nearly everyone participated in the 'myth' of God's existence and in all the myths derivative from that one." *The Failure of Theology in Modern Literature* (New York: Abingdon, 1963), 127. Peter S. Hawkins makes the same point specifically in relation to Dante's poem: "The stories and characters that until recently were common knowledge are . . . rapidly passing out of currency, even as the literary style of the Bible, its imagery and cadence, evaporate from our speech." *Dante's Testaments: Essays in Scriptural Imagination* (Stanford, CA: Stanford University Press, 1999), 19. Erich Auerbach comments that "it did not occur to him [Dante] that his work would one day be admired . . . by people to whom the foundation of his faith and worldview had become meaningless and alien." *Dante: Poet of the Secular World*, trans. Ralph Manheim (Chicago: University of Chicago Press, 1961), 157–58.

44 {parallel Christian construct}   The cosmic mythology with new names that Lewis designs is, in fact, so innovative that, as he reported to a friend, "Out of about 60 reviews [of *OSP*] only 2 showed any knowledge that my idea of the fall of the Bent One was anything but an invention of my own." "Letter to Sister Penelope," July [August] 9, 1939, *The Collected Letters of C. S. Lewis*, vol. 2, 262.

44 {Lewis on Ptolemaic universe}   C. S. Lewis, *The Discarded Image: An Introduction to Medieval and Renaissance Literature* (Cambridge: Cambridge University Press, 1964), 96.

44 {medieval features of Lewis cosmos}   It is true, as Colin Duriez points out, that in "*Out of the Silent Planet*, C. S. Lewis imaginatively recreates the medieval picture of the cosmos he later sets out in his book, *The Discarded Image*." *The C. S. Lewis Handbook: A Comprehensive Guide to His Life, Thought, and Writings* (Eastbourne, UK: Monarch, 1990), 152. Downing, *Planets in Peril*, notes this as

well (p. 66). However, neither author gives any specific details or examples.

44 {interpretations tied to Dante}   One of the main factors that make Lewis's cosmos specifically Dantean rather than merely medieval is noted by Gisbert Kranz: "Unlike all the other mediaeval authors, Dante's cosmology is filled with sublime religious ardor." "Dante in the Work of C. S. Lewis," *Deutches Dante-Jahrbuch*, vol. 47, trans. Hope Kirkpatrick, *The Bulletin of the New York C. S. Lewis Society* 4, no. 10 (August 1973): 3. Lewis himself highlighted this point, saying that the medieval model "is not fused with high religious ardour in any writer I know except Dante." *The Discarded Image*, 19. Michael Ward believes, "It was in large part through his love of Dante that Lewis grew to be so enchanted by the Ptolemaic universe" and, concerning the Christianizing of the universe, he adds, "Dante is no longer alone in this . . . respect because Lewis has joined him." *Planet Narnia: The Seven Heavens in the Imagination of C. S. Lewis* (Oxford: Oxford University Press, 2008), 41.

44 {ascribing same interpretations}   Failure to understand the medieval Dantean model Lewis is adapting can lead to such odd comments as this one from science fiction writer William Atheling, Jr. [James Blish], that Lewis's space novels "set out to impose upon the solar system a strange Anglican-cum-Babylonian theology and cosmogony." He does concede, however, that Lewis achieved "amazingly convincing results." "Cathedrals in Space," in *Turning Points: Essays in the Art of Science Fiction*, ed. Damon Knight (New York: Harper & Row, 1977), 148.

45 {Nature and Sky}   Aristotle *Metaphysics* 12.7.1072b.

45 {*Par.* 28.41–42}   *Par.* 28.41–42: ". . . Da quel punto / depende il cielo e tutta la natura." Lewis refers to this verse both in *The Discarded Image*, 116, and in his essay "Imagination and Thought," *Studies in Medieval and Renaissance Literature*, coll. Walter Hooper (Cambridge: Cambridge University Press, 1966), 62.

45 {*Par.* 1.139–140}   *Par.* 1.139–140: ". . . privo / d'impedimento." In fact, Beatrice tells the pilgrim when he first leaves the earth that his effortless upward movement is completely natural: "You should not be more amazed at your rising than at a stream on a mountain if it flows down to the bottom" (*Par.* 1.136–138: "Non dei più ammirar . . . / lo tuo salir, se non come d'un rivo / se d'alto monte scende giuso ad imo.")

45 {*Par.* 2.19–20}   *Par.* 2.19–20: "The innate and perpetual thirst for God's realm carried us upward" ("La concreata e perpetüa sete / del deïforme regno cen portava").

46 {nine orders} The nine orders of angels were first postulated by Dionysius the Areopagite. See *The Celestial Hierarchy* (Whitefish, MT: Kessinger, 2004). Dionysius considers angels to be pure unembodied minds, but Lewis does not follow him in that supposition.

46 {Plato, celestial beings} See Plato *Timaeus* 40.

46 {Aristotle, spiritual intelligences} See Aristotle *Metaphysics* 12.7.

46 {*Par.* 8.109–110} *Par.* 8.109–110: "... 'l intelletti che muovon queste stelle."

46 {characteristics of planets} Lewis uses this same approach in his next science fiction novel, *Perelandra*, in which that planet's Oyarsa (Venus) is feminine and sensuous. With its floating islands and lush vegetation, her planet is rainbow colored.

46 {Oyarsa as angelic intelligence} See Lewis's discussion of Intelligences in *The Discarded Image*, 115–16. In the last novel of the Ransom trilogy, Dr. Dimble clarifies that "they aren't exactly angels in the same sense as our guardian angels are. Technically they are Intelligences." *That Hideous Strength* (London: John Lane, 1945; repr., New York: Macmillan, 1965), 284.

46 {angels collaborate in creation} Lewis refers to this function of angels in *The Discarded Image*, 121.

47 {Perelandrian Oyarsa and planet} C. S. Lewis, *Perelandra* (London: John Lane, 1943; repr., New York: Macmillan, 1965), 195–96.

47 {"We have often wondered..."} Ibid., 206.

47 {Plato, *daimones*} See Plato *Symposium* 202.

47 {Apuleius, *daimones*} See Apuleius *De Deo Socratis* 6.8–16.

47 {Augustine, *daimones* restricted} See Saint Augustine, *The City of God*, 8.14–15, trans. Henry Bettenson (New York: Penguin, 1972), 318–21.

47 {Augustine, *daimones* as evil} Ibid., 9.19, 365–66.

47 {"smash ... female angel"} "Letter to Mary Willis Shelburne", March 4, 1953, *The Collected Letters of C. S. Lewis*, vol. 3, 130.

47 {Dante's angels best} Lewis, preface, paperback ed., *The Screwtape Letters* (New York: Macmillan, 1961), ix.

47 {"best angel ... poet"} C. S. Lewis, "Dante's Similes," *Studies in Medieval and Renaissance Literature*, coll. Walter Hooper (Cambridge: Cambridge University Press, 1966), 69.

47 {Lewis's twentieth-century angels} Peter Kreeft believes that Lewis's angels are one of the "two things Lewis describes better than anyone who has ever written." *C. S. Lewis for the Third Millennium: Six*

Essays on "The Abolition of Man" (San Francisco: Ignatius, 1994), 173. However, others, like Downing, still give Dante the prize: "Lewis's eldils have some of the majesty and self-possession of Dante's stern messenger [the angel of Dis], but none of his over-whelming presence." *Planets in Peril*, 43. Still others, like Kranz, see it as a draw: "The angelic sovereigns . . . are with Lewis just as majestic and numinously fearful as Dante's angels." "Dante in the Work of C. S. Lewis," 6.

48 {seven-note chord}   See Cicero *Republic* 6.17–18.

48 {eight-note chord}   See Plato *Republic* 10.617.

48 {music of the spheres}   See Lewis's comments on the music of the spheres in *The Discarded Image*, 112.

48 {Earth silent}   See Cicero *Republic* 6.18.

48 {". . . no message comes from it"}   C. S. Lewis, *Out of the Silent Planet* (1938; repr., New York: Macmillan, 1965), 120. All quotes are from this edition and will be indicated by "*OSP*" and page number(s).

48 {visible patterned after invisible}   See Plato *Timaeus* 29–30.

48 {blessed lives shadowed}   In the three "shadowed spheres," the lowest spheres of Paradise, souls on the Moon were inconstant in their religious vows, those on Mercury were too concerned with worldly ambition, and the souls on Venus led lives tainted by sexual sin.

49 {Lewis's corporeal angels}   Lewis follows Renaissance Platonic theology and Milton, among others, in giving his angels bodies in contrast to the tradition of scholastic and Thomist philosophy in which angels are considered pure-spirit beings.

49 {blessed located higher and higher}   I am indebted to Ward for pointing out the different dwelling locations. *Planet Narnia*, 81.

49 {*Par.* 3.85}   *Par.* 3.85: "E 'n la sua volontade è nostra pace."

50 {Jesus as Lord of universe}   In Chad Walsh's wonderful phrasing, through his cosmic myth Lewis "baptized the solar system and filled it with the radiant presence of Maleldil." *C. S. Lewis: Apostle to the Skeptics* (New York: Macmillan, 1978), 134.

50 {*Par.* 1.1–2}   *Par.* 1.1–2: "La gloria di colui che tutto move / per l'universo penetra. . . ."

50 {Ransom and Tolkien}   Jared C. Lobdell, "The Ransom Stories and Their Eighteenth-Century Ancestry," in *Word and Story in C. S. Lewis*, eds. Peter J. Schakel and Charles A. Huttar (Columbia: University of Missouri Press, 1991), 213; Michael Coren, *The Man Who Created Narnia: The Story of C. S. Lewis* (Grand Rapids, MI: Eerdmans, 1994), 42; and Colin Duriez, "Into the Library: Composition and Context,"

in *Reading the Classics with C. S. Lewis*, ed. Thomas L. Martin (Grand Rapids, MI: Baker Academic, 2000), 352.

50 {Ransom and Barfield} Lobdell combines references to both Tolkien and Barfield as models for Ransom in "The Ransom Stories," 213, and again in *The Scientifiction Novels of C. S. Lewis: Space and Time in the Ransom Stories* (Jefferson, NC: McFarland, 2004), 44. Duriez also refers to Tolkien and Barfield in connection to Ransom. *The C. S. Lewis Handbook*, 1.

50 {Ransom and Williams} Christopher, *C. S. Lewis*, 100. Downing says that once Ransom becomes the Pendragon (Arthur's successor) in *That Hideous Strength*, he resembles Williams. *Planets in Peril*, 127. Sanford Schwartz makes the same observation in *C. S. Lewis on the Final Frontier: Science and the Supernatural in the Space Trilogy* (New York: Oxford University Press, 2009), 92. Robert Boenig believes that Ransom's character starts off as "a tribute to Tolkien . . . but he ends up as a portrait of Charles Williams." *C. S. Lewis and the Middle Ages* (Kent, OH: Kent State University Press, 2012), 111. Similarly, but more tentatively, Ward believes that Ransom at first "may be partly based" on Tolkien and later "may be partly based" on Williams. *Planet Narnia*, 82, 175.

50 {Ransom and Lewis} Evan K. Gibson believes that there are "a number of characteristics which make him almost the alter ego of his creator." *C. S. Lewis, a Spinner of Tales: A Guide to His Fiction* (Grand Rapids, MI: Christian University Press, 1980), 34. Donald E. Glover also points out some of Ransom's similarities to Lewis. *C. S. Lewis: The Art of Enchantment* (Athens, OH: Ohio University Press, 1981), 77. Downing adds Lewis to his list as well and says that "when Lewis presents his protagonist as a soul-in-progress, Ransom most resembles Lewis himself." *Planets in Peril*, 127. William Gray believes that Ransom in the first two books "is based on Lewis himself as much as on anyone else." *C. S. Lewis* (Plymouth, UK: Northcote House, 1998), 36. David G. Clark points out that both Lewis and Ransom "were unmarried professors and philologists who enjoyed long walks." *C. S. Lewis: A Guide to His Theology* (Malden, MA: Blackwell, 2007), 83.

50 {pilgrim as Everyman} Prue Shaw comments on Dante's use of "our" in the opening line of the poem—"In the midst of *our* life"—that "it is *our* life too, not just his." *Reading Dante: From Here to Eternity* (New York: Norton, 2014), 78.

50 {pilgrim's name later} The pilgrim is called "Dante" only in the Garden of Eden when he needs to admit *his* personal wrongdoings— which are different for every individual (see *Purg.* 31.34–36).

50 {Ransom as Everyman} William Luther White, discussing Lewis's shaping of characters, notes that Lewis "was more concerned to evoke a sense of the numinous than he was to delineate character. He was more concerned with Everyman than he was with any particular man." *The Image of Man in C. S. Lewis* (Nashville: Abingdon, 1969), 68.

50 {Ransom called "Pedestrian"} I am indebted to Gibson for this detail. *Spinner of Tales*, 34.

50 {Ransom in "Dantean Dark Wood"} Greg Wolfe, "Essential Speech: Language and Myth in the Ransom Trilogy," in *Word and Story in C. S. Lewis*, eds. Peter J. Schakel and Charles A. Huttar (Columbia: University of Missouri Press, 1991), 63. However, Wolfe does not list any specific similarities apart from this one between Ransom and Dante's pilgrim.

50 {*Inf.* 1.1} *Inf.* 1.1: "Nel mezzo del cammin di nostra vita."

50 {Ransom's interest in languages} Verlyn Flieger notes, "It is not an accident that Ransom is a philologist, thus ideally suited to correlate language, thought, and reality, and more than ordinarily sensitive to how they affect one another." "The Sound of Silence: Language and Experience in *Out of the Silent Planet*," in *Word and Story in C. S. Lewis*, eds. Peter J. Schakel and Charles A. Huttar (Columbia: University of Missouri Press, 1991), 47. Colin N. Manlove comments, "It is not for nothing that Ransom is a philologist," but he emphasizes only the significance of Ransom's ability and desire to communicate. *C. S. Lewis: His Literary Achievement* (London: Macmillan, 1987), 34.

50 {"dark wood" experience} Paul Piehler, speaking of heroes in general, aptly describes "the dark wood experience" as "the ordeal of disorientation . . . [that] purges the hero of . . . his tendency to think of the reality conventions of his civilization as prevailing in the universe as a whole." "Myth or Allegory? Archetype and Transcendence in the Fiction of C. S. Lewis," in *Word and Story in C. S. Lewis*, eds. Peter J. Schakel and Charles A. Huttar (Columbia: University of Missouri Press, 1991), 210. Piehler clarifies this point when he notes, "There is nothing precisely equivalent to Dante's dark wood in Lewis's fiction. But if we think about the way in which the experience of the wood prepares us for the reading of Dante's adventures in the afterworlds, the structural function of the wood . . . , then we can find many equivalences." Ibid., 205.

51 {Ransom as Bunyan character} Downing, *Planets in Peril*, 101.

51 {pilgrim transported in boat} In classical literature, Charon typically transports souls across the Acheron river to the underworld in

his boat. Dante leaves the actual transport ambiguous since he never describes the pilgrim's experience in the boat; his pilgrim awakens to find himself across the river.

51 {punishment as essence of sin}   Dante's concept of *contrapasso*, a "counterpoint," is the basis for each of hell's punishments (see *Inf.* 28.139–142).

52 {Ransom embarrassed by history}   When he is with the Hrossa, Ransom similarly "did not want to tell them too much of our human wars and industrialisms" (*OSP* 70).

52 {Dante's fearful pilgrim}   See, for instance, *Inf.* 2.45, 9.1, 17.85–88, etc. In *Inf.* 34.8–9 the pilgrim even shrinks back for cover behind his guide at what he sees.

52 {Ransom's fears}   The words *fear, terror,* and *alarm* occur regularly throughout Ransom's adventures; see pp. 25, 33, 36, 52, 54, etc.

52 {*Inf.* 34.71–72}   *Inf.* 34.71–72: "ed el prese di tempo e luogo poste; / . . . quando l'ali fuoro aperte assai [appigliò sè]."

52 {"science fiction element" in Dante}   "Letter to William L. Kinter," March 28, 1953, *The Collected Letters of C. S. Lewis*, vol. 3, 314. It is, therefore, not surprising that Lewis would have included a parallel to that event in *his* science fiction novel. In one of his essays, Lewis mentions that the pilgrim and Virgil "have to climb down his [Satan's] shaggy sides . . . [but] climb *up* to his feet." "Imagination and Thought," *Studies in Medieval and Renaissance Literature*, coll. Walter Hooper (Cambridge: Cambridge University Press, 1966), 49. Michael Ward's comment that Dante "climbed down from Lucifer's shoulders to his waist" needs a slight adjustment, since he and Virgil were never on Lucifer's shoulders. "On Suffering," in *The Cambridge Companion to C. S. Lewis*, eds. Robert MacSwain and Michael Ward (Cambridge: Cambridge University Press, 2010), 213.

52 {*Inf.* 34.138}   *Inf.* 34.138: ". . . per un pertugio tondo."

53 {Dante's use of number nine}   Since three is the number of the Trinity, its multiples, and especially nine, are significant for Dante. According to Dante's earlier work, *La Vita Nuova* (*New Life*), he met Beatrice when they were both *nine* (*VN* 2) and then again *nine* years later (*VN* 3). In *VN* 29, he says that at her birth all *nine* spheres of heaven were in perfect relationship and that she died in the *ninth* hour of the day on the *ninth* month. The number nine becomes important in *The Divine Comedy* as well: there are *nine* circles in hell, *nine* areas in purgatory (ante-purgatory, seven ledges, the Garden of Eden), and *nine* heavenly spheres. Lewis echoes Dante's famous num-

ber nine here in the length of the journey. Lewis later echoes Dante's use of three and its multiples to describe the time periods connected to Ransom's journey to Malacandra; according to MacPhee, the resident Ulsterman at St. Anne's, Ransom went to Malacandra for *nine* months *six* years ago and was sick for *three* months after he came home. *That Hideous Strength* (London: John Lane, 1945; repr., New York: Macmillan, 1965), 190.

53 {*Par.* 1.88–90}   *Par.* 1.88–90: ". . . Tu stesso ti fai grosso / col falso imaginar, sì che non vedi / ciò che vedresti se l'avessi scosso." "False perceptions" also occur at other times when the pilgrim does not understand what he sees: for instance, he thinks the giant-guardians of the ninth circle are towers at first (*Inf.* 31.20); on the ledge of pride he does not understand the objects that seem bent over and only later recognizes them as souls carrying heavy burdens on their backs (see *Purg.* 10.114); in the garden the pilgrim thinks he sees golden trees, but they are actually candlesticks (see *Purg.* 29.44).

53 {*Par.* 2.61–61}   *Par.* 2.61–62: ". . . sommerso / nel falso [è] il creder tuo. . . ."

53 {"the black . . . worlds"}   His preconception is based on Wells's description of Bedford's experience of space, as he felt it "closing in on me, embracing me ever nearer . . . that which was before the beginning and that which triumphs in the end; that enormous void . . . the infinite and final Night of space." H. G. Wells, *First Men in the Moon*, in *The Works of H. G. Wells*, vol. 6 (London: T. Fisher Unwin, 1925), 182. As Dorothy L. Sayers aptly points out, "It is the deliberate choosing . . . to see God and the universe as hostile to one's ego that is of the very essence of Hell." *Introductory Papers to Dante* (London: Methuen, 1954), 66.

54 {Dante's jewel metaphors}   Dante mentions sapphires (see *Par.* 23.101); rubies (see *Par.* 9.68; 19.4–5; 30.66); and emeralds (Beatrice's eyes first noted in *Purg.* 31.115–117). Lewis's "pin-pricks of burning gold," are reminiscent of the hundred little glittering globes of light representing the contemplatives (see *Par.* 22.24) and of the golden sparks representing angels (see *Par.* 30.61–64). Dante also refers to groups of the blessed as "jewels" (see *Par.* 10.71–73; 18.115) and to an individual soul in heaven as a "jewel" twice (see *Par.* 9.37; 15.22).

54 {"*empyrean* ocean"}   Lewis says that "the substitution of heaven for space . . . is my favourite idea in the book." "Letter to Mrs. Stuart Moore" [Evelyn Underhill], October 29, 1938, *The Collected Letters of C. S. Lewis*, vol. 2, 235.

54–55 {"moral standards . . . vary"} C. S. Lewis, "De Futilitate," in *Christian Reflections*, ed. Walter Hooper (Grand Rapids, MI: Eerdmans, 1971), 61.

55 {amoral, ruthless Earthmen} Walter Hooper points out in this regard that Lewis "was probably the first writer to introduce the idea of having *fallen* terrestrial invaders discover on other planets . . . *unfallen* rational beings." *Christian Reflections*, 174, n. 1.

55 {Cicero, view earth from heaven} In *Scipio's Dream*, Africanus minor, viewing the earth from the sphere of Fixed Stars, is embarrassed by the size of Earth, which "looked so small as to make me ashamed of our empire, which was a mere point on its surface." *The Basic Works of Cicero*, ed., intro., and notes Moses Hadad (New York: Modern Library, 1951), 164. His celestial experience diminishes the glory of his empire and consequently his pride in it. Lewis refers to this event from *Scipio's Dream* as "the prototype of many ascents to Heaven in later literature" in *The Discarded Image*, 24, but he follows Dante's expanded meaning of the event in this novel.

55 {Boethius, view earth from heaven} Lady Philosophy, attempting to dissuade Boethius from a desire for earthly fame, asks him to picture Earth's size relative to the rest of the universe: "The circumference of the earth has the size of a point; that is to say, compared with the magnitude of the celestial sphere, it may be thought of as having no extent at all." *The Consolation of Philosophy*, 2.7, trans. V. E. Watts (Middlesex, England: Penguin, 1969), 73.

55 {*Par.* 22.134–135} *Par.* 22:134–135: ". . . vidi questo globo / tal, ch'io sorrisi del suo vil sembiante."

55 {*Par.* 22.151} *Par.* 22.151: "L'aiuola che ci fa tanto feroci."

55 {Dante's moral contrast} When he later looks down a second time at the Earth from that sphere, the emphasis—again a moral one—is on his awareness of the current wretched lives of human beings (see *Par.* 28.1–2).

56 {viewing Earth precedes revelation} In the *Paradiso* this incident occurs right before his first symbolic vision of Christ with all the redeemed. In *Out of the Silent Planet*, this incident occurs right before the Malacandrian Oyarsa presents a full account of cosmic history to Ransom.

56 {Ransom and Gulliver interviews} James Osler Bailey, *Pilgrims through Space and Time* (New York: Argus, 1947), 203; Robert Plank, "Some Psychological Aspects of Lewis's Trilogy," *Shadows of Imagination: The Fantasies of C. S. Lewis, J. R. R. Tolkien, and Charles*

Williams, ed. Mark Robert Hillegas (Carbondale: Southern Illinois University Press, 1969), 58; Dabney Adams Hart, *Through the Open Door: A New Look at C. S. Lewis* (Tuscaloosa: University of Alabama Press, 1984), 34; Jeanette Hume Lutton, "The Feast of Reason: *Out of the Silent Planet* as the Book of Hnau," *Mythlore* 47 (Autumn 1986): 39; and Flieger, "The Sound of Silence," 56. For several points of similarity with Swift in addition to the interview scenes, see Lobdell, "The Ransom Stories," 213–31, and David C. Downing, "Rehabilitating H. G. Wells: C. S. Lewis's *Out of the Silent Planet*," in *C. S. Lewis: Life, Works, Legacy,* ed. Bruce L. Edwards, vol. 2 (London: Praeger, 2007), 28–29.

56 {Ransom and Cavor interviews}   See, for instance, Plank, "Some Psychological Aspects," 58, and Kath Filmer, *The Fiction of C. S. Lewis: Mask and Mirror* (New York: St. Martin's, 1993), 63. Downing lists some similarities between the plot structure of this novel and Wells's *The Time Machine.* "Science Fiction," 303.

56 {*Purg.* 28.23}   *Purg.* 28.23: "dentro alla selva antica. . . ."

57 {*Purg.* 28.5}   *Purg.* 28.5: ". . . lento, lento."

57 {*Purg.* 28.1}   *Purg.* 28.1: "Vago già di cercar dentro e dintoro."

57 {*Purg.* 29.16–17}   *Purg.* 29.16–17: ". . . un lustro subito trascorse / da tutte parti per la gran foresta." In fact, "that [light], which remained, shone more and more brightly" (*Purg.* 29.20: "e quel, durando, più e più splendeva").

57 {*Purg.* 30.46–47}   *Purg.* 30.46–47: ". . . Men che dramma / di sangue m'è rimaso che non tremi."

57 {*Purg.* 30.97–98}   *Purg.* 30.97–98: "lo gel che m'era intorno al cor ristretto, / spirito e acqua fessi. . . ."

57 {*Purg.* 31.7–9}   *Purg.* 31.7–9: "Era la mia virtù tanto confusa, / che la voce si mosse, e pria si spense / che dalli organi suoi fosse dischiusa."

57 {*Purg.* 30.129–131}   *Purg.* 30.129–131: "I was less valued and appreciated by him, and he turned his steps to a false path, following after deceptive images of good" ("fu' io a lui men cara e men gradita; / e volsi i passi suoi per via non vera, / imagini di ben seguendo false").

58 {*Purg.* 30.133–135}   *Purg.* 30.133–135: "Nè l'impetrare ispirazion mi valse, / con le quali ed in sogno e altrimenti / lo rivocai. . . ."

58 {Beatrice, unasked questions}   See *Par.* 4.13–18; 7.10–17; 14.10–15; 15.70–71; 21.49–51; 27.103–104; 29.10–12. Virgil at times seems to know the pilgrim's thoughts (for example, see *Purg.* 19.39), but that comes from his psychological understanding of the pilgrim and not

because he sees the pilgrim's questions mirrored in God's mind the way Beatrice does. In the *Paradiso* all the blessed, in fact, can gaze into the mirror (God) that makes the pilgrim's thoughts plain (see *Par.* 15.61–63).

58 {Dante as "lively 'scientifictionist'"} "Letter to Dorothy L. Sayers," November 11, 1949, *The Collected Letters of C. S. Lewis*, vol. 2, 996.

58 {Dante's "two literary undertakings"} C. S. Lewis, *A Preface to "Paradise Lost"* (1942; repr., London: Oxford University Press, 1961), 114.

59 {Lindsay, "father of my planet books"} "Letter to Charles A. Brady," October 29, 1944, *The Collected Letters of C. S. Lewis*, vol. 2, 630.

59 {". . . Christian casuistry and science fiction"} Rabkin and Scholes, *Science Fiction: History, Science, Vision*, 16.

59 {"Ransom's *enfances*"} "Letter to William L. Kinter," November 27, 1951, in *The Collected Letters of C. S. Lewis*, vol. 3, 146.

Chapter 4: *The Screwtape Letters*

61 {"advice . . . diabolical"} C. S. Lewis, preface, *The Screwtape Letters* (London: Geoffrey Bles, 1942; repr., New York: Macmillan, 1961), v. Subsequent quotes are from this edition and are indicated in the text with Lewis's numbering for the letters.

62 {"blacks all white"} Ibid., xii. Lewis's phrase here describes the technique of moral inversion that he says inspired him in Stephen McKenna's *The Confessions of a Well-Meaning Woman*, where a female letter-writer mistakenly perceives good as evil and evil as good.

62 {symbol for Hell . . . fear and greed"} Ibid., x.

63 {"aimed . . . by the sound"} Ibid., xiii.

63 {circumlocution for God} The only exception in the *Inferno* occurs when Vanni Fucci makes an obscene gesture at God and curses him directly (see *Inf.* 25.3). The name of Christ, however, is never spoken in the *Inferno*. The name "Christ" occurs five times in the *Purgatorio*, but even there, Dante uses circumlocution once for it: "O Jove supreme, who was crucified on earth for us" (*Purg* 6.118–119: ". . . o sommo Giove / che fosti in terra per noi crucifisso"). In the *Paradiso* Christ is named thirty-nine times, but when that name ends a verse, it rhymes with itself and with no other word (see *Par.* 12.71–75; 14.104–108; 19.104–108; 32.83–87).

63 {"adverse judge"} *Inf.* 6.96: ". . . la nimica podèsta." Although it is Virgil who uses this phrase, it represents hell's view of Christ.

63 {God as "the Enemy"}   Wayne Martindale counts 149 times that the name "Enemy" is used for God or Christ, and another nine times in the "Toast." *Beyond the Shadowlands: C. S. Lewis on Heaven and Hell* (Wheaton, IL: Crossway, 2005), 163.

64 {*Inf.* 18.99}   *Inf.* 18.99: ". . . color che 'n sè assanna."

64 {*Inf.* 31.142–143}   *Inf.* 31.142–143: ". . . [il] fondo che divora / Lucifero. . . ."

64 {*Inf.* 7.114}   *Inf.* 7.114: "troncandosi co' denti a brano a brano."

64 {*Inf.* 13.125–129}   *Inf.* 13.125–129: ". . . nere cagne . . . / . . . / . . . miser li denti, / e quel dilaceraro a brano a brano; / poi sen portar quelle membra dolenti."

64 {*Inf.* 30.28–29}   *Inf.* 30.28–29: ". . . in sul nodo / del collo l'assanno. . . ."

64 {*Inf.* 33.1}   *Inf.* 33.1: ". . . fiero pasto."

64 {Ugolino and Ruggieri}   They are both in ice in the circle of traitors: Ugolino betrayed his country, and Ruggieri betrayed his close associate.

64 {Satan's three faces}   Satan's head with "three *faces*" can easily be confused with "three *heads*" even by a good scholar such as Barbara Reynolds. *The Passionate Intellect: Dorothy L. Sayers' Encounter with Dante* (Kent, OH: Kent State University Press, 1989), 109. A being with three heads would have multiple consciousnesses and would therefore no longer be a single, undivided being.

64 {prototype of evil}   As Charles S. Singleton points out, "Satan aspired to be as God, and the justice of his punishment is that now he is what he aspired to be . . .—a grotesque monstrous counterpart of the triune Godhead." *Dante Studies*, vol. 1, *"Commedia": Elements of Structure* (Cambridge, MA: Harvard University Press, 1954), 35.

64 {Brutus and Cassius gnawed}   David C. Downing inaccurately comments that Satan is gnawing on "the skulls of Brutus and Cassius." *Planets in Peril: A Critical Study of C. S. Lewis's Ransom Trilogy* (Amherst: University of Massachusetts Press, 1992), 98. It is only Judas who has the upper half of his body being gnawed; Dante is making a nuanced distinction between the punishment for treachery against the church and against the state.

65 {connection between sin and punishment}   The ninth ditch of fraud punishes sowers of division and discord. Betran de Born, a twelfth-century poet, caused division between Prince Henry and his father Henry II, the king of England, so he is now carrying his own severed

head by its hair: "Because I separated people who were so closely joined, I carry my separated head, alas!. . . . Thus one can see in me the *contrapasso*" (*Inf.* 28.139–140, 142: "Perch'io parti' così giunte persone, / partito porto il mio cerebro, lasso! / . . . / Così s'osserva in me lo contrapasso").

66 {*Par.* 3.45}   *Par.* 3:45: ". . . vuol simile a sè tutta sua corte."

66 {*Inf.* 3.35–36}   *Inf.* 3.35–36: ". . . coloro / che visser sanza infamia e sanza lodo."

66 {*Inf.* 3.49}   *Inf.* 3.49: "Fama di loro il mondo esser non lassa."

66 {*Inf.* 7.53–54}   *Inf.* 7.53–54: "la sconoscente vita che i fè sozzi / ad ogni conoscenza or li fa bruni."

66 {*Par.* 3.85}   *Par.* 3.85: "E 'n la sua volontade è nostra pace."

66 {prayer from loved ones}   For souls asking for prayers, see *Purg.* 3.142–145; 8.71–72; 13.147; 16.50–51. For the effectiveness of prayer, see, for example, *Purg.* 11.31–33.

67 {*Purg.* 24.26}   *Purg.* 24.26: "e del nomar parean tutti contenti." As Irma Brandeis notes, "Everyone in Purgatory knows who he is and why he is here." *The Ladder of Vision: A Study of Dante's "Comedy"* (1960; repr., Garden City, NY: Anchor, 1962), 68. See also *Purg.* 14.81.

67 {*Inf.* 3.95–96, 5.23–24}   *Inf.* 3.95–96 and 5.23–24: ". . . colà dove si puote / ciò che si vuole. . . ." It is interesting to note that this phrase is not only repeated verbatim but also occupies the exact same placement at the end and the beginning of two verses.

67 {*Inf.* 9.94–95}   *Inf.* 9.94–95: "Perchè recalcitrate a quella voglia / a cui non può il fin mai esser mozzo [?]"

67 {*Inf.* 21.83–84}   *Inf.* 21.83–84: ". . . nel cielo è voluto / ch' i' mostri altrui questo cammin silvestro."

67 {*Inf.* 21.85–86}   *Inf.* 21.85–86: "Allor li fu l'orgoglio sì caduto, / che si lasciò cascar l'uncino a' piedi."

67 {*Inf.* 23.55–57}   *Inf.* 23.55–57: ". . . l'alta provedenza . . . / . . . / poder di partirs' indi a tutti tolle."

68 {"torcere" in moral sense}   For Dante's variant uses of "twist" in a moral sense, see *Inf.* 19.36; 30.21; *Purg.* 8.31; 10.3; 17.100; 18.45; 23.126; and *Par.* 1.135; 3.33; 6.123; 8.145; 9.11; 10.16; 13.129; 16.5; 26.62; 29.90.

68 {*Par.* 1.134–135}   *Par.* 1.134–135: ". . . l'impeto primo / s'atterra torto da falso piacere."

69 {"dainty morsel"}   Lewis notes that it is characteristic of Dante (in the *Paradiso*) "that what is generally compared to food is the satisfac-

tion of spirital or intellectual desire." "Imagery in Dante's *Comedy*," *Studies in Medieval and Renaissance Literature*, coll. Walter Hooper (Cambridge: Cambridge University Press, 1966), 87. In this case it is the perverse satisfaction of a perverse desire.

69   {*Purg.* 17.96}   *Purg.* 17.96: "... per troppo ... di vigore"; *Purg.* 17.100: "... con più cura / ... che non dee. ..."

70   {*Purg.* 17.136}   *Purg.* 17.136: "L'amor ch'ad esso troppo s'abbandona."

70   {*Purg.* 16.75}   *Purg.* 16.75: "lume v'è dato a bene e a malizia."

70   {*Inf.* 3.18}   *Inf.* 3.18: "c'hanno perduto il ben dell' intelletto." Brandeis describes the good of the intellect as "the primal truth from which all men's splinter truths derive." *The Ladder of Vision*, 227.

70   {truth as purpose of intellect}   Dante states that "our minds are never satisfied unless the truth—beyond which no truth exists—illumines them" (*Par.* 4.124–126: "... già mai non si sazia / nostro intelleto, se 'l ver non lo illustra / di fuor dal qual nessun vero si spazia."

70   {*Inf.* 9.61}   *Inf.* 9.61: "... li 'ntelletti sani."

70   {"rebellion ... intelligence"}   "Letter to Edward J. Dell," March 28, 1947, *The Collected Letters of C. S. Lewis*, vol. 2, *Books, Broadcasts, and the War 1931–1949*, ed. Walter Hooper (New York: HarperCollins, 2004), 929.

71   {souls in hell not see the present}   Of the sixty-five commentators on the Dante Project at Dartmouth who comment on this inability to see the present (see http://dante.dartmouth.edu/searchview.php?cmd=prevresult), their only solutions are 1) that the damned are farsighted and therefore cannot see near, but no explanation is given for this; and 2) that this defective sight applies only to the circle of heretics. However, other souls in Dante's hell can see the past and the future just like Farinata, since many souls recount things from the past to the pilgrim and know the future as well. For example, Ciacco sees the political future (see *Inf.* 6.64ff.), Brunetto Latini sees part of the pilgrim's future (see *Inf.* 15.61–64), etc. However, it is clear that none of these souls sees the present, because those who already know the pilgrim are unaware of his current journey until his arrival at any given circle.

72   {enemies as friends in *Purgatorio*}   Franco Masciandaro, although speaking about the souls in Limbo, notes that in combining classical heroes and their enemies in the same location peacefully, "Dante fashions a new order, that of ... uniting by contiguity the warriors of opposing camps." *Dante as Dramatist: The Myth of the Earthly Paradise and Tragic Vision in "The Divine Comedy"* (Philadelphia: University of Pennsylvania Press, 1991), 26.

72 {Farinata and Bocca in hell}   Farinata is among the heretics in the sixth circle; Bocca is with the traitors in the ninth circle.

72 {*Purg.* 18.73–74}   *Purg.* 18.68: ". . . innata libertate," and *Purg.* 18.73–74: "La nobile virtù . . . / . . . lo libero arbitrio. . . ."

73 {*Par.* 33.143–145}   *Par.* 33.143–145: "ma già volgeva il mio disio e 'l velle, / sì come rota ch'igualmente è mossa, / l'amor che move il sole e l'altre stelle." According to Joseph Anthony Mazzeo, the orbiting image can indicate "the completion of his divinization." *Structure and Thought in the "Paradiso"* (Ithaca, NY: Cornell University Press, 1958), 158, or, according to Teodolinda Barolini, his orbiting is a visual demonstration of his desire to love God. *The Undivine Comedy: Detheologizing Dante* (Princeton, NJ: Princeton University Press, 1992), 344, n. 33.

73 {fire in Dante's hell}   Dante's hell does occasionally include fire. Scattered fires are burning around the open tombs of the heretics in the sixth circle (*Inf.* 9.118–119); flakes of fire rain down on blasphemers, usurers, and sodomites in one subdivision of the seventh circle of the violent (see *Inf.* 14:28–29); a flame burns the soles of the feet of the simoniacs who are buried upside down in the third ditch of the circle of fraud (see *Inf.* 19.25, 28–30); and fraudulent counselors are wrapped in tongues of flame in the eighth ditch of that circle (*Inf.* 26.40–42). However, given that there are more than twenty different kinds of punishments in Dante's hell, fire is not prevalent, and in the case of the heretics and simoniacs it is an incidental accessory to their primary punishments.

74 {*Inf.* 1.12}   *Inf.* 1.12: ". . . la verace via abbandonai."

74 {walking away from the old mill}   If the mill referred to here is a windmill, it could be an oblique reference to Dante's Satan, because when the pilgrim first sees him he thinks he is seeing a windmill turning its huge sails (*Inf.* 34.6–7). In that context, "walking away from the mill" would signify the patient is "walking away from Satan" during his reconversion.

74 {*Inf.* 15.54}   *Inf.* 15.54: ". . . . reducemi a ca . . ."

75 {pilgrim compared to barbarians}   Lewis refers to this simile in his essay "Imagery in Dante's *Comedy*," 83, and notes it again in "Dante's Similes," saying that its deeper significance is that "the world of time and sin is to Heaven what the barbaric world was to Rome." *Studies in Medieval and Renaissance Literature*, coll. Walter Hooper (Cambridge: Cambridge University Press, 1966), 71.

75 {pilgrim assisted by angels}   His angelic helpers include the angel in the *Inferno* who opens the gate of Dis for access to the four lower

NOTES 241

circles of hell; the angel at the gate of Mount Purgatory who allows him entry to the mount; and the seven angels on Mount Purgatory between the stairs who each remove a "P" indicating the pilgrim's freedom from that particular sinful inclination.

75 {*Inf.* 1.118–119}   *Inf.* 1.118–119: ". . . color che son contenti / nel foco. . . ." Dante also says that divine justice inspires the soul that once desired sin to desire suffering now (see *Purg.* 21.64–66).

75 {*Purg.* 23.72}   *Purg.* 23.72: "io dico pena, e dovrìa dir sollazzo."

75 {desire for purification}   As James Collins points out, "Purgatory is not a series of punishments imposed by an external tyrant on the soul. . . . On the contrary, it is self-purgation undertaken willingly." *Pilgrim in Love: An Introduction to Dante and His Spirituality* (Chicago: Loyola University Press, 1984), 156.

76 {hag-siren dream}   V. Stanley Benfell notes that this dream "illustrates the process of sinfully attaching our desire to false goods and the fact that grace is often necessary to change those desires." *The Biblical Dante* (Toronto: University of Toronto Press, 2011), 131.

77 {*Par.* 10.93}   *Par.* 10.93: "la bella donna ch'al ciel t'avvalora."

77 {"to remove . . . state of happiness"}   Dante, "Letter to Can Grande," 15, *Dantis Alagherii Epistolae*, trans. Paget Toynbee, 2nd ed. (Oxford: Clarendon Press, 1966), 200. This is his dedication letter for the *Paradiso* to his patron, an Italian nobleman.

77–78 {"not speculate . . . life of men}   Lewis, preface, *The Screwtape Letters*, xii.

Chapter 5: *Perelandra*

79 {". . . sequel to *Out of the Silent Planet*"}   C. S. Lewis, preface, *Perelandra* (1943; repr., New York: Macmillan, 1965), n.p. Subsequent quotes are taken from this edition and will be referred to hereafter as "*Per.*" with the page number(s).

80 {links with *Paradise Lost*}   See, among others, Margaret Patterson Hannay, "A Preface to *Perelandra*," in *The Longing for a Form: Essays on the Fiction of C. S. Lewis*, ed. Peter J. Schakel (Kent, OH: Kent State University Press, 1977), esp. 74–86. A. N. Wilson, on the other hand, believes "the plot of *Perelandra* is borrowed from Milton's *Comus*, and its chief ideological failing stems from this." *C. S. Lewis: A Biography* (New York: Norton, 1990), 184. First of all, the plot of *Comus*, in which a lady is tempted to a lack of chastity, does not parallel Lewis's narrative in the least, and second, it is unclear what

"ideological failing" Lewis is being accused of. Wilson also believes that this novel is "an artistic failure" (p. 183), which I, among many others, quite disagree with. In terms of its connections to *Paradise Lost*, Lewis avoids what he considered three problem areas in Milton. See Lewis's *A Preface to "Paradise Lost"* (London: Oxford University Press, 1942; repr., Oxford University Press, 1961), chapters 12 to 18, published the previous year in 1942. Lewis does not present "unfallen sexuality," since his Edenic couple is separated during their time of testing. Second, he does not present God directly: Ransom occasionally hears an inner voice, but Maledil never appears or speaks at length. Third, Lewis depicts the satanic character in the novel as wholly devoid of dignity—even fallen dignity—and presents an unadulterated portrait of evil in its essence. Lewis makes this last point explicit through Ransom for whom "even a somber tragic Satan of *Paradise Lost* . . . would have been a welcome release from the thing he was actually doomed to watch" (*Per.* 128).

80 {links with *The Faerie Queene*}   See David C. Downing, *Planets in Peril: A Critical Study of C. S. Lewis's Ransom Trilogy* (Amherst: University of Massachusetts Press, 1992), 130.

80 {links with Wells's novels}   See, for example, Doris T. Myers, for parallels between *Perelandra* and Wells's *The Time Machine. C. S. Lewis in Context* (Kent, OH: Kent State University Press, 1994), 56ff. David C. Downing believes Lewis's narrative structure echoes Wells's structure for *The Time Machine*, but he notes the distinction that Wells diagnoses problems as political while Lewis sees them as moral. "Science Fiction," in *Reading the Classics with C. S. Lewis*, ed. Thomas L. Martin (Grand Rapids, MI: Baker Academic, 2000), 303.

80 {Ransom resembles Dante's pilgrim}   See Chapter 3, pp. 50–54.

81 {*Inf.* 2.1}   *Inf.* 2.1: "Lo giorno se n'andava, e l'aere [era] bruno."

81 {*Inf.* 2.35}   *Inf.* 2.35: "temo che la venuta non sia folle."

81 {*Inf.* 8.102}   *Inf.* 8.102: "ritroviam l'orme nostre insieme ratto."

81 {Virgil as "reason"}   See, among others, Mark Musa, note for *Inf.* 16.106–108, in *Inferno*, trans. Mark Musa (Bloomington: Indiana University Press, 1971), 221.

81 {*Inf.* 29.52–53, 65}   *Inf.* 29.52–53, 65: "Noi discendemmo in su . . . / . . . pur da man sinistra"; ". . . quella oscura valle."

81 {Dante references to madness}   Juno made King Athamas go insane and smash his son against a rock, leading his wife to drown herself and her other son (*Inf.* 30.1–12); Hecuba went mad and barked like a dog when Polyxena died and Polydorus was left unburied (*Inf.*

30.13–21); and finally, Dante notes the fury of madmen from Troy and Thebes (*Inf.* 30.22–23).

82 {*Inf.* 29.113}   *Inf.* 29.113: "I' mi saprei levar per l'aere a volo."

82 {*Inf.* 9.121}   *Inf.* 9.121: "Tutti li lor coperchi eran sospesi." See also *Inf.* 10.8–9.

82 {*Inf.* 29.22–24}   *Inf.* 29.22–24: ". . . Non si franga / lo tuo pensier da qui innanzi sovr'ello: / attendi ad altro, ed ei là si rimanga."

83 {*Inf.* 30.134–135}   *Inf.* 30.134–135: ". . . [ero] con tal vergogna, / ch'ancor per la memoria mi si gira."

83 {"first chapters need rewriting"}   "Letter to Sister Penelope," May 11, 1942, *The Collected Letters of C. S. Lewis*, vol. 2, *Books, Broadcast, and the War 1931–1949*, ed. Walter Hooper (New York: HarperCollins, 2004), 520.

83 {Christians "right" and "left"}   C. S. Lewis, *The Discarded Image: An Introduction to Medieval and Renaissance Literature* (Cambridge: Cambridge University Press, 1964), 48–49. For Lewis's reference to Augustine, see *Confessions*, 7.9, trans., intro., notes by John K. Ryan (New York: Image Books, 1960), 168–70. Augustine contrasts what pagan philosophy says about the Word (*Logos*) with the explanation of the Word found in the New Testament. In this passage he makes his famous comparison between Christians adopting whatever good they find in pagan thinking and the Israelites taking the gold out of Egypt when they left during the Exodus.

84 {Dante adjustments to pagan truth}   When something like Plato's idea that souls come from and return to the stars (*Timaeus* 42–43) is at complete variance with Christian doctrine, Dante clearly denies the literal aspect of this theory (see *Par.* 4.50ff.). However, in an effort to reconcile as much ancient material to Christian truth as possible, he reinterprets that theory to be potentially admissible on a metaphoric level: "If he [Plato] means to assign the honor and blame of influence to these spheres, then perhaps his bow strikes upon some truth" (*Par.* 4.58–60: "S'elli intende tornare a queste ruote / l'onor della influenza e 'l biasmo, forse / in alcun vero suo arco percuote.")

84 {"real though unfocused glean"}   C. S. Lewis, *Miracles: A Preliminary Study*, rev. ed. (New York: Macmillan, 1978), 134.

85 {angels mistaken for gods}   The classical characteristics of Lewis's planetary eldils are again demonstrated when five of them descend to Ransom's manor to empower Merlin. See *That Hideous Strength* (London: John Lane, 1945; repr., New York: Macmillan, 1965), 320–27.

85 {*Par*. 8.6} *Par*. 8.6: "le genti antiche nell'antico errore." Dante also comments that the ancients misunderstood planetary influence, which "led almost the whole world astray so that it named [the planets] Jove, Mercury, and Mars" (*Par*. 4.61–63: "... torse / già tutto il mondo quasi, sì che Giove, / Mercurio e Marte a nominar trascorse").

85 {*Purg*. 28.139–141} *Purg*. 28.139–141: "Quelli ch'anticamente poetaro / l'età dell'oro e suo stato felice, / forse ... esto loco sognaro."

85 {convergence of myth and Christian truth} Paul Piehler points out that in medieval allegories and Dante's *Purgatorio*, "The garden is the place where the intellectual and emotional problems ... find their solution, as intellect, emotion, and intuition achieve a harmony transcending all other expectations of happiness." "Myth or Allegory?" in *Word and Story in C. S. Lewis* eds. Peter J. Schakel and Charles A. Huttar (Columbia: University of Missouri Press, 1991), 209. For Ransom, both the Garden of Hesperides and the garden at Perelandra's summit function as settings for this integrating experience.

86 {*Purg*. 28.118–120} *Purg*. 28.118–120: "... la campagna santa / dove tu se' ... / ... frutto ha in sè che di là non si schianta."

86 {Matilda} According to most scholars, Matilda could represent the German Benedictine nun Mechtilde von Hackeborn (1240?–1298) who was called the "nightingale" because she had a beautiful voice in singing sacred songs. In her *Book of Special Grace* (pt. I, c. xiii) she describes the place of purification as a seven-terraced mountain, and she was also believed to have had visions of the earthly paradise. Others scholars suggest different historical figures. For example, Diana Glen suggests Matilda could be the eleventh-century Countess of Tuscany who is an example of a political leader who cooperated with the pope but also kept her independence from him. *Dante's Reforming Mission and Women in the "Comedy"* (Leicester, UK: Troubadour, 2008), 90.

86 {*Purg*. 28.40–41} *Purg*. 28.40–41: "una donna soletta che si gìa / cantando e scegliendo fior da fiore." Prior to his arrival in Eden and before meeting Matilda, Dante's pilgrim has a dream of Leah, who is also a lovely young girl in a meadow singing as she picks flowers, but she also weaves them into garlands (see *Purg* 27.97ff.). Lewis incorporates the detail of Leah weaving a garland for his description of the Green Lady.

86 {"owes something to Matilda"} "Letter to Charles A. Brady," October 29, 1944, *The Collected Letters of C. S. Lewis*, vol. 3, *Narnia, Cambridge, and Joy 1950–1963*, ed. Walter Hooper (New York: HarperCollins, 2007), 630.

86 {*Purg.* 28.55–56}   *Purg.* 28.55–56: "volsesi . . . /verso me. . . ."

86 {*Purg.* 28.49–51}   *Purg.* 28.49–51: "You remind me of where Proserpina was and what she was like at the time her mother lost her" ("Tu mi fai rimembrar dove e qual era / Proserpina nel tempo che perdette / la madre lei. . . .").

87 {*Purg.* 7.73–74}   *Purg.* 7.73–74: "gold, fine silver, cochineal [red dye] . . . and wood-indigo" ("Oro e argento fine, cocco e . . . / indaco, legno . . .").

87 {*Purg.* 8.98–99}   *Purg.* 8.98–99: ". . . una biscia, / forse qual diede ad Eva il cibo amaro."

87 {Lewis's Green Lady}   According to Walter Hooper, Lewis "said the idea [of a green person] came from Richard Burton's *Anatomy of Melancholy* (1621)" in which two green children are mentioned as being among inhabitants of other planets. "C. S. Lewis and the Anthropological Approach," in *C. S. Lewis's "Perelandra": Reshaping the Image of the Cosmos*, eds. Judith Wolfe and Brendan Wolfe (Kent, OH: Kent State University Press, 2013), 7. However, since Lewis's approach is often multilayered with several sources, this might be only one source he told Hooper about.

87 {*Purg.* 8.28–29}   *Purg.* 8.28–29: "Verdi come fogliette pur mo nate / erano in veste . . . [con] verdi penne."

87 {*Purg.* 29.124–125}   *Purg.* 29.124–125: ". . . era come se le carni e l'ossa / fossero state di smeraldo fatte."

88 {rejuvenation of both pilgrims}   Dante's pilgrim in fact emerges from his experiences in purgatory "renewed the way new plants are renewed with new foliage" (*Purg.* 33.143–144: "rifatto sì come piante novelle / rinovellate di novella fronda)." Ransom emerges from his experiences on Perelandra so renewed and even physically rejuvenated that he appears to be "almost a new Ransom, glowing with health . . . and seemingly ten years younger" (*Per.* 30).

88 {three ladies}   See *Inf.* 2.97–114 for the description of the three ladies who are helping him—Mary, Lucia, and Beatrice—and their reasons for doing so. All three ladies, as James Collins points out, are "God-bearing images" for the pilgrim. *Pilgrim in Love: An Introduction to Dante and His Spirituality* (Chicago: Loyola University Press, 1984), 76.

88 {Ransom's moral development}   Evan K. Gibson seems to be a bit premature in saying that *Out of the Silent Planet* "records Ransom's triumph over paralyzing fear and the acquisition of . . . fortitude." *C. S. Lewis, Spinner of Tales: A Guide to His Fiction* (Grand Rapids,

MI: Eerdmans, 1973), 51. It seems to me that Ransom reaches this "triumph" through the process of his mission on Perelandra. The Oyarsa on Malacandra had told him, "*when you have grown a little braver* [you] will be ready to go to Maleldil" (*OSP* 123; italics added). I would agree with Gibson, however, that "on Perelandra he demonstrates that this virtue [fortitude] has become a permanent part of his nature" (p. 51), but I think it takes a good part of the book before he demonstrates its permanence.

89 {seven capital sins}   Pope Gregory the Great (540–604) reorganized the number of vices and their sequence, which had first come from monastic traditions, and his codification became the standard that Dante and others followed.

89 {sequence from pride to lust}   See John's return journey in *The Pilgrim's Regress*; the patient in *The Screwtape Letters* after his reconversion; and the sequence of the dialogues in *The Great Divorce*.

90 {Ransom not envious}   Concerning this sinful inclination, Dante's pilgrim states that when he returns to ascend the Mount again (after his death), he will not have to stay long on the ledge of envy because he has seldom sinned that way (see *Purg.* 13.133–135).

91 {*Inf.* 33.129–132}   *Inf.* 33.129–132: ". . . tosto che l'anima trade / come fec' io, il corpo suo l'è tolto / da un demonio, che poscia il governa / mentre che 'l tempo suo tutto sia vòlto."

91 {Alberigo and Branca}   Joe R. Christopher mentions Branca d'Oria in connection to Weston in this context but does not mention Alberigo. *C. S. Lewis* (New York: Twayne, 1987), 96.

91 {*Inf.* 33.145–146}   *Inf.* 33.145–146: ". . . lasciò il diavolo in sua vece / nel corpo suo. . . ."

91 {Alberigo and Branca as traitors}   Alberigo invited two close relatives to dinner and had them killed; Branca invited his father-in-law to dinner and killed him.

91 {Weston as possessed}   Gunnar Urang seems to have misunderstood this point when he complains about Lewis's one-sided characterization of Weston who "is made to seem almost incapable of anything good." *Shadows of Heaven: Religion and Fantasy in the Writing of C. S. Lewis, Charles Williams and J. R .R. Tolkien* (Philadelphia: Pilgrim, 1971), 40. Most critics now characterize the Un-man as being demon-possessed in some way.

91 {Weston's different personality}   At the end of the sea chase when Weston seems to return momentarily to his body, Ransom tells him, "Say a child's prayer if you can't say a man's. Repent your sins" (*Per.*

171). Reminiscent of Christopher Marlowe's Doctor Faustus, Weston refuses the opportunity for repentance and redemption right before he dies.

92 {devils guard sinners} In contrast to the traditional concept of hell as the domain of devils who torture all sinners, Dante's relegation of devils to three areas is another demonstration of his point that the main suffering of souls in hell is the result of their choices; they are eternally punished by the sin that most defines them rather than by devils (see also *Inf.* 18.33ff.; *Inf.* 28.37ff.).

92 {*Inf.* 22.40–41} *Inf.* 22.40–41: "... fa che tu li metti / li unghioni a dosso, sì che tu lo scuoi!"

92 {*Inf.* 34.59–60} *Inf.* 34.59–60: "... tal volta la schiena / rimanea della pelle tutta brulla." Cerberus, Dante's guardian of the gluttons, also has clawed hands and flays souls in his charge (see *Inf.* 6.17–18). However, since he quarters souls as well, his punishment of sinners is not as similar to the Un-man's actions as Satan's is.

92 {physical combat with Un-man} Robert Plank objects that "the fight between good and evil is actually an abstract process. True, to become a narrative it has to be incarnated—but in so much torn flesh? One would think it could be done ... on some level closer to the intrapsychic struggle it really is." "Some Psychological Aspects of Lewis's Trilogy," in *Shadows of Imagination: The Fantasies of C. S. Lewis , J. R. R. Tolkien, and Charles Williams,* ed. Mark Robert Hillegas (Carbondale: Southern Illinois University Press, 1969), 35. Plank is perhaps not taking into account that Lewis was writing this novel during World War II when the recurring bombings of England by Germany could not quite be overcome by "abstract intrapsychic resistance." As Bruce R. Johnson points out, "rational arguments alone are insufficient weapons to fully counter the embodiment of evil present in the Un-man." "Frightful Freedom: *Perelandra* as Imaginative Theodicy," in C. S. Lewis's *"Perelandra": Reshaping the Image of the Cosmos,* eds. Judith Wolfe and Brendan Wolfe (Kent, OH: Kent State University Press, 2013), 136–37.

92 {no physical combat for pilgrim} I find David C. Downing's comment that Ransom's fight scene "frequently parallels the final cantos of the *Purgatorio*" a bit puzzling since Dante's pilgrim is in combat with no one in this part of the poem—or elsewhere for that matter—and the only suffering he goes through in the *Purgatorio* is passage through the wall of fire for a very brief time. *Into the Region of Awe: Mysticism in C. S. Lewis* (Downers Grove, IL: InterVarsity, 2005), 99. On the other hand, I would agree with Downing, with

some qualifications, that the "final quarter" of the *Purgatorio* "is the section Lewis would later draw upon so freely in the final quarter of *Perelandra*." "'*Perelandra*': A Tale of Paradise Retained," *C. S. Lewis: Life, Works, and Legacy*, vol. 2, *Fantacist, Mythmaker, and Poet*, ed. Bruce L. Edwards (Westport, CN: Praeger, 2007), 44. Ransom's ascent of the highest Perelandrian mountain and his meeting with Tor and Tinidril in the garden do have many parallels with the last few cantos of the *Purgatorio*; however, those events are covered only in pages 185–214, which do not mathematically comprise the last quarter of the book. Furthermore, the final quarter of *Perelandra* goes far beyond the *Purgatorio* to include Ransom's internal ascent of the cliff, with its parallels to the *Inferno*, and the Great Dance, with its parallels to the *Paradiso*.

92 {Glaucus}   For the story of Glaucus, see Ovid, *Metamorphoses* 13, 898–968.

92 {*Par.* 1.70–71}   *Par.* 1.70–71: "Trasumanar significar per verba / no si porìa. . . ." Dante invents the verb "*trasumanar.*" Steven Botterill notes that this verb "signifies a profound change of state in Dante *personaggio*, lifting him from his human predicament towards . . . a state of divinity," and it also includes the meaning of "'to travel beyond the confines of the human world,' in a concretely physical sense." *Dante and the Mystical Tradition: Bernard of Clairvaux in the "The Divine Comedy"* (Cambridge: Cambridge University Press, 1994), 226, 232.

93 {cliff ascent like *Inferno*}   Christopher notes that parallels between *The Divine Comedy* and the last part of *Perelandra* include the cavern where Ransom fights the Un-man; the ensuing ascent of a nearby mountain; the meeting with Tor and Tinidril at the top of the mountain; and finally the vision of the Great Dance. However, he gives very few details about these similarities. See his "Dante and the Inklings," *Mythprint* 11 (March 1975): 3, and *C. S. Lewis*, 96–97.

93 {Dante's hell as prison}   See *Inf.* 10.59; 33.56; and *Purg.* 1.41; 22.103.

93 {*Purg.* 1.13}   *Purg.* 1.13: "Dolce color d'orïental zaffiro."

93 {"sweet blue" and "sweet sapphire"}   This might be an example of what Lewis means when he refers to the "apparent '*minutiae*'" a good author attends to in order to create an overall effect. "A Note on *Comus*," in *Studies in Medieval and Renaissance Literature*, coll. Walter Hooper (Cambridge: Cambridge University Press, 1966), 181.

93 {Great Dance like *Paradiso* visions}   Christopher believes that "the plot does not call for the vision [of the Great Dance]," although he does see it as "a substitute for the Beatific vision that ends Dante's

poem." *C. S. Lewis*, 96, 97. On the contrary, I believe that the plot *does* call for that vision because Lewis is deliberately setting up parallels at this point with events in the *Paradiso* journey, particularly its conclusion.

93 {Great Dance in Plato}   See Plato, *Timaeus* 41.

93 {Great Dance in Plotinus}   See Plotinus, *Enneads* 4.4.33.

94 {souls as wheeling circles}   For wheeling circles, see, for example, *Par.* 8.19–20; 10.76–77; 12.19–20.

94 {comparison to dancers}   For images of dancers, see *Par.* 7.5; 10.76–77; 14.20; 25.107–109. At times they circle around Beatrice (see *Par.* 24.23–23) and around the pilgrim (see *Par.* 13.20; 24.151–152).

94 {*cords, bands, ribbons* of light}   In the *Paradiso* lights represent the redeemed, angels, and God, but Lewis's moving lights represent *all* types of created beings. The thin, delicate ribbons of light signify "flowers and insects, a fruit or a storm of rain . . . , rivers, mountains, or even stars" (*Per.* 219) while the larger and brighter ribbons signify "personal beings . . . [and] universal truths or universal qualities" (*Per.* 219). As these moving bands of light intersect, they create other sparks of a different and less substantial nature which represent "peoples, institutions, climates of opinion, civilisations, arts, sciences, and the like" (*Per.* 218)—a profound commentary by Lewis on the ultimate significance of individual human beings represented by the bright ribbons in contrast to nations, races, and cultures represented as less substantial and derivative sparks. Lewis repeats this very point in "The Weight of Glory": "Nations, cultures, arts, civilization—these are mortal, and their life is to ours as the life of a gnat." *"The Weight of Glory" and Other Addresses* (Grand Rapids, MI: Eerdmans, 1949), 15.

94 {*Par.* 26.32–33}   *Par.* 26.32–33: "Any goodness found outside [of God] is nothing but a light reflecting his ray" (". . . ciascun ben che fuor di lei [Dio] si trova / altro non è ch' un lume di suo raggio"). Lewis makes reference to this verse in "Imagery in Dante's 'Comedy,'" *Studies in Medieval and Renaissance Literature*, coll. Walter Hooper (Cambridge: Cambridge University Press, 1966), 90.

94 {*Par.* 29.143–144}   *Par.* 29.143–144: ". . . tanti / speculi fatti s' ha in che [Dio] si spezza." Lewis notes this verse in "Imagery in Dante's 'Comedy,'" 90. Dante also refers to the angels who rule over the seventh sphere as "mirrors" (see *Par.* 9.61).

94 {"mirror . . . return to Him"}   Lewis uses this image in other writings as well. In *Mere Christianity* (Book 4, 9), for instance, he repeats

the idea that if people let him, God will make each person "a bright stainless *mirror* [italics added] which reflects back to God perfectly (though, of course, on a smaller scale) His own boundless power and delight and goodness." *Mere Christianity* (New York: Macmillan, 1952), 175.

95 {*Par.* 33.55–57}   *Par.* 33.55–57: "Da quinci innanzi il mio veder fu maggio / che 'l parlar nostro, ch'a tal vista cede, / e cede la memoria a tanto oltraggio."

95 {memory "dropped farther" behind}   In trying to describe his voyage to Venus, Ransom says, "It is words that are vague. The reason why the thing can't be expressed is that it is too *definite* for language" (*Per.* 33).

95 {*Par.* 33.85–87}   *Par.* 33.85–87: "I saw how it [Eternal Light] held within itself all that is scattered throughout the universe bound by love in one volume" ("Nel suo profondo vidi che s'interna / legato con amore in un volume, / ciò che per l'universo si squaderna").

95 {tranquil simplicity vision}   *Par.* 33.91: the pilgrim sees the "universal form of this knot" ("La forma universal di questo nodo").

95 {*Par.* 33.143–145}   *Par.* 33.143–145: ". . . già volgeva il mio disio e 'l velle, / sì come rota ch'igualmente è mossa, / l'amor che move il sole e l'altre stelle."

95 {"cords of infinite desire"}   Lewis's use of the word *cords* here echoes Dante's vocabulary and concept when his pilgrim is asked by the apostle John to describe "the other cords that drew you to him [God]" (*Par.* 26.49–50: ". . . altre corde / tirarti verso lui. . . "). Lewis refers to Dante's use of "cords" in this verse in "Imagery in Dante's 'Comedy,'" 86.

96 {*Purg.* 28.7–8}   *Purg.* 28.7–8: "Un' aura dolce, sanza mutamento / avere in sè, mi ferìa per la fronte." Dante's pilgrim had once earlier felt a breeze on his forehead when leaving the ledge of gluttony, but in that case it was a "breeze" from the wing of the angel of the stairs removing the "P" of gluttony (see *Purg.* 24.148–149).

96 {wind on Ransom's forehead}   Similarly, right before Ransom meets her, "the warm wind was now strong enough to ruffle his hair" (*Per.* 49).

96 {Ransom looks down}   This reaction occurs again when "he could not long look at her face" (*Per.* 63), and later, recognizing her innocent holiness, he "could not look steadily at her" (*Per.* 68).

97 {"her manner . . . more gracious"}   In a similar instance, when Tinidril declares one of their conversations ended, "she did not move,

[so Ransom] bowed and drew back a step or two. . . . The audience was at an end" (*Per.* 71).

97 {*Purg.* 29.3} In *Purg.* 29.3, Matilda sings this statement in Latin: "Beati quorum tecta sunt peccata," a paraphrase of Psalm 32:1. After the pilgrim's admission of his sin, Beatrice tells him that his sins are no longer held against him (see *Purg.* 31.40–42).

97 {Dante's twenty-four elders} Dante's twenty-four men in pairs represent the books of the Old Testament while the four creatures represent the four Gospels.

97 {*Purg.* 129.148} *Purg.* 129.148: ". . . i rose e d'altri fiore vermigli."

97 {"red lilies" and Dante flowers} Lewis may also have had in mind the "red lily" Dante alludes to in *Par.* 16.152–154 that became the emblem of Florence adopted by the Guelphs in 1251 after they ousted the rival party. Christopher believes that these red lilies are "the substitute for the flames [on the ledge of lust], since there is no purgation of sin on Perelandra." *C. S. Lewis*, 97. However, at the top of the mountain, Ransom's situation is like that of Dante's pilgrim in the Garden of Eden who has already been purified, and he is also similar to him in the *Paradiso*. There is therefore no call at this point for purgation or a substitute for purgation. In addition, when a parallel to Dante's white rose appears in chapter 16 of *The Voyage of the "Dawn Treader"* as the Narnian crew sails through the Silver Sea, the unnamed white flowers there are likewise described as being like lilies. It seems that Lewis may have used lilies twice as substitutes for Dante's white rose.

97 {*Par.* 30.39–40} *Par.* 30.39–40: ". . . pura luce: / luce intelletüale, piena d'amore."

97 {*Purg.* 30.46–47} *Purg.* 30.46–47: ". . . Men che dramma / di sangue m'è rimaso che non tremi."

98 {Ransom's name Elwin} The Oyarsa also indicates that his name means "the friend of the eldila" (*Per.* 195).

98 {titles for Tor and Tinidril} I am indebted to Monika B. Hilder for noting that the titles are in the singular. *The Gender Dance: Ironic Subversion in C. S. Lewis's Cosmic Trilogy* (New York: Peter Lang, 2013), 71.

98 {*Purg.* 31.115–116} *Purg.* 31.115–116: ". . . Fa che le viste non risparmi; / posto t'avem dinanzi alli smeraldi."

98 {royal Perelandrians as "emeralds"} Although it is true, as Lionel Adey says, that Ransom loses his piebald appearance, it is not clear why he believes that in the end Tinidril "has lost her green color," since that color is a permanent feature for both herself and the

King. "Medievalism in the Space Trilogy of C. S. Lewis." *Studies in Medievalism* 3, no. 3 (Winter 1991): 284.

98 {use of "tu" for Beatrice}   Robert Hollander remarks about this pronoun shift that "only when she [Beatrice] is at one with God, where and when there are no human hierarchies, does she become 'tu.'" *Dante: A Life in Works* (New Haven, CT: Yale University Press, 2001), 127. And this is similar to the case for Ransom.

99 {". . . mimesis . . . science fiction"}   C. S. Lewis, *Spenser's Images of Life*, ed. Alastair Fowler (Cambridge: Cambridge University Press, 1967), 1.

99 {"spectator . . . pupil"}   Thomas G. Bergin, *Perspectives on "The Divine Comedy"* (New Brunswick, NJ: Rutgers University Press, 1967), 29.

99 {"enjoyed [writing] . . . most"}   "Letter to Roy W. Harrington," January 19, 1948, *The Collected Letters of C. S. Lewis*, vol. 2, 830.

99 {*Till We Have Faces* and *Perelandra*}   In his "Letter to Audrey Sutherland," April 28, 1960, he says about *Till We Have Faces*, "I think it far and away my best book." *The Collected Letters of C. S. Lewis*, vol. 3, *Narnia, Cambridge, and Joy 1950–1963*, ed. Walter Hooper (New York: HarperCollins, 2007), 1148. See also his "Letter to Joan Lancaster," April 20, 1959, *The Collected Letters of C. S. Lewis*, vol. 3, 1040.

99 {"*Perelandra* . . . best book"}   "Letter to George Sayer," April 10, 1946, *The Collected Letters of C. S. Lewis*, vol. 3, 1564.

99 {"*Perelandra* . . . my favorite too"}   "Letter to Colin Bailey," October 18, 1963, *The Collected Letters of C. S. Lewis*, vol. 3, 1467.

Chapter 6: *That Hideous Strength*

101 {"Ransom Trilogy"}   Although the trilogy has been called Lewis's "space trilogy," the third novel is not science fiction but adult fantasy, so the series is therefore more appropriately called "the Ransom trilogy." See "Letter to Sister Penelope," September 6, 1944, *The Collected Letters of C. S. Lewis*, vol. 2, *Books, Broadcast, and the War 1931–1949*, ed. Walter Hooper (New York: HarperCollins, 2004), 624, and another letter to her on January 3, 1945, *The Collected Letters of C. S. Lewis*, vol. 2, 635.

101 {"'tall story' of devilry"}   C. S. Lewis, *That Hideous Strength* (London: John Lane, 1945; repr., New York: Macmillan, 1965), 7. Subsequent quotes from this edition are referred to hereafter as "*THS*"

with page number(s). The title comes from a verse that refers to the Tower of Babel in Sir David Lyndsay's sixteenth-century poem "Ane Dialog betuix Experience and ane Courteour."

102 {legends of Arthur}   For details about the Arthurian myth in this novel, see, among others, Charles Moorman, *Arthurian Triptych* (Berkeley: University of California Press, 1960), 112–26, and David C. Downing, "*That Hideous Strength*: Spiritual Wickedness in High Places," in *C. S. Lewis: Life, Works, Legacy*, vol. 2, *Fantacist, Mythmaker, and Poet*, ed. Bruce L. Edwards (London: Praeger, 2007), 63ff.

102 {Logres' name}   "Logres" is the Welsh word for England that has traditionally been linked to Arthur's realm.

103 {*Inf.* 32.50–51}   *Inf.* 32.50–51: ". . . come due becchi / cozzaro insieme, tante ira li vinse." I am indebted to David C. Downing for noting this comparison. *Planets in Peril: A Critical Study of C. S. Lewis's Ransom Trilogy* (Amherst: University of Massachusetts Press, 1992), 98. I agree with his interpretation rather than Joe McClatchey's comparison of the scene to Ugolino gnawing on Ruggieri's head in Dante's ninth circle, which is quite different on many levels. "The Affair of Jane's Dreams: Reading *That Hideous Strength* as Iconographic Art," *The Taste of the Pineapple: Essays on C. S. Lewis as Reader, Critic, and Imaginative Writer*, ed. Bruce L. Edwards (Bowling Green, OH: Bowling Green State University Press, 1988), 172.

103 {Belbury character names}   Other major characters at Belbury are not given first names, but Lewis always chooses names suitable for them: Professor Filostrato, referred to as an "Italian eunuch" (see *THS* 70), has a name that means "frustrated love" (or "afflicted love"); the sociologists Steele (hard as steel) and Cosser (the French verb, "to butt" like rams) are stern and quarrelsome men.

104 {Dante's hell as prision}   See *Inf.* 10.59; 33.56; and *Purg.* 1.41; 22.103.

104 {Belbury *contrapasso* punishment}   Although Sanford Schwartz makes the point that "each of the major operatives [at the N.I.C.E.] perishes in a manner commensurate with his own aberrations, following the well-established precedent of Dante's *contrapasso*," he does not describe either how their deaths demonstrate a *contrapasso* or how they might echo specific punishments depicted in Dante's hell. *C. S. Lewis on the Final Frontier: Science and the Supernatural in the Space Trilogy* (New York: Oxford University Press, 2009), 135.

104 {"They despised the word of God . . ."}   The attendees are now like Dante's Nimrod, whose speech no one can understand and who cannot understand the speech of others (see *Inf.* 31.67, 80–81).

105 {trampled by elephant}   Downing notes that there is an image of
Dante's Satan from *Inf.* 34.38–54 when the elephant's ears are described as looking like devil's wings on each side of his head (see
THS 349). *Planets in Peril*, 98. His comment, however, that "at the
epicenter of hell sits Satan, frozen in ice, with batlike wings fluttering
at the sides of his head," needs adjustment. Satan is not sitting but is
standing encased in ice from his mid-chest down, and Dante says
the six bat wings are attached *underneath* each of Satan's three faces
and are vaster than ship sails (see *Inf.* 34.46–48), so it is unclear how
his wings could look like elephant ears "fluttering" at the side of his
head. Downing is correct, however, to connect Mark's reference to
the elephant as "the King of the world" (*THS* 350) with Dante's title
for Satan as "the emperor of his sad world" (*Inf.* 34.28)—although I
would translate "Lo 'mperador del doloroso regno" as "the emperor
of the kingdom of pain."

105 {Wither slits Straik's throat}   Downing says that Straik's decapita-
tion echoes "the beheadings and dismemberments of the schismatics
and heretics in the ninth circle (canto 38)." *Planets in Peril*, 98. There
are a few points to comment on here. First, Straik is not decapitated,
although that was Wither's intention; second, the schismatics are not
in the ninth but in the eighth circle; and third, there is no canto 38
since the *Inferno* ends with canto 34. Unfortunately these same errors
carried over into Downing's otherwise good chapter "*That Hideous
Strength*: Spiritual Wickedness in High Places" in *C. S. Lewis: Life,
Works, Legacy*, vol. 2, *Fantacist, Mythmaker, and Poet*, ed. Bruce L.
Edwards (London: Praeger, 2007), 60.

105 {*Inf.* 3.18}   *Inf.* 3.18: "c' hanno perduto il ben dell'intelletto."

105 {*Inf.* 1.11–12}   *Inf.* 1.11–12: "I was so full of sleep at that point that I
abandoned the true way" ("tant'era pieno di sonno a quel punto / che
la verace via abbandonai").

106 {Hardcastle's death}   Schwartz, for example, believes she is killed
by a tiger. *C. S. Lewis on the Final Frontier*, 134–35. Monika B. Hilder
believes that as well. *The Gender Dance: Ironic Subversion in C. S.
Lewis's Cosmic Trilogy* (New York: Peter Lang, 2013), 101. In contrast,
Michael Ward believes she shoots herself. *Planet Narnia: The Seven
Heavens in the Imagination of C. S. Lewis* (Oxford: Oxford University
Press, 2008), 197. If Lewis is attempting to have her clearly embody
the whole circle of violence, it seems more probable that she commits
suicide.

106 {no normalcy in "Objective Room"}   The room has irregular patterns, unnatural pictures, an anti-religious atmosphere, etc.

106 {traditional hell-fire punishment}   Fire appears intermittently throughout the novel, possibly as a reminder of the traditional hell-fire that is appropriate for this hellish place: Mark's first interview at Belbury occurs in a "room with a blazing fire" (*THS* 52), and the rooms at Belbury generally have fireplaces lit in the background. See, for example, *THS* 68, 97, 103, 128, 208, 217, 263.

106 {earth conquers him}   One of Lewis's main points in *The Abolition of Man* (New York: Macmillan, 1947) is that "Man's conquest of Nature" turns out to be Nature's conquest of Man.

106 {terrible end for N.I.C.E. members}   All of their punishments fit what *The Divine Comedy*'s narrator notes about one of hell's punishments: "O supreme wisdom, how great is the art you demonstrate . . . in this evil world, and how just are your rewards!" (*Inf.* 19.10–12: "O somma sapïenza, quanta è l'arte / che mostri . . . nel mal mondo, / e quanto giusto tua virtù comparte!" Dante's remark here about the punishments for sinners in the third ditch of the circle of fraud applies equally well to all of hell's punishments.

106 {"nasty and inhumane" portrayal}   Kath Filmer, *The Fiction of C. S. Lewis: Mask and Mirror* (London: Macmillan, 1993), 35.

107 {"divine Camilla"}   For Camilla, see Virgil *Aeneid* 11.583–584, 676–706, 726–812, 881–1132.

107 {*Par.* 3.78–79}   *Par.* 3.78–79: ". . . è formale ad esto beato esse / tenersi dentro alla divina voglia."

108 {no battle plan}   Cecil says he was not "asked . . . to join a definitive movement" (*THS* 198); the Dennistons admit that in joining St. Anne's they did not "foresee how [they] were going to be employed" (*THS* 198); and MacPhee says, "We've all been playing blind man's buff" (*THS* 198). Arthur acknowledges that asking Jane to join the group is like "asking her to take a leap in the dark" (*THS* 115) because "you can only take it on trust" (*THS* 116).

108 {to find Merlin}   Robert Boenig mistakenly believes that Camilla is with them on their mission. *C. S. Lewis and the Middle Ages* (Kent, OH: Kent State University Press, 2012), 146. Camilla *does* ask to go, but Ransom does not allow her to (see *THS* 228). She does, however, always have a willing, warrior spirit: "I don't mind anything," she says, "once I'm on a horse" (*THS* 324).

108 {eldils descend}   Ward believes the arrival of the five planetary eldils "is strongly reminiscent of the coming of the Holy Spirit at Pentecost." *Planet Narnia*, 36. Although that could apply quite well to the experience of the residents of St. Anne's, it certainly does not apply to the

people at Belbury since the purpose for which the eldils have come is judgment.

109 {"... become a bridge"}   Ransom uses the word *bridge*, but with a negative connotation, in *Perelandra* when he describes Weston's body as "the *bridge* by which something else had invaded Perelandra" (*Per.* 111; italics added). Earlier in that novel, the narrator-Lewis also uses that word negatively when he is suspicious of Ransom during his mini-journey to Ransom's cottage: "How if my friend were the unwitting bridge [for invaders of the earth], the Trojan Horse?" (*Per.* 12).

109 {Ransom recalls the pilgrim}   Most scholars are in accord that Ransom in this third novel resembles Charles Williams, perhaps because the novel is a supernatural thriller of sorts and is the kind of novel Williams is famous for, but I see no other solid connections. See Joe R. Christopher, *C. S. Lewis* (Boston: Twayne, 1987), 100. William Gray believes Ransom "strikingly resembles" Williams. *C. S. Lewis* (Plymouth UK: Northcote House, 1988), 36. Downing says that once Ransom is the Pendragon (Arthur's successor) in the third novel of the trilogy, he resembles Williams. *Planets in Peril*, 127. Schwartz makes the same kind of comment about Ransom. *C. S. Lewis on the Final Frontier*, 92.

109 {*Purg.* 27.142}   *Purg.* 27.142: "... io te sovra te corono e mitrio."

109 {"... priesthood, mercy, and power"}   When MacPhee comments on Ransom's post-journey appearance, he says, "That is what people are like who come back from the *stars*" (*THS* 194; italics added). If Dante were not in the picture, one would have expected MacPhee to say, "back from the *planets*."

109 {pilgrim commissioned}   He is first commissioned by Beatrice in the garden, "Be sure to write what you see when you have returned from here" (*Purg.* 32.104–105: "... quel che vedi / ritornato di là, fa che tu scrive"). She also tells him, after her prophecy about God's intervention on behalf of the church, "Teach these words to those who are living the life that is a rush to death" (*Purg.* 33.53–54: "... queste parole segna a' vivi / del viver ch' è un correre alla morte"). Next he is commissioned by his ancestor Cacciaguida, "Make known all that you have seen" (*Par.* 17.128: "tutta tua visïon fa manifesta"). Peter Damien tells him to convey to the world that no one can fully penetrate the mystery of God's will (see *Par.* 21.97–99), and the Apostle John tells him to report that his physical body is not yet in heaven (see *Par.* 25.124). Finally St. Peter tells him to repeat his invective against the evils of the church: "When you return down there, open your mouth

and do not hide what I do not hide" (*Par.* 27.65–66: "ancor giù torne-
rai, apri la bocca, / e non asconder quel ch'io non ascondo").

109 {Ransom commissioned}   The Oyarsa of Malacandra had told him
to watch for any evil that Weston and Devine (now Feverstone) might
do: "Fight them. And when you have need, some of our people will
help. Maleldil will show them to you" (*OSP* 143). Ransom resisted
Weston in Perelandra, and now he resists Feverstone and his group
at Belbury.

109 {pilgrim as narrator}   On Dante's narrator as a character in the
poem, see Robert Wilson, *Prophecies and Prophecy in Dante's "The
Divine Comedy"* (Florence: Leo Olschki Editore, 2008), especially pp.
3–4, 9–10. Wilson presents an excellent analysis of the three "Dantes":
Dante the historical poet, Dante the pilgrim, and Dante the narrator.

110 {"assume the role . . . prophet"}   Patrick Boyde also adds that the narrator functions as "chorus, commentator, accomplice and composer."
Perception and Passion in Dante's "Comedy" (Cambridge: Cambridge
University Press, 1993), 111–12. Marguerite Mills Chiarenza points
out that the narrator is presenting "the story of his former self and
his former responses," so the narrator adds his after-thoughts, invec-
tives, etc., as well. His comments are retrospective and are thus not
confined to the pilgrim's initial perceptions during the journey. *"The
Divine Comedy": Tracing God's Art* (Boston: Twayne, 1989), 28–29.
Irma Brandeis notes that the narrator separates his voice from the
pilgrim's "when he wants to affirm some judgment of his mature
thought." *The Ladder of Vision* (Garden City, NY: Anchor, 1962), 29.

110 {Ransom introduced late}   Although Ward believes that Ransom
"has become etiolated by the time of third book" and "has turned
into a passive valetudinarian" (*Planet Narnia*, 69–70), that would be
an inexact and inappropriate description for Ransom if he is, as I
maintain, meant to be echoing the role of Dante-narrator.

110 {"divine fecundity . . . last state"}   Evelyn Underhill, *Mysticism: A
Study in the Nature and Development of Man's Spiritual Consciousness*
(New York: E. P. Dutton, 1910), 367.

110 {"cleanse [hero's] soul . . . the divine"}   Francesca Galligan, "Dante
and Epic: The Artist as Hero," in *Nature and Art in Dante*, eds. Daragh
O'Connell and Jennifer Petrie (Dublin: Four Courts Press, 2013), 113.

110 {*Par.* 25.1–2}   *Par.* 25.1–2: ". . . 'l poema sacro / al quale ha posto
mano e cielo e terra." He also calls it "the consecrated poem" (*Par.*
23.62: ". . . lo sacrato poema").

110   {*Par.* 17.131–132}   *Par.* 17.131–132: ". . . vital nutrimento / . . . quando sarà digesta."

110   {*Purg.* 32.103}   *Purg.* 32.103: ". . . in pro del mondo che mal vive."

110   {spiritual benefit of poem}   Peter S. Hawkins remarks that the pilgrim's "transformation . . . is meant to transform others as well." *Dante's Testaments: Essays in Scriptural Imagination* (Stanford, CA: Stanford University Press, 1999), 263.

111   {Downing on *Inferno*}   See Downing, *Planets in Peril*, 94–96, as well as his chapter "*That Hideous Strength*: Spiritual Wickedness," where he adds a few more details on pp. 53ff.

112   {"moment of his consent . . . a corner"}   Mark's situation illustrates what Screwtape says in Letter XII: "It does not matter how small the sins are. . . . Indeed the safest road to Hell is the gradual one—the gentle slope, soft underfoot, without sudden turnings, without milestones, without signposts."

113   {Mark's necessary path}   Mark realizes that his situation is dire and that he may be killed, so I would disagree with Paul Piehler that "none of Lewis's heroes is ever depicted as being in the intensity of spiritual peril Dante experiences at the start of his visionary journey, and the disorientations in the novels are appropriately milder experiences." "Myth or Allegory? Archetype and Transcendence in the Fiction of C. S. Lewis," in *Word and Story in C. S. Lewis*, eds. Peter J. Schakel and Charles A. Huttar (Columbia: University of Missouri Press, 1991), 207. Mark's experiences do not seem "milder" to me, nor does the intensity of Jane's situation or Orual's spiritual situation in *Till We Have Faces*.

113   {*Purg.* 30.136–138}   *Purg.* 30.136–138: "Tanto giù cadde, che tutti argomenti / alla salute sua eran già corti, / fuor che mostrarli le perdute genti." Virgil makes the same point earlier: "There was no other path [to save the pilgrim's soul] than this one. . . . I showed him all the damned souls" (*Purg* 1.62–64: ". . . non li era altra via [per salvarlo] / che questa. . . . / Mostrata ho lui tutta la gente ria."

113   {"site of his rebirth"}   Hilder, *The Gender Dance*, 153.

113   {Virgil calls pilgrim "son"}   See *Inf.* 3.121; 7.61; 8.67; 11.16; 15.31; and *Purg.* 3.66; 4.46; 17.92; 25.35; 25.58; 27.20; and 27.128.

113   {Hardcastle calls Mark "Sonny"}   See *THS* 69–70, 96–97, 121, 129–30, and 186. She also calls him "honey" twice (*THS* 99, 186) and "lovey" (*THS* 187).

114   {swoon means transition}   In other examples, the pilgrim faints at the end of his first conversation with a soul in hell (Francesca) (see

Inf. 5.142). See also the pilgrim's dream state when he is supernaturally transported to the gate of purgatory (see *Purg.* 9.19ff.); his fainting after his admission of guilt in the garden and before his cleansing in the Lethe (see *Purg.* 31.88–89); and his falling asleep in the Garden of Eden just prior to his allegorical visions of the church's seven catastrophes from its beginning until 1300 (see *Purg.* 32.68–69).

114 {Ransom's loss of consciousness} In other instances, on Perelandra, Ransom stumbles twice and then faints when he sees the Un-man ripping the frogs (*Per.* 111) and realizes the depth of active evil that is present on Perelandra. He also falls to the ground when he learns that things have gone well for the Green Lady right before he meets the King and Queen on the mountain summit (*Per.* 197). When Teodolinda Barolini explains that "transition in the *Commedia* is regularly represented by sleep [and I would add, a loss of consciousness], a quintessentially liminal condition that participates in both life and death, standing on the threshold of both worlds," her comment can be applied equally well to Lewis's use of this kind of transition. *The Undivine Comedy: Detheologizing Dante* (Princeton, NJ: Princeton University Press, 1992), 160.

114 {"Surgi e vieni"} Downing compares Merlin's "Surge" to Virgil's "Lèvati su . . . in piede" when the pilgrim is about to leave hell (*Inf.* 34.94). *Planets in Peril*, 98. Although the context of leaving hell can certainly be considered a parallel to Mark's leaving Belbury, Dante's pilgrim is not asleep or unconscious in the *Inferno* when Virgil says this to him, and, furthermore, Virgil's attitude to the pilgrim in hell is not the negative one of "wretched boy." The event in the *Purgatorio* seems a more likely parallel because of the contextual similarity of the pilgrim needing to be roused to consciousness *and* the linguistic similarity of Virgil's verb to Merlin's verb, i. e., *surge/surgi*. There is one other instance of "Surgi" in the *Purgatorio* that could also be a model for Mark's situation. Matilda tells the pilgrim to get up (see *Purg.* 32.72) after he falls asleep so that he can follow after Beatrice in the garden, and it is time now for Mark to follow after Jane.

115 {Jane as Mark's Beatrice} In Thomas Howard's phrasing, Jane is "the 'God-bearer' to Mark." *Narnia and Beyond: A Guide to the Fiction of C. S. Lewis* (San Francisco: Ignatius, 2006), 162.

115 {*Purg.* 6.47–48} *Purg.* 6.47–48: "tu la vedrai di sopra, in su la vetta / di questo monte, ridere e felice."

116 {Jane as protagonist's wife} A very condensed mini-version of another wife-husband dynamic could be applied to Ivy and Tom Maggs. Despite being a thief in the past, once Tom was with Ivy (who led him

on a righteous path), "he had gone 'as straight, as straight'" (*THS* 302). When he is released from jail for an earlier theft, Ransom tells Ivy, "Go and heal this man" (*THS* 378), echoing the concept that Beatrice has the power to heal the pilgrim's soul (see *Par.* 31.89)

116 {male "Beatrice"}   For an excellent discussion of gender roles and their reversals in Lewis's fiction, see Monika B. Hilder's *Feminine Ethos in C. S. Lewis's Chronicles of Narnia* (New York: Peter Lang, 2012) and *The Gender Dance.*

116 {*Inf.* 1.14–15}   *Inf.* 1.14–15: ". . . quella valle / che m'avea di paura il cor compunto."

116 {*Inf.* 1.52–54}   *Inf.* 1.52–54: ". . . mi porse tanto di gravezza / con la paura . . . / ch'io perdei la speranza. . . ."

116 {*Inferno* as subtext}   Downing, *Planets in Peril*, 94.

116 {"Mark's redemption . . . central element"}   Mona Dunkel, "C. S. Lewis as Allegorist: *The Pilgrim's Regress*," in *C. S. Lewis: Life, Works, Legacy*, vol. 3, *Apologist, Philosopher, and Theologian*, ed. Bruce L. Edwards (London: Praeger, 2007), 44.

117 {*Purg.* 9.32–33}   *Purg.* 9.32–33: "e sì lo 'ncendio imaginato cosse, / che convenne che 'l sonno si rompesse."

117 {east as heavenward direction}   God and/or heaven is represented as the Eastern Mountains (*The Pilgrim's Regress*), as the Mountains off in the east bathed in light (*The Great Divorce*), and as Aslan's dwelling in the east (The Chronicles of Narnia). In Dante's garden, the pilgrim faces east to see Beatrice (see *Purg.* 29.12).

117 {*Purg.* 10.7–8}   *Purg.* 10.7–8: ". . . per una pietra fessa, / che si moveva d'una e d'altra parte."

117 {*Purg.* 9.68–69}   *Purg.* 9.68–69: ". . . 'l duca mio . . . / si mosse, ed io di retro. . . ."

117 {*Purg.* 11.61–62}   *Purg.* 11.61–62: "L'antico sangue e l'opere leggiadre / di miei maggior mi fer sì arrogante."

118 {*Purg.* 11.64}   *Purg.* 11.64: "ogn' uomo ebbi in despetto tanto avante."

118 {barren by choice}   It is "her determination not to have a child—or not for a long time" (*THS* 73).

118 {*Purg.* 10.2–3}   *Purg.* 10.2–3: ". . . 'l malo amore dell'anime . . . / . . . fa parer dritta la via torta."

118 {*Purg.* 12.70–72}   *Purg.* 12.70–72: "Or superbite, e via col viso altero, / . . . non chinate il volto / sì che veggiate il vostro mal sentiero!"

119 {*vive voce* examination}   Lewis uses this same expression when he describes the questioning of Dante's pilgrim as "a *vive voce* examination by three apostles." "Imagery in Dante's 'Comedy,'" *Studies in Medieval and Renaissance Literature*, coll. Walter Hooper (Cambridge: Cambridge University Press, 1966), 79.

120 {*Purg.* 23.84}   *Purg.* 23.84: "dove tempo per tempo si ristora."

121 {"Your trouble . . . Pride"}   She is, in this regard, like Dante's pilgrim who admits that pride is his worst sin that needs cleansing (see *Purg.* 13.136–138).

121 {"brightness . . . dazzled"}   Dazzling brightness is always typical of Dante's angels, and with Camilla's resemblance to the angel at the gate of purgatory at certain points, it is fitting that she now recalls this feature of Dante's angels as well.

122 {*Par.* 17.20}   *Par.* 17.20: ". . . lo monte che l'anime cura."

122 {"Beatrician experience"}   Christopher, *C. S. Lewis*, 102. He also refers to it as the "Beatrician revelation" (p. 100), basing his terminology on phrases found in Charles Williams's *The Figure of Beatrice: A Study in Dante* (London: Faber and Faber, 1943): "Beatrician experience" (p. 47), "Beatrician revelation" (p. 48), and "Beatrician discovery" (p. 95). In yet another phrasing, Peter S. Hawkins calls it the "Beatrician moment," saying it "reveals that the people we are given to love . . . can open us to the divine." *Dante: A Brief History* (Malden, MA: Blackwell, 2006), 94.

122 {garden meetings so far}   The one exception *could* be in *The Screwtape Letters*, but the reader is never told where the patient meets the young Christian woman he loves.

123 {*Purg.* 31.19}   *Purg.* 31.19: ". . . scoppia' io sott'esso grave carco."

123 {*Purg.* 31.20–21}   *Purg.* 31.20–21: "fuori sgorgando lacrime e sospiri, / e la voce allentò per lo suo varco."

123 {*Purg.* 30.78}   *Purg.* 30.78: "tanta vergogna mi gravò la fronte."

123 {*Purg.* 32.3}   *Purg.* 32.3: ". . . li altri sensi m'eran tutti spenti."

123 {*Purg.* 32.93}   *Purg.* 32.93: "quella ch'ad altro intender m'avea chiuso."

123 {*Purg.* 32.106–107}   *Purg.* 32.106–107: ". . . tutto ai piedi / de' suoi comandamenti era divoto." He also says he did as he was told (see *Purg.* 33.22).

123 {*Par.* 31.93}   *Par.* 31.93: "poi si tornò all'etterna fontana." Lewis quotes this line, without citing its reference, to end his book *A Grief Observed*.

Chapter 7: *The Great Divorce*

127 {*The Great Divorce* (1946)}   The original title in 1944 was *Who Goes Home? or the Grand Divorce*. The title was changed to *The Great Divorce: A Dream* at the book's first printing in 1946. According to Walter Hooper, the novel's printing was mistakenly dated November 1945 when it was actually January 1946. *The Collected Letters of C. S. Lewis*, vol. 2, 698, note.

127 {dream-vision narrative}   In his comparison of Lewis's novel and *The Divine Comedy*, Robert Boenig believes that both are dream narratives, even calling Dante's poem the "culmination" of the dream-vision genre. *C. S. Lewis and the Middle Ages* (Kent, OH: Kent State University Press, 2012), 98–99. However, Dante, unlike most medieval writers, presents his narrative poem as a *vision* and *not* as a dream narrative. Dream narratives did not have the same weight or elicit the same level of acceptance as visions did for medieval readers, and Dante wanted his readers to take what he was saying seriously. See Charles Singleton's famous saying that "the fiction of the *Divine Comedy* is that it is not a fiction"—which clearly excludes it from the dream-vision category. *Dante Studies*, vol. 1, *"Commedia": Elements of Structure* (Cambridge, MA: Harvard University Press, 1954), 62. As Prue Shaw points out, "The poem begins not with a moment of falling asleep but of awakening." *Reading Dante: From Here to Eternity* (New York: Norton, 2014), 82.

127 {MacDonald's name}   Although Lewis used the spelling "Macdonald" in his writings, today's preferred spelling tends to be "MacDonald."

127 {similarity between Dante's poem and *The Great Divorce*}   Green and Walter Hooper call it "Lewis's *Divine Comedy*," noting that "the parallels between the two books are numerous," but they note only the similarities concerning the guides and between Dante's popes in hell and Lewis's apostate bishop. *C. S. Lewis: A Biography*, 222. Joe R. Christopher calls it "an obvious (if truncated) imitation of *The Commedia* as a whole." "Dante and the Inklings," *Mythprint* 11 (March 1975): 3. He repeats this point in his book on Lewis, calling it simply "an imitation of *La Divina Commedia*." *C. S. Lewis* (Boston: Twayne, 1987), 105. Chad Walsh says it is "obviously inspired by Dante's *Divine Comedy*" (*The Literary Legacy of C. S. Lewis* [New York: Harcourt Brace Jovanovich, 1979], 69), and Margaret Patterson Hannay says it "is clearly modeled on Dante's *Divine Comedy*" (*C. S. Lewis* [New York: Frederick Unger, 1981], 111), but neither Walsh nor Hannay gives explanations or evidence. A. N. Wilson calls it "Lewis's *Commedia*,"

but the examples he gives as similarities are highly inaccurate both about Lewis's narrative and Dante's poem: he compares the rain in Grey Town to the rain in the sixth circle of heretics, where there is fire but no rain; he says the journey from Grey Town goes "to the heights of Paradise," but the Grey Towners reach only the Plain, the outskirts of heaven; and he incorrectly equates the Tragedian at the end of the novel with Dante himself. *C. S. Lewis: A Biography* (New York: Norton, 1990), 201. Peter S. Hawkins lists it as one of the ten novels in the last hundred years that owe "a more or less obvious debt" to Dante's poem. *Dante: A Brief History* (Malden, MA: Blackwell, 2006). 145.

127 {*The Great Divorce* and *Inferno*}   Colin N. Manlove says, "This book owes some affinity" to the *Inferno. C. S. Lewis: His Literary Achievement* (London: Macmillan, 1987), 99. Although there is some truth to that, the links with Inferno are minor. In his "Letter to Dorothy Sayers," January 22, 1946, Lewis says *The Great Divorce* "owes more to the Purgatorio [*sic*] than to the Inferno [*sic*]." *The Collected Letters of C. S. Lewis*, vol. 2, *Books, Broadcasts, and the War 1931–1949*, ed. Walter Hooper (New York: HarperCollins, 2004), 700.

127 {*The Great Divorce* and *Purgatorio*}   Robert Boenig's remark that this is Lewis's "version of the *Purgatorio*" is closer to the mark, but he gives no details and omits mention of any features from the *Inferno* and the *Paradiso*. "Critical and Fictional Pairing in C. S. Lewis," *The Taste of the Pineapple: Essays on C. S. Lewis as Reader, Critic, and Imaginative Writer*, ed. Bruce L. Edwards (Bowling Green, OH: Bowling Green State University Press, 1988), 138.

127 {*The Great Divorce* and *Paradiso*}   David C. Downing believes that "Lewis used the 'Paradiso' [*sic*] as his structural subtext in *The Great Divorce*." *Planets in Peril: A Critical Study of C. S. Lewis's Ransom Trilogy* (Amherst: University of Massachusetts Press, 1992), 94. However, evidence seems to point to the *Purgatorio* as the primary subtext, while the *Paradiso* plays a much lesser role.

127 {MacDonald as Virgil}   MacDonald's similarity to Virgil is noted by the following: Gisbert Kranz, "Dante in the Work of C. S. Lewis," *Deutches Dante-Jahrbuch*, vol. 47, trans. Hope Kirkpatrick, *The Bulletin of the New York C. S. Lewis Society*, 4, no. 10 (August 1973): 6; Green and Hooper, *C. S. Lewis*, 222; Kath Filmer, *The Fiction of C. S. Lewis: Mask and Mirror* (New York: St. Martin's, 1993], 57; William Gray, *C. S. Lewis* (Plymouth, UK: Northcote House, 1998), 26; Dominic Manganiello, "*The Great Divorce*: C. S. Lewis's Reply to Blake's Dante," *Christian Scholar's Review*, 27, no. 4 (Summer 1998):

479; Wayne Martindale *Beyond the Shadowlands: C. S. Lewis on Heaven and Hell* (Wheaton, IL: Crossway, 2005), 76; and Boenig, *C. S. Lewis and the Middle Ages*, 98.

127　{MacDonald as Beatrice}　Chad Walsh says MacDonald "was his [the narrator's] Beatrice." "The Man and the Mystery," *Shadows of Imagination: The Fantasies of C. S. Lewis, J. R. R. Tolkien and Charles Williams,* ed. Mark Robert Hillegas (Carbondale: Southern Illinois University Press, 1969), 4.

127　{MacDonald as Virgil and Beatrice}　A more accurate analysis compares MacDonald to *both* Dantean guides. See Joe R. Christopher in three works: "Considering *The Great Divorce*: Parts I and II," *Mythcon Proceedings* (Los Angeles: Mythopoeic Society, 1971), 40; "Dante and the Inklings," 3; and *C. S. Lewis*, 106. This dual interpretation is also given by Hannay, *C. S. Lewis*, 111, and by Sebastian D. G. Knowles, *A Purgatorial Flame: Seven British Writers in the Second World War* (Philadelphia: University of Pennsylvania Press, 1990), 148.

128　{Jeremy Taylor and Prudentius}　According to Roger Lancelyn Green and Walter Hooper, Lewis said his idea of access to heaven by souls from hell is based on the concept of *Refrigerium* found in one of Jeremy Taylor's sermons ("Christ's Advent to Judgement," in *Whole Works*, ed. Reginald Heber [London, 1822], vol. 5, 45), where the damned are occasionally allowed temporary excursions out of hell. *C. S. Lewis: A Biography* (New York: Harcourt Brace Jovanovich, 1974), 220–21. In an earlier work by the fourth-century Latin poet, Prudentius Aurelius Clemens, "Hymn for the Lighting of the Lamp" (in *Liber Cathemerinon*), the punishments of hell are relaxed on the day of Christ's resurrection. However, neither writer indicates that souls may leave hell and go to heaven; that proposition is found only in Dante.

128　{"emperor Trajan did"}　C. S. Lewis, *The Great Divorce* (London: Geoffrey Bles, 1945; repr., New York: Macmillan, 1946), 66. Subsequent quotes are taken from this edition and are hereafter indicated by "*GD*" and page number(s)

128　{*Par.* 20.106–117}　According to a medieval legend, Pope Gregory the Great prayed for Trajan to be brought back to life so that he could preach the gospel to him; Trajan then became a believer in Christ and was saved.

128　{Dante as authoritative source}　Joe R. Christopher also notes that Lewis is using Dante as an authority for the possible salvation of souls from Grey Town. "The Dantean Structure of *The Great Divorce*," *Mythlore* 29, no. 3/4 (Spring/Summer 2011): 82.

128 {"by his merits . . . by justice"}   Dante, *Dantis Alagherii Epistolae*, trans. Paget Toynbee, 2nd ed. (Oxford: Clarendon, 1966), 200.

128 {freely choose hell or heaven}   Wilson's comment that "behind [Lewis's] story is the idea—*more generous than anything in Dante*—that all may be saved if they so choose" seems to misunderstand the very point of Dante's poem that people *do indeed* freely choose their eternal abodes. *A Biography*, 201. As Joseph Anthony Mazzeo states, the inhabitants of Dante's hell "are not sent there by anything external to them, but because Hell is what they really wanted." "Dante's Three Communities: Mediation and Order," in *The World of Dante: Six Studies in Language and Thought*, eds. Bernard Chandler and J. A. Molinaro (Toronto: University of Toronto Press, 1966), 70.

128 {"All that are . . . miss it"}   Lewis makes this same point in other places: "A man can't be *taken* to hell, or *sent* to hell: you can only get there on your own steam." *"The Dark Tower" and Other Stories*, ed. Walter Hooper (New York: Harcourt, 1977), 49.

129 {"Blake . . . perennial"}   Lewis, preface, *The Great Divorce*, 5.

129 {"written of their divorce"}   Ibid.

129 {divorce between two regions}   In the preface to this novel, Lewis clarifies that his afterlife is an analogue for earth: "Earth, I think, will not be found by anyone to be in the end a very distinct place. I think earth, if chosen instead of Heaven, will turn out to have been, all along, only a region in Hell: and earth, if put second to Heaven, to have been from the beginning a part of Heaven itself" (*GD* 7).

129 {*Purg.* 1.5–6}   *Purg.* 1.5–6: "dove l'umano spirito si purga / e di salire al ciel diventa degno."

130 {*Purg.* 4.89–90}   *Purg.* 4.89–90: ". . . sempre al cominciar di sotto è grave; / e quant' uom più va su, e men fa male."

130 {accurate interpretation of purgatory}   Lewis believes that the concept of purgatory found in Thomas More's *Supplication of Souls* and in John Fisher's *Sermon on Psalm VI*—where sinners' pain is retributive rather than purifying—is mistaken. *Letters to Malcolm: Chiefly on Prayer* (New York: Harcourt Brace Jovanovich, 1963), 108. See also *English Literature in the Sixteenth Century Excluding Drama* (Oxford: Clarendon, 1954; repr., New York: Oxford University Press, 1973), 163–64, 172.

130 {"I don't think . . . purgation"}   Lewis, *Letters to Malcolm*, 109.

131 {nonbeing in Augustine}   Augustine, making the equation between evil and lack of substance, says, "I found that it [evil] is not a substance. It is perversity of will, twisted away from the supreme

substance, yourself, O God, and towards lower things." *The Confessions of Saint Augustine*, 7.16, trans., intro., and notes by John K. Ryan (New York: Image Books, 1960), 175. He also correlates evil with nothingness in 3.7: "Evil is only the privation of a good, even to the point of complete nonentity" (Ibid., 85). In *The City of God*, he repeats this philosophical analysis: "To exist in oneself, that is to please oneself, is not immediately to lose all being; but it is to come nearer to nothingness." *The City of God*, 14.13, trans. Henry Bettenson (New York: Image Books, 1958), 122.

131 {nonbeing in Boethius}   Boethius's Lady Philosophy says that when men abandon goodness and consciously turn to evil, "they not only cease to be powerful, but cease to be at all." *The Consolation of Philosophy*, 4.2, trans. and intro. V. E. Watts (Baltimore, MD: Penguin, 1969), 122. "Men who give up the common good of all things that exist, thereby cease to exist themselves. . . . I am not trying to deny the wickedness of the wicked; what I do deny is that their existence is absolute and complete existence" (Ibid.).

131 {nonbeing in Thomas Aquinas}   See Thomas Aquinas, *Summa Theologica*, Ia, q. 49, a.1–3.

131 {perpetually drizzling rain}   This is similar to Dante's third circle of hell that has "eternal rain . . . with never any change to its rhythm or its quality" (*Inf.* 6.79: ". . . piova / etterna . . . / regola e qualità mai non l'è nova").

131 {Grey Town and nonbeing}   Lewis defines hell similarly elsewhere as "the outer rim where being fades into nonentity." *The Problem of Pain* (New York: Macmillan, 1962), 127. He elsewhere describes this concept of hell more fully as "the last outpost, the rim, the place where being is nearest to non-being, where positive unbeing . . . asymptotically approaches that zero it can never reach." "Imagination and Thought," *Studies in Medieval and Renaissance Literature*, coll. Walter Hooper (Cambridge: Cambridge University Press, 1966), 62.

132 {"in the light . . . stains"}   Kathryn Lindskoog sees a parallel between Lewis's insubstantial souls and "the phantom souls that Dante described in *The Inferno*." *Finding the Landlord: A Guidebook to C. S. Lewis's "Pilgrim's Regress"* (Chicago: Cornerstone, 1995), 56. While this is true, it is worth noting that the souls in the *Purgatorio* are also "phantom souls." Dante's depiction of souls as "phantoms" is not an index of whether they are good or evil but is simply meant to indicate they do not have their bodies.

132 {grassy shores of mount}   Christopher considers this rural imagery to be reminiscent of Dante's Garden of Eden at the top of the mount.

C. S. Lewis, 108. I believe Lewis's intent was to depict similarities between the Plain and the shore of the Island of Purgatory and that Dante's garden makes its primary appearance in the episode of Sarah and her husband because of Sarah's intended similarity to Beatrice.

132 {*Purg.* 2.52–54}   *Purg.* 2.52–54: "La turba che rimase lì, selvaggia / parea del loco, rimirando intorno / come colui che nove cose assaggia."

132 {*Inf.* 9.82–83}   *Inf.* 9.82–83: "Dal volto rimovea quell'aere grasso, / menando la sinistra innanzi spesso."

133 {"bus-driver . . . gates of Dis"}   "Letter to William L. Kinter," March 28, 1953, *The Collected Letters of C. S. Lewis*, vol. 3, *Narnia, Cambridge, and Joy 1950–1963*, ed. Walter Hooper (New York: HarperCollins, 2007), 313–14. See also "Letter to William L. Kinter," July 30, 1954, *The Collected Letters of C. S. Lewis*, vol. 3, 498. Christopher also notes this similarity in "Considering *The Great Divorce*: Parts I and II," 40, and in *C. S. Lewis*, 108, as does Kranz in "Dante in the Work," 6. Lewis says that Dante's angel of Dis is "surely the best angel ever made by a poet." "Dante's Similes," *Studies in Medieval and Renaissance Literature*, coll. Walter Hooper (Cambridge: Cambridge University Press, 1966), 69. It is therefore not surprising that Lewis included a version of that angel in *The Great Divorce*.

133 {*Inf.* 9.101–103}   *Inf.* 9.101–103: ". . . fè sembiante / d'omo cui altra cura stringa e morda / che quella di colui che li è davante."

133 {"look of authority . . . his job"}   Lewis makes reference to this attitude of Dante's angel in "Dante's Similes," 70.

133 {angel pilots vessel}   This is perhaps a case where people did not ask Lewis enough questions. He might have responded that this Bus-Driver is also meant to be like the angel of transport to purgatory because many of the details just noted about the Driver do *not* fit the angel of Dis but do fit the purgatorial boatman. Knowles notes a parallel with Dante's angelic boatman but fails to mention the angel of Dis. "A Purgatorial Flame," 144.

133 {suggests hell and purgatory}   These are the same sort of subtle clues that Lewis gives in *Perelandra* to indicate that the planet is an unfallen Eden where temptation will occur. No reader needs to notice or even heed the cues to enjoy the story, but they indirectly indicate the situation.

133 {"Only the Greatest . . . Hell"}   Christopher believes that the Bus-Driver being an angel is "perhaps the only logical inconsistency" in the novel since one of MacDonald's statements (see *GD* 123–24) indicates that only Christ could have entered Grey Town. *C. S. Lewis*,

108. In a later article, Christopher posits that MacDonald's statement could be "a hint at an allegorical level" that "the Driver is Christ, not an Angel." "The Dantean Structure of *The Great Divorce*," *Mythlore* 29, no. 3/4 (Spring/Summer 2011): 86. Martindale believes that the Bus-Driver does represent Christ. *Beyond the Shadowlands*, 78. Given the doctrine that Christ is the one who extends to people the offer of salvation, it seems fitting that the Driver is facilitating that possibility for Grey Towners and thus represents Christ. However, since Lewis often conflates some of Dante's characters into one new character, the Driver can easily represent Christ as well as Dante's two angels. In *The Great Divorce*, it is generally not a question of "either/or" but of "both/and."

133 {combines two trees}   Knowles, "A Purgatorial Flame," 146–47, notes the similarity of Lewis's tree to Dante's two trees.

133 {*Purg.* 22.137–138}   *Purg.* 22.137–138: ". . . un liquor chiaro / . . . si spandeva per le foglie suso."

133 {"Wet with spray"}   Lewis comments on the shape of this particular tree in "Dante's Similes," 74.

133 {probably an apple tree}   This could be an apple tree—if tradition about the apple tree in the Garden of Eden is correct—because Virgil intimates as much: "There is a tree higher up [in the Garden of Eden] that Eve ate of, and this shoot comes from that tree" (*Purg.* 24.116–117: "legno è più su che fu morso da Eva, / e questa pianta si levò da esso").

134 {*Purg.* 22.141}   *Purg.* 22:141: ". . . 'Di questo cibo avrete caro'"; *Purg.* 24.115: "'Trapassate oltre sanza farvi presso.'"

134 {"a little like Lethe"}   Christopher notes this Dantean allusion to Lethe as well in *C. S. Lewis*, 105, and "Considering *The Great Divorce*: Parts I and II," 42.

134 {redeemed radiate light}   See *Par.* 4.140, 5.94, 6.128, 7.17, 8.53, etc.

135 {Virgil as physical support}   See, for example, the times when Virgil has to carry the pilgrim if the path is treacherous or if he has to protect him in other ways: Virgil needing to carry the pilgrim down into a ditch and back up in *Inf.* 18.43–44 and *Inf.* 19.124–128; Virgil sliding on his back into a ditch as he holds the pilgrim in *Inf.* 23.37–45 and carrying him back out in *Inf.* 24.32; Virgil interposing himself between the pilgrim and the stinging tail of Geryon when they are transported to the eighth circle in *Inf.* 17.94–96; Virgil holding the pilgrim as the giant Antaeus lowers them by hand into the ninth circle in *Inf.* 31.134–135; and Virgil offering his shoulder on the ledge of anger because of the blinding smoke (see *Purg.* 16.9).

135 {Beatrice and Mountain-Dwellers}   Christopher notes these parallels with Beatrice. *C. S. Lewis*, 108.

135 {pilgrim's two main guides}   Two other characters are sometimes called guides for Dante's pilgrim, but their appearances are brief and they function differently from the pilgrim's two main guides. Matilda is considered by some to be a guide in the Earthly Paradise, but she does not lead the pilgrim away from there into any new places. Some also consider Bernard, a twelfth-century mystic, as a guide when Dante's pilgrim is in the Empyrean. However, the pilgrim's journeying has ceased at this point, so Bernard's "guidance" is spiritual instruction in preparing the pilgrim for his ultimate heavenly visions (see *Par.* 31.58ff.).

136 {*Purg.* 1.40–41}   *Purg* 1.40–41: "Chi siete voi che . . . / fuggita avete la pregione etterna?"

136 {*Purg.* 1.32}   *Purg.* 1.32: "degno di tanta reverenza in vista."

136 {*Purg.* 9.85}   *Purg.* 9.85: ". . . che volete voi?"

136 {MacDonald calls narrator "Son"}   MacDonald calls the narrator "son" at other times as well (see note to page 147), but it is significant that he does so here.

137 {*Par.* 17.34–35}   *Par.* 17.34–35: ". . . per chiare parole e con preciso / latin. . . ."

137 {*Par.* 17.116–117}   *Par.* 17.116–117: "ho io appreso quel che s' io redico, / a molti fia sapor di forte agrume."

137 {*Par.* 17.122–123}   *Par.* 17.122–123: ". . . si fè prima corusca, / quale a raggio di sole specchio d'oro."

138 {episodes function like ledges}   Lewis tells a friend concerning *The Great Divorce*, "Spiritual unity I hope it has: but a book needs . . . architectural unity as well." "Letter to Dom Bede Griffiths," May 10, 1945, *The Collected Letters of C. S. Lewis*, vol. 2, 648. I believe that Lewis drew on Dante for the "architectural unity" of this novel.

138 {organizing principle of Dante's mount}   Although Christopher earlier believed that the "book is episodic and without Dante's thematic, underlying structures" (see *C. S. Lewis*, 105), he later discusses many of this novel's Dantean structures in "The Dantean Structure of *The Great Divorce*," 77–99. For example, in addition to analyzing episodes, he describes some similarities between Dante's hell and Grey Town and between souls in the City of Dis and Grey Towners before they arrive on the Plain (pp. 83–85).

138 {main episodes}   Since the descriptions of other ghosts take up less than one page, they could be called embellishing vignettes rather than episodes.

138 {structure of perverted and disordered love}   Donald E. Glover believes "there is no attempt to categorize ghosts or place them on ordered levels." *C. S. Lewis: The Art of Enchantment* (Athens, OH: Ohio University Press, 1981), 129. Christopher says, "There seems to be no pattern to the episodes of choice," and therefore "the whole work suffers in its organization." *C. S. Lewis*, 106–7. Martindale also refers to "a series of loosely organized encounters." *Beyond the Shadowlands*, 78. Some scholars, however, have attempted to identify patterns for the ghosts. Despite saying that "the structure is haphazard and fragmentary . . . [and this] is Lewis's intent," Evan K. Gibson speaks of the first five ghosts as "turning in upon themselves" and the second five as desiring "to control and exploit others." *C. S. Lewis: Spinner of Tales* (Grand Rapids, MI: Eerdmans, 1980), 121. Manlove classifies the ghosts as having "faults relating mainly to the self . . . [and] faults that involve others" *C. S. Lewis*, 115. Martindale points out that most in the second group "exhibit some kind of perverted family relationship." *Beyond the Shadowlands*, 79. Gibson, Manlove, and Martindale have identified generally defensible patterns, but they do not connect any of them to Dante. Christopher says, "even though there is a . . . resemblance to the attitudes being corrected on the stone ledges of Mount Purgatory, still there is no pattern which suggests Dante." "Considering *The Great Divorce*: Parts III, IV, & V," *Mythcon Proceedings* (Los Angeles: Mythopoeic Society, 1972), 14. Knowles, on the other hand, works out a scheme that parallels the seven ledges on Dante's Mount, but he has to omit some major interviews to do so. "A Purgatorial Flame," 146–48.

138 {episode ten, Sarah and Frank}   Although episode ten fits this scheme of disordered love, Lewis sets it apart by designing it to echo Dante's scene of Beatrice and the pilgrim in the garden. This leaves episodes one through nine as possible parallels to the different ledges of Dante's mount. Although these nine attitudes of the Grey Towners do not strictly correspond to the sinful dispositions on Dante's mount, Lewis's episodes begin with pride (Dante's first ledge) and the ninth concerns lust (Dante's seventh ledge). A general pattern that begins with pride and ends with lust also appears in John's return journey in *The Pilgrim's Regress* when he sees the true beings who rule the land, and in the patient's series of temptations after his reconversion in Letters XIV through XX in *The Screwtape Letters*.

139 {no classification of sin}   Lewis similarly avoids categorizing sin in *The Screwtape Letters*, and sin has only one generic punishment in that novel's hell.

139 {souls belong on ledge of pride} Christopher believes that "all of the sketches of the damned were sketches of pride (or self-centeredness)." "Considering *The Great Divorce*: Parts III, IV, & V," 16.

139 {one soul vanishes} Robert's wife adamantly insists that she is justified in maintaining her hellish attitude and becomes, in the context of Lewis's kind of hell, totally insubstantial and disappears completely (see *GD* 89).

139 {souls' choices left in doubt} The narrator does not see the end of the interview in the case of the Vanity Ghost (see *GD* 63) or in the case of the mother Pam, for whom MacDonald says there may some hope (*GD* 96); the fate of some characters in very brief episodes is similarly left unclear (see *GD* 74, 79, 96). Martindale's statement that "all but one return to Hell" therefore needs some qualification. *Beyond the Shadowlands*, 181.

140 {Casella hinder pursuit of holiness} Ricardo J. Quinones has a somewhat different interpretation for the Casella incident: "Immediately a warning is raised against the dangers of using art as a substitute gratification for the processes of moral purification." *Dante Alighieri* (Boston: Twayne, 1979), 133.

140 {*Par.* 1.1–3} *Par.* 1.1–3: "La gloria di colui che tutto move / per l'universo penetra e risplende / in una parte più e meno altrove."

141 {*Purg.* 11.94–96} *Purg.* 11.94–96: "Credette Cimabue nella pintura / tener lo campo, e ora ha Giotto il grido, / sì che la fama di colui è scura." Cimabue (1240–1302) was a Florentine painter who was succeeded in popularity by another Florentine painter, Giotto (1267–1337).

141 {"You and I . . . out of fashion"} David C. Clark mistakenly believes it is "a poet [who] refuses Heaven when he learns he has been forgotten on earth." *C. S. Lewis: A Guide to His Theology* (Malden, MA: Blackwell, 2007), 144. However, Dante says that what applies to the displacement of painters applies to poets as well (see *Purg.* 11.94–99).

141 {*Purg.* 11.115–116} *Purg.* 11.115–116: "La vostra nominanza è color d'erba, / che viene e va. . . ."

141 {same point, different outcome} Mazzeo points out that "artistic achievement . . . [is] not necessarily a means of grace for the possessor of artistic gifts, however paradoxically his life and work may have channeled grace to others." "Dante's Three Communities," 74.

141 {ninth episode prototype} John Randall Willis believes that Lewis is at his finest for his descriptions in this episode, and "nowhere else in all his writings does he ever surpass this incident. *The Great Divorce*

could conceivably be his greatest work." *Pleasures Forevermore: The Theology of C. S. Lewis* (Chicago: Loyola University Press, 1983), 16. It is unclear why this incident, among so many others to choose from in Lewis's works, stands out for this critic. Although this novel could be considered by some to be Lewis's greatest work, it might not be due primarily to this incident.

141 {angels greet Grey Towners}   The waterfall-angel who speaks to the Grey Towner who is stealing the golden apple is a stationary figure on the Plain and is not there to greet him.

141 {*Purg.* 27.59–60}   *Purg.* 27.59–60: ". . . un lume . . . / che mi vinse e guardare nol potei." See also *Purg.* 2.39, 15.10–12, 17.57, 24.142.

141 {*Inf.* 12.88}   *Inf.* 12.88: ". . . si partì da cantare allelulia."

142 {*Purg.* 24.137–139}   *Purg.* 24.137–139: "e già mai non si videro in fornace / vetri o metalli sì lucenti e rossi / com' io vidi un. . . ."

142 {kill the red lizard}   Gibson believes that the lizard "does not represent the vice of lust, *per se*, but man's animal nature." *Spinner of Tales*, 124. However, MacDonald refers to the "man's sensuality" (*GD* 105) as the young man's obstacle to the journey and makes an analogy between the lizard and lust (*GD* 104–5).

142 {lizard whispering and whining}   The lizard, who is "whispering things in his ear" (*GD* 98), complains that if the angel kills him, "Then you'll be without me for ever and ever. . . . How could you live?" (*GD* 101). This of course recalls Augustine's pre-conversion state of mind concerning his sinful habits: "They plucked at my fleshly garment, and they whispered softly: . . . 'From that moment we shall no more be with forever and ever!' . . . An overpowering habit kept saying to me, 'Do you think you can live without them?'" *Confessions*, 8.11, 200.

142 {*Purg.* 27.34–35}   *Purg.* 27.34–35: ". . . pur fermo e duro, / turbato un poco. . . ."

142 {*Purg.* 27.21}   *Purg.* 27.21: "qui può esser tormento, ma non morte."

142 {*Purg.* 27.49–50}   *Purg.* 27.49–50: ". . . in un bogliente vetro / gittato mi sarei per rinfrescarmi."

142 {"gave a scream . . . on Earth"}   Gilbert Meilander believes that we can ask "whether there may not be a bit too much more of More and Fisher and not quite enough Dante" in this passage about the young man. *The Taste for the Other: The Social and Ethical Thought of C. S. Lewis* (Grand Rapids: Eerdmans, 1978), 121. This comment seems to misunderstand (1) that Lewis is giving us the very same kind of suffering (the pain of fire) that Dante includes in his episode; (2) that the suffering is for the identical sin of lust; and (3) that the

suffering in both episodes is not the "suffering for its own sake" that
Lewis objected to in More and Fisher (see note to page 130 {accurate
interpretation of purgatory}). Lewis says elsewhere, "That purification must, in its own nature, be painful, we hardly dare to dispute."
English Literature in the Sixteenth Century, 164. In both narratives the
suffering is a purification that advances a character on his journey to
God rather than being merely retributive punishment.

142 {*Purg.* 27.121–123}   *Purg.* 27.121–123: "Tanto voler sopra voler mi
venne / dell'esser su, ch'ad ogni passo poi / al volo mi sentìa crescer le
penne."

143 {*Purg.* 27.142}   *Purg.* 27.142: ". . . io te sovra te corono e mitrio."

143 {pilgrim as king and priest}   Dorothy L. Sayers notes in this regard
that the soul "must die to sin with Christ and make free its will so
that it may become one with the will of Christ within it. This done, it
can be crowned and mitred over itself." *Introductory Papers to Dante*
(London: Methuen, 1954), 121.

143 {master of himself and Nature}   Kranz believes, "The 27th canto
of the *Purgatorio* was obviously the inspiration for a whole chapter
[chapter 11] in *The Great Divorce*." "Dante in the Work," 6. First, this
episode in Lewis's story occurs in only the second half of chapter
11, and, second, the one parallel Kranz notes between this chapter
and *Purg.* 27 is mistaken: "*In the one as in the other* [italics added],
Nature hails that man, her conqueror, whom God has appointed as
her King and high priest." Kranz's one example overlooks the fact that
it is Virgil, not Nature, who pronounces the pilgrim king and priest—
and Nature is not personified in Dante's episode (or elsewhere in his
poem for that matter). Lewis's personification of Nature is his addition to Dante's episode.

143 {soul advances, mountain trembles}   Irma Brandeis notes that a soul
moves upward when it "completes its work on any terrace, reaching
the point where temptation is annulled and the habit of virtue locked
in place." *The Ladder of Vision: A Study of Dante's "Comedy"* (1960;
repr., Garden City, NY: Anchor, 1962), 205.

145 {Dante's experiences transposed to pilgrim}   In addition to his love
for Beatrice Potinari and his admiration for Virgil and other classical and contemporary poets discussed in the poem, Dante mentions,
among other examples, being present at the defeat of the Aretines in
the battle at Campaldino (1289) in *Inf.* 22.1–9 and refers in *Par.* 25.8–9
to the baptismal font in which he was baptized.

145 {*Inf.* 1.85}   *Inf.* 1.85: "Tu se' lo mio maestro e 'l mio autore."

145 {MacDonald inspiration and insight}   Christopher says that "here MacDonald (standing for his works) is a God-bearing image for Lewis the character as well as for Lewis the man." *C. S. Lewis*, 108.

145 {"I fancy ... from him"}   C. S. Lewis, "Introduction," *George MacDonald: An Anthology*, ed. C. S. Lewis (London: Geoffrey Bles, 1946), 20. Lewis also says in this introduction, "I have never concealed the fact that I regard him as my master" (p. 20). However, in selecting the passages for this anthology, Lewis clearly states that he is "concerned with MacDonald not as a writer but as a Christian teacher" (p. 18); in fact, three-fourths of the extracts in this book are from MacDonald's sermons and religious writings rather than from his literary works. He says of *Unspoken Sermons*, "My own debt to this book is almost as great as one man can owe another" (p. 22). Lewis's statement about MacDonald being his master, then, does not contradict my contention that Dante was Lewis's *literary* master for his *fiction*.

145 {*Phantastes*}   MacDonald's *Phantastes: A Faerie Romance for Men and Women* was published in 1858. See pages 25–27 of Lewis's preface to *George MacDonald* for more of his remarks about *Phantastes*.

146 {*The New Life*}   See this collection of poems linked by prose in the English translation by Mark Musa, *Dante's "Vita Nuova"* (Bloomington: Indiana University Press, 1973). According to Robert Hollander, there is "no earlier example in the history of Western literature of a writer who gathered *his own* poems into a collection and then wrote commentaries on them." *Dante: A Life in Works* (New Haven, CT: Yale University Press, 2001), 14.

146 {author of *Phantastes* as Beatrice}   Christopher notes that strictly speaking it is the *novel* and not MacDonald that the narrator compares to Beatrice. "The Dantean Structure of *The Great Divorce*," 81. However, I believe MacDonald can be identified with his novel and thus function as a Beatrice here himself.

146 {"I ... crossed a great frontier"}   Lewis, preface, *George MacDonald*, 25.

146 {"as if I ... alive in the new"}   C. S. Lewis, *Surprised by Joy* (New York: Harcourt, Brace & World, 1955).

146 {from atheism to Christianity}   Ibid., 181, 228. See Alister E. McGrath's challenge to the dates Lewis gives for his conversion to theism and to Christianity in *C. S. Lewis—A Life: Eccentric Genius, Reluctant Prophet* (Carol Stream, IL: Tyndale House, 2013), 131–51. Lewis himself admits in one letter, about another matter, "I'm weak on dates." "Letter to William L. Kinter," January 14, 1951, *The Collected Letters of C. S. Lewis*, vol. 3, 87.

146 {"figura," historical character} For a fuller explanation of the nature of Dante's historical characters, see Erich Auerbach's groundbreaking essay on "Figura," trans. Ralph Manheim in *Scenes from the Drama of European Literature* (New York: Meridian, 1959), 11–76.

147 {Virgil calls pilgrim "son":} For Virgil calling the pilgrim "son," see *Inf.* 3.121; 7.61; 8.67; 11.16, and *Purg.* 1.112; 3.66; 4.46; 17.92; 23.4; 25.35; 25.58; 27.20; 27.35; 27.128.

147 {MacDonald calls him "Son"} For MacDonald calling the narrator "son," see *GD* (sometimes twice on one page) 65, 67, 74, 97, 104, 120, 127.

147 {Virgil called "teacher"} For the pilgrim calling Virgil "teacher/master" ("maestro"), see *Inf.* 1.85; 2.140; 3.121; 4.31, 46; etc., for a total of 41 times in the *Inferno*; see *Purg.* 1.25; 2.25, 115; 3.53, 61; etc., for a total of 23 times in the *Purgatorio*. (The pilgrim refers to him less often as "teacher" using the term "dottore": see *Inf.* 5.70, 123; 16.13, 48; and *Purg.* 18.2; 21.22, 131; 24.143.) For the pilgrim calling Virgil "sir" ("segnore"), see *Inf.* 2.140; 4.46, 95; 8.20, 103, 116; 16.55; 19.38; and *Purg.* 4.109; 6.49; 7.61; 9.46; 19.85. In contrast, he refers to him as "guide" ("guida") only three times: *Inf.* 1.113 and *Purg.* 5.62; 19.53.

147 {MacDonald called "Teacher"} For MacDonald being referred to as "Teacher," see *GD* (sometimes twice on one page) 66, 69, 71, 74–76, 78–79, 96, 104, 108, 120, 122, 126, 128. For MacDonald being called "Sir," see *GD* (sometimes more than once per page) 65–66, 68, 74, 96–97, 104–105, 120, 124, 127. Similar to Dante's pilgrim who refers to Virgil as "guide" ("guida") only three times (*Inf.* 1.113 and *Purg.* 5.62; 19.53), the narrator calls MacDonald "my guide" only once (*GD* 107). Dante's pilgrim most often refers to Virgil as "leader" ("duca")—56 times in the *Inferno* and 23 times in the *Purgatorio*—but Lewis never calls MacDonald "leader," perhaps because there is very little actual journeying.

147 {MacDonald 's three major teachings} Walsh objects that "the book . . . is preachy, and many of the episodes turn into didactic lectures." *The Literary Legacy of C. S. Lewis*, 76. However, precisely the same could be said about the sections of Dante's poem that Lewis was consciously reflecting in his novel.

147 {*Purgatorio* Lewis's favorite} See "Letter to Dorothy L. Sayers," December 16, 1953, *The Collected Letters of C. S. Lewis*, vol. 3, 387, where he says the *Purgatorio* "is perhaps my favourite part of the Comedy [sic]."

147 {stopped walking for the teaching} Similarly, when Virgil explains the structure of hell to the pilgrim, they are stopped at the edge of a

steep bank (see *Inf.* 11.1–2). Whenever Virgil gives complex teachings about the structure of a realm, they cease walking and are stationary.

147 {justice of God, soul's choice}   The concept of souls being given what they choose is also alluded to in Virgil's *Aeneid*, 6.624. The Sibyl, describing evil souls imprisoned in buildings encircled by the fiery Phlegethon in Hades, tells Aeneas, "These souls all purposed dreadful deeds *and got their way*." Lewis translates this verse and adds the italics himself in *The Discarded Image: An Introduction to Medieval and Renaissance Literature* (Chicago: University of Chicago Press, 1961), 86.

148 {love as cause of virtue and sin}   Erich Auerbach notes that "the ethical order of the *Purgatorio* is governed by the Thomist-Aristotelian principle that the vices are perversions of love." *Dante: Poet of the Secular World*, trans. Ralph Manheim (Chicago: University of Chicago Press, 1961), 112. That principle applies to the lower ledges of Dante's mount and characterizes the sinful attitudes of the first group of Lewis's ghosts as well.

148 {*Purg.* 17.94}   *Purg.* 17.94: "Lo naturale [amore] è sempre sanza errore."

148 {*Purg.* 17.97–99}   *Purg.* 17.97–99: "Mentre ch'elli è nel primo ben diretto, / e ne' secondi sè stesso misura, / esser non può cagion di mal diletto."

148 {*Purg.* 17.100–102}   *Purg.* 17.100–102: "ma quando al mal si torce, o con più cura / o con men che non dee corre nel bene, / contra 'l fattore adovra sua fattura."

149 {*Purg.* 17.95}   *Purg.* 17.95: ". . . puote errar per malo obietto."

149 {*Purg.* 17.96}   *Purg.* 17.96: ". . . per troppo o per poco di vigore."

149 {*Par.* 5.19–22}   *Par.* 5.19–22: "Lo maggior don che Dio per sua larghezza / fesse creando ed alla sua bontate / più conformato e quel ch'e' più apprezza, / fu della volontà la libertate."

149 {*Par.* 7.97–100}   *Par.* 7.97–100: "Non potea l'uomo ne' termini suoi / mai sodifar, per non potere ir guiso / con umiltate obedïendo poi, / quanto disobediendo intese ir suso."

149 {name of city through sorcery}   See Musa, commentary, on *Inferno*, 257.

151 {*Purg.* 29.34–35}   *Purg.* 29.34–35: ". . . tal quale un foco acceso / ci si fè l'aere sotto i verdi rami."

151 {*Purg.* 29.22–23}   *Purg.* 29.22–23: ". . . una melodia dolce correva / per l'aere luminoso. . . ."

151 {*Purg.* 31.98–99}   *Purg.* 31.98–99: ". . . sì dolcemente udissi, / che nol so rimembrar, non ch' io lo scriva." For other heavenly songs that bypass the pilgrim's memory, see *Par.* 19.38–39; 20.11–12; 24.23–24.

151 {*Purg.* 30.18–20}   *Purg.* 30.18–20: "ministri e messaggier di vita etterna / . . . . / e fior gittando di sopra e dintorno."

151 {*Purg.* 29.124–125}   *Purg.* 29.124–125: ". . . come se le carni e l'ossa / fossero state di smeraldo fatte." She represents the theological virtue of hope.

151 {"I really am Beatrice"}   I am indebted to Christopher for noting this detail. "Considering *The Great Divorce*: Parts I and II," 42.

152 {Frank called "Tragedian"}   Wilson's remark that "perhaps none of Lewis's portraits is more cruel than that of the figure of Dante himself, who appears at the end . . . as a dwarf leading the other part of himself, the Tragedian, round on a chain," defies comment in terms of misunderstanding both Lewis and Dante. *A Biography*, 201.

152 {"the meeting . . . these resemblances"}   See "Letter to William L. Kinter," March 28, 1953, *The Collected Letters of C. S. Lewis*, vol. 3, 314. See also "Letter to William L. Kinter," July 30, 1954, *The Collected Letters of C. S. Lewis*, vol. 3, 498. Failure to understand the parallels Lewis was deliberately making here may be what led Gunnar Urang to remark that there are "a few overwritten pages near the end about the apotheosis of Sarah Smith of Golders Green." *Shadows of Heaven* (Philadelphia: Pilgrim, 1971), 12.

152 {*Purg.* 30.74–75}   *Purg.* 30.74–75: "Come degnasti d'accedere al monte? / non sapei tu che qui è l'uom felice?"

153 {*Inf.* 2.91–92}   *Inf.* 2.91–92: "Io son fatta da Dio, sua mercè, tale, / che la vostra miseria non mi tange."

153 {"You . . . infect our light"}   Filmer considers these particular statements as "smug remonstrations," which is consistent with her interpretation that all of Sarah's remarks have "hectoring tones." *The Fiction of C. S. Lewis: Mask and Mirror*, 94. Since Sarah is designed to reflect the normally gracious Beatrice, rather than the Beatrice-as-judge that Dante's pilgrim first meets in the garden, Filmer's objections are perhaps better directed to Dante and his Beatrice than to Lewis and his Sarah.

153 {"connections . . . tenuous"}   Glover, *C. S. Lewis: The Art of Enchantment*, 129.

154 {free will, heart of story}   In the edition I am using, MacDonald enters the scene to give this teaching on page 64 of a 128-page novel. Gibson, using a different edition, counts 47 pages preceding MacDonald's initial appearance and 46 pages following. *Spinner of Tales*, 111. The point is that in whatever edition a person uses, the narrator's guide arrives in the middle of the book to teach on free will.

154 "miniature replica"}   Kathryn Lindskoog, *Surprised by C. S. Lewis, George MacDonald, & Dante: An Array of Original Discoveries* (Macon, GA: Mercer University Press, 2001), 35.

Chapter 8: The Chronicles of Narnia

155 {unmarried scholar}   Lewis did not marry until 1956 after the entire Narnian series was written.

155 {no intention of a series}   Lewis stated in fact in a "Letter to William L. Kinter," January 19, 1951, that *The Lion, the Witch and the Wardrobe* "is a single story not a collection." *The Collected Letters of C. S. Lewis*, vol. 3, *Narnia, Cambridge, and Joy 1950–1963*, ed. Walter Hooper (New York: HarperCollins, 2007), 86.

155 {"When I wrote . . . wrong"}   "Letter to Laurence Krieg," April 21, 1957, *The Collected Letters of C. S. Lewis*, vol. 3, 847–48. The contracted titles here are Lewis's own.

155 {"All . . . in my head"}   C. S. Lewis, "It All Began with Pictures . . . ," in *Of Other Worlds: Essays and Stories*, ed. Walter Hooper (New York: Harcourt Brace Jovanovich, 1966), 42.

155 {"The Form . . . fairy tale"}   C. S. Lewis, "Sometimes Fairy Stories May Say Best What's to Be Said," in *Of Other Worlds*, 36. In the second half of the twentieth century, scholars began to distinguish between fairy tales and children's fantasy, so the Narnia stories are now generally categorized as children's fantasy. Lewis referred to his stories as fairy tales, so I will follow his categorization for this chapter.

155 {"pulled . . . after Him"}   Lewis, "It All Began with Pictures . . ." 42.

156 {Narnia and *The Faerie Queene*}   Doris T. Myers believes that *The Faerie Queene* is a model for the chronicles, calling them Lewis's "miniature *Faerie Queene*." *C. S. Lewis in Context* (Kent, OH: Kent State University Press, 1994), 126. Colin Duriez believes it could be argued that Spenser's poem "provides a pattern for . . . the Narnian Chronicles." "In the Library: Composition and Context," in *Reading the Classics with C. S. Lewis*, ed. Thomas L. Martin (Grand Rapids, MI: Baker Academic, 2000), 365.

156 {Narnia and *Morte Darthur*}   For Lewis's appreciation of Malory, see C. S. Lewis, "The 'Morte Darthur,'" *Studies in Medieval and Renaissance Literature*, coll. Walter Hooper (Cambridge: Cambridge University Press, 1966), 104.

156 {Narnia and Ptolemaic heavens}   Michael Ward, *Planet Narnia: The Seven Heavens in the Imagination of C. S. Lewis* (Oxford: Oxford University Press, 2008).

157 {wand of angel of Dis} Dante intends the angel's small wand to recall the wand that the Sibyl uses in Virgil's *Aeneid* when she leads
Aeneas through the underworld, but in Virgil's poem the wand itself
has the magical power to overcome resistance to Aeneas's journey.

157 {*Par.* 2.19–20} *Par.* 2.19–20: "La concreata e perpetüa sete / del deïforme regno cen portava."

157 {Narnian magic, spiritual forces} Thomas Williams says, "Narnia
affirms the supernatural by taking it for granted. . . . [It is] woven
into the fabric of the stories so thoroughly that it can't be extricated
from it." *The Heart of the "Chronicles of Narnia": Knowing God Here
by Finding Him There* (Nashville: W. Publishing, 2005), 158.

157 {gifts not for owners} The gifts are given to them by Father
Christmas in *The Lion, the Witch and the Wardrobe.*

158 {"it was part . . . they weren't"} C. S. Lewis, *The Lion, the Witch and
the Wardrobe* (New York: Macmillan, 1950), 135. Future references to
this work are indicated by *LWW* and page number(s).

158 {typological approach to biblical narratives} For a comprehensive
discussion of biblical typology and Dante's appropriation of that technique for literary purposes, see A. C. Charity's clear and enlighten-
ing discussion in *Events and Their After-Life* (Cambridge: Cambridge
University Press, 1966). See also the series of classic essays collected
and republished in *Dante and Theology: The Biblical Tradition and
Christian Allegory*, vol. 4, *Dante: The Critical Complex*, ed. Richard
Lansing (New York: Routledge, 2003).

158 {"a way . . . earlier one"} I. Howard Marshall et al., eds., *New Bible
Dictionary*, 3rd ed. (Downers Grove, IL: InterVarsity, 1996), 1214.

158 {*prefigurement, fulfillment, reenactment*} There are many terms
to describe these interrelationships. Biblical scholars tend to use
the terms "type" and "antitype" (which people can find confusing when Christ in this scheme turns out to be an *antitype*). The
Latin terms *umbra* (shadow) and *veritas* (truth) are at times used
instead of *prefigurement* and *fulfillment*; and *reenactment* can also
called *recapitulation* or *sub-fulfillment*. For an in-depth description
of biblical typology in general, see Henri de Lubac, *Medieval Exegesis*,
trans. Mark Sebanc (Grand Rapids, MI: Eerdmans, 1998), and Jean
Daniélou, *From Shadows to Reality: Study in the Biblical Typology of
the Fathers*, trans. Wulstan Hibberd (London: Burns & Oates, 1960).
For an overview of the history of typological interpretation, see
George T. Montague, *Understanding the Bible: A Basic Introduction
to Biblical Interpretation* (New York: Paulist Press, 1997), especially

chapter 2 on the church fathers (pp. 29–51) and chapter 3 on the
Middle Ages (pp. 52–72).

159 {narration recalls prototype}   In a secondary, less important mode
of biblical typology, an event can also be a *prefigurement* or a *reenactment* only because of parallel details. As examples of this second
mode, Abraham's departure from Egypt to the land of Israel (see Gen.
13:1) prefigures the Exodus, and Christ's departure (as a child) from
Egypt to Israel (see Matt. 2:21) reenacts the Exodus. In both cases the
only similarity is in the detail of a biblical personage leaving Egypt
to return to Israel.

159 {poem reenacts Exodus event}   There is general agreement among
Dante scholars that Dante's poem is meant to be a metaphoric parallel to the Exodus. Mark Musa, for example, says that "the Exodus,
with all its concomitant significance, is quite simply the figure or pattern for the action of the entire *Comedy*." Trans. and notes, Dante,
The Divine Comedy, vol. 2, *Purgatorio* (New York: Penguin, 1985), 24,
n. 46. Peter S. Hawkins maintains that the Exodus "provides one of
the deep structures of the entire poem." *Dante's Testaments: Essays
in Scriptural Imagination* (Stanford, CA: Stanford University Press,
1999), 42.

159 {*Par.* 25.55–56}   *Par.* 25.55–56: ". . . li è conceduto che d'Egitto /
venga in Ierusalemme, per vedere."

159 {Exodus applies to any soul}   See V. Stanley Benfell, *The Biblical
Dante* (Toronto: University of Toronto Press, 2011), 107. See also
Dante's "Letter to Can Grande," #7, in which he spells out a fourfold spiritual interpretation of the Exodus. *Dantis Alagherii Epistolae*,
trans. Paget Toynbee, 2d ed. (Oxford: Clarendon, 1966), 199.

159 {*Par.* 31.85}   *Par.* 31.85: "Tu m'hai di servo tratto a libertate." Virgil
earlier describes the pilgrim to Cato as "seeking freedom" (see *Purg.*
1.71: "libertà va cercando. . . .").

159 {singing Psalm 114}   Dante's souls sing the psalm in Latin: "*In exitu
Israël de Aegypto*" (*Purg.* 2.46).

159 {reenacting St. Paul's journey}   Paul does not know if it was an out-of-body experience (2 Cor. 12:3), and neither does Dante's pilgrim: "If
it was only that part of me which you [God] created last [my soul] . . .
you know" (*Par.* 1.73–75: "S' i' era sol di me quel che creasti / novellamente . . . / tu 'l sai . . ."). Paul "heard unspeakable words, which it is
not lawful for a man to utter" (2 Cor 12.4b), and Dante's pilgrim is told
to remain silent about some things he sees and hears both by Charles
Martel (see *Par.* 9.2–5) and by Cacciaguida (see *Par.* 17.91–93). Paul's

blindness on the road to Damascus is healed by Ananias (see Acts 9:10–18), and when the pilgrim is blinded by the light in the eighth sphere (see *Par.* 25.118–121), Beatrice can heal him because she has the same power as Ananias (see *Par.* 26.10–12). Dante compares his pilgrim and Paul on some of these points in his dedication letter of the *Paradiso*, the "Letter to Can Grande," #27–29, in *Dantis Alagherii Epistolae*, 209–210. In addition to Dante's clear intention to parallel his pilgrim's journey through the heavens with Paul's, this journey could also be classified as "one of several medieval astral journeys to wisdom modeled on Cicero's *Dream of Scipio*" as Alison Cornish comments. *Reading Dante's Stars* (New Haven, CT: Yale University Press, 2000), 1.

159 {purpose of Paul's and Dante's visions}   While Paul's visions were a help to him in his mission of preaching the gospel to pagan gentiles, Dante's vision is a help for him to "spread the gospel to his fellow Christians, . . . to the nominal Christians of his own day." Ronald Herzman, "'Io non Enëa, io non Paulo sono': Ulysses, Guido da Montefeltro, and Franciscan Traditions in the *Commedia*," *Dante Studies*, ed. Richard Lansing (Bronx: Fordham University Press, 2005), 57.

159 {Narnia history, biblical history}   Charles A. Huttar in fact calls it Lewis's "panoramic summary of a world's entire existence" that becomes "a sort of Bible for a Bibleless age." "C. S. Lewis's Narnia and the 'Grand Design,'" in *The Longing for a Form: Essays on the Fiction of C. S. Lewis*, ed. Peter J. Schakel (Kent, OH: Kent State University Press, 1977), 126. Michael Ward, in his *Planet Narnia*, posits that the Ptolemaic planets are the prevailing organizing principle of the Narnia series. Although there is clear evidence of that patterning, I agree with Huttar that the salvation history recorded in the Bible is the *major* organizing principle. Ward's theory would seem stronger to me if there were no (or few) biblical events echoed in the series and if Lewis had pre-planned the whole series, but, according to Lewis, "the series was not planned beforehand." "Letter to Laurence Krieg," April 21, 1957, *The Collected Letters of C. S. Lewis*, vol. 3, 847.

160 {apocalyptic end of Narnia}   Ward believes that only three of the Narnia stories have "Christocentric explanations." *Planet Narnia*, 12. He omits *The Horse and His Boy* from his list, but I believe that story is typologically meant to represent an Exodus story. Insofar as Lewis may have had Dante in mind when writing *The Silver Chair*, it is also possible that this story is meant to be a typological reflection of the tradition in some Christian theologies of the "harrowing of hell"

(Christ's descent into hell after his crucifixion to rescue faithful souls in hell) that Dante mentions in *Inf.* 12.38–41.

160 {allusion to other biblical events}   At the end of *The Silver Chair*, Aslan's power to resurrect King Caspian parallels Christ's power to raise people from the dead.

160 {Narnia stories not allegory}   Even though Lewis clearly states in several letters to several people that he was not writing allegory, the number of people who continue to call the echoes of biblical events in Narnia "allegory" are too numerous to list. Nor is Lewis writing symbolically, for he says, "I'm not exactly 'representing' the real (Christian) story in symbols," and goes on to say that his stories are "supposals": "Suppose there were a world like Narnia and it needed rescuing and the Son of God . . . went to redeem *it*, . . . what might it . . . all have been like?" "Letter to Patricia Mackey," June 8, 1960, *The Collected Letters of C. S. Lewis*, vol. 3, 1157–58. Lewis repeats this "supposal" explanation in several letters; see, for example, "Letter to Sophia Storr," December 24, 1959, vol. 3, 1113; "Letter to Anne Jenkins," March 3, 1961, vol. 3, 1244.

160 {different details than the Bible}   See Lewis's "Letter to Patricia Mackey," June 8, 1960, *The Collected Letters of C. S. Lewis*, vol. 3, 1157–58 in which he lists seven instances of events or characters in the Narnia series whose prototypes are from the Bible. Although he does not list the book titles, his examples come from *The Lion, the Witch and the Wardrobe*, *The Magician's Nephew*, *The Voyage of the "Dawn Treader,"* and *The Last Battle*.

160 {Ape like anti-Christ}   Ibid.

161 {Beatrice reenacts Christ}   Dante's pilgrim also "reenacts Christ" in the time line of the poem through his descent into hell on Good Friday, his emergence from under the earth on Easter, and his subsequent ascension into Paradise. However, this reenactment is only in the details that parallel Christ's death, resurrection, and ascension. As a sinful human being, the pilgrim cannot reenact the essence of Christ's actions that redeem the world. This reenactment belongs to the secondary category of typology that follows the details but not the substance of a biblical event.

161 {Aslan not allegory}   See note above for 160 {Narnia stories not allegory} since it applies to Lewis's characterization of Aslan as well.

161 {"an invention . . . in ours"}   "Letter to Mrs. Hook," December 29, 1958, *The Collected Letters of C. S. Lewis*, vol. 3, 1004.

161 {*The Voyage of the "Dawn Treader"* as last book}   See "Letter to Laurence Krieg," April 2, 1947, *The Collected Letters of C. S. Lewis*, vol. 3, 848.

161 {Aslan as Christ}   I would whole-heartedly agree with Peter J. Schakel that "Aslan does not 'stand for' Christ because in his [Lewis's] suppositional world he *is* Christ." *Reading with the Heart: The Way into Narnia* (Grand Rapids, MI: Eerdmans, 1979), 27. John Hicks likewise says "the figure of Aslan . . . is the divine logos incarnate as a mighty lion." *The Metaphor of God Incarnate* (London: SCM Press, 1993), 90. Lewis writes in response to a mother who had a young son worried about loving Aslan too much, "Laurence can't *really* love Aslan more than Jesus. . . . The things he loves Aslan for doing are simply the things Jesus really did and said, so that when Laurence thinks he is loving Aslan, he is really loving Jesus." "Letter to Philinda Krieg," May 6, 1955, *The Collected Letters of C. S. Lewis*, vol. 3, 603.

161 {"I don't . . . Christian"}   "Letter to Sophia Storr," December 24, 1959, *The Collected Letters of C. S. Lewis*, vol. 3, 1113.

161 {capitals for "He" and "Him"}   Speaking of his wife's illness before their wedding, Lewis writes to a young boy, "*Aslan* [italics added] has done great things for us and she is now walking about again." "Letter to Laurence Krieg," December 23, 1957, *The Collected Letters of C. S. Lewis*, vol. 3, 909.

161 {"The whole . . . about Christ"}   "Letter to Anne Jenkins," March 3, 1961, *The Collected Letters of C. S. Lewis*, vol. 3, 1244.

162 {occasional echoes of Dante}   When, for example, the dwarfs at the end of *The Last Battle* choose to worship neither the Calormene god Tash nor Aslan and proclaim, "the Dwarfs are for the Dwarfs" (*LB* 148), they are reminiscent of the fallen angels in the vestibule of Dante's hell "who were neither faithful nor unfaithful to God but were *only for themselves*" (*Inf.* 3.38–39; italics added: ". . . angeli che non furon ribelli / nè fur fideli a Dio, ma per se foro"). In another instance, when the resurrected Caspian, for example, is told he cannot want wrong things anymore, he is reminiscent of Dante's pilgrim after his ascent of the mount who cannot desire wrong things because his will has become free, upright, and whole (see *Purg.* 27.148). I am indebted to Wayne Martindale for noting this last example. *Beyond the Shadowlands: C. S. Lewis on Heaven and Hell* (Wheaton, IL: Crossway, 2005), 113.

163 {structure not Homeric}   I would disagree with William Gray who believes that the episodic plot of this story "with its loosely linked

adventures at sea is obviously based on the *Odyssey*, though possibly no more than on the medieval *Voyage of St. Brendan.*" C. S. Lewis (Plymouth, UK: Northcote, 1998), 71.

163 {no Homeric episodes} The one exception is that, in an echo of Ulysses who abandons his duties to his wife, son, and country in his selfish pursuit of knowledge, Caspian is tempted to abandon his duty to his country and go instead to Aslan's Mountains. It during this temptation that the name Ulysses appears (*VDT* 264).

163 {recalls *Purgatorio* and *Paradiso* journeys} Colin N. Manlove believes that *The Voyage of the "Dawn Treader"* has "episodic adventures with little narrative connection among them." *C. S. Lewis: His Literary Achievement* (London: Macmillan, 1987), 156. However, Dante's poem seems to provide the pattern for the structural connecting links. Manlove does say in a later book that the Narnian series is "imbued with complex and subtle artistic patterns," although he does not give examples or possible sources for those patterns. "*The Chronicles of Narnia*": *The Patterning of a Fantastic World* (New York: Twayne, 1993), 12.

163 {"everything . . . slouching manner"} C. S. Lewis, *The Voyage of the "Dawn Treader"* (New York: Macmillan, 1952; repr., New York: HarperCollins, 1980). Subsequent quotes from this edition will be listed as *VDT* with page number(s).

164 {*Purg.* 1.23–24} *Purg.* 1.23–24: "vidi quattro stelle / non viste mai."

164 {*Purg.* 4.40} *Purg.* 4.40: "Lo somma er' alto che vincea la vista." See also *Purg.* 4.86–87, where the pilgrim says his eyes cannot climb as high as the steep cliff. Dante's Ulysses in the *Inferno*, who sailed toward but failed to reach the Island of Purgatory, describes it as "higher than any mountain anyone had ever seen" (*Inf.* 26.134–135: ". . . alta tanto / quanto veduta non avea alcuna."

164 {sin . . . dragon body} Gray believes that "the particular punishment of dragonization . . . seems harsh . . . [and] contains some rather unsettling sado-masochistic connotations." *C. S. Lewis*, 73. On the contrary, I find Eustace's "dragonization" quite apt as a Dantean *contrapasso* and as a parallel to the P's initially inscribed on Dante's forehead. Children seem to have no problem understanding the underlying concepts that Lewis is presenting through this image. Commenting on how some adults think that *The Lion, the Witch and the Wardrobe* might frighten children, Lewis says, "The real children like it, and I am astonished at how some *very* young ones understand it. I think it frightens some adults, but very few children." "Letter to

'Mrs. Lockley' " (L), March 5, 1951, *The Collected Letters of C. S. Lewis*, vol. 3, 93.

165   {top of a mountain}   Although Lewis does not specify the location, Eustace could have been brought to the high mountain on Dragon Island or to Aslan's Mountain in the east.

165   {Eustace, Garden of Eden}   Christopher notes that there "seem to be a number of Garden of Eden-topped hills in Narnia" that recall Dante's *Purgatorio* (as well as Milton's *Paradise Lost*), and Aslan's Mountain is "another Dantean variation." *C. S. Lewis*, 119. Michael Morris notes the same connection, saying that Lewis "borrows [from Dante] the notion of an immeasurably high mountain which has no frigid zone." "The Multiple Worlds of the Narnia Stories," in *Word and Story in C. S. Lewis*, eds. Peter J. Schakel and Charles A. Huttar (Columbia: University of Missouri Press, 1991), 244.

165   {Eustace similar restoration}   See, for instance, Myers, *C. S. Lewis in Context* (Kent, OH: Kent State University Press, 1994), 146.

165   {Eustace "remade"}   Myers compares Eustace's plunge in water to Dante's plunge in the river Lethe. *C. S. Lewis in Context*, 146. However, cleansing in the Lethe makes a person forget the emotional guilt and shame of past sin (see *Purg.* 31.94–102), but Eustace remembers and is ashamed of his past sin. It is the river Eunoë that restores a person, and restoration is what Eustace primarily needs and seems to experience.

165   {sin as "wounds"}   For sin as a "wound," see also *Purg.* 9.114; 15.80; 25.139; and *Par.* 32.4. Lewis notes that in *Par.* 32.4 Dante describes "the sin of Adam as a wound (*piaga*)." "Imagery in Dante's 'Comedy,'" *Studies in Medieval and Renaissance Literature*, coll. Walter Hooper (Cambridge: Cambridge University Press, 1966), 86.

165   {*Par.* 17.20}   *Par.* 17.20: ". . . lo monte che l'anime cura." Lewis uses this same kind of terminology when he says that when someone repents of sin, "the Christ-life [is] inside him, *repairing* [italics added] him all the time." *Mere Christianity* (New York: Macmillan, 1952), 64.

165   {arrive at *ninth* island}   By presenting three Lone Isles and six uncharted islands—for a total of nine—Lewis is using one of Dante's favorite mathematical structuring numbers: Dante posits nine circles in hell, nine distinct areas in purgatory (ante-purgatory, seven ledges, and the Garden of Eden), and nine spheres in the heavens. Lewis uses the number nine in other novels as well. In *Out of the Silent Planet* it takes ninety days to return to earth (see *OSP* 141), and in *That Hideous Strength* MacPhee describes Ransom's time in Malacandra

in multiples of three: he was gone for *nine* months *six* years ago and was ill for *three* months afterward (see *THS* 190).

166 {Nimrod and pine cone}   This thirteen-foot high first-century bronze sculpture of a pine cone is now on display in the courtyard of the Vatican Museum in Rome.

166 {"randomness . . . not characteristic"}   Ward, *Planet Narnia*, 11.

166 {three sleeping lords}   After they quarreled about whether to remain on the island, to sail back home, or to continue sailing east, these lords were cast into an enchanted sleep when one of them touched the knife that had been used to kill Aslan.

166 {Dante's Ulysses}   Dante adds to Ovid's story of Ulysses *in Metamorphoses* 13–14 by carrying his narrative beyond the point when Ulysses is sailing off. See also Mark Musa, trans. and notes, *The Divine Comedy*, vol. 1, *Inferno* (Bloomington: Indiana University Press, 1971), 311.

166 {*Inf.* 26.114–120}   *Inf.* 26.114–120: "a questa tanto picciola vigilia / de' nostri sensi ch'è del rimanente, / non vogliate negar l'esperïenza, / di retro al sol, del mondo sanza gente. / Considerate la vostra semenza: / fatti non foste a viver come bruti, / ma per seguir virtute e canoscenza."

167 {whirlpool sank them}   Ulysses refers to his voyage as his "mad flight" (*Inf.* 26.125: ". . . folle volo"). As Franco Masciandaro points out, "Like Adam, [Dante's] Ulysses transgressed an interdiction against going beyond human limits." *Dante as Dramatist: The Myth of the Earthly Paradise and Tragic Vision in "The Divine Comedy"* (Philadelphia: University of Pennsylvania Press, 1991), 140. There have recently been some scholarly comparisons of Dante and Ulysses in terms of "transgressing limits" that seem somewhat off the mark to me. Teodolinda Barolini, for example, believes that Dante the poet, by writing a poem that judges historical human beings and fixes them in their eternal states, "has embarked on a voyage whose Ulysses component [of transgression] he recognizes, fears, and never fully overcomes." *The Undivine Comedy: Detheologizing Dante* (Princeton, NJ: Princeton University Press, 1992), 52. However, Dante seems to believe he was appointed to write this poem, so doing so would not involve any transgression, and, as a Christian, his only fear would have been *not* to fulfill that task. When the pilgrim refers to Ulysses' journey as "the mad crossing" (*Par.* 27.82–83: ". . . il varco / folle . . ."), he does not sound afraid of having done a similar thing.

167 {metaphoric made literal}   Leanne Payne points out about Lewis's writings that "the embodiment of spiritual reality in material form

is the principle of the Incarnation." *Real Presence: The Christian Worldview of C. S. Lewis as Incarnational Reality* (Grand Rapids, MI: Baker, 2002), 20.

167 {ship metaphors} See *Purg.* 1.1–2, *Par.* 2.3, and 23.69.

167 {*Purg.* 1.1–2} *Purg.* 1.1–2: "... alza le vele / omai la navicella del mio ingegno."

167 {literally sailing} This occurs before Lucy, Edmund, and Eustace join the Narnians on their sea voyage.

167 {*Par.* 2.7} *Par.* 2.7: "L'acqua ch' io prendo già mai non si corse." According to Ricardo J. Quinones, Dante is referring to the fact that he is "the first poet to put the Christian story, told though the history of his times, into epic form and style derived from the classics." *Dante Alighieri* (Boston: Twayne, 1979), 159.

168 {"There was ... steadily"} What Virgil says about Mount Purgatory, using a boat comparison, applies here as well: "When climbing the mountain seems as easy to you as floating along with the current in a boat, then you will be at the end of this road" (*Purg.* 4.91–94: "... quand'ella [montagna] ti parrà soave / tanto, che su andar ti fia leggero, / com'a seconda giù andar per nave / allor sarai al fin d'esto sentero").

168 {*Par.* 1.63} *Par.* 1.63: "avesse il ciel d'un altro sole adorno."

168 {*Par.* 30.88–89} *Par.* 30.88–89: "... di lei bevve la gronda / delle palpebre mie...."

168 {increasing light for pilgrim} See, for example, the last time this happens when he is in the Empyrean. The light that envelops him transforms his sight so that he may withstand the ultimate visions of heaven: "And new vision was so kindled in me that no light would be so bright that my eyes could not withstand it" (*Par.* 30.58–60: "e di novella vista mi raccesi / tale, che nulla luce è tanto mera / che li occhi miei non si fosser difesi").

169 {*Par.* 30.129} *Par.* 30.129: "quanto è 'l convento delle bianche stole!"

169 {*Par.* 30.116–117} *Par.* 30.116–117: "... quanta è la larghezza / di questa rosa nell'estreme foglie!"

169 {*Par.* 33.94, 96} *Par.* 33.94, 96: "Un punto solo ... / ... / che fè Nettuno ammirar l'ombra d'Argo." Much critical ink has been spilled over the meaning of these verses with no clear resolution, so I am following the comparison that Lewis seems to be making. Lewis comments that this metaphor places us "at once in the dawn of time, in the old untravelled world when the shadow of a ship was a wonder." "Imagery in Dante's 'Comedy,' " 83.

169 {invent notion about Neptune}   Catullus' poem #64, describing the marriage of Thetis and Peleus, mentions in lines 14–15 that when the *Argo* first sailed, "wild shy faces emerged from the foaming eddies, / deepwater Nereïds, in wonder at this portent." *The Poems of Catullus*, trans. Peter Green (Berkeley: University of California Press, 2005), 135. However, there is no ancient text that speaks of a similar reaction by Neptune.

169 {*Par.* 33.109}   *Par.* 33.109: "... vivo lume...." See also *Par.* 31.46, "the living light" ("... la viva luce..."), and *Par.* 33.77, "living ray" ("... vivo raggio...").

169 {mind inadequate}   "My own wings were not sufficient for that" (*Par.* 33.139: "ma non eran da ciò le proprie penne").

170 {too shallow for boat}   Reepicheep manages to sail up and through the wave to enter Aslan's country in the tiny coracle retrieved from Burnt Island that had been brought on board.

170 {"the last canto ... reached"}   C. S. Lewis, "Shelley, Dryden, and Mr Eliot," *Selected Literary Essays*, ed. Walter Hooper (Cambridge: Cambridge University Press, 1969), 203. The quote is from Eliot's book *Dante* (1929, repr., New York: Haskell House, 1974), 34.

170 {represents spiritual life}   "Letter to Anne Jenkins," March 5, 1961, *The Collected Letters of C. S. Lewis*, vol. 3, 1245.

170 {Aslan identified as Jesus}   Lewis is here alluding to two biblical names for Christ: "the Lamb of God" and "the Lion of Judah."

171 {journey to underworld}   Lewis describes its theme as "the continued war against the power of darkness." "Letter to Anne Jenkins," March 5, 1961, *The Collected Letters of C. S. Lewis*, vol. 3, 1245.

171 {parallels with the giant scenes}   I am indebted to John D. Cox for noting three of the parallel details I list in this scene: the parallel of "towers," the nonsense syllables, and the giants' stupidity. "Epistemological Release in *The Silver Chair*," in *Longing for A Form: Essays in the Fiction of C. S. Lewis*, ed. Peter J. Schakel (Kent, OH: Kent State University Press, 1997), 163–64.

171 {*Inf.* 31.20}   *Inf.* 31.20: "... me parve veder molte alte torri."

171 {"little towers of rock"}   C. S. Lewis, *The Silver Chair* (New York: Macmillan, 1953; repr., New York: HarperCollins, 1981), 79. All quotes are from this edition and will be referred to as *SC* with page number(s).

171–72 {"stormed ... words"}   Dabney Adams Hart notes this similar detail as well. *Through the Open Door: A New Look at C. S. Lewis* (Tuscaloosa: University of Alabama Press, 1984), 39.

172 {*Inf.* 31.70}   *Inf.* 31.70: ". . . 'Anima sciocca.'"

172 {deceiving the children}   Ward likens their deception (in the queen's assurance of warm baths, soft beds, and good food at Harfang) to the "false imagining" (see *Par.* 1.89) of Dante's pilgrim when he has arrived on the sphere of the Moon. *Planet Narnia*, 134. However, the pilgrim has a *false perception* because he thinks he is still on earth, so he does not understand what he sees. Lewis's travelers, on the other hand, are given *false information*, so they have been lied to and misled, which is quite another matter.

174 {"From reading . . . to me"}   "Letter to Arthur Greeves," October 17, 1929, *The Collected Letters of C. S. Lewis*, vol. 1, 835.

174 {"serpent" in *Purgatorio*}   In *Purg.* 8.38 Dante refers to an unidentified "serpente" that will be coming to the valley garden at night, and in *Purg.* 8.98–99 he refers to it as a "biscia," a "snake." He says that *perhaps* it was the snake that gave Eve the fruit. However, since Dante's Satan is encased in ice in hell, it is likely that he was using this image mainly to suggest that temptation could occur in this valley garden, rather than using it as an alternate description or name for Satan. He refers to Satan in only two other ways: "the ancient adversary" (*Purg.* 14.146: ". . . antico avversaro") and "the evil worm" in *Inf.* 34.108.

174 {*Inf.* 34.108}   *Inf.* 34.108: ". . . vermo rea che 'l mondo fora." Dante also refers to the dog Cerberus as a "great worm" (*Inf.* 6.22: ". . . gran vermo"). With his three heads he prefigures the three-faced ruler of the underworld and is thus similar to Satan. See Mark Musa, trans. and notes, *Inferno*, 125.

174 {"worm" from other sources}   Lewis may also have had in mind E. R. Eddison's *The Worm Ouroboros* (1922), referring to a serpent or dragon that swallows its tail, an ancient Egyptian symbol of eternal, cyclic repetition. A variation of that word occurs when Wither and Straik chant "Ouroborindra" in worship of the severed head at the N.I.C.E (see *THS* 354).

174 {*Inf.* 34.139}   *Inf.* 34.139: ". . . a reveder le stelle." As a structural parallel, Dante ends each of the three major sections of his poem with the word *stelle* ("stars"). John D. Sinclair notes that "the stars mean for Dante all the good that is beyond the world, all the perfect order and the working providence of God." Commentary on the *Inferno* (London: The Bodley Head, 1939–1946; repr., Oxford: Oxford University Press, 1961), 432. In another interpretation, Peter S. Hawkins believes that ending each cantiche with the word *stars* suggests Dante's "orientation of the reader heavenward." *Dante's Testaments*, 6.

175 {"is telling . . . itself"}   C. S. Lewis, *A Preface to "Paradise Lost"* (London: Oxford University Press, 1942; repr., Oxford University Press, 1961), 132–33.

176 {"child reader . . . man"}   C. S. Lewis, "On Three Ways of Writing for Children," *Of Other Worlds: Essays and Stories*, ed. Walter Hooper (New York: Harcourt Brace Jovanovich, 1966), 34.

176 {We must . . . equals"}   Ibid.

176 {"in the moral . . . as we"}   Ibid., 33.

176 {"by casting . . . potency"}   Lewis, "Sometimes Fairy Stories May Say Best What's to Be Said," 37.

176 {"everything . . . our minds"}   Lewis, "On Three Ways of Writing for Children," 33–34.

Chapter 9: *Till We Have Faces*

177 {Christian story as myth}   Wayne Martindale notes that Lewis's use of a classical myth for this novel "is yet another way of slipping 'past the watchful dragons' of assumption and prejudice." *Beyond the Shadowlands: C. S. Lewis on Heaven and Hell* (Wheaton, IL: Crossway, 2005), 124. In fact, he says, "The biblically uninformed reader would never know that this is the true Christian myth in another form because none of the names or precise events are given." The phrase about "watchful dragons" that Martindale quotes is from Lewis's essay "Sometimes Fairy Stories May Say Best What's to Be Said" and refers to inhibitions and obligations concerning religion that "can freeze feelings" and block people from looking with fresh eyes at what they consider to be well-known or familiar religious truths. *Of Other Worlds: Essays and Stories*, ed. Walter Hooper (New York: Harcourt Brace Jovanovich, 1966), 37. Joe R. Christopher believes that "a Christian reading of this book is possible" because of its "Dantean parallels." *C. S. Lewis* (New York: Twayne, 1987), 124–25.

177 {Psyche tasks}   Sorting seeds into appropriate piles, acquiring golden fleece, getting a cup of water from Styx, and bringing back some of Proserpine's beauty from the underworld.

178 {pagan version of Christ}   Psyche, in identifying the Shadowbrute as "West-Wind," says, "He was in human shape. But you couldn't mistake him for a man." C. S. Lewis, *Till We Have Faces: A Myth Retold* (London: Geoffrey Bles, 1956), 111. Subsequent quotes from this edition are indicated by *TWHF* with page number(s). When

Orual catches a glimpse of him, "This great light stood over me. . . . In the center of the light was something like a man" (*TWHF* 172).

178 {"condensed . . . *Divine Comedy*"}   Christopher, *C. S. Lewis*, 123.

179 {Dante incorporates myths}   Dante also uses myth in similes and metaphors "as a decoration of his Christian theme." See Robin Kirkpatrick, *Dante's "Paradiso" and the Limitations of Modern Criticism* (Cambridge: Cambridge University Press, 1978), 174.

180 {Cerberus's three mouths}   According to George Holmes, "Dante tended to use all his characters, biblical and pagan, for moral purposes with the difference that the Bible carried traditional significance which he could hardly escape, while the pagan world was a freer field for invention." *Dante* (New York: Hill & Wang, 1980), 46.

180 {*Par*. 8.6}   *Par*. 8.6: "le genti antiche nell'antico errore."

180 {Lewis's modification of the myth}   Karen Rowe aptly notes that in his version of the myth, Lewis "foreground[s] the mortals in their interactions with the gods rather than the gods' interaction with mortals." "*Till We Have Faces*: A Study of the Soul and the Self," in *C. S. Lewis: Life, Works, Legacy*, ed. Bruce L. Edwards, vol. 2, *Fantacist, Mythmaker, and Poet* (London: Praeger, 2007), 141.

180 {Fox like Virgil}   Peter J. Schakel notes a resemblance of the Fox to Virgil as a symbol of reason and as a guide. *Reason and Imagination in C. S. Lewis: A Study of "Till We Have Faces"* (Grand Rapids, MI: Eerdmans, 1984), 80. Doris T. Myers compares the Fox to Virgil in the *Purgatorio* when he leads Orual to paintings that come alive on three walls of a chamber (see *TWHF* 297ff.). *Bareface: A Guide to C. S. Lewis's Last Novel* (Columbia: University of Missouri Press, 2004), 132. Gareth Knight sees a parallel in the fact that just as Virgil has to give way to Beatrice as a guide, "so too the Fox has to give way to the guidance of Psyche herself" in the garden scene at the end. *The Magical World of the Inklings* (Cheltenham, England: Skylight Press, 2010), 113.

180 {Fox represents philosophy}   According to Lewis, "the Fox expresses . . . Stoicism." "Letter to Clyde S. Kilby," November 22, 1962, in *The Collected Letters of C. S. Lewis*, vol. 3, *Narnia, Cambridge, and Joy 1950-1963*, ed. Walter Hooper (New York: HarperCollins, 2007), 1382.

180 {*Purg*. 21.32-33}   *Purg*. 21.32-33: ". . . mosterrolli / oltre, quanto 'l potrà menar mia scola." When they reach the Garden of Eden, he informs the pilgrim, "you have come to the place where I can discern no farther" (*Purg*. 27.128-129: ". . . se' venuto in parte / dov' io per me

più oltre non discerno"), so "do not expect any more words or signs from me" (*Purg.* 27.139: "Non aspettar mio dir più nè mio cenno").

180 {reasonable causes}   The only kinds of invisible things he believes in include "Justice, Equality, Soul, or musical notes" (*TWHF* 142).

181 {Virgil as "Father"}   For the pilgrim referring to Virgil as "father," see *Inf.* 8.110, and *Purg.* 4.44; 13.34; 15.25, 124; 17.82; 18.7, 13; 23.4, 13; 25.17; 26.97; 27.52.

181 {pilgrim as "son"}   For Virgil calling the pilgrim "son," see *Inf.* 3.121, 7.61, 8.67, 11.16, and *Purg.* 1.112, 3.66, 4.46, 17.92, 23.4, 25.35, 25.58, 27.20, 27.35, 27.128.

181 {Fox as "grandfather"}   For Orual's addresses to the Fox, see pp. 14, 17, 20, 23, 82–86, 140–44, 146–47, 149, 177, 207, 210, 296, 299–301, 305.

181 {Orual as "daughter"}   Before she is queen and then later in Orual's final dream-vision, the Fox calls her either "daughter" (see pp. 14–15, 17–18, 21, 28, 141–42, 146, 148–49, 177, 189, 194, 198, 208–210, 301) or "child" (pp. 14, 17, 82, 84, 86–87, 140, 142–43, 148, 178, 294, 296–97, 300). Once she is queen the Fox uses Bardia's address for her, calling her "Lady" (p. 178).

182 {unreliable narrator}   This is also the case for the narrator in *The Screwtape Letters* and for Eustace's diary entries in *The Voyage of the "Dawn Treader."*

182 {*Inf.* 3.18}   *Inf.* 3.18: "ch' hanno perduto lo ben dell'intelleto."

183 {*Inf.* 11.51}   *Inf.* 11.51: ". . . chi, spregiando Dio col cor, favella."

183 {*Inf.* 14.69–70}   *Inf.* 14.69–70: ". . . ebbe e par ch'elli abbia / Dio in disdegno, e poco par che 'l pregi."

183 {*Inf.* 14.65–66}   *Inf.* 14.65–66: "nullo martiro, fuor che la tua rabbia, / sarebbe al tuo furor dolor compito."

183 {*Inf.* 14.59–60}   *Inf.* 14.59–60: "a me saetti con tutto sua forza; / non ne potrebbe aver vendetta allegra."

184 {*Inf.* 14.46–48}   *Inf.* 11.46–48: "Puossi far forza nella deitade, / . . . / e spregiando ['n] natura sua bontade." Dante scholars generally interpret those who "despise nature" to be sodomites, but it depends on the translation of "*sua* bontade": is it *God's* goodness in nature or *nature's* goodness that is being despised? The only other time Dante uses the word *bontade* is in *Inf.* 11.96 when it again refers to God's goodness. Elsewhere when he uses the spelling *bontate*, it most often still applies to God: see *Inf.* 19.2, *Par.* 5.20, 13.58, 29.59. Lewis's description of Orual's disdain for nature seems to be following the interpretation that she is scorning God's goodness.

184 {"the whole . . . God's love"} James Collins, *Pilgrim in Love: An Introduction to Dante and His Spirituality* (Chicago: Loyola University Press, 1984), 165–66. It was a commonplace in medieval theology that nature, alongside the Bible, was the other book written by God. Joseph Anthony Mazzeo makes the interesting point that "seeing God through his creatures is a natural process in which all men share, and it simply requires a clear mind, not sanctity or any special grace." *Structure and Thought in the "Paradiso"* (Ithaca, NY: Cornell University Press, 1958), 86.

184 {*Purg.* 1.19–20} *Purg.* 1.19–20: "Lo bel pianeta . . . / faceva tutto rider l'orïente."

184 {*Par.* 28.83–84} *Par.* 28.83–84: ". . . 'l ciel ne ride / con le bellezze."

184 {*Par.* 5.97} *Par.* 5.97: ". . . la stella si cambiò e rise."

184 {*Par.* 14.86} *Par.* 14.86: ". . . l'affocato riso della stella."

184 {*Par.* 27.4–5} *Par.* 27.4–5: "Ciò ch' io vedeva mi sembiava un riso / dell'universo. . . ."

184 {*Purg.* 16.89} *Purg.* 16.89: ". . . lieto fattore." Peter S. Hawkins comments that one of the contributions Dante made to the tradition of Christian imagination "is a notion that joy is at the heart of reality, even at the heart of God" and that the "the smile is . . . perhaps his most original and indeed useful contribution to medieval theology." *Dante: A Brief History* (Malden, MA: Blackwell, 2006), 123, 129.

185 {"If we . . . hostility"} Dorothy L. Sayers, *Introductory Papers to Dante* (London: Methuen, 1954), 64. She goes on to say, "It is the deliberate choosing to remain in illusion and to see God and the universe as hostile to one's ego that is the very essence of hell" (p. 66).

185 {Lewis read Sayers} See "Letter to Dorothy L. Sayers," November 14, 1954, *The Collected Letters of C. S. Lewis*, vol. 3, 523–27.

185 {"rejoicing universe"} Sayers, *Introductory Papers*, 174.

185 {Orual's fraudulent counsel} In Dante's hell, fraudulent counselors are in the eighth ditch of the circle of fraud. Like the fraudulent counsel of Dante's Ulysses, who convinced his elderly crew to sail into forbidden waters, which led to their deaths (see *Inf.* 26.56ff.), Orual's fraudulent counsel has dire consequences as well.

186 {pagans not absolved} As Paul says in Romans, God's existence and power are visible through his creation so that people "are without excuse" (Rom. 1:20).

186 {classical figures punished} Dante, for example, does not place Dido in the circle of suicides because suicide in ancient times was

often a noble admission of wrongdoing rather than a sin. However, she put her obsessive love for Aeneas over her duty as queen to her country, thereby also breaking a vow to her dead husband, so she is now punished in the circle of lust (see *Inf.* 5.61–62). Jason, despite his heroic feat of building the first ship, the *Argo*, and of accomplishing the difficult task of acquiring the golden fleece, deceived and seduced Hypsipyle, so Dante places him in hell with other seducers (see *Inf.* 18.86–96). Patrick Boyde points out that a soul's particular punishment in Dante's hell is "the consequence and the symbol of [a soul's] *dominant* [italics added] obsession." *Perception and Passion in Dante's "Comedy"* (Cambridge: Cambridge University Press, 1993), 329, n. 36.

186 {*Par.* 17.112}   *Par.* 17.112: "... lo mondo sanze fine amaro."

187 {Orual's three vices}   Jane Studdock manifests these same three dispositions in her first visit to St. Anne's in *That Hideous Strength*.

187 {Aglauros}   See Ovid, *Metamorphoses*, 2.737–832.

187 {"clear ... petted thing"}   Even when Bardia is absent from court because he is dying, Orual objects to "how that wife of his cockered and cosseted him, like a hen with one chicken ... to keep him at home and away from the palace" (*TWHF* 248).

187 {Orual's anger at family}   For instance, when Psyche speaks of her palace, Orual says, "Fury ... fell on me" (*TWHF* 118), and when Psyche refers to her husband-god, Orual could "feel her rage coming back" (*TWHF* 122).

188 {*Purg.* 18.34–36}   *Purg.* 18.34–36: "... quant'è nascosa / la veritate alla gente ch'avvera / ciascun amore in sè laudabil cosa."

188 {"I learned ... loves"}   Lewis explains that Orual "is an instance ... of human affection" that becomes "tyrannically possessive and ready to turn into hatred when the beloved ceases to be its possession." "Letter to Clyde S. Kilby," February 10, 1957, *The Collected Letters of C. S. Lewis*, vol. 3, 831. He gives an example of a "close parallel" to Orual's situation as occurring today when "someone [in the family] becomes a Christian. ... The others suffer a sense of outrage. What they love is being taken away from them." Ibid.

188 {Orual in love with Bardia}   When Bardia has to leave after Orual's victorious fight against Argan because his wife is about to deliver a child, her "impossible fool's dream ... was that all should have been different from the very beginning and he would have been my husband" (*TWHF* 224).

189 {Psyche loves mountain god}   Psyche says, "The sweetest thing in all my life has been the longing—to reach the Mountain, to find the

place where all the beauty came from. . . . I am going to my lover" (*TWHF* 75–76).

189 {"How can . . . I die?"}   Speaking of marriage, Psyche says, "To leave your home . . . or to lose one's maidenhood—to bear a child—they are all deaths" (*TWHF* 73).

189 {*Par.* 5.105}   *Par.* 5.105: "Ecco chi crescerà li nostri amori." Lewis quotes this verse in *The Four Loves* (London: Collins, 1960), 64, and he repeats that concept in a letter to Mrs. Johnson, November 18, 1953: "When I have learnt to love God better than my earthly dearest, I shall love my earthly dearest better than I do now." *The Collected Letters of C. S. Lewis*, vol. 3, 247.

189 {"encounters . . . in Psyche"}   Schakel, *Reason and Imagination in C. S. Lewis*, 105.

190 {"deserving . . . punishment"}   Dante, "Letter to Can Grande," *Dantis Alagherii Epistolae*, 8, trans. Paget Toynbee. 2nd ed. Oxford: Clarendon, 1966), 200.

190 {"it is by . . . good"}   "Letter to Mrs. Frank L. Jones," *The Collected Letters of C. S. Lewis*, vol. 2, *Books, Broadcasts, and the War 1931–1949*, ed. Walter Hooper (New York: HarperCollins, 2004), 764.

190 {*Purg.* 13.88–90}   *Purg.* 13.88–90: "se tosto grazia resolve la schiume / di vostra cosci̇enza sì che chiaro /per essa scenda della mente il fiume."

191 {*Par.* 20.106–107}   *Par.* 20.106–107: ". . . u' non si riede / già mai a buon voler. . . ."

191 {*Inf.* 14.51}   *Inf.* 14.51: ". . . Qual io fui vivo, tal son morto."

192 {*Purg.* 13.121–122}   *Purg.* 13.121–122: ". . . io volsi in su l'ardita faccia, / gridando a Dio, 'Omai più non ti temo!'"

192 {*Purg.* 13.124–125}   *Purg.* 13.124–125: "Pace volli con Dio in su lo stremo / della mia vita. . . ."

192 {*Purg.* 8.120}   *Purg.* 8.120: "a' miei portai l'amor che qui raffina."

193 {*Inf.* 3.56–57}   *Inf.* 3.56–57: ". . . io non averei creduto / che morte tanta n'avesse disfatta." Christopher also notes the echo of this verse from Dante's poem. *C. S. Lewis*, 124.

193 {*Inf.* 5.7–8}   *Inf.* 5.7–8: ". . . quando l'anima mal nata / li vien dinanzi, tutta si confessa."

193 {*Inf.* 5.18}   *Inf.* 5.18: "lasciando l'atto di cotanto offizio."

193 {"a plaintiff . . . her case"}   Christopher believes that this judge of the dead is "not treated in Dantean terms," but these details indicate that perhaps he is. *C. S. Lewis*, 124.

194 {*Purg.* 16.31–32}   *Purg.* 16.31–32: ". . . che ti mondi / per tornar bella a colui che ti fece." In *The Divine Comedy*, this comment is made to Marco Lombardo, the character who begins the lengthy discussion on the doctrine of free will in the *Purgatorio*.

194 {a forgiving God}   Her final statement before her death—in a cadence reminiscent of St. Augustine's "Late have I loved thee"—is "Long did I hate you, long did I fear you" (*TWHF* 308).

194 {*Par.* 26.62–63}   *Par.* 26.62–63: "tratto m'hanno del mar dell'amor torto, / e del diritto m'han posto alla riva."

194 {*Purg.* 20.142}   *Purg.* 20.142: ". . . cammin santo."

195 {echoes of Matilda and Beatrice}   Myers also connects Psyche here both to the Green Lady in *Perelandra*, who is reminiscent of Matilda, and to Matilda herself. *Bareface*, 56. However, since Psyche is a channel of grace to lead Orual to her god, I believe she represents far more than Matilda. Just as Lewis's Green Lady recalls *both* Matilda and Beatrice, so too does Psyche in this instance (for the discussion of the Green Lady as both Beatrice and Matilda see pages 86, 96–99).

195 {*Inf.* 2.55}   *Inf.* 2.55: "Lucevan li occhi suoi più che la stella."

196 {*Purg.* 12.67}   *Purg.* 12.67: "Morti li morti e i vivi parean vivi."

196 {*Purg.* 10.37–39}   *Purg.* 10.37–39: "dinanzi a noi pareva sì verace / . . . / che non sembiava imagine che tace."

196 {*Purg.* 10.95}   *Purg.* 10.95: ". . . visibile parlare."

196 {paintings on chamber walls}   Myers says the Fox explains the pictures in this scene "just as Virgil explained visions and images to Dante on the terraces of Mount Purgatory." *Bareface*, 132. However, Virgil at times comments on, but does not need to explain, the pilgrim's visions, and the images displayed on the ledge of pride do not need explanation either. Christopher conjectures that the fourth task of Psyche depicted on the wall is reshaped into pictures "replacing perhaps the allegorical pageants Dante saw on the top of Mount Purgatory." *C. S. Lewis*, 123. Lewis could be echoing that here, but the sculptures on the ledge of pride seem more analogous for several reasons.

196 {Dante's "I see"}   See *Purg.* 12.22, 25, 28, 31, 34, 38, 43, 61.

196 {Lewis's "I saw"}   Sometimes more than once per page; see *TWHF* 297–300, 302–3. Lewis also uses "we saw" once (p. 302).

196 {Orual's suffering for Psyche}   Christopher believes Lewis is suggesting that this is "a lesser instance of Jesus bearing the burden of mankind's sins." *C. S. Lewis*, 123.

196 {*Purg.* 29.20} *Purg.* 29.20: "e quel [lustro], durando, più e più splendeva."

197 {Fox disappears} Christopher notes the similarity of the Fox's disappearance to Virgil's at the top of the mount. *C. S. Lewis*, 124.

197 {*Purg.* 31.83} *Purg.* 31.83: "vincer parìemi più sè stessa antica."

197 {Psyche repeats prophecy} On the mountain Psyche had prophesied, "We shall meet here again with no cloud between us" (*TWHF* 128), and now she repeats, "Did I not tell you . . . that a day was coming when you and I would meet in my house and no cloud between us?" (*TWHF* 306).

197 {Psyche's God like Beatrice} Christopher also sees Orual's meeting with Psyche's god as "in a general way parallel to the end of *The Divine Comedy* with Dante's symbolic vision of God." *C. S. Lewis*, 124. Although this is true, the narrative is also structured to parallel some features from the scene in the Garden of Eden.

197 {*Purg.* 29.34–35} *Purg.* 29.34–35: ". . . un fuoco accese, / ci si fè l'aere. . . ."

197 {*Purg.* 30.76–77} *Purg.* 30.76–77: "Li occhi mi cadder giù nel chairo fonte; / ma veggendomi in esso, i trassi all'erba."

198 {"*Perelandra* . . . written"} "Letter to George Sayer," April 10, 1946, *The Collected Letters of C. S. Lewis*, vol. 3, 1564.

198 {"I think . . . best book"} "Letter to Audrey Sutherland," April 28, 1960, *The Collected Letters of C. S. Lewis*, vol. 3, 1148. See also "Letter to Joan Lancaster," April 20, 1959, *The Collected Letters of C. S. Lewis*, vol. 3, 1040. Nevertheless, *Perelandra* did not lose a favored status with Lewis because, in answer to the question about which he *liked* best, Lewis responded, "The answer wd. be *Till We Have Faces* and *Perelandra*." "Letter to Meredith Lee," December 6, 1960, *The Collected Letters of C. S. Lewis*, vol. 3, 1214.

198 {"Pagan stories . . . itself"} "Letter to Arthur Greeves," November 18, 1931, *The Collected Letters of C. S. Lewis*, vol. 2, 12–13.

198 {"Paganism . . . dream"} C. S. Lewis, *Surprised by Joy: The Shape of My Early Life* (New York: Harcourt, Brace & World, 1955), 235. As John learns in *The Pilgrim's Regress*, "Myth is my [God's] inventing, the veil under which I have chosen to appear even from the first until now" (*PR* 171).

198 {"Psyche . . . saved"} "Letter to Anne and Martin Kilmer," August 7, 1957, *The Collected Letters of C. S. Lewis*, vol. 3, 874.

198 {"I think . . . know him"} "Letter to Mrs. Johnson," November 8, 1952, *The Collected Letters of C. S. Lewis*, vol. 3, 245. Lewis points

to the parable of the sheep and goats in Matthew 25 to support this concept.

199 {*Purg.* 7.7–8} *Purg.* 7.7–8: ". . . per null' altro rio / lo ciel perdei che per non aver fè."

199 {*Inf.* 4.34–36} *Inf.* 4.34–36: ". . . s'elli hanno mercedi, / non basta, perchè non ebber battesmo, / ch' è porta della fede. . . ."

199 {*Par.* 20.111} *Par.* 20.111: "sì che potesse sua voglia esser mossa."

199 {*Par.* 20.114} *Par.* 20.114: "credette in lui che potea aiutarla."

199 {baptism access to heaven} Baptism, however, does not provide automatic admission into heaven according to Dante. Echoing Matthew 7:21–23, Dante's eagle points out that "there are many crying, 'Christ, Christ!' who will be less close to him on judgment day than someone who does not know Christ" (*Par.* 19.106–108: ". . . molti gridan 'Cristo, Cristo!,' / che saranno in giudicio assai men prope / a lui, che tal che non conosce Cristo."

199 {Rhipeus in *Aeneid*} For Virgil's mentions of Rhipeus, see *Aeneid* 2.426–427; and 2.339, 394.

199 {*Par.* 20.119–10} *Par.* 20.119–120: ". . . per grazia che da sì profonda / fontana stilla, che mai creatura / non pinse l'occhio infino alla prima onda."

199 {*Par.* 20.122–124} *Par.* 20.122–124: ". . . Dio li aperse / l'occhio alla nostra redenzion futura: / ond'ei credette in quella. . . ."

199 {*Par.* 19.103–105} *Par.* 19.103–105: ". . . A questo regno / non salì mai chi non credette 'n Cristo, / vel pria vel poi ch'ei si chiavasse al legno."

200 {*Par.* 20.127–29} *Par.* 20.127–129: ". . . li fur per battesmo / . . . . / dinanzi al battezzar più d'un millesmo."

200 {baptism by desire} For baptism by desire, see, for example, Augustine, *Commentary on Psalm 57*, or Thomas Aquinas, *Summa Theologica*, III, q. 68, and II–II, q. 2, a. 7, a. 3. The other two baptisms include "baptism by water" (the normative mode for the administration of that sacrament), and "baptism by fire," which occurs when an unbaptized person dies for the Christian faith.

200 {Lewis knew the two examples} In his essay "Dante's Statius," Lewis refers to "exceptional mercies [that] might raise a Trajan or a Rhipeus." *Studies in Medieval and Renaissance Literature*, coll. Walter Hooper (Cambridge: Cambridge University Press, 1966), 97. In *The Great Divorce*, MacDonald mentions Trajan as an example of someone who comes from hell and is allowed to stay in heaven (see *GD* 66). In his "Letter to Margaret Pollard," May 22, 1954, Lewis refers to "uncov-

enanted mercies" and uses the example that Dante placed Trajan and Rhipeus in heaven. *The Collected Letters of C. S. Lewis*, vol. 3, 478.

200 {"Lewis . . . Christ"}   Walter Hooper, *The Collected Letters of C. S. Lewis*, vol. 2, 135, n. 9.

200 {Emeth demonstration}   This young Calormene, a worshipper of Tash, was accepted by Aslan because of his heart's intentions. Aslan's dialogue with Emeth is his longest dialogue with any character in The Chronicles of Narnia.

Chapter 10: Conclusion: In the Footsteps of Dante

201 {"By studying . . . narrative"}   David C. Downing, *Planets in Peril: A Critical Study of C. S. Lewis's Ransom Trilogy* (Amherst: University of Massachusetts Press, 1992), 121.

201 {Dante quotes in other writings}   Many of the direct quotes in his other writings find narrative echoes in Lewis's novels and are often clues as to what ideas and images from Dante were significant for him.

202 {Lewis's female protagonists}   Young girls are main protagonists in the five Chronicles of Narnia stories that are not discussed in this book.

203 {allusions to other segments}   For example, on his Malacandrian journey when he is learning about sin and evil on earth, Ransom looks down at the earth from his position high in the heavens like Dante's pilgrim in the *Paradiso*. Flashes of the *Inferno* occur in *The Voyage of the "Dawn Treader"* at the very juncture in Lewis's story that separates the *Purgatorio* segment from the *Paradiso* segment of that ship's voyage, etc.

205 {"written . . . Jerusalem"}   Chad Walsh, *C. S. Lewis: Apostle to the Skeptics* (New York: Macmillan, 1949), 156.

205 {use tailored to genre}   Lewis's appropriation of medieval elements from Dante's Ptolemaic cosmos is fitting for novels that include journeys into the heavens but would be not be suitable in fairy tales, etc.

205 {"Lewis often . . . Lewis"}   Downing, *Planets in Peril*, 122.

205 {"Parrot critics . . . *splende*"}   C. S. Lewis, *Surprised by Joy: The Shape of My Early Life* (New York: Harcourt, Brace & World, 1955), 53.

206 {"the real . . . imitative"}   Northrop Frye, *Anatomy of Criticism* (Princeton: Princeton University Press, 1957), 97.

206 {much Dante unseen}   The authors who have noted the most concrete connections between Dante and Lewis are Joe R. Christopher in

his book *C. S. Lewis* (New York: Twayne, 1987) and his many essays and Downing's *Planets in Peril* and his many essays.

206 {"no artist . . . strategy"}   Michael Ward, *Planet Narnia: The Seven Heavens in the Imagination of C. S. Lewis* (Oxford: Oxford University Press, 2008), 7.

206 {"It is past . . . ingredients"}   Walter Hooper, "Narnia: the Author, the Critic, and the Tale," in *The Longing for a Form: Essays on the Fiction of C. S. Lewis*, ed. Peter J. Schakel (Kent, OH: Kent State University Press, 1977), 112.

206 {"in some . . . species alone"}   C. S. Lewis, "Dante's Similes," *Studies in Medieval and Renaissance Literature*, coll. Walter Hooper (Cambridge: Cambridge University Press, 1966), 64. Lewis is paraphrasing a verse from the first stanza from Abraham Cowley's poem "The Praise of Pindar in Imitation of Horace His Second Book 4": "The phoenix Pindar is a vast species alone."

206 {"champion . . truth"}   Robin Kirkpatrick, *Dante: "The Divine Comedy"* (Cambridge: Cambridge University Press, 2004), 112.

206 {"They may . . . truths"}   "Letter to Tony Pollock," May 3, 1954, *The Collected Letters of C. S. Lewis*, vol. 3, *Narnia, Cambridge, and Joy 1950–1963*, ed. Walter Hooper (New York: HarperCollins, 2007), 465.

206 {"the imagination . . . effect"}   C. S. Lewis, "Imagery in the Last Eleven Cantos of Dante's 'Comedy,'" *Studies in Medieval and Renaissance Literature*, coll. Walter Hooper (Cambridge: Cambridge University Press, 1966), 78.

Bibliography

Bibliography: Lewis

Lewis, Clive Staples. *The Abolition of Man*. New York: Macmillan, 1947.

———. *The Allegory of Love: A Study in Medieval Tradition*. London: Oxford University Press, 1936. Reprint, New York: Oxford University Press, 1969.

———. *Christian Reflections*. Edited by Walter Hooper. Grand Rapids, MI: Eerdmans, 1971.

———. *The Collected Letters of C. S. Lewis*. Edited by Walter Hooper. 3 vols. New York: Harper Collins, 2004–2007.

———. *"The Dark Tower" and Other Stories*. Edited by Walter Hooper. New York: Harcourt, 1977.

———. *The Discarded Image: An Introduction to Medieval and Renaissance Literature*. Cambridge: Cambridge University Press, 1964.

———. *English Literature in the Sixteenth Century Excluding Drama*. Oxford: Clarendon, 1954. Reprint, New York: Oxford University Press, 1973.

———. *An Experiment in Criticism*. Cambridge: Cambridge University Press, 1965.

———. *The Four Loves*. London: Collins, 1960.

———. *The Great Divorce; A Dream*. London: Geoffrey Ellen, 1945. Reprint, New York: Macmillan, 1946.

———. *The Horse and His Boy*. New York: Macmillan, 1954.

———. *The Last Battle*. New York: Macmillan, 1955.

———. *Letters of C. S. Lewis*. Edited with a memoir by W. H. Lewis. New York: Harcourt Brace Jovanovich, 1966.

————. *Letters to an American Lady*. Edited by Clyde S. Kilby. Grand Rapids, MI: Eerdmans, 1967.

————. *Letters to Malcolm: Chiefly on Prayer*. New York: Harcourt Brace Jovanovich, 1964.

————. *The Lion, the Witch and the Wardrobe*. New York: Macmillan, 1950.

————. *The Magician's Nephew*. New York: Macmillan, 1955.

————. *Mere Christianity*. New York: Macmillan, 1952.

————. *Miracles: A Preliminary Study*. New York: Macmillan, 1947; reprint ed., New York: Macmillan paperbacks, 1978.

————. *Of Other Worlds: Essays and Stories*. Edited by Walter Hooper. New York: Harcourt Brace Jovanovich, 1966.

————. *Out of the Silent Planet*. London: John Lane, 1938. Reprint, New York: Macmillan, 1965.

————. *Perelandra*. London: John Lane, 1943. Reprint, New York: Macmillan, 1965.

————. *The Pilgrim's Regress: An Allegorical Apology for Christianity, Reason, and Romanticism*. London: Geoffrey Bles, 1933; 2nd ed. revised with a new preface. London: Geoffrey Bles, 1944.

————. *A Preface to "Paradise Lost."* London: Oxford University Press, 1942. Reprint, London: Oxford University Press, 1961.

————. *Prince Caspian*. New York: Macmillan, 1951.

————. *The Problem of Pain*. New York: Macmillan, 1962.

————. *The Screwtape Letters*. London: Geoffrey Bles, 1942. Reprinted with a new preface. New York: Macmillan, 1961.

————. *Selected Literary Essays*. Edited by Walter Hooper. Cambridge: Cambridge University Press, 1969.

————. *The Silver Chair*. New York: Macmillan, 1953.

————. *Spenser's Images of Life*. Edited by Alastair Fowler. Cambridge: Cambridge University Press, 1967.

————. *Studies in Medieval and Renaissance Literature*. Collected by Walter Hooper. Cambridge: Cambridge University Press, 1966.

————. *Surprised by Joy: The Shape of My Early Life*. New York: Harcourt, Brace & World, 1955.

————. *That Hideous Strength*. London: John Lane, 1945. Reprint, New York: Macmillan, 1965.

————. *Till We Have Faces: A Myth Retold*. London: Geoffrey Bles, 1956.

————. *The Voyage of the "Dawn Treader."* New York: Macmillan, 1952.

————. *'The Weight of Glory' and Other Addresses.* Grand Rapids, MI: Eerdmans, 1949.

————. *"The World's Last Night" and Other Essays.* New York: Harcourt Brace Jovanovich, 1960.

Lewis, C. S., ed. *Essays Presented to Charles Williams.* Oxford: Oxford University Press, 1947.

————, ed. *George MacDonald: An Anthology.* London: Geoffrey Bles, Centenary, 1946.

Lewis, C. S., and E. M. W. Tillyard, *The Personal Heresy: A Controversy.* Oxford: Oxford University Press, 1939.

Secondary Sources for Lewis

Adey, Lionel. *C. S. Lewis: Writer, Dreamer & Mentor.* Grand Rapids, MI: Eerdmans, 1998.

————. "Medievalism in the Space Trilogy of C. S. Lewis." *Studies in Medievalism* 3, no. 3 (Winter 1991): 279–89.

Amis, Kinglsey. *New Maps of Hell.* New York: Harcourt Brace, 1960.

Arnott, Anne. *The Secret Country of C. S. Lewis.* London: Hodder & Stoughton, 1976.

Bailey, James Osler. *Pilgrims through Space and Time.* New York: Argus, 1947.

Barfield, Owen, *Owen Barfield on C. S. Lewis.* Edited by G. B. Tennyson. Middleton, CT: Wesleyan University Press, 1989.

Boenig, Robert. *C. S. Lewis and the Middle Ages.* Kent, OH: Kent State University Press, 2012.

Bramlett, Perry. *C. S. Lewis: A Life at the Center.* Macon, GA: Peak Road, 1996.

Brown, Devin. *Inside Narnia: A Guide to Exploring the "Lion, the Witch and the Wardrobe."* Grand Rapids, MI: Baker, 2005.

Carnell, Corbin Scott. *Bright Shadows of Reality: C. S. Lewis and the Feeling Intellect.* Grand Rapids, MI: Eerdmans, 1974.

Carpenter, Humphrey. *The Inklings: C. S. Lewis, J. R. R. Tolkien, Charles Williams, and Their Friends.* Boston: Houghton Mifflin, 1979.

Caughey, Shanna, ed. *Revisiting Narnia: Fantasy, Myth and Religion in C. S. Lewis's Chronicles.* Dallas: BenBella, 2005.

Chard, Jean Marie. "Some Elements of Myth and Mysticism in C. S. Lewis' Novel *Till We Have Faces*." *Mythlore* 5 (1978): 15–18.

Christensen, Michael J. *C. S. Lewis on Scripture*. London: Hodder & Stoughton, 1979.

Christopher, Joe R. *C. S. Lewis*. New York: Twayne, 1987.

———. "Considering *The Great Divorce*: Parts I and II." *Mythcon Proceedings* (Los Angeles: Mythopoeic Society, 1971). 40–48.

———. "Considering *The Great Divorce*: Parts III and IV." *Mythcon Proceedings* (Los Angeles: Mythopoeic Society, 1972). 12–22.

———. "Dante and the Inklings." *Mythprint* 11 (March 1975). 2–4.

———. "The Dantean Structure of *The Great Divorce*." *Mythlore* 29, no. 3/4 (Spring/Summer 2011): 77–99.

Clark, David G. *C. S. Lewis: A Guide to His Theology*. Malden, MA: Blackwell, 2007.

Colbert, David. *The Magical Worlds of Narnia: The Symbols, Myths, and Fascinating Facts behind the Chronicles*. New York: Berkley, 2005.

Como, James T. *Branches to Heaven: The Geniuses of C. S. Lewis*. Dallas: Spence, 1998.

Como, James T., ed. *"C. S. Lewis at the Breakfast Table" and Other Reminiscences*. New York: Macmillan, 1980.

Coren, Michael. *The Man Who Created Narnia: The Story of C. S. Lewis*. Grand Rapids, MI: Eerdmans, 1994.

Cunningham, Richard B. *C. S. Lewis: Defender of the Faith*. Philadelphia: Westminster, 1967.

Dickerson, Matthew, and David O'Hara. *Narnia and the Fields of Arbol: The Environmental Vision of C. S. Lewis*. Lexington: University Press of Kentucky, 2009.

Downing, David C. *C. S. Lewis's Journey to Faith: The Most Reluctant Convert*. Downers Grove, IL: InterVarsity, 2002.

———. *Into the Region of Awe: Mysticism in C. S. Lewis*. Downers Grove, IL: InterVarsity, 2005.

———. *Into the Wardrobe: C. S. Lewis and the Narnia Chronicles*. San Francisco: Jossey Bass, 2005.

———. *Planets in Peril: A Critical Study of C. S. Lewis's Ransom Trilogy*. Amherst: University of Massachusetts Press, 1992.

Duriez, Colin. *The C. S. Lewis Handbook: A Comprehensive Guide to His Life, Thought, and Writings*. Eastbourne, UK: Monarch, 1990.

Edwards, Bruce L., ed. *C. S. Lewis: Life, Works, Legacy*. 4 vols. London: Praeger, 2007.

———. *The Taste of the Pineapple: Essays on C. S. Lewis as Reader, Critic and Imaginative Writer*. Bowling Green, OH: Bowling Green State University Popular Press, 1988.

Filmer, Kath. *The Fiction of C. S. Lewis: Mask and Mirror*. London: Macmillan, 1993.

Freshwater, Mark Edwards. *C. S. Lewis and the Truth of Myth*. Lanham, MD: University Press of Americas, 1988.

Fuller, Edmund. *Books with Men behind Them*. New York: Random House, 1962.

Gerber, Richard. *Utopian Fantasy*. London: Routledge & Paul, 1955.

Gibb, Jocelyn, ed. *Light on C. S. Lewis*. New York: Harcourt, Brace & World, 1965.

Gibson, Evan K. *C. S. Lewis, Spinner of Tales: A Guide to His Fiction*. Grand Rapids, MI: Eerdmans, 1980.

Gilbert, Douglas, and Clyde Kilby. *C. S. Lewis: Images of His World*. Grand Rapids, MI: Eerdmans, 1973.

Glaspey, Terry W. *Not a Tame Lion: The Spiritual Legacy of C. S. Lewis*. Nashville: Cumberland, 1996.

Glover, Donald E. *C. S. Lewis: The Art of Enchantment*. Athens, OH: The Ohio University Press, 1981.

Glyer, Diana Pavlac. *The Company They Keep: C. S. Lewis and J. R. R. Tolkien as Writers in Community*. Kent, OH: Kent State University Press, 2007.

Graham, David, ed. *We Remember C. S. Lewis: Essays and Memoir*. Nashville: Broadman & Holman, 2001.

Gray, William. *C. S. Lewis*. Plymouth, UK: Northcote House, 1998.

Green, Roger Lancelyn. *C. S. Lewis*. London: Bodley Head, 1963.

Green, Roger Lancelyn, and Walter Hooper. *C. S. Lewis: A Biography*. New York: Harcourt Brace Jovanovich, 1974.

Griffin, William. *C. S. Lewis: The Authentic Voice*. Oxford, England: Lion, 1986.

———. *C. S. Lewis: Spirituality for Mere Christians*. New York: Crossroad, 1998.

Hannay, Margaret Patterson. *C. S. Lewis*. New York: Frederick Ungar, 1981.

Harris, Richard. *C. S. Lewis: The Man and His God*. London: Collins, 1987.

Hart, Dabney Adams. *Through the Open Door: A New Look at C. S. Lewis*. Tuscaloosa: University of Alabama Press, 1984.

Hick, John. *The Metaphor of God Incarnate*. London: SCM Press, 1993.

Hilder, Monika B. *The Feminine Ethos in C. S. Lewis's Chronicles of Narnia*. New York: Peter Lang, 2012.

———. *The Gender Dance: Ironic Subversion in C. S. Lewis's Cosmic Trilogy*. New York: Peter Lang, 2013.

Hillegas, Mark Robert. *The Future as Nightmare: H. G. Wells and the Anti-Utopians*. New York: Oxford University Press, 1967.

Hillegas, Mark Robert, ed. *Shadows of Imagination: The Fantasies of C. S. Lewis, J. R. R. Tolkien, and Charles Williams*. Carbondale: Southern Illinois University Press, 1979.

Holmer, Paul. *C. S. Lewis: The Shape of His Faith and Thought*. New York: Harper & Row, 1976.

Honda, Mineko. *The Imaginative World of C. S. Lewis: A Way to Participate in Reality*. Lanham, MD: University Press of America, 2000.

Hooper, Walter. *C. S. Lewis: A Companion and Guide*. London: HarperCollins, 1996.

———. *Past Watchful Dragons: A Guide to C. S. Lewis's "Chronicles of Narnia."* London: Collins, 1980.

Howard, Thomas. *C. S. Lewis, Man of Letters: A Reading of His Fiction*. San Franciso: Ignatius, 1987.

———. *Narnia and Beyond: A Guide to the Fiction of C. S. Lewis*. San Francisco: Ignatius, 2006.

Huttar, Charles A., ed. *Imagination and the Spirit*. Grand Rapids, MI: Eerdmans, 1971.

Jacobs, Alan. *The Narnian: The Life and Imagination of C. S. Lewis*. New York: Harper Collins, 2005.

Keefe, Carolyn, ed. *C. S. Lewis: Speaker and Teacher*. Foreword by Thomas Howard. Grand Rapids, MI: Zondervan, 1971.

Kilby, Clyde S. *The Christian World of C. S. Lewis*. Grand Rapids, MI: Eerdmans, 1964.

———. *Images of Salvation in the Fiction of C. S. Lewis*. Wheaton, IL: Harold Shaw, 1978.

Killinger, John. *The Failure of Theology in Modern Literature*. New York: Abingdon, 1963.

King, Don W. *C. S. Lewis, Poet: The Legacy of His Poetic Impulse*. Kent, OH: Kent State University Press, 2001.

Knight, Damon, ed. *Turning Points: Essays on the Art of Science Fiction.* New York: Harper & Row, 1977.

Knight, Gareth. *The Magical World of the Inklings.* Cheltenham, England: Skylight Press, 2010.

Kreeft, Peter. *C. S. Lewis: A Critical Essay.* Grand Rapids, MI: Eerdmans, 1969.

————. *C. S. Lewis for the Third Millennium: Six Essays on "The Abolition of Man."* San Francisco: Ignatius, 1994.

Lindskoog, Kathryn. *Dante's 'Divine Comedy'; Purgatory: Journey to Joy.* Translation with notes. Macon, GA: Mercer University Press, 1997.

————. *Finding the Landlord: A Guidebook to C. S. Lewis's "Pilgrim's Regress."* Chicago: Cornerstone, 1995.

————. *Journey into Narnia.* Pasadena, CA: Hope, 1998.

————. *The Lion of Judah in Never-Never Land: The Theology of C. S. Lewis Expressed in His Fantasies for Children.* Grand Rapids, MI: Eerdmans, 1973.

————. *Surprised by C. S. Lewis, George MacDonald, & Dante: An Anthology of Original Discoveries.* Macon, GA: Mercer University Press, 2001.

Lobdell, Jared. *The Scientifiction Novels of C. S. Lewis: Space and Time in the Ransom Stories.* Jefferson, NC: McFarland, 2004.

Macdonald, Michael H., and Andrew A. Tadie. *G. K. Chesterton and C. S. Lewis: The Riddle of Joy.* London: Collins, 1989.

MacSwain, Robert, and Michael Ward, eds. *The Cambridge Companion to C. S. Lewis.* Cambridge: Cambridge University Press, 2010.

Manlove, Colin N. *C. S. Lewis: His Literary Achievement.* London: Macmillan, 1987.

————. *Christian Fantasy: From 1200 to the Present.* Notre Dame, IN: University of Notre Dame Press, 1992.

————. *"The Chronicles of Narnia": The Patterning of a Fantastic World.* New York: Twayne, 1993.

————. *Modern Fantasy: Five Studies.* New York: Cambridge University Press, 1975.

Marshall, Cynthia, ed. *Essays on C. S. Lewis and George MacDonald: Truth, Fiction, and the Power of Imagination.* Lampeter, NY: Edwin Mellen, 1991.

Martin, Thomas L., ed. *Reading the Classics with C. S. Lewis.* Grand Rapids, MI: Baker Academic, 2000.

Martindale, Wayne. *Beyond the Shadowlands: C. S. Lewis on Heaven and Hell*. Wheaton, IL: Crossway, 2005.

May, Stephen. *Stardust and Ashes: Science Fiction in Christian Perspective*. London: SPCK, 1998.

McGrath, Alister E. *C. S. Lewis—A Life: Eccentric, Genius, Reluctant Prophet*. London: Hodder and Stoughton, 2013.

———. *The Intellectual World of C. S. Lewis*. Malden, MA: John Wiley and Sons, 2014.

Meilander, Gilbert. *The Taste for the Other: The Social and Ethical Thought of C. S. Lewis*. Grand Rapids, MI: Eerdmans, 1978.

Menuge, Angus, J. L., ed. *C. S. Lewis, Lightbearer in the Shadowlands: The Evangelistic Vision of C. S. Lewis*. Wheaton, IL: Crossway, 1997.

Mills, David, ed. *The Pilgrim's Guide: C. S. Lewis and the Art of Witness*. Grand Rapids, MI: Eerdmans, 1998.

Milward, Peter. *A Challenge to C. S. Lewis*. London: Associated University Presses, 1995.

Montgomery, John Warwick, ed. *Myth, Allegory, and Gospel: An Interpretation of J. R. R. Tolkien, C. S. Lewis, G. K. Chesterton, Charles Williams*. Minneapolis: Bethany Fellowship, 1974.

Moorman, Charles. *Arthurian Triptych*. Berkeley: University of California Press, 1960.

Murphy, Brian. *C. S. Lewis*. Mercer Island, WA: Stormont, 1983.

Myers, Doris T. *Bareface: A Guide to C. S. Lewis's Last Novel*. Columbia: University of Missouri Press, 2004.

———. *C. S. Lewis in Context*. Kent, OH: Kent State University Press, 1994.

Nicolson, Marjorie Hope. *Voyages to the Moon*. New York: Macmillan, 1948.

Patterson, Nancy-Lou. "'Miraculous Bread . . . Miraculous Wine': Eucharistic Motifs in the Fantasies of C. S. Lewis." *Mythlore* 84 (Summer 1998): 28–46.

Payne, Leanne. *Real Presence: The Christian Worldview of C. S. Lewis as Incarnational Reality*. Grand Rapids, MI: Baker, 2002.

Peters, John. *C. S. Lewis: The Man and His Achievement*. Exeter, UK: Paternoster, 1985.

Peters, Thomas C. *Simply C. S. Lewis: A Beginner's Guide to the Life and Works of C. S. Lewis*. Wheaton, IL: Crossway, 1997.

Poe, Harry Lee, and Rebecca Whitten Poe. *C. S. Lewis Remembered.* Grand Rapids, MI: Zondervan, 2006.

Rabkin, Eric S., and Robert Scholes. *Science Fiction: History, Science, Vision.* New York: Oxford University Press, 1977.

Reppert, Victor. *C. S. Lewis's Dangerous Idea: In Defense of the Argument from Reason.* Downers Grove, IL: InterVarsity, 2003.

Reynolds, Barbara. *The Passionate Intellect: Dorothy L. Sayers' Encounter with Dante.* Kent, OH: Kent State University Press, 1989.

Rigney, Joe. *Live Like a Narnian: Christian Discipleship in Lewis's Chronicles.* Minneapolis: Eyes & Pen Press, 2013.

Rossi, Lee D. *The Politics of Fantasy. C. S. Lewis and J. R. R. Tolkien.* Ann Arbor: University of Michigan Research Press, 1984.

Ryken, Leland, ed. *The Christian Imagination: The Practice of Faith in Literature and Writing.* Colorado Springs, CO: Shaw, 2002.

———. *Realms of Gold: The Classics in Christian Perspective.* Wheaton, IL: Harold Shaw, 1991.

———. *Triumphs of the Imagination: Literature in Christian Perspective.* Downers Grove, IL: InterVarsity, 1979.

Ryken, Leland, and Marjorie Lamp Mead. *A Reader's Guide to Caspian: A Journey into C. S. Lewis's Narnia.* Downers Grove, IL: InterVarsity, 2008.

Sammons, Martha C. *"A Far-Off Country": A Guide to C. S. Lewis's Fantasy Fiction.* Lanham, MD: University Press of America, 2000.

———. *A Guide through C. S. Lewis's Space Trilogy.* Westchester, IL: Cornerstone, 1980.

———. *A Guide through Narnia.* London: Hodder & Stoughton, 1979.

Sayer, George. *Jack: C. S. Lewis and His Times.* San Francisco: Harper & Row, 1988.

Schakel, Peter J. *Imagination and the Arts in C. S. Lewis.* Columbia: University of Missouri Press, 2002.

———. *Reading with the Heart: The Way into Narnia.* Grand Rapids, MI: Eerdmans, 1979.

———. *Reason and Imagination in C. S. Lewis: A Study of "Till We Have Faces."* Grand Rapids, MI: Eerdmans, 1984.

———. *The Way into Narnia: A Reader's Guide.* Grand Rapids, MI: Eerdmans, 2005.

Schakel, Peter J., ed. *The Longing for a Form: Essays on the Fiction of C. S. Lewis.* Kent, OH: Kent State University Press, 1977.

Schakel, Peter J., and Charles A. Huttar, eds. *Word and Story in C. S. Lewis.* Columbia: University of Missouri Press, 1991.

Schwartz, Sanford. *C. S. Lewis on the Final Frontier: Science and the Supernatural in the Space Trilogy.* New York: Oxford University Press, 2009.

Schofield, Stephen, ed. *In Search of C. S. Lewis.* South Plainfield, NJ: Bridge, 1983.

Smith, Robert Houston. *Patches of Godlight: The Pattern of Thought in C. S. Lewis.* Athens, GA: University of Georgia Press, 1981.

Tripp, Raymond P., ed. *Man's Natural Powers: Essays for and about C. S. Lewis.* Church Stretton, UK: Onny, 1975.

Urang, Gunnar. *Shadows of Heaven: Religion and Fantasy in the Writing of C. S. Lewis, Charles Williams, and J. R. R. Tolkien.* Philadelphia: Pilgrim, 1971.

Veith, Gene Edward, Jr. *Reading between the Lines: A Christian Guide to Literature.* Wheaton, IL: Crossway, 1990.

Walker, Andrew, and James Patrick, eds. *A Christian for All Christians: Essays in Honour of C. S. Lewis.* London: Hodder and Stoughton, 1990.

Walsh, Chad. *C. S. Lewis: Apostle to the Skeptics.* New York: Macmillan, 1949.

———. *The Literary Legacy of C. S. Lewis.* New York: Harcourt Brace Jovanovich, 1979.

Ward, Michael. *The Narnia Code: C. S. Lewis and the Secret of the Seven Heavens.* Carol Stream, IL: Tyndale, 2010.

———. *Planet Narnia: The Seven Heavens in the Imagination of C. S. Lewis.* Oxford: Oxford University Press, 2008.

Watson, George, ed. *Critical Essays on C. S. Lewis.* Aldershot, UK: Scolar, 1992.

White, William Luther. *The Image of Man in C. S. Lewis.* Nashville: Abingdon, 1969.

Williams, Charles. *Arthurian Torso:* Containing the Posthumous Fragment of *The Figure of Arthur* by Charles Williams, and a Commentary on the Arthurian Poems of Charles Williams by C. S. Lewis. New York: Oxford University Press, 1948.

Williams, Donald T. *Mere Humanity: G. K. Chesterton, C. S. Lewis, and J. R. R. Tolkien on the Human Condition.* Nashville: Broadman & Holman, 2006.

Williams, Thomas. *The Heart of the "Chronicles of Narnia": Knowing God Here by Finding Him There.* Nashville: W Publishing, 2005.

Willis, John Randolph. *Pleasures Forevermore: The Theology of C. S. Lewis.* Chicago: Loyola University Press, 1983.

Wilson, A. N. *C. S. Lewis: A Biography.* New York: Norton, 1990.

Wolfe, Judith, and Brendan Wolfe, eds. *C. S. Lewis's "Perelandra": Reshaping the Image of the Cosmos.* Kent, OH: Kent State University Press, 2013.

Bibliography: Dante

Alighieri, Dante. *Dantis Alagherii Epistolae.* Translated by Paget Toynbee. 2d ed. Oxford: Clarendon, 1966.

———. *La Divina Commedia.* Rev. Scartazziniano ed. Edited and revised by Guiseppe Vandelli. Milan: Ulrico Hoepli, 1965.

———. *The Divine Comedy.* Translated with commentary by Mark Musa. 6 vols. Bloomington: Indiana University Press, 1996–2004.

———. *The Divine Comedy.* Translated with commentary by John D. Sinclair. 3 vols. London: The Bodley Head, 1939–1946. Reprint, Oxford: Oxford University Press, 1961.

———. *The Divine Comedy.* Translated with commentary by Charles S. Singleton. 3 vols. Princeton: Princeton University Press, 1970–1975.

———. *Literary Criticism of Dante Alighieri.* Edited and translated by Robert S. Haller. Lincoln: University of Nebraska Press, 1973.

Secondary Sources for Dante

Auerbach, Erich. *Dante: Poet of the Secular World.* Translated by Ralph Manheim. Chicago: University of Chicago Press, 1961.

———. *Mimesis: The Representation of Reality in Western Literature.* Translated by Willard Trask. Princeton; NJ: Princeton University Press, 1953. Reprint, Garden City, NY: Doubleday, 1957.

———. *Scenes from the Drama of European Literature.* New York: Meridian, 1959.

Barnes, John C., and Jennifer Petrie, eds. *Word and Drama in Dante: Essays on "The Divine Comedy."* Dublin: Irish Academic Press, 1993.

Barbes, John C., and Michelangelo Zaccarello, eds. *Language and Style in Dante: Seven Essays.* Dublin: Four Courts Press, 2013.

Barolini, Teodolinda. *The Undivine Comedy: Detheologizing Dante.* Princeton, NJ: Princeton University Press, 1992.

Barolini, Teodolinda, and H. Wayne Storey, eds. *Dante for the New Millennium.* New York: Fordham University Press, 2003.

Baur, Christine O'Connell. *Dante's Hermeneutics of Salvation: Passages to Freedom in the "Divine Comedy."* Toronto: University of Toronto Press, 2007.

Benfell, V. Stanley. *The Biblical Dante.* Toronto: University of Toronto Press, 2011.

Bergin, Thomas G. *A Diversity of Dante.* New Brunswick, NJ: Rutgers University Press, 1969.

———. *Perspectives on "The Divine Comedy."* New Brunswick, NJ: Rutgers University Press, 1967.

Botterill, Steven. *Dante and the Mystical Tradition: Bernard of Clairvaux in the "The Divine Comedy."* Cambridge: Cambridge University Press, 1994.

Boyde, Patrick. *Perception and Passion in Dante's "Comedy."* Cambridge: Cambridge University Press, 1993.

Brandeis, Irma. *The Ladder of Vision: A Study of Dante's "Comedy."* 1960. Reprint, Garden City, NY: Anchor, 1962.

Brinton, Henry Griffith. *Church Divinity 1986.* Edited by John H. Morgan. Bristol, IN: Wyndam Hall Press, 1986.

Carroll, John S. *In Patria: An Exposition of Dante's "Paradiso."* Port Washington, NY: Kennikat Press, 1911.

Cassell, Anthony K. *"Inferno" I.* Foreword by Robert Hollander. Philadelphia: University of Pennsylvania Press, 1989.

Chandler, S. Bernard, and J. A. Molinaro, eds. *The World of Dante: Six Studies in Language and Thought.* Toronto: University of Toronto Press, 1966.

Charity, A. C. *Events and Their Afterlife.* Cambridge: Cambridge University Press, 1966.

Chiarenza, Marguerite Mills. *"The Divine Comedy": Tracing God's Art.* Boston: Twayne, 1989.

Cicero, Marcus Tullius. *The Basic Works of Cicero*. Edited and introduction by Moses Hadas. New York: Modern Library, 1951.

Colish, Marcia L. *The Mirror of Language: A Study in the Medieval Theory of Knowledge*. New Haven, CT: Yale University Press, 1968.

Collins, James. *Pilgrim in Love: An Introduction to Dante and His Spirituality*. Chicago: Loyola University Press, 1984.

Cornish, Allison. *Reading Dante's Stars*. New Haven, CT: Yale University Press, 2000.

Demaray, John G. *The Invention of Dante's "Commedia."* New Haven, CT: Yale University Press, 1974.

DiScipio, Giuseppe. *The Presence of Pauline Thought in the Works of Dante*. Lewiston, NY: Edwin Mellen, 1995.

Eliot, T. S. *Dante*. 1929. Reprint, New York: Haskell House, 1974.

Fergusson, Francis. *Dante's Drama of the Mind*. Princeton, NJ: Princeton University Press, 1953.

Foster, Kenelm. *The Two Dantes and Other Studies*. Berkeley: University of California Press, 1977.

Foster, Kenelm, and Patrick Boyde, eds. *Cambridge Readings in Dante's Comedy*. Cambridge: Cambridge University Press, 1981.

Franke, William. *Dante and the Sense of Transgression: "The Trespass of the Sign."* New York: Bloomsbury, 2013.

Havely, Nick. *Dante*. Malden, MA: Blackwell, 2007.

Hawkins, Peter S. *Dante: A Brief History*. Malden, MA: Blackwell, 2006.

———. *Dante's Testaments: Essays in Scriptural Imagination*. Stanford, CA: Stanford University Press, 1999.

Herzman, Ronald. "'Io non Enëa, io non Paolo sono': Ulysses, Guido da Montefeltro, and Franciscan Traditions in the *Commedia*." *Dante Studies*. Vol. 123, edited by Richard Lansing. Bronx: Fordham University Press, 2005.

Hollander, Robert. *Allegory in Dante's" Commedia."* Princeton: Princeton University Press, 1969.

———. *Dante: A Life in Works*. New Haven, CT: Yale University Press, 2001.

———. *Dante and Paul's Five Words with Understanding*. Binghamton, NY: Medieval and Renaissance Texts and Studies, 1992.

———. "Dante Theologus-Poeta." *Dante Studies*. Vol. 94, edited by Christopher Kleinhenz. Albany: State University of New York Press, 1976.

Holmes, George. *Dante*. New York: Hill & Wang, 1980.

Hunt, Patrick, ed. *Critical Insights: The "Inferno" by Dante*. Hackensack, NJ: Salem Press, 2012.

Iannucci, Amilcare A., ed. *Dante: Contemporary Perspectives*. Toronto: University of Toronto Press, 1997.

Jacoff, Rachel, ed. *The Cambridge Companion to Dante*. New York: Cambridge University Press, 1993.

Jacoff, Rachel, and William A. Stephany. *"Inferno" II*. Philadelphia: University of Pennsylvania Press, 1989.

Jacoff, Rachel, and Jeffrey T. Schnapp, eds. *The Poetry of Allusion: Virgil and Ovid in Dante's "Commedia."* Stanford, CA: Stanford University Press, 1991.

Kay, Richard. *Dante's Christian Astrology*. Philadelphia: University of Pennsylvania Press, 1994.

Kirkpatrick, Robin. *Dante: "The Divine Comedy."* Cambridge: Cambridge University Press, 2004.

———. *Dante's "Paradiso" and the Limitations of Modern Criticism*. Cambridge: Cambridge University Press, 1978.

Lansing, Richard, ed. *Dante and Theology: The Biblical Tradition and Christian Allegory*. New York: Routledge, 2002.

Masciandaro, Franco. *Dante as Dramatist: The Myth of the Earthly Paradise and Tragic Vision in "The Divine Comedy."* Philadelphia: University of Pennsylvania Press, 1991.

Mazzeo, Joseph Anthony. *Structure and Thought in the "Paradiso."* Ithaca, NY: Cornell University Press, 1958.

Mazzotta, Giuseppe, ed. *Critical Essays on Dante*. Boston: G. K. Hall, 1991.

Montgomery, Marion. *The Reflective Journey toward Order: Essays on Dante, Wordsworth, Eliot, and Others*. Athens, GA: University of Georgia Press, 1973.

Moore, Edward. *Studies in Dante*. Fourth Series. Oxford: Clarendon, 1917.

Nolan, David, ed. *Dante Commentaries: Eight Studies of the "Divine Comedy."* Totowa, NJ: Rowman & Littlefield, 1977.

Nuttall, Geoffrey F. *The Faith of Dante Alighieri*. London: SPCK, 1969.

O'Connell, Daragh, and Jennifer Petrie, eds. *Nature and Art in Dante*. Dublin: Four Courts Press, 2013.

Ó Cuilleanáin, Cormac, and Jennifer Petrie, eds. *Patterns in Dante*. Dublin: Four Courts Press, 2005.

Quinones, Ricardo J. *Dante Alighieri*. Boston: Twayne, 1979.

Raffa, Guy P. *Divine Dialectic: Dante's Incarnational Poetry*. Toronto: University of Toronto Press, 2000.

Sayers, Dorothy L. *Christian Letters to a Post-Christian World*. Selected with introduction by Roderick Jellema. Grand Rapids, MI: Eerdmans, 1969

————. *Further Papers on Dante*. London: Methuen, 1957.

————. *Introductory Papers to Dante*. London: Methuen, 1954.

Scott, John A. *Understanding Dante*. Notre Dame, IN: University of Notre Dame Press, 2004.

Shaw, Prue. *Reading Dante: From Here to Eternity*. New York: Norton, 2014.

Singleton, Charles S. *Dante Studies*. 2 vols. Cambridge, MA: Harvard University Press, 1954–1958.

Thompson, David. *Dante's Epic Journeys*. Baltimore, MD: Johns Hopkins University Press, 1974.

Underhill, Evelyn. *Mysticism: A Study in the Nature and Development of Man's Spiritual Consciousness*. New York: E. P. Dutton, 1912.

Wicksteed, Philip Henry. *Dante and Aquinas*. New York: E. P. Dutton, 1913.

Williams, Charles. *The Figure of Beatrice: A Study in Dante*. London: Faber and Faber, 1943.

Wilson, Robert. *Prophesies and Prophecy in Dante's "Commedia."* Florence: Leo S. Olschki, 2008.

Index

155; as non-allegorical figure, 161,
282; false Aslan, 160
Athamas, King, 242
Atheling, William, Jr. [James Blish],
227
Auerbach, Erich, 216, 218, 226, 275–76
Augray, 55
Augustine, 12, 47, 83, 131, 243, 265,
272, 296, 298; *City of God*, 228;
Confessions, 243, 265–66, 272
avarice. *See* seven capital sins.

Babel, 104, 253
Bailey, James Osler, 234
Banquet, The (*Convivio*), 210
Bardia, 180–81, 185, 187–88, 190, 192,
194–95, 292, 294; as Virgil-figure,
181, 194–95
Barfield, Owen, 13, 50, 209, 214, 224,
230; Lewis letter to, 224; similarity
to Ransom, 50, 230
Barolini, Teodolinda, 240, 259, 286
Bate, Walter Jackson, 213
Battle of Benevento, 72
Battle of Montaperti, 72
Beatrice (character in *Divine
Comedy*), 3, 19, 34–39, 45, 55–62,
74, 77, 80, 87, 94, 96–99, 108,
113–16, 122–23, 127, 135–36, 144–47,
149, 150–53, 159, 161, 168, 174, 181,
194–98, 203–5, 222, 227, 232–33,
236, 245, 249, 251–52, 256, 259–60,
267, 269, 270, 274, 277, 281–82,
291, 296; in the Garden of Eden,
4, 18–19, 34, 37, 56, 74, 114, 151; as
channel of grace, 3, 135, 145–46,
152, 194; as guide, 2, 16, 19, 32, 34,
53, 55, 74, 77, 135, 159, 291; as judge,
19, 37, 57, 146, 152, 194, 197, 251, 277
Beatrice-figures in Lewis, 5, 6, 36, 43,
58, 77, 102, 116, 125, 154, 200, 203–4,
210; Green Lady as, 80, 96–97; island as, 34–39, 203; Jane Studdock
as, 115–16, 204, 259; Jill as, 174–75,
204; MacDonald as, 145–47, 149,
204; Mountain-Dwellers as, 135,
269; Oyarsa of Malacandra as, 4,
56–62, 203; Psyche as, 6, 181, 194–
98, 200, 204; Ransom as, 122–24,
204; Sarah Smith as, 150–53, 204,
267, 270, 277; Tor and Tinidril as,

5, 93, 96–99, 203, 296–97; young
Christian woman as, 4, 76–77, 203
Beatrice Portinari, 2, 135, 146, 232,
273
Beatrician experience, 34, 38, 58, 80,
97, 99, 122, 195, 222–23, 261
Bedford (character), 42, 225, 233
Belbury, 101, 110, 103–4, 106–8, 111–16,
119, 124–25, 202, 253, 255–57, 259.
See also N.I.C.E.
Benedict (character name for
Spinoza), 29
Benfell, V. Stanley, 241, 280
Bent Eldil, 43, 59, 79, 90–91, 101,
106, 109, 124. *See also* eldil; Satan;
Thulcandra
Bergin, Thomas G., 252
Bernard of Clairvaux, 19, 269
Bernardus Silvestris, 226
Bertran de Born, 105, 237–38
Bible, 6, 22–23, 105, 162, 173, 179, 216,
218, 226, 281–82, 291, 293; exodus
event, 243, 280–81; quotations
from, Psalm 32:1, 251; Psalm 84:11,
219; Psalm 90:10, 50; Psalm 91, 153;
Psalm 110, 143; Psalm 114, 280;
Isaiah 2:11, 217; Romans 1:20, 293;
Romans 1:21, 189; Philippians 4:8,
212. *See also* typology
Bilbro, Jeffrey L., 217
Bloom, Harold, 213
Bocca degli Abati, 72, 240
Boenig, Robert, 224, 230, 255,
262–64
Boethius, 55, 131; *Consolation of
Philosophy*, 234, 266
Botterill, Steven, 248
Boyde, Patrick, 257, 294
Bracton College, 101, 104, 111
Branca d'Oria, 91, 246
Brandeis, Irma, 238–39, 257, 273
Bright People, 132, 135–36, 152. *See
also* Mountain-Dwellers
Brobdingnagians, 56
Brutus, 64, 237
Bunyan, John, 22–25, 27, 30, 38, 51,
217, 219, 226, 231. *See also* allegory.
Burton, Richard, 245
Bus-Driver, 132–33, 154, 267; like
angel of Dis, 132–33; like boat
angel, 133; like Christ, 133, 267